D0070637

ON SPEECH COMMUNICATION

An Anthology of Contemporary Writings and Messages

ON SPEECH COMMUNICATION

An Anthology
of Contemporary Writings
and Messages

CHARLES J. STEWART

Department of Communication
Purdue University

HOLT, RINEHART and WINSTON, INC.

New York	Chicago	San Francisco
Atlanta	Dallas	Montreal
Toronto	London	Sydney

A revision of *On Speech and Speakers*
by Charles J. Stewart and H. Bruce Kendall

© 1972, 1968 by Holt, Rinehart and Winston, Inc.

Library of Congress Catalog Card No.: 75-187109
ISBN: 0-03-086734-7

PRINTED IN THE UNITED STATES OF AMERICA

2 3 4 5 6   090   9 8 7 6 5 4 3 2 1

To the memory of Bruce Kendall,
a colleague and friend

PREFACE

Never before has man had such a variety of means to communicate. Radio, television, telephone, teletype, satellites, and the press are at man's disposal to aid him in communicating with his fellow man. Ironically, we have probably never been so plagued with failures to communicate. Indeed, the means of communication have frequently accentuated the very problems and differences we thought they would help us solve. It has become painfully apparent to many of us that we must learn to communicate before our marvelous devices can attain their expected potentials.

This edition, like the first, is designed to offer the student a combination of varied readings related to the medium and subject matter of speech communication and of sample messages involving a variety of speakers and issues. The emphasis is on the contemporary with special attention given to the relevance of speech communication to our society.

Part One of this book contains recent articles on communication in a confused and sometimes violent society, on the process of communication and its components (speaker, message, audience), on communication in small groups and dyads (one-to-one situations), and on criticism of attempts to communicate. Some articles have the layman's touch while others are products of specialists.

Part Two contains messages by students, politicians, reformers, and observers of the American scene. They treat issues such as human rights, divorce, ecology, the mass media, campus unrest, and politics. These messages are presented for analysis and criticism. They are not meant to be imitated, but I hope they will provide inspiration and a point of departure for the aspiring communicator—public speaker, member of a small group, or part of a dyad.

In conclusion, it is my wish that anyone who reads and uses this book to increase his knowledge and skill in speech communication will have gained true insight into the nature and importance of communication—perhaps the most important key to the survival of our society.

West Lafayette, Indiana   CHARLES J. STEWART

CONTENTS

Alternate Table of Contents for Part II

PART ONE READINGS

I

COMMUNICATION IN OUR SOCIETY

The Selling of the Candidates 1970

This Newsweek article deals with the use and role of mass communication in contemporary American politics. No longer is television used simply to transmit speeches "live" to the home viewer. Media specialists and public relations firms have developed the political commercial into an art form, often directing political campaigns as if they were epic motion pictures. The expenditures for televised spots and programs stagger the imagination.

The picture on the TV screen is more than vaguely reminiscent of Mark Shaw's famous photographs of John F. Kennedy. Down a deserted beach strolls another tall, handsome young man, accompanied by his pretty wife and tow-headed children. Finally, the camera moves in for a flattering view of California Congressman John Tunney, son of the man who beat Jack Dempsey and a Kennedy family friend. Tunney, who is running for a seat in the U.S. Senate, looks into the camera from under a Kennedy-style mop of hair. "We can fly to the moon, we can split the atom, we can build great cities. But we cannot build the ocean or the sky," he tells his unseen audience earnestly. "These are gifts . . . my vote and voice will be with the protection of this great state of ours." It all takes a trifle less than 30 seconds. Then the slogan flashes across the screen: "You need a fighter in your corner. John Tunney is a fighter."

His coat is off, his sleeves rolled up, his collar open. Silver-haired Howard Metzenbaum, the millionaire liberal, is commiserating with a crew of construction workers. Metzenbaum, who is running for the Senate in Ohio, agrees that things are tough these days and he talks about the spiraling inflation and unemployment figures. Within seconds one of the hard hats is weeping over his family's plight. A credit notes that this dramatic slice of life was presented by the Citizens for Metzenbaum Committee.

The face is that of Adlai Stevenson III, the Democratic Senate candidate in Illinois, looking owlish and a bit bemused. But the voice is something else again. "Why doesn't he speak out against busing?" it demands. The camera zooms in closer on Adlai's face. "Why doesn't he denounce those students who try to force our universities to close?" the voice persists. The camera comes closer still. "What has Ad-a-lay got against the FBI and the Chicago police?" The screen is now entirely filled by Stevenson's nose and glassy eyeballs. "Why doesn't he admit he's a liberal and put an end to all the pretense?" A question mark flickers briefly onscreen, then the camera goes back to staring into Stevenson's myopic eyes. "Why doesn't he?" insists the voice. Before the picture fades, a tiny message across the bottom of the screen reveals that the instant inquisition was paid for by supporters of Sen. Ralph Smith, Stevenson's Republican opponent.

Scenes of subtle and not-so-subtle campaign hucksterism such as these are almost as common on U.S. television today as Alka-Seltzer's saga of the spicy meatball. From candidates for county boards to contenders for the Statehouse and Capitol Hill, politicians are filling the airwaves with an unprecedented and awesomely expensive onslaught of slick campaign commercials. The escalating war of the spots has transformed the face of American politics (and not a few politicians), elevated to sacerdotal status the elite new band of political filmmakers and TV technologists who fashion the commercials—and it has created a mystique all its own. It is fair to say that the medium is much of the message in this fall's elections—the selling of the candidates 1970 is in many respects a more compelling story than their politics.

Commercials aside, TV news coverage has become perhaps the dominant factor in the nation's day-to-day political environment, its marketplace of ideas. At the Federal Communications Commission and in network executive suites, hard thought is being given to the problem of insuring fair exposure to all viewpoints in an electronic arena that naturally tends to be monopolized by a few powerful spokesmen. The paramount such spokesman is the President, who demonstrated his ability to command the home screen again last week when he announced new proposals to bring an end to the war in Vietnam, his 25th important TV showing since taking office.

Politicians and media professionals themselves are divided over the precise merits of television commercials in political campaigns. Some swear by TV. "Anyone who doesn't spend 80 per cent of his advertising budget on television is throwing money away," says a West Coast campaign manager. Others are not so sure. "Actually," admits one leading practitioner of the art, "I think that most political advertising is [garbage], including some of ours." While a massive television effort is no guarantee of victory, it can boost an unknown candidate to the status of a real contender and it seems to have played a decisive role in an ever-growing list of races.

Most big-league politicians today must be willing—and able—to sink sizable fortunes into the media market. This year, a near-million-dollar TV blitz won a U.S. Senate nomination for relatively obscure Democrat Richard Ottinger in New York and a $1.3 million TV budget made Norton Simon, the shy conglomerator, a reasonably robust challenger for the GOP Senate nomination in California. Skillfully used TV spots are generally credited with saving Nelson Rockefeller's political hide in 1966 (when he spent an estimated $1.5 million on TV and radio and let others do the talking for him, including a now celebrated animated fish). This time around, Rocky is sinking upwards of $2 million into 34 10-, 20-, 30- and 60-second commercials. In some cases (notably Ottinger's) the vast amount of money spent has itself become a campaign issue—although voters are slowly beginning to accept huge media budgets as a fact of modern political life.

According to a report by the FCC, the total cost of air time—mainly television—purchased by all Presidential, gubernatorial and Senatorial candidates in 1968 was $58.9 million—70 per cent more than was spent only four years before. Add the cost of producing all the film and tape that filled those time slots and the total could come close to $90 million. Last month, Congress passed controversial legislation that would limit future campaign spending on TV time in Federal and major state races to 7 cents per vote cast in the previous comparable election. At the weekend, President Nixon, who is dissatisfied with the bill, was pondering whether to sign it. Even if the new measure becomes law, it will not affect the 1970 campaign, and its real impact in the future is problematical.

Free of such limitations, candidates' media budgets are now swelling to record size for an off-year election. Both the Twentieth Century Fund, Inc., and the watchdog National Committee for an Effective Congress have warned that the spending for air time and related costs in 1970 seems likely to reach $50 million—and the total could reach $75 million with all costs included. "This whole thing reminds me of the Mad Hatter's tea party," sighs a Washington media manager. "Elections are the most important transaction in a democracy. Television is a major element in that transaction. The airwaves are owned by the people of the country. Yet political candidates have to pay a ransom to conduct this most important transaction."

What the candidate gets for his media dollar is a sales package of calibrated emotional, ideological and symbolic appeals—and the mix is helping to shape a not entirely rational "new politics" in the U.S. But commercials themselves are only one weapon in the with-it candidate's media arsenal. The pros know that candidates' appearances on TV news shows can impress viewers as much as their commercial spots. Thus, much live campaigning today is aimed not so much at the voters on scene as at television news directors.

HOT AIR

If the locale of a candidate's press conference or walking tour is imaginative or colorful enough, he stands a good chance of winning attention on the evening news shows—probably the most influential TV forum available to a politician. The result is a turn to gimmickry by a growing number of candidates, especially those without large war chests to buy commercial time. California's underdog Democratic gubernatorial candidate Jess Unruh, for example, recently launched an attack on property taxes at the gates to the Bel Air mansion of Henry Salvatori, one of Gov. Ronald Reagan's flushest backers. In New York last spring, Rep. Richard D. Max McCarthy went for a swim in the polluted Hudson River and went aloft in a balloon filled with hot air while he campaigned (in vain) for the Democratic Senate nomination.

The impact of so much political television—commercial and news—has been to further reduce the power of the already weakened party organizations. Mass-media exposure gives a candidate easy access to the voters right in their homes, regardless of clubhouse politics or hostile precinct captains. And it focuses the voters' attention on the candidate as an individual, even a celebrity, rather than as a party standard-bearer. A process of natural selection already at work seems likely to produce an increasing number of youthful Ottinger-style telegenic candidates with large personal fortunes—or some other extraordinary claim on TV time. Broadcasters themselves have entered the political lists in New York, Tennessee and Georgia; even former NBC anchorman Chet Huntley is rumored to be contemplating a race for the House or the Senate in Montana.

The real masters of the art, however, are the men behind the scenes. There are now perhaps half a dozen top professionals in the business of manipulating a candidate's image and marketing it to the electorate. For their services, they can command fees ranging from $30,000 to $100,000 or a flat 10 to 15 per cent of a candidate's advertising budget. Among the best of the new breed:

• *Charles Guggenheim*, 46, a frail-looking, Oscar-winning documentary-film maker ("Nine From Little Rock") who has helped win twenty of the 33 election campaigns in which he has been involved since 1954. The pre-eminent artist of the industry (his sensitive evocations of Robert F. Kennedy and George McGovern are considered models of the art); he is now working in nine major races around the country, including the Senate campaigns of Edward Kennedy in Massachusetts, Philip Hart in Michigan, Metzenbaum in Ohio, Albert Gore in Tennessee and the Rev. Joseph Duffey in Connecticut and the gubernatorial challenge of Arthur Goldberg in New York. Attracted to politics by Adlai Stevenson in 1956, Guggenheim works solely for liberals, mostly Democrats. "The most important thing I can do is make sure I work for the right man," he explains in his cramped Washington office. In the field, Guggenheim has been known to shoot thousands of feet of film (in hand-held, *cinéma vérité* style) to get the 500 or so feet that finally will appear in his political productions. "In putting those things together," he says, "you start with your own belief in a man. You analyze why you believe in him, the things about him you want people to appreciate and understand."

• *David Garth*, 40, a paunchy, cigar-smoking New Yorker who moved into the spotlight with his first major political client—John Vliet Lindsay. Garth handled Lindsay's first campaign well enough, but his greatest triumph was the famous "I've made mistakes" commercial during the mayor's successful campaign for re-election last year. Like Guggenheim, Garth was first drawn into politics by Stevenson, in 1960. Unlike him, however, Garth takes a much more pragmatic, strategic approach to the campaign packages that he produces. He also shoots in cinéma vérité, filming his candidate in "surrogate situations," but there is less wasted effort because Garth has mapped out the key political issues and emotions that he has decided to project. "Garth is the best," graciously admits a competitor. "He perceives the problems, develops extremely good material and then executes it." He has a portfolio bulging with half a dozen political clients this year, including Senate candidates John Tunney in California, Adlai Stevenson III in Illinois and Ottinger in New York. "If you have a guy who is good, he will come across," says Garth bluntly. "And there's nothing very mysterious about that."

• *Robert Goodman*, 42, of Baltimore, who started with Spiro Agnew and is now handling four major Republican candidates. "We try to make the candidate bigger than life and we try to do it emotionally," he says. "Our job is to glamorize them and hide their weaknesses."

• *Robert Squier*, 35, a fast-talking veteran of the craft beginning in his undergraduate days in Minnesota where he worked for Gov. Orville Freeman. Now the head of the Washington-based Communications Company, Squier is creating the TV campaigns for Democratic Senate candidates Edmund Muskie in Maine, Sam Grossman in Arizona and Philip Hoff in Vermont, for Gov. Marvin Mandel in Maryland and for gubernatorial hopeful Milton Shapp in Pennsylvania—and is serving as a TV consultant for the Democratic National Committee.

• *Harry Treleaven*, 48, a veteran ad man and former vice president at the J. Walter Thompson agency (Pan Am, Lark cigarettes, RCA) whose biggest political account, without question, is Richard M. Nixon. As one of the skillful managers of Mr. Nixon's appearances on television and radio during the 1968 campaign, the formal, gray-haired Treleaven won notoriety in Joe McGinniss's "The Selling of the President 1968." Now, operating out of a New York apartment, Treleaven is handling a selection of tough but important (to the President) Republican races. They include the Senate campaigns of Lenore Romney in Michigan, Bill Brock in Tennessee and George Bush in Texas. Treleaven's first political job was the engineering of a "fighting underdog" Congressional campaign for Bush in 1966. Out of that he formulated well-accepted but scarcely mentioned rules of thumb. "Most national issues today are so complicated, so difficult to understand and have opinions on, that they either intimidate or, more often, bore the average voter," he wrote in a post-campaign report. "Probably more people vote for irrational, emotional reasons than professional politicians suspect."

• Roger Ailes, 30, another member of Mr. Nixon's highly touted media team who still lends a hand at times when the President goes on TV (he helped, for example, in setting up the broadcast that announced U.S. intervention in Cambodia). Ailes is best known for the crash courses in on-camera composure that he provides for Republican candidates. He also advises on the most suitable studio lighting and even dabbles in haberdashery. For Massachusetts Gov. Francis Sargent, 55, running against zesty Boston Mayor Kevin White, 41, Ailes prescribed a 25-pound weight loss and longer hair, then selected six conservatively modish suits for Sargent's TV appearances—after which the governor decided he no longer needed a TV consultant.

Can a candidate really be redesigned or programed for television? The truth lies somewhere between the modest disclaimers made by most media men in public and the rather more prideful analyses they make in private. "All you have to do is tell a guy to lift his chin a little and he will go around thinking about his chin for the next three months," says one of the top professionals. But David Garth, for example, was not averse to suggesting that Adlai III practice up a bit on a private TV tape machine (Adlai never did). Sometimes the pros even trick their clients to get the effect they want. Robert Squier feels that a too-tight collar can detract from a man's image. "Some candidate will feel that the collar size he's worn since college is still right for him," Squier says. "He's not ready to admit that he's gotten a fat neck." The solution is simple: Squier supplies such a candidate with a "special" TV blue shirt (actually, the color is immaterial) with a collar one-half size larger.

The end product of all the crafty showmanship is likely to be a "spot" of one minute or less. Even Charles Guggenheim, once a passionate proponent of the serious, evocative, half-hour film biography, has given them up for the season. His longest commercials now run five minutes; the majority are much shorter. "Maybe it is manipulation to show only the best of a candidate," he mused recently to Newsweek's Richard Stout. "What can you really say in 60 seconds?" The answer seems to be plenty—if the messages are kept simple. In California, for example, David Garth is suggesting that Tunney is young and aggressive in the Kennedy mold (though no radic-lib). The Spencer-Roberts agency there is countering with a $500,000 wave of TV suggesting that Republican Senate incumbent George Murphy speaks for the silent majority (one commercial shows President Nixon himself placing a confident hand on Murphy's shoulder).

DAM SYMBOLISM

In Missouri, Medion, Inc., of San Francisco is dramatizing the youthful vigor and empathy of State Attorney General John Danforth, 34, a lawyer, an Episcopal minister and heir to the Ralston Purina Co. fortune. His opponent in the Senatorial race is incumbent Democrat Stuart Symington, who is 69. Pierre Vacho, head of Shelby Storck and Co. in St. Louis (and a former colleague of Guggenheim), has relied heavily on "symbolic" television appeals that show Symington's accomplishments—a dam, for example—as well as the senior senator in the midst of the action on Capitol Hill. In New York, Republican Sen. Charles Goodell is seeking to turn the attacks of Vice President Agnew and other conservatives to his own advantage in a hard-pressed campaign for re-election. "Goodell must be good," wryly argues the slogan at the tail end of his latest commercial. "Look at the enemies he's made."

Referring to one's enemies is a new and rather risky trend in political TV. Not only can the attacking candidate come off sounding too shrill, he also provides free air time to an opponent. But Sen. Ralph T. Smith's tough spot on Adlai's eyeballs in Illinois has helped persuade Adlai to take a stronger law-and-order line (Newsweek, Oct. 12).

In Michigan, Treleaven tried a somewhat similar approach briefly with Lenore Romney. TV spots excerpted from an address to the GOP state convention last August had her taking the fight to liberal Sen. Philip Hart. "Good grief," she exclaimed at one point. "Haven't we had enough Hart trouble?" But a recent poll showed her still trailing Hart and now Treleaven has led Lenore back to a more ladylike posture—posed in front of an unadorned background, appealing for votes so that she can go to Washington to help Richard Nixon. Guggenheim's strategy, in behalf of Hart, includes a commercial in which the senator visits a local precinct house and praises the work of the police.

Treleaven and Guggenheim stand lens to lens in the Tennessee Senate race, too, and the difference in their hard- and soft-sell approaches shows up dramatically. By all odds, Guggenheim's candidate, Albert Gore, should be a dead dove in a state full of Southern hawks. But Guggenheim viewed him as a gallant, stick-to-your-guns kind of guy whose roots are still in the soil of his farm in Carthage after nearly eighteen years in the Senate. For four days, Guggenheim and a small crew trailed Gore round the countryside with a pair of hand-held cameras and a sound recorder. They filmed the senator playing checkers with an old friend outside the Smith County courthouse, talking to young businessmen at the Exchange Club in Murfreesboro and to construction workers on the campus at Vanderbilt University.

The 16,000 feet of film that they shot was later edited down to about a dozen 30-second and one-minute spots, all with homey flavor and lots of jawing with the homefolks about Gore's battles in their behalf on such issues as tax reform, medicare, social security and the TVA. The war is largely sidestepped, except to say that "a man who's stuck his neck out all his life expects some criticism, friendly and otherwise . . ." Among Gore's favorites was one commercial used for the primary in which he gallops along on a white horse while the announcer's voice croons: "The pace and direction a man sets for his life can tell you a lot about his inner spirit . . . Those closest to him value his integrity and his judgment and his determination to take the right path as he sees it."

Treleaven's man Brock is one of the clutch of congressmen persuaded by the President to give up safe House seats to challenge vulnerable, liberal Senate Democrats. He is definitely not the world's most dynamic campaigner, which prompted more than a few anguished grimaces on Treleaven's face as he squinted through his camera. Working with a budget that probably approaches $1 million, Treleaven let others tell a part of Brock's story: old folks in a solicited testimonial to his efforts on their behalf, the wife of a captured U.S. GI expressing gratitude for a Brock-sponsored day of prayer for prisoners of war.

FRANTIC SIGNALS

To film Brock himself on the offensive, Treleaven and a crew of long-haired, bell-bottomed cameramen and technicians followed him to several shopping centers and rallies ("Is that one a girl or a boy?" a portly matron giggled after spotting camera assistant Mike Morris). In Chattanooga, Treleaven commandeered a high-school football field, rounded up 250 GOP partisans on a day's notice and jammed them all in between the 20- and 45-yard lines to give the impression of a crowd. Under drizzly skies, the "rally" got under way, with Brock denouncing Gore ("Why in 1941, Albert Gore voted against the fortification of Guam!"), and Treleaven frantically signaling from the stands for the candidate to smile, gesture, wave.

Too much artifice on TV can backfire. Campaign managers for Richard Roudebush, the Republican Senatorial candidate in Indiana, approved a short spot by m w b inc of Indianapolis in which an actor made up as a Viet Cong guerrilla loaded a rifle, then pointed it directly at the viewer. "The weapons the Viet Cong use to kill American servicemen are given to them by Communist countries," says the voice-over. "Sen. Vance Hartke voted for the bill to permit American trade with those Communist countries. Isn't that like putting a loaded gun into the hands of our enemies? Vote for Dick Roudebush. Roudebush thinks the way you do." Hartke filed a formal complaint with the FCC, and the Roudebush people finally pulled the spot back—but not before as many as 21 Indiana stations had aired it. Roudebush media men also hired eight hippies at $75 each to perform assorted antisocial acts before the cameras (littering, smoking, guzzling wine), but one scruffy leaked the story to The Chicago Sun-Times, and the film never made it to the screen.

Roudebush's foray into political fantasy raises knotty questions of fair play in a medium that can have the most powerful emotional impact. How far should a candidate be able to go with inflammatory imagery? Would specified limits violate his constitutional freedom of speech?

> When making our selections for governors, congressmen, and even presidents, how can we distinguish the real man from the possible myth produced by a public relations firm or by a media specialist? What are the ethical limitations to the "image building" or "image destruction" potential of political "spots?" If legal controls of political spending and media manipulation are possible and desirable, how would they affect freedom of speech and press?

Confrontation at Columbia: A Case Study in Coercive Rhetoric

James R. Andrews

James R. Andrews, associate professor of speech at Indiana University, was on the faculty of Teachers College, Columbia University, when the confrontation occurred in 1968. In this article he describes the incident, distinguishes persuasion from coercion, and carefully traces the arguments, counter-arguments, and strategies employed by radical elements at Columbia. Confrontations on college campuses before and since Columbia have not been mere breakdowns in communication, but have been refusals to communicate. How can we cope with these situations without forfeiting the principles of our democratic system?

On the broad steps leading up to Columbia University's Lowe Memorial Library, dominating College Walk, sits the placid, weather-stained figure of alma mater. On April 30 of last year there swirled about her feet the currents of anger, fear, puzzlement, and frustration; about her neck hung a boldly lettered sign: "Raped by the Cops."

The University had, indeed, been raped; it had been seized, immobilized, and ravished before the eyes of millions of American television viewers and newspaper readers, and word of the assault was reported throughout the world. But the attack that paralyzed the one hundred and fourteen year old institution was not only an attack on Columbia University, it was the rejection of persuasive rhetoric for coercive rhetoric. To say that the "rape" was carried out "by the cops" is simplistic and propagandistic. What occurred on Morningside Heights was much more complex and has serious implications for the student of rhetoric. . . .

Reprinted with permission from Quarterly Journal of Speech, XV (February, 1969), pp. 9–16. This article has been condensed with permission from the author.

The distinction between persuasive and coercive rhetoric focuses on choice. The Columbia incident demonstrates that rhetoric ceases to be persuasive and becomes coercive as the attempt is made to restrict choice. The Columbia incident affords a case study that might point the way to a reasonable distinction between these two types of rhetoric. I propose to examine coercive tendencies as they relate to specific events in the situation: the identification and exploitation of issues; the adaptation to counterarguments; the predictive results of strategy; and the use of physical force. Further, I intend to discuss whether coercive rhetoric is justified, with particular reference to the disruption of Columbia.

COERCIVE TENDENCIES AT COLUMBIA

IDENTIFICATION AND EXPLOITATION OF ISSUES

Two questions had long agitated the Columbia community. First, should the construction of a gymnasium in Morningside Park, city-owned land adjacent to the campus that had been leased to the University with the proviso that it be a shared facility with the Harlem community, be continued in the face of mounting hostility by community groups and growing dissatisfaction with the plan by students and faculty? And, second, should the University modify or sever its relations with the Institute for Defense Analysis? It was on these issues that the Students for a Democratic Society seized.

The use of these issues by the SDS was exploitative. The protestors clearly were not offering, nor encouraging the exploration of, real alternatives. There was no option offered to propose a variety of solutions to the IDA and gymnasium problems. Clearly the SDS was not prepared to debate issues because to them these apparent issues were not real. The aims of the radicals were larger than those that they ostensibly espoused. Mark Rudd, in a position paper drafted in October, 1967, which outlined SDS strategy for the coming year, clearly stated the organization's objectives: "(1) the 'radicalization' of students—showing people the connections in the liberal structure, showing them how our lives really are unfree in this society (and at Columbia), getting them to act in their own interest" and "(2) striking a blow at the Federal Government's war effort ('resistance')."[1] Rudd went on to describe the results of a sustained SDS campaign: Students "will become conscious of their own interests and needs and the way the university acts against them, corrupting and distorting education. . . . We will be able to present our alternative to this

[1] *New York Times*, May 13, 1968, p. 46.

university and this society as we discuss the role of the university under capitalism."[2]

To the SDS far more was involved than the gym and the IDA. The University itself, and through it the society of which it was an agent, was deplored by student radicals; nothing less than an "alternative" was envisioned. The goal was destruction, not reconstruction, of the university. Radical leaders logically discerned that such goals would be unsuccessful in gaining widespread support and that they could "never force the university to submit to our demands unless we have behind us the strength of the majority of students on campus."[3] To gain such backing Rudd proposed a strategy that depended on extensive organization and the statement of specific goals, for "to be militant is to fight to achieve a specific goal."[4] In the halting of gym construction and the abandonment of the IDA, the SDS had found specific goals that could marshal strong campus backing.

The subsidiary nature of these issues, however, became apparent as the crisis evolved. On April 28 the Board of Trustees announced the suspension of construction of the gymnasium, purportedly at the behest of Mayor John Lindsay.[5] Further, many believed that the report of Professor Henkin's committee studying the IDA would deal the Institute the death blow on the Columbia campus. One member of the *Ad Hoc* Faculty Committee, canvassing support for the Committee's mediation efforts, stated to me and to a group of my colleagues that the IDA was a "dead issue," since students and faculty alike believed it to be "on the way out." The apparent issues might have been on the way to resolution with substantial compromises being made by the administration were it not for another issue that the protestors had injected: full amnesty for all students involved in demonstrations. (This argument will be discussed later in another context. What it demonstrates at this point is that the protestors had not focused their efforts exclusively on the apparent issues.)

In "The Rhetoric of Confrontation," Scott and Smith have suggested that student radicals generally see as their goal the destruction of universities and by so "stalemating America's intellectual establishment," they will eventually "paralyze the political establishment as well."[6] Through their seizure of the two most burning Columbia issues, the SDS leaders had attempted to make only two choices available—support the SDS or support the administration's plan to construct the gym and stay with the IDA (for the moment, at least). But support of the SDS did not allow

[2] *Ibid.*
[3] *Ibid.*
[4] *Ibid.*
[5] *Ibid.*, April 28, 1968, p. 74.
[6] Robert L. Scott and Donald K. Smith, "The Rhetoric of Confrontation," *supra*, p. 5.

for a meaningful stand on the issues—it implied so much more. And the unhappy floundering of many faculty members and students during the hiatus between the seizure of the buildings and the police intervention clearly demonstrated their reluctance to accept either alternative. But the SDS would offer no other. Their exploitative manipulation of the issues was decidedly coercive in that it severely limited the kind of choices that could have been explored in a truly persuasive atmosphere.

ADAPTATION TO COUNTERARGUMENTS

Throughout the controversy radical leaders were at pains to prevent counterarguments or compromises from eroding their position. Their actual goal was not to answer objections or persuasively defend rejections of compromise. Their aim was to limit the choice of possibilities offered to the student audience. The answer to official statements and offers to negotiate was an unequivocal "bull shit," from Mark Rudd.[7] The choice then was between the SDS position and "bull shit"; no choice at all. Through a linguistic tactic designed not to answer arguments, but to dismiss them from the realm of the possible, Rudd and other leaders consistently vilified the administration and obscured their offers to talk. Who, for example, could consider the position of a "son-of-a-bitch" who had rejected students' demands "a million times," as Rudd pointed out in a speech at the sundial.[8]

Words are so powerful, as Ogden and Richards observed, that "by the excitement which they provoke through their emotive force, discussion is for the most part rendered sterile."[9] Certainly one of the striking rhetorical tactics employed by the radicals was to use language and description to render counterarguments beyond the pale of consideration. The University itself was repeatedly labeled as "racist," as Rudd had done when he seized the microphone to disrupt a memorial service held for Dr. King earlier in the month.[10] Black militant leaders who invaded the campus contributed their own inflammatory descriptions to the racist theme. Charles 37X Kenyatta, leader of the Mau Mau, pictured the University as the "Columbia octopus," and the Chairman of the Harlem branch of CORE, Victor Solomon, proclaimed that "this community is being raped."[11] In a speech at a teach-in at Teachers College Professor Eric Bentley, a firm supporter of the strike, strongly suggested that President

[7] "Columbia at Bay," *Newsweek*, LXXI (May 6, 1968), 43.
[8] *Columbia Daily Spectator*, April 24, 1968, p. 3.
[9] C. K. Ogden and I. A. Richards, *The Meaning of Meaning* (New York, 1923), p. 45.
[10] *Columbia Daily Spectator*, April 12, 1968, p. 1.
[11] *Newsweek*, LXXI (May 6, 1968), 44.

Kirk was a racist who disliked the recently murdered Martin Luther King. Whether or not the past actions of Columbia University had been in its own best interests, or in the best interests of its Harlem neighbors, or even in the best interests of the liberal, intellectual community at large is beside this particular point. Radical rhetoric offered a choice between support for the protestors or support for their "racist" enemies. Again, no choice at all, but a coercive attempt designed to eliminate real alternatives.

From the very beginning of the crisis many recognized that the police might be called in to clear the buildings. The radicals failed to come to grips with this possibility publicly before the event occurred. When it came radical rhetoric was mobilized to place, once again, the reasonable investigation of the merits and demerits of such action beyond consideration. Their hyperbolic description of the event attempted to equate its defense with defense of fascist totalitarianism. Stories of blood and beating were rife on the campus; there were many examples of rumors and exaggeration. Now it seems apparent from all accounts that some police acted viciously; some took out their frustrations, built up during days and nights of tension and taunts, on unarmed students. It is a sad and distressing sight to see any student with blood running down his face. Nevertheless, the injuries sustained were superficial and none of a serious nature resulted.[12] A press release from the Strike Steering Committee is typical of the use of language to describe this incident:

> Students have been clubbed, beaten, and carted off in police vans by the hundreds. Faculty members have been carried out on stretchers. And with that it is clear. University violence against students and faculty is an extension of its violence against black people in Columbia University owned buildings, against the community in the seizure of park land, against third world struggles in IDA weapons systems, against employees in denial of unions and decent wages. And now, in a 3 a.m. police raid, violence is used against students and faculty.
>
> The nature of the University was clearly revealed. The Trustees

[12] The question of what is or is not "brutal" is a difficult one. The *Columbia Daily Spectator* of April 30 reported that 135 people were treated for injuries in nearby hospitals and at a special infirmary set up at Philosophy Hall. *Newsweek* reported that 132 students, four faculty members, and twelve policemen were injured. No student or faculty member, however, was hospitalized. The Mayor's reaction was based on the reports of his aides on the spot, and is probably the most accurate assessment. Mr. Lindsay admitted that while some members of the police force "used excessive force," the majority demonstrated "great professionalism and restraint," *Newsweek*, LXXI (May 13, 1968), 59–60. To describe the police action as "beyond comprehension," as a flyer distributed by the Ad Hoc Teachers College Strike Committee did, is certainly to overstate the case.

and administration respond only to outside interests, student and faculty demands are met with violence.[13]

To label all counterarguments as total evil, to describe hyperbolically the controversial situation, and to picture the only choice as between the SDS position and brutal racism was to limit reasonable choices coercively.

THE PREDICTIVE RESULTS OF STRATEGY

When rhetorical strategy is so designed that it leaves the opposition no viable persuasive alternative, it is a coercive one. Scott and Smith have forcefully pointed out that "those who would confront have learned a brutal art, practiced sometimes awkwardly and sometimes skillfully, which demands response. But that art may provoke the response that confirms its presuppositions . . . and turns the power-enforced victory of the establishment into a symbolic victory for its opponents."[14] The demand of the radicals for amnesty was indeed coercive; it left no room for maneuvering, compromise, or examination of alternatives. It forced the administration to use coercive measures itself or submit to unconditional surrender.

The demand for amnesty obviously rendered meaningful discussion and compromise impossible. Student radicals could hardly have failed to realize that the administration would view such an action as surrender. Certainly on the subject of amnesty the administration's response, and that of the Trustees who "advised the president that they wholeheartedly support the administration position that there shall be no amnesty accorded to those who have engaged in this illegal conduct," was highly predictable.[15]

While faculty groups worked arduously to achieve a compromise, the demonstrators were adamant. Even the generally sympathetic *Spectator* was moved to comment that "the most serious loss of perspective has been shown by the students negotiating on the side of the demonstrators . . . throughout the latter part of the week, the demonstrators consistently refused to accept any solutions at all that were offered them by the faculty group."[16] As the sit-in continued, reaction began to emerge. Anti-SDS students formed a group called the Majority Coalition and blocked the entry of pro-SDS students with food and supplies into Lowe Library. One disgruntled student, addressing a faculty meeting, asserted, "Three years of the administration giving in to the SDS is a long time to restrain ourselves. . . . And in the last three days we've been sold out several

---

[13] Press statement, April 30, 9 a.m., distributed on campus.
[14] Scott and Smith, *supra*, p. 8.
[15] *New York Times*, April 28, 1968, p. 74.
[16] *Columbia Daily Spectator*, April 29, 1968, p. 4.

times."[17] Pressure on the administration from the alumni was also building. The President of Murray Space Corporation, for example, wired the Almuni Secretary: "As an alumnus I am shocked at the handling of mob rule taking over Columbia University. These people are not supporting the University. How can law respecting alumni be expected to support a university run by hoodlums and law breakers."[18] The tide of sympathy was beginning to run against the demonstrators.

It became extremely likely that, unless a compromise were reached, the administration would feel compelled to call in the police; the demonstrators utterly refused to agree to any compromise. They undoubtedly anticipated police action—one of the students in an occupied building said that he and his compatriots would not leave until their demands were met or until "we are carried out by the cops."[19] Undoubtedly, as Scott and Smith assert, in many cases "altercation with the police is enough. It is consummatory."[20] In the Columbia case, it not only fulfilled the function of unmasking the establishment in its true brutality (as the radicals saw it), but it also served to unite campus opinion behind the SDS leaders. The violent confrontation led to a broader base of support.[21] These supporters had not been persuaded; they had clearly been coerced. By inflexibly pursuing a strategy that almost inevitably led to confrontation, the demonstrators had forced the university community to choose, not between discernible positions, but between the bloodied students, armed only with their intellect and their passion to right hypocritical wrongs, and the unseen, powerful administration moving to protect its plush offices, aided by beasts with blackjacks and billy clubs. The choice of propositions, like the prose, was purple. And it was coercive.

THE USE OF PHYSICAL FORCE

I do not propose to devote much space to this consideration. Actions like pulling down a metal fence,[22] or holding a dean captive[23] seem clearly non-persuasive in that they employ direct physical force or its threat. Likewise the burning of a professor's papers,[24] or the fears one heard expressed that the strikers would retaliate against faculty who refused to

---

[17] *Ibid.*, April 26, 1968, p. 3.

[18] *Connection: A Magazine Supplement of the Columbia Daily Spectator*, I, 2, May 10, 1968, p. c5.

[19] *Columbia Daily Spectator*, April 26, 1968, p. 3.

[20] Scott and Smith, *supra*, p. 7.

[21] The campus reaction is accurately described and documented in "The End of a Siege—and an Era," *Newsweek*, LXXI (May 13, 1968), 60.

[22] *Columbia Daily Spectator*, April 24, 1968, p. 1.

[23] *Ibid.*, and also April 25, 1968, p. 1.

[24] *New York Times*, May 23, 1968, p. 51.

support them, would generally be held to be coercive and not persuasive rhetorical strategies. Suffice it to say that such actions were also a part of the Columbia incident.

IS COERCIVE RHETORIC JUSTIFIED?

Not all demonstrations, as Professor Haiman observes perceptively, are coercive. He clearly differentiates between the actions of a peaceful demonstrator whose act of protest is not inherently coercive, and the hostile audience that chooses "to go forth to do battle with them."[25] Violence, in such a case, is clearly the result of hostile action by anti-demonstrators who seek a confrontation.

At Columbia, however, no choice was given those who dissented from the protest: In the occupied buildings students could not go to classes, professors could not work undisturbed in their offices, administrators could not carry out their duties. The protest was clearly not a persuasive demonstration that gave an audience a choice of responsive alternatives.

Given the distinction between persuasion and coercion that I have suggested, the student radicals at Columbia chose to employ coercive rather than persuasive rhetorical procedures. Their rhetorical strategy was one of polarization; it aimed to admit only two choices, one of which was consistently distorted. Were such procedures justified?[26]

Professor Haiman asserts that "if the channels for peaceful protest and reform become so clogged that they appear to be (and, in fact, may be) inaccessible to some segments of the population, then the Jeffersonian doctrine that 'the tree of liberty must be refreshed from time to time, with the blood of patriots and tyrants' may become more appropriate to the situation than more civilized rules of the game."[27] In the Columbia case, there were, no doubt, some clogs in the channels. The Kirk administration was accused, for example, by as relatively moderate a student as the President of the Student Council of "sitting for almost ten months on a report recommending a greater role for faculty members and students in Columbia's disciplinary machinery," and of "being inaccessible to student leaders."[28] To think, however, in this case of "patriots" and "tyrants"

[25] Haiman, 112.

[26] I have not discussed the question of civil disobedience in the Columbia case. At Columbia the protestors were not breaking a law that was in itself deemed unjust (the laws of trespass), nor were they willing to be punished in any way for their actions. The argument that such incidents as the one at Columbia fall outside the concept of civil disobedience is ably articulated by Mr. Justice Fortas in *The New York Times Magazine*, May 12, 1968, and I could not improve on it here.

[27] Haiman, 105.

[28] *New York Times*, May 13, 1968, p. 47.

is to oversimplify, to make an exceedingly skewed judgment that the facts hardly seem to warrant. This is no doubt the quintessential problem, for it hangs ultimately on the extent to which one may allow himself to go when condoning rhetorical strategies used in behalf of what he considers to be worthy causes. If rhetorical theory in the twentieth century must take into account the change described by Scott and Smith, that "civility and decorum serve as masks for the preservation of injustice,"[29] then rhetorical criticism obviously must also provide for the examination of those cases in which civility and decorum are discarded for ends that are not obviously and unquestionably just. In the film based on Gore Vidal's *The Best Man*, the former President observed to a ruthless young politician that in politics, as in life, "there are no ends, only means. . . ."

> American society has depended upon persuasion, discussion, and compromise for its very existence as a democracy. How can we communicate or persuade when one side—radical element or establishment—limits alternatives to no choice at all or simply refuses to communicate? Where is the line between coercion and persuasion? Is authority inherently coercive? Does force by either side end all hope of persuasion or communication?

[29] Scott and Smith, *supra*, p. 8.

Kennedy on King: The Rhetoric of Control

Karl W. Anatol
John R. Bittner

Karl Anatol and John Bittner, graduate students at Purdue University when Martin Luther King, Jr., was assassinated, studied a television film of Robert Kennedy's speech at Indianapolis and interviewed members of the audience and community. They discovered that a simple, hastily-prepared speech by a politician—himself an assassin's victim just two months later—may have prevented a bloody riot. This article suggests the potential of meaningful communication in times of crisis as well as the possibility and the necessity of cross-cultural communication.

In the heart of the Indianapolis Negro ghetto, shortly after 9 P.M. on April 4, 1968, Senator Robert F. Kennedy addressed a mixed Negro and White crowd of over 1000 persons.[1] Other than the speech being somewhat shorter than usual, it would have had little more significance than countless other political speeches delivered in the course of the Indiana Presidential Primary. However, that same evening, at 7 P.M. in Memphis, Tennessee, Dr. Martin Luther King, Jr. was pronounced dead from an assassin's bullet. The murder touched off racial violence in cities throughout the nation, but Indianapolis with a Negro population of over 95,000 remained quiet.[2]

This article will attempt to explain the background of the Kennedy speech delivered the night Dr. King was shot, describe conditions under which it was delivered, and ascertain the effects of the speech on the Indianapolis Black community.

Reprinted with permission from Today's Speech, XVI (September, 1968), pp. 31–34.

[1] Estimates ran as high as 3000; none, however, were lower than 1000.

[2] 1967 census listed 20.6% of the total population as Negro, out of a total 476,000.

Kennedy had been scheduled to speak in the ghetto at 7:30 P.M. Political workers, both White and Black, were busily obtaining voter registrations. Local and network television crews were present as were police and interested spectators. A Negro band was playing on the speaker's platform, signs were waving, and the few spectators close enough to the platform where some movable space was available were dancing. The crowd was about 75% Negro,[3] filling the basketball court across from the Broadway Christian Center at 17th and Broadway, stretching south to Sixteenth Street and one block east on 17th to College Avenue. As one Negro lady described it, "they were packed in like sardines."[4]

The Kennedy flight to Indianapolis was late, landing just after 8:30 P.M. By that time the news of Dr. King's assassination had reached the ghetto and portions of the crowd. Negro and White confrontations were beginning to take place and yells such as "what are you doing here whitey" and "get out of here you white son of a bitch"[5] caused two White spectators on the outskirts of the crowd to leave the scene immediately. Other Whites in the central crowd area could go nowhere.

Reverend Lewis Deer, White pastor of the Christian Brotherhood Center, noted that "transistor radios began to pop up everywhere." "People were jammed in groups of six or seven listening to developments."[6] Standing in the center of the crowd, as he turned to a familiar Negro who had worked on numerous church projects at the Center, he was met by the Black man's surging upthrust hands and an antagonistic verbal "no!" A Negro lady, grabbing his arm cried, "Dr. King is dead and a White man did it, why does he [Kennedy] have to come here!"[7]

As the news of the assassination spread through the community, a Negro gang known as the "Ten Percenters" began scouring the neighborhood gathering militant support for violence. The seven-man committee which was responsible for local arrangements for the political gathering met in the reception room of the Christian Brotherhood Center. Included in the group was Charles "Snookey" Hendricks, Indianapolis Black Power leader. They had just learned King was officially pronounced dead. The decision was made not to announce publicly the latest development to the crowd. Spectators nearer the speaker's stand and in the basketball

[3] Persons near the rear of the crowd estimated the Negro content of the crowd at about 95%. Those persons nearer the speaker's stand judged the crowd to be about 50% Negro. Negro estimates were usually in terms of numbers they could see. Comments such as "I don't know" or a silent shaking of the head were not infrequent.

[4] Interview of May 3, 1968. The lady noted she attempted to penetrate the crowd at two different points, both unsuccessful.

[5] Interview of April 27, 1968.

[6] Interview with Reverend Lewis Deer, May 3, 1968.

[7] Ibid.

court seemed unaware of the critical situation. A direct announcement, the committee feared, would make the scene erupt into total chaos. The band was instructed to "keep playing" but, as tension increased, the committee began to fear for Kennedy's life. The aid of local Negroes from a nearby recreation center was enlisted to fill the trees and check vacant windows looking for possible assassins.[8] The police in the area were looked upon as "invaders" not capable of keeping anything under control, let alone creating enough surveillance to uncover a would-be killer.

Pierre Salinger met Kennedy at the airport and informed him that King had died. Aware of the unrest in the ghetto, Kennedy made the decision to bypass a planned stop to downtown headquarters and proceeded directly to 17th and Broadway. Many local politicians remained at the downtown headquarters because they feared the crowd reaction.[9]

The entire preparation of the speech took place during the ride from the airport to the ghetto. It consisted mainly of notes the Senator jotted on the back of a white envelope.[10]

By the time Kennedy's motorcade arrived in the ghetto, the Negro gangs had gained considerable support. Militant and Black Power advocates in the crowd apparently numbered upwards of 200.[11] Kennedy mounted the platform, spoke briefly to his aides and then, taking the envelope from his suit coat pocket, turned and faced the noisy sign-waving crowd. He began:

> Ladies and gentlemen, I am only going to talk to you for just a minute or so this evening, because I have some very sad news for all of you.[12]

Perhaps realizing the solemnity of the occasion or the possible effects of television cameras trained on the crowd, he asked, "Would you lower those signs please?" He continued:

> I have some very sad news for all of you, and I think—sad news for all of our fellow citizens and people who love peace all over the world. And that is—that Martin Luther King was shot and killed tonight.[13]

---

[8] The authors could not ascertain if any actual firearms were carried by gang members. A legitimate intent seemed apparent, however. Comments such as "there would have been killing," "people would have lost their lives before they got out of here" seemed to verify this intent.

[9] Many Negroes interviewed were aware of this fact and resented it.

[10] Information obtained for the authors by Connie Chandler of the Kennedy press staff in an interview with Pierre Salinger, May 5, 1968.

[11] Estimates by gang members ranged as high as 350; none were lower than 200.

[12] Transcription of a 16mm. sound motion picture provided the authors by WFBM-TV Indianapolis.

[13] *Ibid.*

Much of the crowd had not had a chance to express outwardly their feelings about King's death, or were unaware that he was actually dead. The crowd reacted with loud continuous screams when Kennedy made the announcement. A Negro lady driving her car two blocks away, unaware of King's death, wondered, "what he [Kennedy] had said." "I could hear the oooo," she said, "it just filled the air."[14] After the reaction subsided, Kennedy looked at the envelope for the first time saying:

> Martin Luther King dedicated his life to love and to justice between fellow human beings. He died for the cause of that effort. In this difficult time for the United States, it is perhaps well to ask what kind of nation we are and what direction we want to move in. For those of you who are Black, concerned [sic] the evidence evidently is that there were White people responsible, you can be filled with bitterness, hatred, and a desire for revenge.[15]

At this point in the speech the crowd became somewhat noisy and isolated shouts were easily distinguishable. Kennedy tried to continue, waited a few moments, then proceeded without referring back to the envelope for the remainder of the speech. He continued:

> We can move in that direction as a country in greater polarization, black amongst blacks and white amongst whites, filled with hatred toward one another; or we can make an effort as Martin Luther King did, to understand and to comprehend, and replace that violence, that stain and bloodshed that has spread across our land, with an effort to understand, compassion and love.[16]

There were continued rumblings of unrest. He then spoke the three sentences which seemed to have the greatest total and lasting effect on the crowd. Kennedy said:

> For those of you who are Black and are tempted to be filled with,— hatred and distrust of the unjustice of such an act, against all white people, I can only say that I can also feel in my own heart the same kind of feeling. I had a member of my family killed, but he was killed by a white man. But we have to make an effort in the United States . . . .[17]

One elderly Black gentleman said that Kennedy "had tears in his eyes, I saw it, he felt it man, he cried," and a friend nearby concurred,

14 *Ibid.*
15 *Ibid.*
16 *Ibid.*
17 *Ibid.*

"yea he did, right there, he had tears."[18] There was no way to determine whether Kennedy actually did shed tears, the result, however, was apparently one of deep emotional impact on the crowd. Continuing, Kennedy quoted briefly from Aeschylus:

> My favorite poem, my favorite poet, was Aeschylus. He once wrote, "even in our sleep pain which cannot forget, falls drop by drop upon the heart, until in our own great despair, against our will comes wisdom through the awful grace of God."[19]

These words may well have been wasted on the illiterate gentry of the ghetto; nevertheless, the crowd had quieted and the rumblings had stopped. He asked them to go to their homes and, amazingly the crowd "dispersed in four to five minutes."[20] Reverend Deer commented further that he had "never seen anything like it."

This "dispersal" would seem to constitute a major factor in determining the effectiveness of the Kennedy speech. It must be remembered that the "Ten Percenters" had obtained a headstart in gathering support and attempting to persuade individuals in the crowd. One gang member expressed, "Man there was going to be trouble," "They kill Martin Luther and we was [sic] ready to move."[21]

Under these conditions effective persuasion was vital. Involvement was Kennedy's choice; confrontation, his method; pacification, the "payoff." The authors attempted through interviews to obtain a greater insight into the processes by which this pacification took place.

Several comments obtained in interviews lend credence to the fact that Kennedy created a new or accentuated an already existing "image" that appealed to the Black community. Reverend Deer, who considered himself "not a Kennedy man" said, "no one else could have done it." He said, "He was a hero, then he was our hero because he was coming."[22] A Negro lady who saw the speech on television noted, "the feeling comes right through the TV, when he speaks it's just like Mr. [Billy] Graham."[23] The religious aura was also expressed in the comment that Kennedy was "like right out of the New Testament. . . . like my life is not complete until I have stood in the presence of such a man."[24]

This same "image" was also a factor in the overall effect. The seven-

18 Interview of May 3, 1968.
19 WFBM film.
20 Deer, May 3, 1968.
21 Interview of May 3, 1968.
22 Deer, May 3, 1968.
23 Interview of May 3, 1968.
24 Interview of May 3, 1968.

man planning committee expressed this when considering whether to notify Kennedy not to appear for the rally, realizing "you don't just tell a United States Senator what to do."[25] A militant who admitted throwing rocks and bottles at Whites on the night prior to April 4, 1968, said about Kennedy, "he knows the law, he was Attorney General, we listen to him."[26]

Another factor contributing to the overall effectiveness of the speech was Kennedy's "pathos" or "identification" with the Black community itself. His remarks, "I can only say that I can also feel in my own heart," were quoted almost verbatim to the authors during many of the interviews. One Black gentleman said, "he [Kennedy] know [sic] the Black people."[27] The authors tested this identification by asking numerous subjects the question, "how can you, a Black poor man, identify with a White rich man?" Not an atypical answer was, "we Black people remember his brother, we know what trouble is, we had all kinds of it."[28] Reverend Deer commented that "They were in grief together; they share a common experience; he reminded them of that; he communicated."[29]

At this point one may conjecture about what could have happened if Kennedy had not appeared in the ghetto and if his counter-persuasion to that of the "Ten Percenters" had not taken place. It would not have been the typical looting and burning that occurred in other cities. A racially mixed, congested crowd would have erupted into physical conflict between Black and White with lives being lost and women and children caught in the melee. Furthermore, if a riot had taken place, a national television audience would have been witness to its commencement. The prospect of chain reactions in other areas cannot be over-ruled. However, there was neither bodily harm nor violence. A young foundry worker bespeaks "effect" of the Kennedy speech when he said, "the Black power guys didn't get no place after the man speak."[30] A "Ten Percenter" commented, "We went there for trouble, after he spoke we couldn't get nowhere, I don't know why, I don't understand."[31] Another gang member with self-evident intentions commented, "After he spoke we realized the

[25] Interview of May 3, 1968.

[26] Interview of May 3, 1968.

[27] Interview of May 3, 1968.

[28] Interview of May 3, 1968.

[29] Deer, May 3, 1968. At a memorial service the Saturday following the assassination, numerous persons mentioned to the pastor, "how wonderful" it was that Mr. Kennedy had been there. He offered the opinion that Kennedy's remarks had given them something to talk about, live with internally, and express verbally among themselves rather than through outward physical violence.

[30] Interview of May 3, 1968.

[31] Interview of May 3, 1968.

sensible way was not to kill him the way they killed his brother."[32] Another subject was less direct in his opinion, but perhaps in his own inarticulate way he succeeded in saying to the writers all that the ghetto wanted to say about its romance with the rhetoric of Robert Kennedy. Placing a grimy hand on the writer's shoulder in an expression of sincerity he said, "Like I say man, . . . the cat tell the truth like it is."[33]

One may speculate concerning the spirit in which Kennedy went to the ghetto that night. He may have been driven by political opportunism or by a sincere humanitarian concern. The fact is that Martin Luther King, Jr. was dead and violence seemed inevitable. But there was no violence.

The greatest lesson learned is that violence and riots can be averted and that cross-cultural communication is a necessary step. In the ghetto it seemed to matter that verbal discourse took place in a critical moment. It is customary that the task of "preachment 'midst crisis" be assigned to countless editorials; the irony is that the illiterate cannot read.

As the nation struggles with its moment of turbulence, it is perhaps vital that the tools of effective verbal communication be sharpened.

Assuming from the evidence presented that Robert Kennedy's appearance prevented a riot, what component or components of the communication process were most crucial? Was it the total speech? Was it only a few phrases of the speech? Or was it merely the man himself—a charismatic leader? Would this speech, delivered by another politician, have had the same effect? If Kennedy's image was the decisive factor, what were the vital components of that image?

[32] Interview of May 3, 1968.
[33] Interview of May 3, 1968.

II

PROCESS OF
COMMUNICATION

The Fateful Process of Mr. A Talking to Mr. B

Wendell Johnson

The late Wendell Johnson, professor of speech pathology and psychology at the University of Iowa, states at the beginning of this article that he is concerned with discovering how man communicates with man in order to better understand why communicative attempts succeed or fail. We obviously must be concerned with the same questions if we hope to succeed in our present and future fields of endeavor. Johnson diagrams the process of communication and then explains each stage of the process.

It is a source of never-ending astonishment to me that there are so few men who possess in high degree the peculiar pattern of abilities required for administrative success. There are hundreds who can "meet people well" for every one who can gain the confidence, goodwill, and deep esteem of his fellows. There are thousands who can speak fluently and pleasantly for every one who can make statements of clear significance. There are tens of thousands who are cunning and clever for every one who is wise and creative.

Why is this so? The two stock answers which I have heard so often in so many different contexts are: (1) administrators are born, and (2) administrators are made.

The trouble with the first explanation—entirely apart from the fact that it contradicts the second—is that those who insist that only God can make a chairman of the board usually think themselves into unimaginative acceptance of men as they find them. Hence any attempt at improving men for leadership is automatically ruled out.

Meanwhile, those who contend that administrators can be tailor-made are far from omniscient in their varied approaches to the practical job of transforming bright young men into the inspired leaders without which our national economy could not long survive. Nevertheless, it is in the self-acknowledged but earnest fumblings of those who would seek out and train our future executives and administrators that we may find our finest hopes and possibilities.

This article does not propose to wrap up the problem of what will make men better administrators. Such an attempt would be presumptuous and foolhardy on anyone's part; there are too many side issues, too many far-reaching ramifications. Rather, this is simply an exploration into one of the relatively uncharted areas of the subject, made with the thought that the observations presented may help others to find their way a little better. At the same time, the objective of our exploration can perhaps be described as an oasis of insight in what otherwise is a rather frightening expanse of doubt and confusion.

The ability to respond to and with symbols would seem to be the single most important attribute of great administrators. Adroitness in

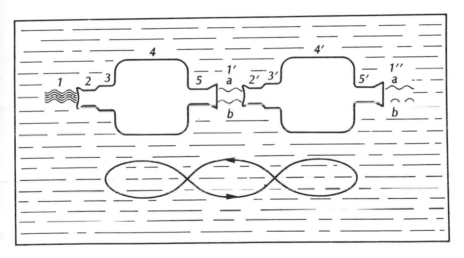

Exhibit 1.   The Process of Communication

Key: Stage 1, event, or source of stimulation, external to the sensory end organs of the speaker; Stage 2, sensory stimulation; Stage 3, pre-verbal neurophysiological state; Stage 4, transformation of pre-verbal into symbolic forms; Stage 5, verbal formulations in "final draft" for overt expression; Stage 1', transformation of verbal formulations into (a) air waves and (b) light waves, which serve as sources of stimulation for the listener (who may be either the speaker himself or another person); Stages 2' through 1" correspond, in the listener, to Stages 2 through 1'. The arrowed loops represent the functional interrelationships of the stages in the process as a whole.

reading and listening, in speaking and writing, in figuring, in drawing designs and diagrams, in smoothing the skin to conceal and wrinkling it to express inner feelings, and in making the pictures inside the head by means of which thinking, imagining, pondering, and evaluating are carried on—these are the fundamental skills without which no man may adequately exercise administrative responsibilities.

Many of the more significant aspects of these administrative pre-requisites may be brought into focus by means of a consideration of what is probably the most fateful of all human functions, and certainly the one function indispensable to our economic life: communication. So let us go on, now, to look at the process of communication and to try to understand the difficulties and disorders that beset us in our efforts to communicate with one another.

THE PROCESS DIAGRAMED

Several years ago I spent five weeks as a member of a group of university professors who had the job of setting up a project concerned with the study of speech. In the course of this academic exploring party we spent a major part of our time talking—or at least making noises—about "communication." By the second or third day it had become plain, and each day thereafter it became plainer, that we had no common and clear notion of just what the word "communication" meant.

After several days of deepening bewilderment, I recalled an old saying: "If you can't diagram it, you don't understand it." The next day I made a modest attempt to bring order out of the chaos—for myself, at least—by drawing on the blackboard a simple diagram representing what seemed to me to be the main steps in the curious process of Mr. A talking to Mr. B. Then I tried to discuss communication by describing what goes on at each step—and what might go wrong. Since sketching that first diagram on the blackboard eight or nine years ago, I have refined and elaborated it, and I have tried from time to time, as I shall again here, to discuss the process of communication in terms of it (see Exhibit 1).[1]

[1] The diagram, with a discussion of it, was first published in my book *People in Quandaries* (New York: Harper & Row Publishers, 1946), Chapter 18, "The Urgency of Paradise." I developed it further in *The Communication of Ideas*, edited by Lyman Bryson (New York: Harper & Row Publishers, 1948), Chapter 5, "Speech and Personality." It was also reproduced in *Mass Communications*, edited by Wilbur Schramm (Urbana: University of Illinois Press, 1949), pp. 261–274. The most recent statement is to be found in my article, "The Spoken Word and the Great Unsaid," *Quarterly Journal of Speech*, December 1951, pp. 419–429. The form of the diagram reproduced here, together with a substantial portion of the text, are used by permission of the *Quarterly Journal of Speech*.

INSIDE MR. A

What appears to take place when Mr. A talks to Mr. B is that first of all, at Stage 1, some event occurs which is external to Mr. A's eyes, ears, taste buds, or other sensory organs. This event arouses the sensory stimulation that occurs at Stage 2. The dotted lines are intended to represent the fact that the process of communication takes place in a "field of reality," a context of energy manifestations external to the communication process and in major part external to both the speaker and the listener.

The importance of this fact is evident in relation to Stage 2 (or Stage 2'). The small size of the "opening" to Stage 2 in relation to the magnitude of the "channel" of Stage 1 represents the fact that our sensory receptors are capable of responding only to relatively small segments of the total ranges of energy radiations.

SENSORY LIMITATIONS

The wave lengths to which the eye responds are but a small part of the total spectrum of such wave lengths. We register as sound only a narrow band of the full range of air vibrations. Noiseless dog whistles, "electronic eyes," and radar mechanisms—to say nothing of homing pigeons—underscore the primitive character of man's sensory equipment. Indeed, we seem little more than barely capable of tasting and smelling, and the narrowness of the temperature range we can tolerate is downright sobering to anyone dispassionately concerned with the efficiency of survival mechanisms.

The situation with regard to the normal individual may appear to be sufficiently dismal; let us not forget, however, how few of us are wholly normal in sensory acuity. We are familiar with the blind and partially sighted, the deaf and hard of hearing; we notice less the equally if not more numerous individuals who cannot taste the difference between peaches and strawberries, who cannot smell a distraught civet cat or feel a fly bite.

All in all, the degree to which we can know directly, through sensory avenues, the world outside (and this includes the world outside the sensory receptors but inside the body) is impressively restricted.

Any speaker is correspondingly limited in his physical ability to know what he is talking about. Relatively sophisticated listeners are likely to judge a speaker's dependability as a communicating agent by the degree to which he discloses his awareness of this limitation. The executive who demonstrates a realistic awareness of his own ignorance will in the long run acquire among his peers and subordinates a far better reputation for good judgment than the one who reveals his limitations by refusing to acknowledge them.

Once a sensory receptor has been stimulated, nerve currents travel quickly into the spinal cord and normally up through the base of the brain to the higher reaches of the cortex, out again along return tracts to the muscles and glands. The contractions and secretions they cause bring about new sensory stimulations which are "fed back" into the cord and brain and effect still further changes. The resulting reverberations of stimulation and response define what we may call a pre-verbal state of affairs within the organism. This state is represented at Stage 3 of the diagram.

Two statements about this pre-verbal state are fundamental: (1) we need to realize that our direct knowledge of this state is slight; (2) at the same time we are justified in assuming that it does occur.

No one has ever trudged through the spinal cord and brain with gun and camera, at least not while the owner of those organs was alive. Nevertheless, we are reasonably sure of certain facts about the nervous system. Observations have been reported by neurosurgeons, electroencephalographers, nerve physiologists, and anatomists. Thousands of laboratory animals have been sacrificed on the altars of scientific inquiry. We know that there are nerve currents, that they travel at known rates of speed, exhibit certain electrical properties, and are functionally related to specified kinds and loci of stimulation and to specified kinds and loci of response.

Thus, though our factual information is meager as yet, certainly it is sufficient to demonstrate that the nervous system is not merely a hypothetical construct. We can say with practical assurance that stimulation of our sensory end organs is normally followed by the transmission of nerve currents into the central nervous system, with a consequent reverberation effect, as described above, and the resulting state of affairs within the organism.

Two specific observations about this state of affairs are crucial: (1) it is truly pre-verbal, or silent; (2) it is this noiseless bodily state that gets transformed into words (or other symbols). Therefore—and these next few words should be read at a snail's pace and pondered long and fretfully—besides talking always to ourselves (although others may be listening more or less too), and whatever else we may also be striving to symbolize, *we inevitably talk about ourselves.*

THE INDIVIDUAL'S FILTER

What the speaker—whether he be a junior executive or the general manager—directly symbolizes, what he turns into words, are physiological or electrochemical goings-on inside his own body. His organism, in this sense, operates constantly as a kind of filter through which facts (in the sense of things that arouse sensory impulses) must pass before they can become known to him and before they can be communicated by him to others in some symbolic form, such as standard English speech.

It follows, to present a single, seemingly trivial, but quite representative example, that when the junior executive says to the general manager, "It's certainly a fine day," he is exhibiting an elaborate variety of confusion; indeed, he appears literally not to know what he is talking about. In the meantime, he is talking about himself—or at least about the weather only as "filtered" by himself. He is symbolizing an inner state, first of all. In this he is the brother of all of us who speak.

I do not mean to imply that we talk solely about our inner states. We often talk about the world outside; but when we do, we filter it through our inner states. To the degree that our individual filters are standardized and alike, we will agree in the statements we make about the world outside—allowing, of course, for differences in time, place, observational set, equipment, sensory acuity, perceptive skill, and manner of making verbal reports.

The existence of the filter at Stage 3 of the process of communication is the basic fact. We may differ in our manner of appreciating and interpreting the significance of the filter, and in so doing make ourselves interesting to each other. But when the administrator—when anyone at all—simply never learns that the filter is there, or forgets or disregards it, he becomes, as a speaker, a threat to his own sanity and a potential or actual menace in a public sense.

SELF-PROJECTION

Because the filter is there in each of us, self-projection is a basic bodily process that operates not only in all our speaking but in other kinds of communicative behavior. To claim to speak literally, then, a person must always say "as I see it," or "as I interpret the facts," or "as I filter the world" if you please, or simply "to me."

An administrator whose language becomes too "is"-y tends to persuade himself that what he says the facts are is the same thing as the facts, and under the numbing spell of this illusion he may become quite incapable of evaluating his own judgments. If he is aware of projection, he must make clear, first of all to himself, that he is not speaking about reality in some utterly impersonal or disembodied and "revealed" sense, but only about reality as the prism of his own nervous system projects it upon the gray screen of his own language—and he must realize that this projection, however trustworthy or untrustworthy, must still be received, filtered, and reprojected by each of his listeners.

Sufficient contemplation of this curious engineering scheme renders one sensitive to the hazards involved in its use. As with any other possibility of miracle, one is well advised not to expect too much of it.

PATTERNS AND SYMBOLS

Stage 4, the first stage of symbolization, is represented in our diagram as a great enlargement in the tunnel through which "the world" passes from Stage 1 to Stage 1'. The words ultimately selected for utterance (at Stage 5) are a very small part of the lush abundance of possible verbalizations from which they are abstracted. Moreover, the bulge is intended to suggest that the state of affairs at Stage 3 becomes in a peculiarly human way much more significant by virtue of its symbolization at Stage 4.

At Stage 4 the individual's symbolic system and the pattern of evaluation reflected in its use come into play. The evaluative processes represented at this stage have been the object of much and varied study and speculation:

Freud. Here, it would appear, was the location of Freud's chief preoccupations, as he attempted to explain them in terms of the so-called unconscious depths of the person, the struggle between the Id and the Super-Ego from which the Ego evolves, the ceaseless brewing of dreamstuff, wish and counterwish, the fabulous symbolism of the drama that we call the human personality.[2] Indeed, at this stage there is more than meets the eye—incredibly more so far as we may dimly but compellingly surmise.

Korzybski. Here, too, were the major preoccupations of the founder of general semantics, Alfred Korzybski: the symbol; the creation of symbols and of systems of symbols; the appalling distortions of experience wrought by the culturally imposed semantic crippling of the young through the witless and artful indoctrination of each new generation by the fateful words of the elders—the words which are the carriers of prejudice, unreasoning aspiration, delusional absolutes, and the resulting

[2] Sigmund Freud, *A General Introduction to Psychoanalysis,* translated by Joan Riviere (New York: Liveright Publishing Corporation, 1935).

attitudes of self-abandonment. But also here we find the unencompassable promise of all that human can suggest, and this Korzybski called upon all men to see, to cherish, and to cultivate with fierce tenderness.[3]

Pavlov. The father of the modern science of behavior, Pavlov, also busied himself with ingenious explanations of occurrences at what we have called Stage 4.[4] In human beings, at least, the learning processes, as well as the drives and goals that power and direct them, appear to function at this stage of incipient symbolization.

It seems useful to conjecture that perhaps the general *patterns* of symbolic conditioning are formed at Stage 4, in contrast to the conditioning of specific symbolic responses (i.e., particular statements) produced at Stage 5. We may put it this way: at Stage 4 the syllogism, for example, as a *pattern* or *form* of possible symbolic response, is laid down, while at Stage 5 there occur the specific verbal responses patterned in this syllogistic mold.

Again, at Stage 4 we find the general form, "X affects Y", at Stage 5 we see its specific progeny in such statements as "John loves Mary," "germs cause disease," "clothes make the man," and so on. In this relationship between general forms or patterns at Stage 4 and the corresponding specific utterances at Stage 5 we find the substantial sense of the proposition that our language does our thinking for us.

In fact, one of the grave disorders that we may usefully locate at Stage 4 consists in a lack of awareness of the influence on one's overt speech of the general symbolic forms operating at Stage 4. The more the individual knows about these forms, the more different forms he knows—or originates—and the more adroit he is in the selective and systematic use of them in patterning specific statements at Stage 5, the more control he exercises over "the language that does his thinking for him." The degree of such control exercised over the verbal responses at Stage 5 represents one of the important dimensions along which speakers range themselves, all the way from the naïveté of the irresponsible robot—or compulsive schizophrenic patient—to the culture-shaping symbolic sophistication of the creative genius.

(Generally speaking, most of the disorders of abstracting described and emphasized by the general semanticists are to be most usefully thought of as operating chiefly at Stage 4. These disorders include those

[3] Alfred Korzybski, *Science and Sanity: An Introduction to Non-Aristotelian Systems and General Semantics* (Lancaster, Pennsylvania: Science Press, 3rd ed. 1948).

[4] I. P. Pavlov, *Conditioned Reflexes: An Investigation of the Physiological Activity of the Cerebral Cortex,* translated and edited by G. V. Anrep (London: Oxford University Press, 1927).

involving identification or lack of effective discrimination for purposes of sound evaluation.[5])

THE FINAL DRAFT

The fact has been mentioned, and should be emphasized, that the "final draft" formulated at Stage 5, the words that come to be spoken, represents as a rule a highly condensed abstract of all that might have been spoken. What enters into this final draft is determined, in a positive sense, by the speaker's available knowledge of fact and relationship, his vocabulary, and his flexibility in using it, his purposes, and (to use the term in a broad sense) his habits. What enters into it is determined negatively by the repressions, inhibitions, taboos, semantic blockages, and ignorances, as well as the limiting symbolic forms, operating at Stage 4.

MR. A TO MR. B

As the communication process moves from Stage 5 to Stage 1′, it undergoes another of the incredible transformations which give it a unique and altogether remarkable character: the words, phrases, and sentences at Stage 5 are changed into air waves (and light waves) at Stage 1′. At close quarters, Mr. A may at times pat the listener's shoulder, tug at his coat lapels, or in some other way try to inject his meaning into Mr. B by hand, as it were, but this transmission of meaning through mechanical pressure may be disregarded for present purposes.

INEFFICIENCY OF AIR WAVES

In general, it seems a valid observation that we place an unwarranted trust in spoken words, partly because we disregard, or do not appreciate, the inefficiency of air waves as carriers of information and evaluation. The reasons for this inefficiency lie both in the speaker and in the listener, of course, as well as in the air waves themselves. What the listener ends up with is necessarily a highly abstracted version of what the speaker intends to convey.

The speaker who sufficiently understands this—the wise administrator —expects to be misunderstood and, as a matter of fact, predicts quite well the particular misunderstandings with which he will need to contend. Consequently, he is able not only to forestall confusion to some extent

---

[5] Alfred Korzybski, *Science and Sanity,* and Wendell Johnson, *People in Quandaries,* particularly Chapters 5 through 10.

but also to give himself a chance to meet misunderstanding with the poise essential to an intelligent handling of the relationships arising out of it. A minimal requirement for the handling of such relationships is that either the speaker or the listener (or, better, both) recognize that the fault lies not so much in either one of them as in the process of communication itself —including particularly the fragile and tenuous air waves, whose cargo of meaning, whether too light to be retained or too heavy to be borne, is so often lost in transit.

Such an executive takes sufficiently into account the fact that words, whether spoken or written, are not foolproof. He will do all he can, within reason, to find out how his statements, his letters and press releases, his instructions to subordinates, and so on are received and interpreted. He will not take for granted that anyone else thinks he means what he himself thinks he means. And when he discovers the misunderstandings and confusions he has learned to expect, he reacts with disarming and constructive forbearance to the resentments and disturbed human relationships that he recognizes as being due, not to men, but to the far from perfect communications by means of which men try to work and live together.

INSIDE MR. B

The air waves (and light waves) that arrive at Stage 2′—that is, at the ears and eyes of the listener—serve to trigger the complex abstracting process which we have just examined, except that now it moves from 2′ through 5′ instead of 2 through 5. That is, the various stages sketched in the speaker are now repeated in the listener. To understand speech, or the communication process in general, is to be aware of the various functions and the disorders operating at each stage in the process—and to be conscious of the complex pattern of relationships among the various stages, as represented schematically by the double-arrowed loops in the diagram.

EFFECT OF FEEDBACK

Always important, these relationships become particularly significant when the speaker and listener are one and the same individual. And this, of course, is always the case, even when there are other listeners. The speaker is always affected by "feedback": he hears himself. What is significant is precisely the degree to which he is affected by feedback. It may, in fact, be ventured as a basic principle that the speaker's responsiveness to feedback—or, particularly important, the *administrator's* responsiveness to feedback—is crucial in determining the soundness of his spoken evaluations. It is crucial, also, in determining his effectiveness in maintaining good working relationships with his associates.

APPLICATION TO PROBLEMS

This view of the process of Mr. A speaking to Mr. B may be applied to any one of a great many specific problems and purposes. The diagram can be used especially well as a means of directing attention to the disorders of communication, such as those encountered daily in the world of trade and industry.

PREVENTING TROUBLES

In this connection, let me call attention to the fact that Professor Irving Lee of the School of Speech at Northwestern University has written a book on *How to Talk with People,*[6] which is of particular interest to anyone concerned with such disorders. Its subtitle describes it as "a program for preventing troubles that come when people talk together." The sorts of troubles with which Professor Lee is concerned in this book are among those of greatest interest and importance to personnel managers and business administrators and executives generally, and there would seem to be no better way to make my diagram take on a very practical kind of meaning than to sketch briefly what Professor Lee did and what he found in his studies of men in the world of business trying to communicate with one another.

Over a period of nearly ten years Professor Lee listened to the deliberations of more than 200 boards of directors, committees, organization staffs, and other similar groups. He made notes of the troubles he observed, and in some cases he was able to get the groups to try out his suggestions for reducing such troubles as they were having; and as they tried out his suggestions, he observed what happened and took more notes.

Among the many problems he describes in *How to Talk with People* there are three of special interest, which can be summarized thus:

(1) First of all, misunderstanding results when one man assumes that another uses words just as he does. Professor Quine of Harvard once referred to this as "the uncritical assumption of mutual understanding." It is, beyond question, one of our most serious obstacles to effective thinking and communication. Professor Lee suggests a remedy, deceptively simple but profoundly revolutionary: better habits of listening. We must learn, he says, not only how to define our own terms but also

[6] New York, Harper & Row, Publishers, 1952.

how to ask others what they are talking about. He is advising us to pay as much attention to the righthand side of our diagram as to the left-hand side of it.

(2) Another problem is represented by the person who takes it for granted that anyone who does not feel the way he does about something is a fool. "What is important here," says Lee, "is not that men disagree, but that they become disagreeable about it." The fact is, of course, that the very disagreeable disagreer is more or less sick, from a psychological and semantic point of view. Such a person is indulging in "unconscious projection." As we observed in considering the amazing transformation of the physiological goings-on at Stage 3 into words or other symbols at Stage 4, the only way we can talk about the world out-side is to filter it through our private inner states. The disagreeable dis-agreer is one who has never learned that he possesses such a filter, or has fogotten it, or is so desperate, demoralized, drunk, or distracted as not to care about it.

A trained consciousness of the projection process would seem to be essential in any very effective approach to this problem. The kind of training called for may be indicated by the suggestion to any administrator who is inclined to try it out that he qualify any important statements he makes, with which others may disagree, by such phrases as "to my way of thinking," "to one with my particular background," "as I see it," and the like.

(3) One more source of trouble is found in the executive who thinks a meeting should be "as workmanlike as a belt line." He has such a business-only attitude that he simply leaves out of account the fact that "people like to get things off their chests almost as much as they like to solve problems." Professor Lee's sensible recommendation is this: "If people in a group want to interrupt serious discussion with some diversion or personal expression—let them. Then bring them back to the agenda. Committees work best when the talk swings between the personal and the purposeful."

CONSTRUCTIVE FACTORS

Professor Lee saw something, however, in addition to the "troubles that come when people talk together." He has this heartening and important observation to report:

"In sixteen groups we saw illustrations of men and women talking together, spontaneously, cooperatively, constructively. There was team-play and team-work. We tried to isolate some of the factors we found there: (1) The leader did not try to tell the others what to do or how to think; he was thinking along with them. (2) No one presumed to know it all; one might be eager and vigorous in his manner of talking, but he was amenable and attentive when others spoke. (3) The people thought of the accomplishments of the group rather than of their individual exploits."

This can happen. And where it does not happen, something is amiss. The diagram presented in Exhibit 1, along with the description of the process of communication fashioned in terms of it, is designed to help us figure out what might be at fault when such harmony is not to be found. And it is intended to provide essential leads to better and more fruitful communication in business and industry, and under all other circumstances as well.

CONCLUSION

Mr. A talking to Mr. B is a deceptively simple affair, and we take it for granted to a fantastic and tragic degree. It would surely be true that our lives would be longer and richer if only we were to spend a greater share of them in the tranquil hush of thoughtful listening. We are a noisy lot; and of what gets said among us, far more goes unheard and unheeded than seems possible. We have yet to learn on a grand scale how to use the wonders of speaking and listening in our own best interests and for the good of all our fellows. It is the finest art still to be mastered by men.

Is Johnson's diagram of the process of communication too complicated for a "simple" process, or would you add to it? What parts or stages of the process would you consider to be most important or are they all of equal importance? Perhaps we can see how this process takes place when we are communicating face-to-face with another individual, but does this process of communication occur when we are speaking to large audiences? If not, how can we as speakers assure its taking place? Of what importance is "feedback" to the process of communication?

Barriers and Gateways to Communication

Carl R. Rogers

This article was originally divided into two parts: the first part analyzed communication from the standpoint of human behavior, and the second illustrated it in an industrial context. In the first part reprinted here, Carl Rogers, professor of psychology and psychiatry at the University of Wisconsin, analyzes and provides a solution to a problem of vital concern to all of us—breakdowns in our communications with individuals and groups. He asserts that the causes of most communicative breakdowns are our emotions and our natural tendency to evaluate statements of others. Rogers openly admits that his solution—listening with understanding—is not easily applied.

It may seem curious that a person like myself, whose whole professional effort is devoted to psychotherapy, should be interested in problems of communication. What relationship is there between obstacles to communication and providing therapeutic help to individuals with emotional maladjustments?

Actually the relationship is very close indeed. The whole task of psychotherapy is the task of dealing with a failure in communication. The emotionally maladjusted person, the "neurotic," is in difficulty, first, because communication within himself has broken down and, secondly, because as a result of this his communication with others has been damaged. To put it another way, in the "neurotic" individual parts of himself which have been termed unconscious, or repressed, or denied to awareness, become blocked off so that they no longer communicate themselves to the conscious or managing part of himself; as long as this is true, there are distortions in the way he communicates himself to others, and so he suffers both within himself and in his interpersonal relations.

The task of psychotherapy is to help the person achieve, through a special relationship with a therapist, good communication within himself. Once this is achieved, he can communicate more freely and more effectively with others. We may say then that psychotherapy is good communication, within and between men. We may also turn that statement around and it will still be true. Good communication, free communication, within or between men, is always therapeutic.

It is, then, from a background of experience with communication in counseling and psychotherapy that I want to present two ideas: (1) I wish to state what I believe is one of the major factors in blocking or impeding communication, and then (2) I wish to present what in our experience has proved to be a very important way of improving or facilitating communication.

BARRIER: THE TENDENCY TO EVALUATE

I should like to propose, as a hypothesis for consideration, that the major barrier to mutual interpersonal communication is our very natural tendency to judge, to evaluate, to approve (or disapprove) the statement of the other person or the other group. Let me illustrate my meaning with some very simple examples. Suppose someone, commenting on this discussion, makes the statement, "I didn't like what that man said." What will you respond? Almost invariably your reply will be either approval or disapproval of the attitude expressed. Either you respond, "I didn't either; I thought it was terrible," or else you tend to reply, "Oh, I thought it was really good." In other words, your primary reaction is to evaluate it from *your* point of view, your own frame of reference.

Or take another example. Suppose I say with some feeling, "I think the Republicans are behaving in ways that show a lot of good sound sense these days." What is the response that arises in your mind? The overwhelming likelihood is that it will be evaluative. In other words, you will find yourself agreeing, or disagreeing, or making some judgment about me such as "He must be a conservative," or "He seems solid in his thinking." Or let us take an illustration from the international scene. Russia says vehemently, "The treaty with Japan is a war plot on the part of the United States." We rise as one person to say, "That's a lie!"

This last illustration brings in another element connected with my hypothesis. Although the tendency to make evaluations is common in almost all interchange of language, it is very much heightened in those situations where feelings and emotions are deeply involved. So the stronger our feelings, the more likely it is that there will be no mutual element in the communication. There will be just two ideas, two feelings, two judgments, missing each other in psychological space.

I am sure you recognize this from your own experience. When you have not been emotionally involved yourself and have listened to a heated discussion, you often go away thinking, "Well, they actually weren't talking about the same thing." And they were not. Each was making a judgment, an evaluation, from his own frame of reference. There was really nothing which could be called communication in any genuine sense. This tendency to react to any emotionally meaningful statement by forming an evaluation of it from our own point of view is, I repeat, the major barrier to interpersonal communication.

GATEWAY: LISTENING WITH UNDERSTANDING

Is there any way of solving this problem, of avoiding this barrier? I feel that we are making exciting progress toward this goal, and I should like to present it as simply as I can. Real communication occurs, and this evaluative tendency is avoided, when we listen with understanding. What does that mean? It means to see the expressed idea and attitude from the other person's point of view, to sense how it feels to him, to achieve his frame of reference in regard to the thing he is talking about.

Stated so briefly, this may sound absurdly simple, but it is not. It is an approach which we have found extremely potent in the field of psychotherapy. It is the most effective agent we know for altering the basic personality structure of an individual and for improving his relationships and his communications with others. If I can listen to what he can tell me, if I can understand how it seems to him, if I can see its personal meaning for him, if I can sense the emotional flavor which it has for him, then I will be releasing potent forces of change in him.

Again, if I can really understand how he hates his father, or hates the company, or hates Communists—if I can catch the flavor of his fear of insanity, or his fear of atom bombs, or of Russia—it will be of the greatest help to him in altering those hatreds and fears and in establishing realistic and harmonious relationships with the very people and situations toward which he has felt hatred and fear. We know from our research that such empathic understanding—understanding with a person, not about him— is such an effective approach that it can bring about major changes in personality.

Some of you may be feeling that you listen well to people and yet you have never seen such results. The chances are great indeed that your listening has not been of the type I have described. Fortunately, I can suggest a little laboratory experiment which you can try to test the quality of your understanding. The next time you get into an argument with your wife, or your friend, or with a small group of friends, just stop the discussion for a moment and, for an experiment, institute this rule: "Each person can speak up for himself only *after* he has first restated the ideas and feelings of the previous speaker accurately and to that speaker's satisfaction."

You see what this would mean. It would simply mean that before presenting your own point of view, it would be necessary for you to achieve the other speaker's frame of reference—to understand his thoughts and feelings so well that you could summarize them for him. Sounds simple, doesn't it? But if you try it, you will discover that it is one of the most difficult things you have ever tried to do. However, once you have been able to see the other's point of view, your own comments will have to be drastically revised. You will also find the emotion going out of the discussion, the differences being reduced, and those differences which remain being of a rational and understandable sort.

Can you imagine what this kind of an approach would mean if it were projected into larger areas? What would happen to a labor-management dispute if it were conducted in such a way that labor, without necessarily agreeing, could accurately state management's point of view in a way that management could accept; and management, without approving labor's stand, could state labor's case in a way that labor agreed was accurate? It would mean that real communication was established, and one could practically guarantee that some reasonable solution would be reached.

If, then, this way of approach is an effective avenue to good communication and good relationships, as I am quite sure you will agree if you try the experiment I have mentioned, why is it not more widely tried and used? I will try to list the difficulties which keep it from being utilized.

NEED FOR COURAGE

In the first place it takes courage, a quality which is not too widespread. I am indebted to Dr. S. I. Hayakawa, the semanticist, for pointing out that to carry on psychotherapy in this fashion is to take a very real risk, and that courage is required. If you really understand another person in this way, if you are willing to enter his private world and see the way life appears to him, without any attempt to make evaluative judgments, you run the risk of being changed yourself. You might see it his way; you might find yourself influenced in your attitudes or your personality.

This risk of being changed is one of the most frightening prospects many of us can face. If I enter, as fully as I am able, into the private world of a neurotic or psychotic individual, isn't there a risk that I might become lost in that world? Most of us are afraid to take that risk. Or if we were listening to a Russian Communist, or Senator Joe McCarthy, how many of us would dare to try to see the world from each of their points of view? The great majority of us could not *listen*; we would find ourselves compelled to *evaluate*, because listening would seem too dangerous. So the first requirement is courage, and we do not always have it.

HEIGHTENED EMOTIONS

But there is a second obstacle. It is just when emotions are strongest that it is most difficult to achieve the frame of reference of the other person or group. Yet it is then that the attitude is most needed if communication is to be established. We have not found this to be an insuperable obstacle in our experience in psychotherapy. A third party, who is able to lay aside his own feelings and evaluations, can assist greatly by listening with understanding to each person or group and clarifying the views and attitudes each holds.

We have found this effective in small groups in which contradictory or antagonistic attitudes exist. When the parties to a dispute realize that they are being understood, that someone sees how the situation seems to them, the statements grow less exaggerated and less defensive, and it is no longer necessary to maintain the attitude, "I am 100% right and you are 100% wrong." The influence of such an understanding catalyst in the group permits the members to come closer and closer to the objective truth involved in the relationship. In this way mutual communication is established, and some type of agreement becomes much more possible.

So we may say that though heightened emotions make it much more difficult to understand *with* an opponent, our experience makes it clear that a neutral, understanding, catalyst type of leader or therapist can overcome this obstacle in a small group.

SIZE OF GROUP

That last phrase, however, suggests another obstacle to utilizing the approach I have described. Thus far all our experience has been with small face-to-face groups—groups exhibiting industrial tensions, religious tensions, racial tensions, and therapy groups in which many personal tensions are present. In these small groups our experience, confirmed by a limited amount of research, shows that this basic approach leads to improved communication, to greater acceptance of others and by others, and to attitudes which are more positive and more problem-solving in nature. There is a decrease in defensiveness, in exaggerated statements, in evaluative and critical behavior.

But these findings are from small groups. What about trying to achieve understanding between larger groups that are geographically remote, or between face-to-face groups that are not speaking for themselves but simply as representatives of others, like the delegates at Kaesong? Frankly we do not know the answers to these questions. I believe the situation might be put this way: As social scientists we have a tentative test-tube solution of the problem of breakdown in communication. But to confirm the validity of this test-tube solution and to adapt it to the enormous problems of communication breakdown between classes, groups, and nations would involve additional funds, much more research, and creative thinking of a high order.

Yet with our present limited knowledge we can see some steps which might be taken even in large groups to increase the amount of listening *with* and decrease the amount of evaluation *about*. To be imaginative for a moment, let us suppose that a therapeutically oriented international group went to the Russian leaders and said, "We want to achieve a genuine understanding of your views and, even more important, of your attitudes and feelings toward the United States. We will summarize and resummarize these views and feelings if necessary, until you agree that our description represents the situation as it seems to you."

Then suppose they did the same thing with the leaders in our own country. If they then gave the widest possible distribution to these two views, with the feelings clearly described but not expressed in name-calling, might not the effect be very great? It would not guarantee the type of understanding I have been describing, but it would make it much more possible. We can understand the feelings of a person who hates us much more readily when his attitudes are accurately described to us by a neutral third party than we can when he is shaking his fist at us.

FAITH IN SOCIAL SCIENCES

But even to describe such a first step is to suggest another obstacle to this approach of understanding. Our civilization does not yet have enough faith in the social sciences to utilize their findings. The opposite is true of the physical sciences. During the war when a test-tube solution was found to the problem of synthetic rubber, millions of dollars and an army of talent were turned loose on the problem of using that finding. If synthetic rubber could be made in milligrams, it could and would be made in the thousands of tons. And it was. But in the social science realm, if a way is found of facilitating communication and mutual understanding in small groups, there is no guarantee that the finding will be utilized. It may be a generation or more before the money and the brains will be turned loose to exploit that finding.

SUMMARY

In closing, I should like to summarize this small-scale solution to the problem of barriers in communication, and to point out certain of its characteristics.

I have said that our research and experience to date would make it appear that breakdowns in communication, and the evaluative tendency which is the major barrier to communication, can be avoided. The solution is provided by creating a situation in which each of the different parties comes to understand the other from the other's point of view. This has been achieved, in practice, even when feelings run high, by the influence of a person who is willing to understand each point of view empathically, and who thus acts as a catalyst to precipitate further understanding.

This procedure has important characteristics. It can be initiated by one party, without waiting for the other to be ready. It can even be initiated by a neutral third person, provided he can gain a minimum of cooperation from one of the parties.

This procedure can deal with the insincerities, the defensive exaggerations, the lies, the "false fronts" which characterize almost every failure in communication. These defensive distortions drop away with astonishing speed as people find that the only intent is to understand, not to judge.

This approach leads steadily and rapidly toward the discovery of the truth, toward a realistic appraisal of the objective barriers to communication. The dropping of some defensiveness by one party leads to further dropping of defensiveness by the other party, and truth is thus approached.

This procedure gradually achieves mutual communication. Mutual communication tends to be pointed toward solving a problem rather than toward attacking a person or group. It leads to a situation in which I see how the problem appears to you as well as to me, and you see how it appears to me as well as to you. Thus accurately and realistically defined, the problem is almost certain to yield to intelligent attack; or if it is in part insoluble, it will be comfortably accepted as such.

This then appears to be a test-tube solution to the breakdown of communication as it occurs in small groups. Can we take this small-scale answer, investigate it further, refine it, develop it, and apply it to the tragic and well-nigh fatal failures of communication which threaten the very existence of our modern world? It seems to me that this is a possibility and a challenge which we should explore.

Do you agree with Rogers that the causes of most communication breakdowns are our emotions and natural tendency to evaluate statements of others? Can you suggest other causes? More important ones? Is Rogers' suggested solution just another simple but idealistic solution being offered to meet the problems of our shrunken world? Can we expect people to "listen with understanding" to ideas and proposals that are contrary to their beliefs and interests? Does our educational system, even college, train students to so listen? Can you think of ways to implement Rogers' proposal? He stresses the importance of "frames of reference" and the "risk" of having these changed. What does Rogers mean by "frame of reference," and what role does it play in communication breakdowns?

Making Phrases at Each Other

Irving J. Lee

Irving J. Lee, late professor of speech at Northwestern University, was long concerned with the language symbols employed in man's attempt to communicate with man. In this reading, he discusses phrases that can halt communication between individuals and groups —the use of stigmas. According to Lee, our feelings range from approving, to indifferent, to disapproving. He points out that both identical and different words and phrases may be used in interpreting the same situation, but the meanings may be vastly different. Read carefully the solution that Lee proposes to improve our communication.

Harry Hershfield tells of a cop who clubbed a spectator at a parade, calling him a Communist. "But I'm an anti-Communist!" the spectator protested. "I don't care what kind of a Communist you are!" said the cop. "Get outa here!"—Earl Wilson, *The New York Post*, April 16, 1948, p. 52.

One of the tantalizing phenomena of the discussion process is the "stopper." Men go along easily, asserting, questioning, denying. Then, someone says or does something. There is a moment of uncertainty. The talk stops. The talk picks up again, but it is off the track. It wanders. The men have lost direction. They fumble a bit. Sometimes they get back on the track. Sometimes they don't.

Some stoppers:

- A man reminisces about something only dimly related to the subject at hand; when he is finished no one quite knows what the point was.
- Two or three pursue some topic by themselves as if they were alone in the room; then they are noticed.

"Making Phrases at Each Other" from How to Talk with People by *Irving J. Lee.* Copyright 1952 by Harper & Row, Publishers.

- A man gets wound up, going on and on until the others lose interest. He stops and no one knows where to begin.
- One man insults another or the group.
- A man loses his head and talks wildly. His listeners' sympathy is mixed with embarrassment.
- A man gets off the subject and another tells him about it. The issue is a new one: is he on the subject?

These stoppers seem violations of the common courtesies, demonstrations of what used to be called bad manners. This is not the place for an analysis of the means of correcting them.

But there is one stopper that we have tried to do something about, probably because it seemed to have nothing in common with the others. It is the "stigma."

A man describes a situation, takes a position, or makes a proposal. A listener says:

"But that's ——!"
"Why that is nothing but ——!"
"You're proposing ——!"
"Jim, you are a ——!"
"A clear example of ——!"
"Well, of course, they're ——!"

Substitute for the blank any word or phrase used in connection with something considered undesirable—any one of these, for example: un-American, fascist, communist, socialism, New Dealer, capitalist, Wall Street lackey, conservative, reactionary, fundamentalist, radical, drunkard, thief, liar, delinquent, coward, childish, fool, politician, demagogue, warmonger, pacifist, militarist, a racket, appeasement, fifth columnist, Quisling . . .

The first speaker is now identified with the stigma. Sometimes it stops him cold. Sometimes he denies its relevance. Sometimes he finds a stigma for his listener. The talk turns on the implication of the stigma. The subject fades away.

THE STIGMA: ITS USE AND ABUSE

A word becomes a stigma by a process both historical and psychological. For our purposes a rather simple theory of the stigma's functioning may be enough. It begins with the notion that words go with or reflect attitudes or feelings.

Every minute of every waking hour a man has some sort of awareness, some feelings or attitudes. These awarenesses shift rapidly or one may persist or several may blend—but let a man be alive and awake and he will feel something. He may be pleased, frightened, angry, satisfied, surprised, ashamed, bored, tired, disgruntled, comfortable, in pain, hopeful, despairing, forgiving, ambitious, numb, excited, dizzy, resigned, confident, pitying, sorrowful, aghast, wondering, adamant, worshipful, cynical, optimistic, pessimistic, expectant, eager, uncertain, assured, uneasy, happy, terrified—the list of possible feelings is a long one.

It matters little whether they be classified one way or another. In one catch-all view these feelings can be arranged in this form:

The painful, disapproving, uncomfortable, negative, despairing	The mildly painful, etc.	The indifferent or inexplicit	The mildly pleasant, etc.	The pleasant, approving, comfortable, positive, hopeful

Suppose, further, that every expression of a man's relationship with a thing, person, or situation will involve some feeling to it, which feeling will be reflected or involved in what he says.

The senator is in front of the audience for thirty minutes. At the end three people comment:

A: "Mere rhetoric and bombast."

B: "He spoke about foreign affairs and the audience clapped hands for five minutes when he finished."

C: "Eloquence and great speaking."

After questioning the three further, an interviewer is assured that the feeling in A was disapproval, in B indifference, in C approval.

The same word can be used in settings which reflect different feelings. Three people are referring to three different men:

A: "He is a bastard."

B: "He is a bastard."

C: "He is a bastard."

In the particular settings it is found that the feeling in A is one of disapproval, that the man was born out of wedlock; in B the feeling is of indifference, the speaker wishing only to distinguish the birth from one when the parents are married; in C at the beer party one lodge brother refers in friendly fashion to another.

Any word in English, then, may be used as a *stigma* when the feeling involves disapproval or negativeness, as an *inexplicit* term when the feeling is one of unconcern or non-interest, and as a *halo* when the feeling involves approval or positiveness. In short, a word has a stigma- or halo-function only when somebody uses or takes it so.

Most of the time this is no conscious, deliberate process. A person doesn't sit back and say to himself, "I want to say something about the proposal just advanced. I feel negative about it. What is a good word to express my attitude so the others will know I don't like the proposal?" Something like that may happen, but for the most part one has at hand a vocabulary organized and ready for this kind of evaluative indication.

There is nothing intrinsic in a word that makes us use it for either approval or disapproval. Custom is a sufficient explanation. Though each of us develops his own ways of characterization there are broad tendencies in our usage. When Jon Stone said that it was "damned nonsense," his hearers could assume with considerable assurance that he was not expressing approval. When a man was referred to as an "infamous impostor" it is likely that that phrase reflected feelings different from those involved when he was called a "prophet, seer, and revelator"—even though on occasion a man might have contrary feelings and use these words in an ironic or just nonconventional way.

That usage does become established is rather well revealed in Ben W. Palmer's illustration. Do you have any doubt which terms you would choose if you liked or disliked the President?

The President achieved $\frac{\text{notoriety}}{\text{fame}}$ by $\begin{array}{l}\text{stubbornly, bitterly, fanati-}\\\text{tenaciously, vigorously, zeal-}\end{array}$ $\begin{array}{l}\text{cally}\\\text{ously}\end{array}$ asserting his $\frac{\text{impudent pretensions}}{\text{bold claims}}$ even in legislative councils through his $\frac{\text{tools}}{\text{agents}}$ who $\frac{\text{cunningly insinuated}}{\text{skillfully introduced}}$ themselves into those councils. The Senate being in accord with his $\frac{\text{prejudices succumbed}}{\text{principles yielded}}$ to his $\frac{\text{domination.}}{\text{leadership.}}$ He was a man of $\frac{\text{superstition}}{\text{faith}}$ and of $\frac{\text{obstinacy}}{\text{strength of}}$ $\begin{array}{l}\text{purpose}\end{array}$ whose policy combined $\frac{\text{bigotry and arrogance}}{\text{firmness and courage}}$ with $\frac{\text{cowardice.}}{\text{caution.}}$

He was a $\frac{\text{creature}}{\text{man}}$ of strong $\frac{\text{biases}}{\text{convictions}}$ and belonged in the camp of the $\frac{\text{reactionaries.}}{\text{conservatives.}}$ His conduct of the presidency $\frac{\text{portended}}{\text{foreshadowed}}$ a $\frac{\text{degeneration}}{\text{change}}$ of that office into one of $\frac{\text{dictatorship.}}{\text{leadership.}}$[1]

If talking necessarily involves naming people and actions and indicating how the talker feels about them, what does this have to do with discussion?

[1] *American Bar Association Journal*, July, 1949, p. 559.

There is nothing about a stigma word as such which leads to trouble. It is as necessary a phase of the talk process as the halo or inexplicit term. Nevertheless, when a man is moved to stigmatize a person or situation or argument, in our experience the result very often is a dramatic dead end. Once something is stigmatized it tends to be located and fixed. A barrier is set up around it and further discussion is shunted away. It is as if the speaker said, "Nothing can be said further, I've catalogued the thing and there is no other way to do it."

A staff had considered hiring a research agency to survey job assignments. There were pros and cons. Then Jon Stone said, "They're a bunch of racketeers." Somehow this "fixed" the issue. An anti-Stoneite could reply, "No, they are not. They're an honest outfit." But the barrier was up. The agency was tagged. And it was not easy to get out from under the influence of the stigma. It was like an umbrella which kept men from seeing the heavens beyond.

Organizations at work on behalf of "the handicapped," those released from "insane asylums," "juvenile delinquents," "epileptics," "lepers" have had to fight long and hard against the imprisoning effects of the stigma. People seem stopped by the label from looking beyond it to what it points to. Though an epileptic is thoroughly normal when he is not having a seizure, and a man released from a leper colony is by no means dangerous, it still takes a strong sort of evaluating penetration to see beyond the feeling of suspicion derived from negative associations with the words.

What Dr. William Alanson White wrote in connection with physicians fits here: "Giving something a name seems to have a deadening influence upon all our relations to it. It brings matters to a finality. Nothing further seems to need to be done. The disease has been identified. The necessity for further understanding of it has ceased to exist. And so classifications . . . had a sterilizing effect upon further inquiries."[2]

Again it should be said, the stigma word is inevitable and unavoidable. To outlaw it would be to prevent the expression of a tremendous area of human concern. Would it be humanly possible to stop people from saying they dislike something? Would you want to?

There would be values, however, in a tactic by which a group could be sensitized to the stigma's dead-end effect.

We have found but one way to get at it. We work through the leader. He is urged to recognize that

- A stigma word may well be an accurate indication of how someone feels about a person or situation.
- A stigma word describes a situation from a particular point of view. It

2 William A. White, *William Alanson White: The Autobiography of a Purpose* (Garden City, N.Y.: Doubleday & Company, 1938), p. 53.

applies to an aspect of things as one person sees it. It is a fractional indicator. Every name gets to a bit of something, not all of it.

- A stigma word may put a brake on further discussion of an issue. This is the danger the leader must watch for. Should a stigma word be an invitation to more scrutiny on the issue, then it is to be welcomed. When it limits analysis or cuts off consideration, then its braking influence must be exposed.

What should a leader do when the stopper is at work? He is urged to say something like

- "The gentleman said 'the agency is a racket!' That is certainly one way of looking at it. Is there any other?"
- "Certainly Mr. Stone's feeling about the agency is clear. Does it exhaust what can be said about it?"
- "Mr. Stone has pegged the agency. Is that true all the time? Is it always that?"

This direct attack by the leader on the stigma does not guarantee that the limiting effects will be removed. But it does invite and encourage more talk. If it doesn't remove the effect, it undercuts it. In groups where the leader or anyone else does something similar the uncertainty and stoppage of talk are less apparent. Under the prodding of his question the talk usually starts again. When he has spotted stigmas long enough, he may even find that the practice is picked up by others.

What are "stigmas" and why are they used? Do you agree with Lee that our feelings range on a scale from the approving, to the indifferent, to the disapproving? Are we ever totally indifferent to communications or to communicating? If so, when and under what circumstances? How as speakers can we be certain of accurately communicating the meaning we desire? How as listeners can we be assured of interpreting the message as the sender desired?

The Field of Nonverbal Communication: An Overview

Mark L. Knapp

In this reading Mark L. Knapp, associate professor of communication at Purdue University, defines nonverbal communication, discusses the interrelation of verbal and nonverbal communication, and reviews research findings in eight areas of nonverbal behavior. The reading is an overview of research and theory in topics such as physical appearance and dress, gestures, touch, facial expressions, eye contact, and voice.

In many respects the field of nonverbal communication is like a newborn baby. It was conceived many years ago and slowly began to take shape in the work of some isolated scholars. Within the last few years the child was born, and we are just now beginning to gain a greater perspective on its role in the total process of human communication.

WHAT IS NONVERBAL COMMUNICATION?

Traditionally, educators, researchers, and laymen have used the following definition when discussing nonverbal communication: Nonverbal communication designates all those human responses which are not described as overtly manifested words (either spoken or written). Whereas this definition provides a common referent for discussing this phenomenon, it does not offer us much insight into the complex nature of nonverbal communication.

For instance, some scholars have questioned the term nonverbal to describe the range of vocal and nonvocal events generally studied under

This article is printed here for the first time.

this label.[1] Indeed, this position has some validity when verbal symbols are used to decode (or encode) a message. For example, you respond to someone by making a circle with your thumb and first finger and the other person says to himself, "Everything is OK." An analysis of this transaction makes it difficult to affirm that such behavior was literally *nonverbal*. Certainly we may engage in nonverbal behavior, but the moment we begin to interpret this behavior in terms of words the verbal-nonverbal dichotomy becomes hazy. In the previous example we used a gesture to illustrate the verbal-nonverbal confusion; the same argument could be made for vocal sounds. Some theorists would describe the sound of a long drawn-out groan as nonverbal because it does not overtly manifest words; to others, as soon as a person attaches meaning to the groan it becomes a verbal phenomenon.

Regardless of our position concerning the preceding discussion, we are reminded of the intimate relationship that exists between verbal and nonverbal communication systems. Any time we separate verbal and non-verbal communication it is an artificial distinction. Usually, such separation is used primarily for focusing a discussion or for experimental control in research. In everyday human interaction, however, verbal and nonverbal systems are intimately interwoven and subtly represented in one another. Ray Birdwhistell, a noted nonverbal scholar, was once quoted as saying that studying *nonverbal* communication is like studying *noncardiac* physiology. His point was this: human transactions cannot be dissected and diagnosed in such a way that one diagnosis concerns verbal behavior and the other is concerned only with nonverbal behavior. They work together.

INTERRELATION OF VERBAL
AND NONVERBAL BEHAVIOR

Ekman and Friesen[2] discuss five ways in which these two systems interact. Perhaps the most obvious role of nonverbal communication in relation to spoken communication is *repetition*. Through the use of gestures and body movements the spoken message is repeated. If an irate instructor orders a mischievous student to leave the room and then points at the door, we have a case of repetition of the verbal by the nonverbal.

Another common situation in human communication behavior is when messages sent verbally and nonverbally seem to *contradict* one

---

[1] F. E. X. Dance, "Toward a Theory of Human Communication," in F. E. X. Dance (ed.) *Human Communication Theory* (New York: Holt, Rinehart and Winston Inc., 1967).

[2] P. Ekman and W. V. Friesen, "The Repertoire of Nonverbal Behavior: Categories, Origins, Usage, and Coding," *Semiotica*, 1 (1969), 49–98.

another. A case in point is the instructor who states his deep-felt belief in student conferences and claims he has plenty of time to talk to students. When a student arrives for a conference, however, the instructor begins to pack his briefcase, straighten his papers, look at his watch and out the window. He leaves the student with the impression that he has better things to do than talk to him. Sarcasm is another good example of a situation in which vocal cues contradict verbal cues. Your parents see you going out on a date in levis, a tee shirt, and no shoes, and they say to you, "Well, you certainly outdid yourself in dressing up for the occasion." The tone of voice, however, suggests they are disapproving your attire. Some nonverbal scholars have suggested that we are likely to place more reliance on non-verbal messages when we are confronted with contradictory verbal and nonverbal messages. They explain that we have grown up in a verbally-oriented world, have been sensitized to deceptions on the verbal level and perceive nonverbal cues as harder to fake—hence, more reliable. We should be cautious in accepting this position. Some nonverbal behaviors are harder to fake than others, and some individuals are particularly skilled at such deception. Those who have studied nonverbal deceptive behavior[3] suggest we can do much better at deceiving others with our facial expressions than we can with our hands or especially our legs and feet. Skill at deception depends upon how much external feedback we previously have received concerning the particular nonverbal mode being used, how motivated we are to carry out the deception successfully, how rapidly we can neurologically handle internal message transmission to make alterations in behavior, and how likely the perceiver is to attend to the particular type of nonverbal behavior being used. We might expect children to place a great deal of reliance on nonverbal cues of any sort when confronted with contradictory messages, but Bugental and his colleagues[4] found just the opposite. Young children placed less credence in certain nonverbal cues than adults did when they were confronted with a speaker who smiled while making a critical comment. Children generally thought the overall impact of the message was negative, particularly when the speaker was a woman. Another study casts even more doubt on the theory that we generally rely on nonverbal cues in contradictory situations. Shapiro[5] found that some people consistently rely on one type of cue (either facial expressions or verbal statements) across a wide range of subjects and situations.

3 P. Ekman and W. V. Friesen, "Nonverbal Leakage and Clues to Deception," *Psychiatry*, 32 (1969), 88–106.

4 D. E. Bugental, J. W. Kaswan, L. R. Love, and M. N. Fox, "Child Versus Adult Perception of Evaluative Messages in Verbal, Vocal, and Visual Channels," *Developmental Psychology*, 2 (1970), 367–75.

5 J. G. Shapiro, "Responsivity to Facial and Linguistic Cues," *Journal of Communication*, 18 (1968), 11–17.

Nonverbal behavior can also *substitute* for verbal messages. This is particularly frequent among persons who have had considerable experience interacting with one another. For example, by mid-semester an instructor may not have to tell you, "I've had a bad day; I'm tired; I really don't want to conduct this class." Instead, the message is communicated by the way he walks into the classroom, his facial expression, his posture, and a host of other cues. If he perceives that such cues are not being monitored by his students, and they are not in turn communicating, "We got your message and we sympathize; we'll try to make it a good class for you," he may resort to the verbal level and tell them about his problems.

Another function of nonverbal behavior is that of *complementing* the verbal messages. Here we find the antithesis of the contradictory situation. In this case nonverbal behaviors reflect one's attitudes and intentions toward the other person. In short, if you were trying to indicate a higher status, a positive attitude, seeking approval, etc., your nonverbal behavior would tend to support or complement the verbal exchange.

Nonverbal behavior can also be used to *accent* certain parts of the verbal message. Consider this familiar scene during courtship. In the course of explaining how much he loves his female companion, the male begins holding her hand. In order to emphasize a particularly meaningful statement, he may give her hand a short squeeze. His words may be further accented by a lingering eye glance and a slight smile. We do the same thing when we *underline* words in order to accent them.

We also use nonverbal behavior to *regulate* the flow of communication. A head nod may encourage the speaker to continue; engaging in eye contact as you pass by another person may suggest the initiation of verbal exchange. Any number of signals may be used to activate or stop the flow of verbal utterances.

Now that we have some idea of how the term *nonverbal communication* has been used and the general functions it performs, we can further clarify the scope of such study by examining some specific dimensions of nonverbal human communication.

SPECIFIC AREAS OF NONVERBAL STUDY

Generally, the research in nonverbal communication has been conducted under the following broad headings: (1) environmental factors which impinge on and influence human interaction; (2) proxemics, or the study of man's use and perception of his social and personal space; (3) physical appearance and dress; (4) gestures, postures, and other body movements—or kinesics; (5) touch behavior; (6) facial expressions; (7) eye behavior; and (8) vocal behavior. As we discuss each of these areas, we must keep in mind the shortcomings of an "overview." Only a fraction of the research and theory extant is discussed under each heading.

ENVIRONMENTAL FACTORS

The setting chosen for our communicative encounters may have a profound influence on the responses we obtain. Have you ever explained a particularly dissatisfactory encounter with another person by saying he was "hot and irritable." It is a common phrase and suggests there may be some relationship between heat and humidity and one's interpersonal responses. This idea formed the basis for experiments by Griffitt[6] in which he varied temperature conditions for students in a laboratory setting. When he measured the interpersonal attraction of these persons for each other, he found evaluative responses became more negative under conditions of increased temperature and humidity. Further evidence of the influence of temperature was seen in the report of the U.S. Riot Commission[7] which stated: "In most instances, the temperature during the day on which the violence erupted was quite high." It is not uncommon to find that conditions of personal discomfort caused by the environment will elicit negative and sometimes hostile reactions to other persons. A related study by Maslow and Mintz[8] used three different types of rooms in which subjects evaluated negative print photographs of faces. Some subjects were placed in a "beautiful" room, some in an "average" room, and some in an "ugly" room. As predicted, more negative evaluations of the faces were obtained from those experiencing the ugly room. A follow-up study found that graduate students, who were testing the subjects, tried to avoid the ugly room and if they could not, they tried to complete their experiments rapidly and leave.

The architectural structure of our environment also seems to affect who communicates with whom and how frequently. Homes located in the middle of the block seem to draw more communication from neighbors than those located on the corners. Apartment complexes may be so structured that dwellers most frequently see and talk to those on their own floor

---

[6] W. Griffitt, "Environmental Effects of Interpersonal Affective Behavior: Ambient Effective Temperature and Attraction," *Journal of Personality and Social Psychology*, 15 (1970), 240–44.

[7] U.S. National Advisory Commission on Civil Disorders, "Report of the National Advisory Commission on Civil Disorders," (Washington, D.C.: U.S. Government Printing Office, 1968), p. 71.

[8] A. H. Maslow and N. L. Mintz, "Effects of Esthetic Surroundings: I. Initial Effects of Three Esthetic Conditions Upon Perceiving 'Energy' and 'Well-Being' in Faces," *Journal of Psychology*, 41 (1956), 247–54. Also see: N. L. Mintz, "Effects of Esthetic Surroundings: II. Prolonged and Repeated Experience in a 'Beautiful' and 'Ugly' Room," *Journal of Psychology*, 41 (1956), 459–66.

or those who use the same stairway or those located near the mailboxes. Some research suggests these architectural features do indeed influence interpersonal contacts, and in turn influence friendship choices.[9]

Take a moment to reflect on your own classroom. Do immovable chairs inhibit interaction? What would happen if the windows were removed? Do students who sit opposite the instructor—those within his range of eye contact—participate more? Do students toward the back participate as much as those in front? Do large classes inhibit participation? Are there physical barriers between you and your instructor—namely, a desk, table, or lectern? What would happen if these were removed? Are there other aspects of the classroom which may be affecting your responses —e.g., noise, lighting, color schemes, etc.? There seems to be little doubt that any analysis of interpersonal transactions must consider the role of environmental and architectural features.

OUR USE OF SPACE

A great many people have been concerned about problems that may arise from overpopulation. Some of these problems can be seen in the context of the invasion of one's territorial space. Man and other animals have a tendency to develop strong identification with a particular area or space which they call their "own." What happens when someone invades our territory? For your own tests: try sitting in another student's chair before he enters the class; try standing very close to someone on a bus; try tailgating the car in front of you; or try sitting down next to someone studying in the library.

The invasion of territory in a library was the subject of an actual experiment conducted by Russo.[10] Over a period of two years, several techniques of invasion were used on female college students seated in a college library. The quickest departure or flight resulted when the researcher sat down next to the person and moved her chair closer, but perhaps the most interesting results from this study concerned the methods used to defend territory. Some had positioned themselves against a wall; some had spread materials such as books, magazines, and coats all over the study table; and a few used verbal methods such as profanity to get rid of the intruder. Obviously there are many ways of defending "our" space, and the intensity of the defense is strongly correlated with the perceived threat of the invader. Overpopulation of an area will obviously result in more territorial violations; several studies show very disruptive behavioral reac-

---

[9] L. Festinger, S. Schachter, and K. Back, *Social Pressures in Informal Groups: A Study of Human Factors in Housing* (New York: Harper & Row, Publishers, 1950).

[10] Robert Sommer, *Personal Space* (Englewood Cliffs, N.J.: Prentice-Hall, Inc., 1969).

tions to such situations. Calhoun[11] deliberately overpopulated a colony of rats and observed behavior over a period of three generations of rats. Some rats withdrew from social contact completely; others became very aggressive—killing and eating other rats. Although such studies have not been replicated with human groups, Hutt and Vaizey[12] found that increasing the density of children in a playroom also tended to result in aggressive/destructive behavior by some children and complete withdrawal by others.

Another way of studying man's use of space is to observe his conversational distance. You may have had the experience of suddenly realizing you have been backing up as you talked to another person. This simply suggests the other person's optimum conversational distance was smaller than yours. As he tried to get closer, you tried to get farther apart. Each of us seems to have a "comfortable" amount of distance, but this may vary depending on: (1) our relationship to the other person; (2) the physical characteristics of the other person, (3) the topic being discussed; (4) the social setting; and (5) perceived attitudinal and personality characteristics of the other person.

Studies of spatial relationships in small group settings suggest that seating is not always random or accidental. For instance, it is part of our cultural heritage that "leaders" sit at the head (or end) of the table. Dominant personalities have been found to seek focal positions (1, 3, and 5 at right) in small groups, while those who are more anxious and want to stay out of the discussion seek nonfocal positions (2 and 4).[13] We also have some information on how people sit with one another when facing different kinds of tasks. When cooperating at a common task (studying for the same exam) we would predict side by side seating, When conversing before class, we would predict either across seating, , or corner seating, . The most popular seating for co-acting or studying for different exams showed a more distant pattern, , while the most popular pattern for competing on a task required some visibility of the opponent by sitting across,[14] .

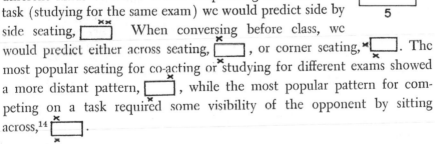

[11] J. B. Calhoun, "Population Density and Social Pathology," *Scientific American*, 206 (1962), 139–48.

[12] C. Hutt and M. J. Vaizey, "Differential Effects of Group Density on Social Behavior," *Nature*, 209 (1966), 1371–72.

[13] A. Hare and R. Bales, "Seating Position and Small Group Interaction," *Sociometry*, 26 (1963), 180–86.

[14] Robert Sommer, "Further Studies of Small Group Ecology," *Sociometry*, 28 (1965), 337–48.

PHYSICAL APPEARANCE AND DRESS

We pay a lot of attention to the way we look. Does it make a difference? Judge for yourself. In April, 1971, the United Press International reported the story of a man in Castro Valley, California, who shot and killed his son because of the youth's long hair and his negative attitude toward society. In January, 1971, the placement officer at Stanford University reported: "The length of a male's hair is directly proportionate to the job opportunities he can find . . . the longer the hair, the fewer the jobs."[15] Visitors to Taiwan in 1970 were greeted with cards saying, "Welcome to the Republic of China. No long hair or long beards, please!" Not all reactions to hair are negative, however. Some women seem to feel a man's beard heightens his sexual magnetism.[16]

Other aspects of one's appearance also seem to have strong communicative potential. We need not review the impact of one's skin color on interpersonal responses. Singer[17] conducted a study which confirmed what many college professors and students had hypothesized for a long time. He found that female students used physical attractiveness as a manipulative device to obtain higher grades from college professors. Attractive females also seem to be able to modify attitudes of male students more than their unattractive counterparts.[18] Numerous studies show physical attractiveness to be a critical factor in mate selection. One representative study was conducted with 752 college students randomly paired for a freshman dance.[19] Considerable information was gathered from each student—a self-report on popularity, religious preference, height, race, expectations for the date, self-esteem, high school academic percentile rank, scholastic aptitude score, and personality test score. In addition, each student was rated by several judges on attractiveness. Physical attractiveness was by far the most important determinant of how much a date would be liked by his or her partner.

There is also a clear indication that we have definite stereotypes which

[15] *Personnel Management Week* (Long Beach, Calif.: Executive's Research Council, January 25, 1971).

[16] D. G. Freedman, "The Survival Value of the Beard," *Psychology Today*, 3 (1969), 36–39.

[17] J. E. Singer, "The Use of Manipulative Strategies: Machiavellianism and Attractiveness," *Sociometry*, 27 (1964), 128–51.

[18] J. Mills and E. Aronson, "Opinion Change as a Function of the Communicator's Attractiveness and Desire to Influence," *Journal of Personality and Social Psychology*, 1 (1965), 73–77.

[19] E. Walster, V. Aronson, D. Abrahams, and L. Rohmann, "Importance of Physical Attractiveness in Dating Behavior," *Journal of Personality and Social Psychology*, 4 (1966), 508–16.

accompany general body types—e.g., endomorph, mesomorph, and ecto-morph. These stereotypes may or may not be accurate, but they do exist. For instance, judges made the following observations about a silhouette drawing of an endomorph:[20] fatter, older, and shorter than other body types (although drawings were all the same height); more old fashioned; less strong physically; less good-looking; more talkative; more warmhearted and sympathetic; more good-natured and agreeable; more dependent on others, and more trusting of others—all derived from a drawing similar to this:

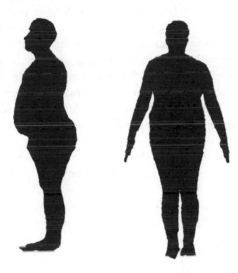

FIG. 1

Although we are not able at this time to specify the exact influence of each aspect of one's physical appearance in any given social situation, it seems fair to conclude that they may be profoundly important in some situations. Adding to the complexity of our responses to physical appear-ance is the influence of clothing, cosmetics, jewelry, glasses, and other artifacts—a subject of little recent research.

GESTURES, POSTURES, AND OTHER
BODY MOVEMENTS

I think we are all aware that our body has a language—but what does it say? We can't review everything that can be communicated through body language, but here are some typical areas of study:

20 W. Wells and B. Siegel, "Stereotyped Somatypes," *Psychological Reports*, 8 (1961), 77–78.

1. Our body positions and movements seem to help us indicate liking and disliking for other communicators. The use of the arms-akimbo position by standing communicators seems to be used with greater frequency when interacting with disliked persons than with liked. Both males and females perceived a person leaning backward from them as having a more negative attitude than when they were leaning forward.[21]

2. Status is also associated with certain positions. In standing positions, shoulder orientation was found to be more direct with a high status addressee, regardless of the attitude toward him. Again, the arms-akimbo position is more likely when talking to a person you think has a lower status than your own. Subjects in Mehrabian's experiments also seemed to raise their heads more when speaking to a high status person—especially males interacting with high status males. It is a frequent observation, however, that people who perceive themselves to be in an inferior role will often lower their heads while high status persons often maintain a raised head. Differences are probably associated with whether or not one has respect, liking, or need for approval from the high status person.

3. Affective states or moods are also reflected in our body movements. Although some feel that high degrees of emotional arousal are associated with much bodily movement, this movement will probably vary with the particular mood.[22, 23]

4. Rosenfeld[24] designed an experiment in which female undergraduate students were trying either to win approval or to avoid approval from another female student. Smiles, nodding, and a generally higher level of gestural activity characterized approval seekers. Closely related was a study which attempted to identify the nonverbal components of being perceived as a "warm" person. "Warmth" included a shift of posture toward the other person, a smile, direct eye contact, and hands remaining still.[25]

5. Scheflen[26] believes we have a whole body repertoire of quasi-courtship behavior—courtship readiness which is characterized by constant manifestations of high muscle tone, reduced eye bagginess and jowl sag, lessening of slouch and shoulder hunching, and decreasing belly sag; preening

[21] A. Mehrabian, "Significance of Posture and Position in the Communication of Attitude and Status Relationships," *Psychological Bulletin*, 71 (1969), 359–72.

[22] P. Sainesbury, "Gestural Movement During Psychiatric Interviews," *Psychosomatic Medicine*, 17 (1955), 458–69.

[23] A. T. Dittman, "The Relationship Between Body Movements and Moods in Interviews," *Journal of Consulting Psychology*, 26 (1962), 480.

[24] H. Rosenfeld, "Instrumental Affiliative Functions of Facial and Gestural Expressions," *Journal of Personality and Social Psychology*, 4 (1966), 65–72.

[25] M. Reece and R. Whitman, "Expressive Movements, Warmth, and Verbal Reinforcement," *Journal of Abnormal and Social Psychology*, 64 (1962), 234–36.

[26] A. E. Scheflen, "Quasi-Courtship Behavior in Psychotherapy," *Psychiatry*, 27 (1965), 245–57.

behavior—characterized by stroking of the hair, rearrangement of makeup, glancing in the mirror, rearranging clothes in a sketchy fashion, leaving buttons open, adjusting suit coats, tugging at socks, and readjusting tie knots; actions of appeal or invitation—characterized by flirtatious glances, gaze-holding, rolling of the pelvis, crossing legs to expose a thigh, exhibiting wrist or palm, and protruding the breasts; and finally, positional cues which suggest to others, "We're not open to interaction with anyone else." These cues involve placement of legs, arms, and torsos in such a way as to inhibit others from entering the conversation.

6. Some of our body movements are known as interaction markers. That is, they mark special points in the interaction. For instance, one may note downward head, eyelid, and hand movements at the end of statements and upward movements at the end of questions.

The foregoing factors associated with body movements must be kept in contextual perspective—e.g., whereas a given configuration of nonverbal cues seems to convey the feeling of interpersonal "warmth," we must be aware that the same configuration may reveal a completely different meaning in a context in which "warmth" behaviors are neutralized, added to, or cancelled by other factors.

TOUCH BEHAVIOR

Tactile communication is probably the most basic or primitive of all forms of communication—with tactual sensitivity the first sensory process to become functional. In a very real sense our first experiences with our world come through touch. We touch things around us, and in turn we learn the touch of our mother, father, siblings, relatives, doctors, and others while they are performing a variety of tasks for us. Several studies suggest that children who are deprived of this early handling and touching may have later problems in their mental and emotional development. Initially, touching behavior is often accompanied by words; gradually, touch is replaced by words. By the time we reach adulthood the amount and kind of touching behavior varies considerably with age and with the relationship of the parties involved. In this culture, many children have been trained that touching is only performed in extremely personal and intimate encounters; children are frequently punished for touching certain objects, certain parts of their own bodies, and even certain parts of their companions' bodies! To my amazement, my five-year-old daughter returned from school recently to inform me there was something "yucky" about men kissing men and women kissing women.

Just where are people frequently touched and by whom? Jourard[27]

---

[27] S. M. Jourard, "An Exploratory Study of Body-Accessibility," *British Journal of Social and Clinical Psychology*, 5 (1966), 221–31.

administered a questionnaire to students asking which of 24 body parts they had seen or touched, or which had been seen or touched by four other persons—mother, father, same-sexed friend, and opposite-sexed friend—within the preceding year. Fig. 2 shows the results of his work. Among other findings, Jourard's study found females considerably more accessible to touch than males. Opposite-sexed friends and mothers were those who did the most touching, while fathers touched not much more than the hands of the subjects.

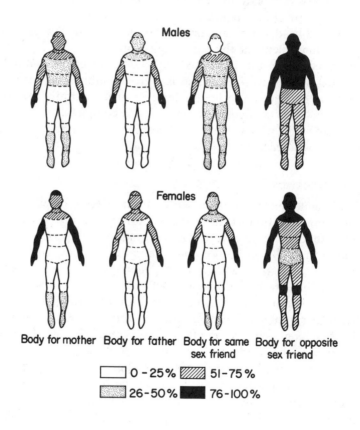

Body for mother Body for father Body for same Body for opposite
                                   sex friend   sex friend

☐ 0 - 25%   ▨ 51-75%
▨ 26-50%   ■ 76-100%

Fig. 2

FACIAL EXPRESSIONS

The face is rich in communicative potential. It is the primary site for communicating emotional states; it reflects interpersonal attitudes; it provides nonverbal feedback on the comments of others; and some say that,

·next to human speech, it is the primary source of giving information. For these reasons and because of its visibility, we pay a great deal of attention to what we see in the faces of others.

One of the heated disputes in the study of facial expressions concerns the question of whether there are facial expressions which are universal— i.e., performed in the same way and meaning the same thing to people all over the world—in both literate and preliterate cultures. The work of Ekman and his colleagues[28] during the last five years supports the universality theory. Facial expressions of happiness, sadness, anger, fear, disgust, and surprise were not only recognized, but expressed, with the same facial musculature in five literate and two preliterate cultures. While this seems to suggest that man has a "facial affect program," it does not discount cultural differences in the stimuli which evoke the expressions or the culturally-bound display rules which man uses to intensify, deintensify, neutralize, or mask the expressions.

Another important consideration in analyzing facial expressions concerns facial blends. Many facial expressions contain aspects of more than one expression. For instance, you may react to your own anger by getting disgusted with yourself. Thus, your expression, when photographed, would show some characteristics of disgust and some of anger.

The shortcomings of some of the previous research on facial expressions have pointed out optimum conditions for accurately judging facial expressions of emotion: (1) judges should have experience and previous training in judging emotion in faces; (2) judges should have exposure to the face they will be judging prior to the actual test and see it in emotional states other than the one to be judged; (3) the face itself should accurately reflect all the facial movements associated with the particular emotion; (4) the judge's discriminatory task should be easy and familiar terminology should be used; (5) judges should have ample time for observation, and they should be able to see the entire face. Obviously, any other contextual information may help to identify the expression if it cannot be clearly identified by the face alone.

EYE BEHAVIOR

Eye-related terms are plentiful in our society: "Shifty eyes," "the evil eye," "the jaundiced eye," "all eyes," "gleam in her eye," "seeing eye to eye," "looking right through you," "icy stare," "looking daggers," etc. The research on eye behavior has generally focused on two main areas—eye contact and pupil dilation.

[28] P. Ekman, P. Ellsworth, and W. V. Friesen, The Face and Emotion (New York: Pergamon Press Inc., 1971).

Generally, eye contact will occur when people are seeking feedback. We find that speakers tend to look at the other person as they come to the end of an utterance, and that they tend to look more closely when they are listening than when they are speaking—especially when discussing difficult material.

Eye contact also occurs when one wants to signal that the communication channel is open. You may have found yourself trying to avoid the eye contact of an instructor who had just asked a question, when you wanted to avoid the suggestion that you were ready to interact. Avoiding eye contact in some instances suggests the disavowal of social contact.

Eye contact frequently is indicative of the nature of the relationship between the interactants. It may be used when affiliation or inclusion is desired. We tend to look at those things which are rewarding to us. A person will engage in more eye contact with someone perceived as being friendly and helpful and will avoid the eyes of a person who comments unfavorably upon his performance. In situations where competition is occurring, or where there is dislike, tension, or a recent deception, the participants are likely to engage in less eye contact. Possibly the avoidance of eye contact in these situations helps to insulate a person against threats or discovery. Eye contact also seems to increase with high status addresses and to decrease for low status persons. One can use prolonged eye contact to indicate aggressiveness or to produce anxiety in others. Usually a gaze of longer than ten seconds will produce an uncomfortable response.

Finally, eye contact can be used to psychologically reduce the physical distance which may exist between communicators. If the two communicators are too close, avoiding eye contact will help psychologically to increase the distance.

Almost all the experiments on pupil dilation associate dilation with emotional arousal, attentiveness, or interest. A few studies suggest the possibility that we can identify a person's attitudes by measuring his pupil dilation, but several well-controlled studies by Woodmansee[29] offer no support that pupil dilation and constriction can be used as an index of attitudes toward Negroes.

A legitimate question for those interested in human communication is: Do we ever respond to pupil dilation in everyday encounters? An interesting study by Stass and Willis[30] gives us only a hint. Subjects were told that they would be in an experiment, and they were requested to choose a partner—one whom they could trust and one who would be

[29] J. J. Woodmansee, "The Pupil Response as a Measure of Social Attitudes," in G. F. Summers (ed.) *Attitude Measurement* (Chicago: Rand McNally & Company, 1970), pp. 514–33.
[30] J. W. Stass and F. N. Willis, Jr., "Eye Contact, Pupil Dilation, and Personal Preference," *Psychonomic Science*, 7 (1967), 375–76.

pleasant and easy to talk with on an intimate basis. The subjects were taken to a room where two other persons waited. These two persons previously had been rated approximately the same in general attractiveness. Eye contact and pupil dilation (through use of a drug) were varied. When the naïve subject left the waiting room, the experimenter asked him to choose one of the two persons and to give reasons for the choice. Results showed that eye contact was an overwhelming factor in choice-making, and that pupil dilation also seemed to be a factor—even though few subjects were consciously aware of reacting to the dilated eyes.

VOCAL BEHAVIOR

We use our voices to communicate in many ways. Sometimes it is a part of the spoken words; sometimes it is used to make sounds which are not part of the formal language code. We may deliberately use our voices to emphasize words by adding volume; we may indicate a question by raising our voice; or we may reveal anxiety or uncertainty through uneven vocal quality, pauses, or nonfluencies such as "uh" or "um." On the other hand, people may associate certain personality or emotional states with our voices when we are not deliberately trying to manipulate them.

Can people judge our personalities solely from our voices? For many years researchers have been trying to determine whether people consistently associate certain personality characteristics with vocal cues. Naturally, attempts have been made to eliminate any possible influence of the particular words spoken. This is done by having speakers recite the alphabet or, more recently, by using electronic filtering which eliminates the words but allows most of the vocal characteristics to remain. Consistently, judges listening to these voices will agree with each other regarding the occupation, race, sociability, introversion, or other personality characteristics, but such judgments usually have little validity when compared to the actual speaker. These results suggest there are definite stereotypes associated with vocal cues which may be influential in judging other persons. However, the probability of these judgments being accurate is only about fifty-fifty. So far it is difficult to identify any personality trait which can be judged with consistent accuracy. This is partly due, of course, to the imperfect nature of personality measures. This does not imply, however, that a particular person, judging a particular voice, cannot be very accurate in judging the personality behind that voice. Accurate judgments of age, sex, and status using vocal cues alone tend to be supported by research completed thus far.

Other researchers have been interested in judging emotions using vocal cues. This research shows we often can make accurate judgments of emotions and feelings from wordless vocal messages. We should remember, however, that any individual may vocally express the same emotion differently on different days, in different situations, and with different stimuli.

Do vocal cues influence listener comprehension or attitude changes? Several studies indicate that moderately poor vocal behaviors do not interfere significantly with the listener's comprehension. Other evidence tells us that if public speakers use variety in their volume, pitch, and rate of speaking they may increase their chances of achieving audience comprehension. Probably the use of an unchanging vocal behavior detracts from the goal of achieving audience comprehension. Nonfluencies do not seem to affect attitude changes, but listeners base some decisions concerning a speaker's credibility on his wordless behavior—and credibility may have a profound effect on changing attitudes.

Considered as a whole, these findings show that vocal cues can add much information about a speaker and that our total reaction to another individual is at least somewhat influenced by our reactions to those vocal cues.

CONCLUSION

Admittedly, this has been a hurried glance at the field of nonverbal communication. It was designed to give the reader an initial perspective on an important and often neglected part of the total process of human communication. We must incorporate an understanding of nonverbal behavior in any analysis of human transactions, if we are to understand them fully. This brief introduction has been successful if it has brought to the reader's attention any types of behavior he formerly was likely to ignore.

Can we separate verbal from nonverbal communication, or are they too interrelated? Which kinds of nonverbal behavior are most important in communication? Does importance vary with audience size— a speech before a large audience, a small group discussion, an interview? Are we aware of our nonverbal behavior? Do we plan it in advance of communication efforts? How can we keep our nonverbal behavior from sending messages we have not intended?

III

SPEAKER

Creating an Image

Joe McGinniss

This chapter from Joe McGinniss' book The Selling of the President 1968 focuses on the image a president must attain, the role of television in creating that image, and the selling of President Nixon to the electorate in 1968. He raises some serious ethical questions about image making and suggests that we are more interested in the wrapping than what is actually inside the package. This phenomenon has serious implications for our society, not only in politics but in education, religion, the professions.

Politics, in a sense, has always been a con game.

The American voter, insisting upon his belief in a higher order, clings to his religion, which promises another, better life; and defends passionately the illusion that the men he chooses to lead him are of finer nature than he.

It has been traditional that the successful politician honor this illusion. To succeed today, he must embellish it. Particularly if he wants to be President.

"Potential presidents are measured against an ideal that's a combination of leading man, God, father, hero, pope, king, with maybe just a touch of the avenging Furies thrown in," an adviser to Richard Nixon wrote in a memorandum late in 1967. Then, perhaps aware that Nixon qualified only as father, he discussed improvements that would have to be made—not upon Nixon himself, but upon the image of him which was received by the voter.

That there is a difference between the individual and his image is human nature. Or American nature, at least. That the difference is exaggerated and exploited electronically is the reason for this book.

Advertising, in many ways, is a con game, too. Human beings do not need new automobiles every third year; a color television set brings little enrichment of the human experience; a higher or lower hemline no expansion of consciousness, no increase in the capacity to love.

It is not surprising then, that politicians and advertising men should have discovered one another. And, once they recognized that the citizen did not so much vote for a candidate as make a psychological purchase of him, not surprising that they began to work together.

The voter, as reluctant to face political reality as any other kind, was hardly an unwilling victim. "The deeper problems connected with advertising," Daniel Boorstin has written in *The Image*, "come less from the unscrupulousness of our 'deceivers' than from our pleasure in being deceived, less from the desire to seduce than from the desire to be seduced. . . .

"In the last half-century we have misled ourselves . . . about men . . . and how much greatness can be found among them. . . . We have become so accustomed to our illusions that we mistake them for reality. We demand them. And we demand that there be always more of them, bigger and better and more vivid."

The Presidency seems the ultimate extension of our error.

Advertising agencies have tried openly to sell Presidents since 1952. When Dwight Eisenhower ran for re-election in 1956, the agency of Batton, Barton, Durstine and Osborn, which had been on a retainer throughout his first four years, accepted his campaign as a regular account. Leonard Hall, national Republican chairman, said: "You sell your candidates and your programs the way a business sells its products."

The only change over the past twelve years has been that, as technical sophistication has increased, so has circumspection. The ad men were removed from the parlor but were given a suite upstairs.

What Boorstin says of advertising: "It has meant a reshaping of our very concept of truth," is particularly true of advertising on TV.

With the coming of television, and the knowledge of how it could be used to seduce voters, the old political values disappeared. Something new, murky, undefined started to rise from the mists. "In all countries," Marshall McLuhan writes, "the party system has folded like the organization chart. Policies and issues are useless for election purposes, since they are too specialized and hot. The shaping of a candidate's integral image has taken the place of discussing conflicting points of view."

Americans have never quite digested television. The mystique which should fade grows stronger. We make celebrities not only of the men who cause events but of the men who read reports of them aloud.

The televised image can become as real to the housewife as her husband, and much more attractive. Hugh Downs is a better breakfast companion, Merv Griffin cozier to snuggle with on the couch.

Television, in fact, has given status to the "celebrity" which few real men attain. And the "celebrity" here is the one described by Boorstin: "Neither good nor bad, great nor petty . . . the human pseudo-event . . . fabricated on purpose to satisfy our exaggerated expectations of human greatness."

This is, perhaps, where the twentieth century and its pursuit of illusion have been leading us. "In the last half-century," Boorstin writes, "the old heroic human mold has been broken. A new mold has been made, so that marketable human models—modern 'heroes'—could be mass-produced, to satisfy the market, and without any hitches. The qualities which now commonly make a man or woman into a 'nationally advertised' brand are in fact a new category of human emptiness."

The television celebrity is a vessel. An inoffensive container in which someone else's knowledge, insight, compassion, or wit can be presented. And we respond like the child on Christmas morning who ignores the gift to play with the wrapping paper.

Television seems particularly useful to the politician who can be charming but lacks ideas. Print is for ideas. Newspapermen write not about people but policies; the paragraphs can be slid around like blocks. Everyone is colored gray. Columnists—and commentators in the more polysyllabic magazines—concentrate on ideology. They do not care what a man sounds like; only how he thinks. For the candidate who does not, such exposure can be embarrassing. He needs another way to reach the people.

On television it matters less that he does not have ideas. His personality is what the viewers want to share. He need be neither statesman nor crusader; he must only show up on time. Success and failure are easily measured: how often is he invited back? Often enough and he reaches his goal—to advance from "politician" to "celebrity," a status jump bestowed by grateful viewers who feel that finally they have been given the basis for making a choice.

The TV candidate, then, is measured not against his predecessors—not against a standard of performance established by two centuries of democracy—but against Mike Douglas. How well does he handle himself? Does he mumble, does he twitch, does he make me laugh? Do I feel warm inside?

Style becomes substance. The medium is the massage and the masseur gets the votes.

In office, too, the ability to project electronically is essential. We were willing to forgive John Kennedy his Bay of Pigs; we followed without question the perilous course on which he led us when missiles were found in Cuba; we even tolerated his calling of reserves for the sake of a bluff about Berlin.

We forgave, followed, and accepted because we liked the way he looked. And he had a pretty wife. Camelot was fun, even for the peasants, as long as it was televised to their huts.

Then came Lyndon Johnson, heavy and gross, and he was forgiven nothing. He might have survived the sniping of the displaced intellectuals had he only been able to charm. But no one taught him how. Johnson was syrupy. He stuck to the lens. There was no place for him in our culture.

"The success of any TV performer depends on his achieving a low-pressure style of presentation," McLuhan has written. The harder a man tries, the better he must hide it. Television demands gentle wit, irony, understatement: the qualities of Eugene McCarthy. The TV politician cannot make a speech; he must engage in intimate conversation. He must never press. He should suggest, not state; request, not demand. Nonchalance is the key word. Carefully studied nonchalance.

Warmth and sincerity are desirable but must be handled with care. Unfiltered, they can be fatal. Television did great harm to Hubert Humphrey. His excesses—talking too long and too fervently, which were merely annoying in an auditorium—became lethal in a television studio. The performer must talk to one person at a time. He is brought into the living room. He is a guest. It is improper for him to shout. Humphrey vomited on the rug.

It would be extremely unwise for the TV politician to admit such knowledge of his medium. The necessary nonchalance should carry beyond his appearance while on the show; it should rule his attitude toward it. He should express distaste for television; suspicion that there is something "phony" about it. This guarantees him good press, because newspaper reporters, bitter over their loss of prestige to the television men, are certain to stress anti-television remarks. Thus, the sophisticated candidate, while analyzing his own on-the-air technique as carefully as a golf pro studies his swing, will state frequently that there is no place for "public relations gimmicks" or "those show business guys" in his campaign. Most of the television men working for him will be unbothered by such remarks. They are willing to accept anonymity, even scorn, as long as the pay is good.

Into this milieu came Richard Nixon: grumpy, cold, and aloof. He would claim privately that he lost elections because the American voter was an adolescent whom he tried to treat as an adult. Perhaps. But if he treated the voter as an adult, it was as an adult he did not want for a neighbor.

This might have been excused had he been a man of genuine vision. An explorer of the spirit. Martin Luther King, for instance, got by without being one of the boys. But Richard Nixon did not strike people that way.

He had, in Richard Rovere's words, "an advertising man's approach to his work," acting as if he believed "policies [were] products to be sold the public—this one today, that one tomorrow, depending on the discounts and the state of the market."

So his enemies had him on two counts: his personality, and the convictions—or lack of such—which lay behind. They worked him over heavily on both.

Norman Mailer remembered him as "a church usher, of the variety who would twist a boy's ear after removing him from church."

McLuhan watched him debate Kennedy and thought he resembled "the railway lawyer who signs leases that are not in the best interests of the folks in the little town."

But Nixon survived, despite his flaws, because he was tough and smart, and—some said—dirty when he had to be. Also, because there was nothing else he knew. A man to whom politics is all there is in life will almost always beat one to whom it is only an occupation.

He nearly became President in 1960, and that year it would not have been by default. He failed because he was too few of the things a President had to be—and, because he had no press to lie for him and did not know how to use television to lie about himself.

It was just Nixon and John Kennedy and they sat down together in a television studio and a little red light began to glow and Richard Nixon was finished. Television would be blamed but for all the wrong reasons.

They would say it was makeup and lighting, but Nixon's problem went deeper than that. His problem was himself. Not what he said but the man he was. The camera portrayed him clearly. America took its Richard Nixon straight and did not like the taste.

The content of the programs made little difference. Except for startling lapses, content seldom does. What mattered was the image the viewers received, though few observers at the time caught the point.

McLuhan read Theodore White's *The Making of the President* book and was appalled at the section on the debates. "White offers statistics on the number of sets in American homes and the number of hours of daily use of these sets, but not one clue as to the nature of the TV image or its effects on candidates or viewers. White considers the 'content' of the debates and the deportment of the debaters, but it never occurs to him to ask why TV would inevitably be a disaster for a sharp intense image like Nixon's and a boon for the blurry, shaggy texture of Kennedy." In McLuhan's opinion: "Without TV, Nixon had it made."

What the camera showed was Richard Nixon's hunger. He lost, and bitter, confused, he blamed it on his beard.

He made another, lesser thrust in 1962, and that failed, too. He showed the world a little piece of his heart the morning after and then he moved East to brood. They did not want him, the hell with them. He was going to Wall Street and get rich.

He was afraid of television. He knew his soul was hard to find. Beyond that, he considered it a gimmick; its use in politics offended him. It had not been part of the game when he had learned to play, he could see no reason to bring it in now. He half suspected it was an eastern liberal trick: one more way to make him look silly. It offended his sense of dignity, one of the truest senses he had.

So his decision to use it to become President in 1968 was not easy. So much of him argued against it. But in his Wall Street years, Richard Nixon had traveled to the darkest places inside himself and come back numbed. He was, as in the Graham Greene title, a burnt-out case. All feeling was behind him; the machine inside had proved his hardiest part. He would run for President again and if he would have to learn television to run well, then he would learn it.

America still saw him as the 1960 Nixon. If he were to come at the people again, as candidate, it would have to be as something new; not this scarred, discarded figure from their past.

He spoke to men who thought him mellowed. They detected growth, a new stability, a sense of direction that had been lacking. He would return with fresh perspective, a more unselfish urgency.

His problem was how to let the nation know. He could not do it through the press. He knew what to expect from them, which was the same as he had always gotten. He would have to circumvent them. Distract them with coffee and doughnuts and smiles from his staff and tell his story another way.

Television was the only answer, despite its sins against him in the past. But not just any kind of television. An uncommitted camera could do irreparable harm. His television would have to be controlled. He would need experts. They would have to find the proper settings for him, or if they could not be found, manufacture them. These would have to be men of keen judgment and flawless taste. He was, after all, Richard Nixon, and there were certain things he could not do. Wearing love beads was one. He would need men of dignity. Who believed in him and shared his vision. But more importantly, men who knew television as a weapon: from broadest concept to most technical detail. This would be Richard Nixon, the leader, returning from exile. Perhaps not beloved, but respected. Firm but not harsh; just but compassionate. With flashes of warmth spaced evenly throughout.

Nixon gathered about himself a group of young men attuned to the political uses of television. They arrived at his side by different routes.

One, William Gavin, was a thirty-one-year-old English teacher in a suburban high school outside Philadelphia in 1967, when he wrote Richard Nixon a letter urging him to run for President and base his campaign on TV. Gavin wrote on stationery borrowed from the University of Pennsylvania because he thought Nixon would pay more attention if the letter seemed to be from a college professor.

> Dear Mr. Nixon:
> May I offer two suggestions concerning your plans for 1968?
> 1. Run. You can win. Nothing can happen to you, politically speaking, that is worse than what has happened to you. Ortega y Gassett in his *The Revolt of the Masses* says: "These ideas are the only genuine ideas; the ideas of the shipwrecked. All the rest is rhetoric, posturing, farce. He who does not really feel himself lost, is lost without remission . . ." You, in effect, are "lost"; that is why you are the only political figure with the vision to see things the way they are and not as Leftist or Rightist kooks would have them be. Run. You will win.
> 2. A tip for television: instead of those wooden performances beloved by politicians, instead of a glamorboy technique, instead of safety, be bold. Why not have live press conferences as your campaign on television? People will see you daring all, asking and answering questions from reporters, and not simply answering phony "questions" made up by your staff. This would be dynamic; it would be daring. Instead of the medium using you, you would be using the medium. Go on "live" and risk all. It is the only way to convince people of the truth: that you are beyond rhetoric, that you can face reality, unlike your opponents, who will rely on public relations. Television hurt you because you were not yourself; it didn't hurt the "real" Nixon. The real Nixon can revolutionize the use of television by dynamically going "live" and answering everything, the loaded and the unloaded question. Invite your opponents to this kind of a debate.
> Good luck, and I know you can win if you see yourself for what you are; a man who had been beaten, humiliated, hated, but who can still see the truth.

A Nixon staff member had lunch with Gavin a couple of times after the letter was received and hired him.

William Gavin was brought to the White House as a speech writer in January of 1969.

Harry Treleaven, hired as creative director of advertising in the fall of 1967, immediately went to work on the more serious of Nixon's personality problems. One was his lack of humor.

"Can be corrected to a degree," Treleaven wrote, "but let's not be too obvious about it. Romney's cornball attempts have hurt him. If we're going to be witty, let a pro write the words."

Treleaven also worried about Nixon's lack of warmth, but decided that "he can be helped greatly in this respect by how he is handled. . . . Give him words to say that will show his *emotional* involvement in the issues. . . . Buchanan wrote about RFK talking about the starving children in Recife. *That's* what we have to inject. . . .

"He should be presented in some kind of 'situation' rather than cold in a studio. The situation should look unstaged even if it's not."

Some of the most effective ideas belonged to Raymond K. Price, a former editorial writer for the *New York Herald Tribune*, who became Nixon's best and most prominent speech writer in the campaign. Price later composed much of the inaugural address.

In 1967, he began with the assumption that, "The natural human use of reason is to support prejudice, not to arrive at opinions." Which led to the conclusion that rational arguments would "only be effective if we can get the people to make the emotional leap, or what theologians call [the] 'leap of faith.' "

Price suggested attacking the "personal factors" rather than the "historical factors" which were the basis of the low opinion so many people had of Richard Nixon.

"These tend to be more a gut reaction," Price wrote, "unarticulated, non-analytical, a product of the particular chemistry between the voter and the *image* of the candidate. *We have to be very clear on this point: that the response is to the image, not to the man.* . . . It's not what's there that counts, it's what's projected—and carrying it one step further, it's not what he projects but rather what the voter receives. It's not the man we have to change, but rather the *received impression*. And this impression often depends more on the medium and its use than it does on the candidate himself."

So there would not have to be a "new Nixon." Simply a new approach to television.

"What, then, does this mean in terms of our uses of time and of media?" Price wrote.

"For one thing, it means investing whatever time RN needs in order to work out firmly in his own mind that vision of the nation's future that he wants to be identified with. This is crucial. . . ."

So, at the age of fifty-four, after twenty years in public life, Richard Nixon was still felt by his own staff to be in need of time to "work out firmly in his own mind that vision of the nation's future that he wants to be identified with."

"Secondly," Price wrote, "it suggests that we take the time and the money to experiment, in a controlled manner, with film and television techniques, with particular emphasis on pinpointing those *controlled* uses of the television medium that can best convey the *image* we want to get across . . .

"The TV medium itself introduces an element of distortion, in terms of its effect on the candidate and of the often subliminal ways in which the image is received. And it inevitably is going to convey a partial image —thus ours is the task of finding how to control its use so the part that gets across is the part we want to have gotten across. . . .

"Voters are basically lazy, basically uninterested in making an *effort* to understand what we're talking about . . . ," Price wrote. "Reason requires a high degree of discipline, of concentration; impression is easier. Reason pushes the viewer back, it assaults him, it demands that he agree or disagree; impression can envelop him, invite him in, without making an intellectual demand. . . . When we argue with him we demand that he make the effort of replying. We seek to engage his intellect, and for most people this is the most difficult work of all. The emotions are more easily roused, closer to the surface, more malleable. . . ."

So, for the New Hampshire primary, Price recommended "saturation with a film, in which the candidate can be shown better than he can be shown in person because it can be edited, so only the best moments are shown; then a quick parading of the candidate in the flesh so that the guy they've gotten intimately acquainted with on the screen takes on a living presence—not saying anything, just being seen. . . .

"[Nixon] has to come across as a person larger than life, the stuff of legend. People are stirred by the legend, including the living legend, not by the man himself. It's the aura that surrounds the charismatic figure more than it is the figure itself, that draws the followers. Our task is to build that aura. . . .

"So let's not be afraid of television gimmicks . . . get the voters to like the guy and the battle's two-thirds won."

So this was how they went into it. Trying, with one hand, to build the illusion that Richard Nixon, in addition to his attributes of mind and heart, considered, in the words of Patrick K. Buchanan, a speech writer, "communicating with the people . . . one of the great joys of seeking the Presidency"; while with the other they shielded him, controlled him, and controlled the atmosphere around him. It was as if they were building not a President but an Astrodome, where the wind would never blow, the temperature never rise or fall, and the ball never bounce erratically on the artificial grass.

They could do this, and succeed, because of the special nature of the man. There was, apparently, something in Richard Nixon's character which sought this shelter. Something which craved regulation, which flourished best in the darkness, behind clichés, behind phalanxes of anti-septic advisers. Some part of him that could breathe freely only inside a hotel suite that cost a hundred dollars a day.

And it worked. As he moved serenely through his primary campaign, there was new cadence to Richard Nixon's speech and motion; new confidence in his heart. And, a new image of him on the television screen.

TV both reflected and contributed to his strength. Because he was winning he looked like a winner on the screen. Because he was suddenly projecting well on the medium he had feared, he went about his other tasks with assurance. The one fed upon the other, building to an astonishing peak in August as the Republican convention began and he emerged from his regal isolation, traveling to Miami not so much to be nominated as coronated. On live, but controlled, TV.

Are we seeking a combination of leading man, God, father, hero, Pope, and king for the position of president of the United States? What are the characteristics we desire in a leader? Are they simply safety, dynamism, and qualification? When an image is created by television, the press, or events, how can we discern the real from the make-believe? What are the dangers when politicians become celebrities and when images replace issues? Of what importance are our own images when we communicate? What is your image when speaking before fellow students?

Developing Confidence

Otis M. Walter

Stage fright is both an emotional and physical response to situations in which we place our reputations and prestige on the line. We may hide our fears and ignorance in silence; but once we begin to speak, we are displaying ourselves in a frighteningly open manner. Otis M. Walter, professor of speech at the University of Alabama, offers a variety of suggestions for reducing stage fright and developing confidence.

Because stage fright is caused by conflict, its solution lies in the reduction of conflict. Conflicts are reduced by increasing some desires and by nullifying, preventing, or weakening desires that pull in other directions. The medieval donkey need not have starved to death between the two stacks of hay had he reduced the desire for one of the stacks and increased the desire for the other. He might have remembered that he was a "left-footed" donkey and taken the stack of hay to the left, and thereby reduced the conflict sufficiently to permit his survival. The speaker is not given so simple a choice; on the other hand, so many possibilities for reinforcing the desire to speak and reducing the fear of speaking exist that he has a strong chance of reducing conflict in the speech situation. Look next at the ways in which he can unify himself so that when he must speak, he will want to.

RESOLVING CONFLICT: SOME AUTOMATIC TREATMENTS

There are some "instant" ways of reducing stage fright that can help a speaker once he knows of them. A speaker can take heart from the knowledge that if he has stage fright, the audience will not realize that fact. Experiments demonstrate that audiences—including even experienced speech instructors—are notoriously poor judges of the degree of stage fright experienced by a speaker. These observers, whether experts in speech or otherwise, greatly underrate the amount of stage fright they believe the speaker has.[1] When a speaker realizes that his stage fright will not be noticed, some of his apprehension may vanish.

A second bit of reassurance may come from the realization that stage fright decreases with age. Adolescents in the tenth grade experience less stage fright than those in grades below them, and by the time one reaches twenty, stage fright will have dropped even more. Inasmuch as time seems to decrease stage fright, you may trust that time will also help you to feel more confident.[2]

Thirdly, and far more importantly, experience in speaking reduces stage fright enormously. "All the investigations . . . showed that on the high school as well as on the college and adult level, practice was a significant factor in influencing gains in confidence."[3] Most students gain confidence as they proceed through a course in public speaking. Practice is so certain to reduce stage fright that it is the most frequently recommended treatment in textbooks,[4] and is recommended as a treatment by instructors more than any other single remedy.[5] The more frequently one speaks, the less will his stage fright be a problem. Especially does stage fright lessen in a classroom where the attitudes of the instructor and of the classmates are unthreatening, and when the student is taught so well that he receives genuine insight into the means of preparing and delivering fine speeches. In any event, students can expect a reduction in stage fright as a result of speaking frequently.

Finally, the student may take heart from realizing that nearly all beginners feel stage fright.[6] Inasmuch as his classmates have the same disadvantage, he need not feel upset.

These four automatic helps are at least reassuring: The speaker knows in advance that the audience can't recognize how much stage fright he

---

[1] See Theodore Clevenger, Jr., "A Synthesis of Experimental Research in Stage Fright," *Quarterly Journal of Speech*, XLV (April, 1959), p. 137.

[2] Clevenger, pp. 141–142.

[3] William Hamilton, "A Review of Experimental Studies of Stage Fright," *Pennsylvania Speech Annual*, XVII (September, 1960), pp. 44–45.

[4] Edward R. Robinson, "What Can the Speech Teacher Do About Students' Stage-fright?" *The Speech Teacher* VIII (January, 1959), pp. 10–11.

[5] Lawrence Edward Cole, Jr., *A Critical Evaluation of Methods of Controlling Stage Fright*, Unpublished M.A. Thesis, Emerson College, 1964.

[6] Elma Dean Orr Wrenchy, *A Study of Stage Fright in a Selected Group of Experienced Speakers*, Unpublished M.A. Thesis, University of Denver, 1948, p. 37.

has; as he grows older, his stage fright will lessen; experience in speaking will greatly reduce his fears; his classmates have the same difficulty that he does. These automatic helps will reduce the fear of speaking, but there is much more that the speaker can do to increase his desire to speak. Here are some further sources of reassurance.

COMBATING UNFORTUNATE PREVIOUS
EXPERIENCES RESOLVING CONFLICT

Some students may have had an alarming experience with speaking in which they may have felt publicly embarrassed. The fifth grader, who, on Parents' Night, was asked to recite a poem, but who, when he stood in front of his classmates, parents and teacher, couldn't remember the first line, may have become so frightened that he is afraid to get up in front of another audience. The young actor who accidentally stumbled against the canvas scenery during the class play and pushed his arm through the canvas "wall" may feel alarmed at the thought of being before people again. Usually such experiences are passed off lightly, but once in a while, the experience may cause undue stage fright. The student who has had such an experience should take the following steps to reduce or nullify the effect of it:

1. Recall the experience fully. The process of recalling may be temporarily painful, but to "forget" the experience may cause harm. Such "forgetting," which psychologists call *repression*, may be harmful and may continue to cause trouble. A standard treatment for phobias —unjustified fears—is to trace the origin of the phobia to the incident that caused it. This incident usually is painful to the person, and difficult to recall, because the experience makes him feel guilty. The guilty feelings, however, are unjustified, and as soon as the incident is fully recalled, the unjustified guilt feelings disappear, as *does the fear itself*. The best way, therefore, to reduce any feelings of anxiety caused by such an incident, is to recall the incident completely.
2. Discuss the experience with the instructor. The instructor will probably want to know if there are students who have been "traumatized" in front of an audience. Moreover, the act of talking over the experience with a sympathetic listener is, itself, therapeutic. Discussion of the episode with others not only reduces the repression further, but often helps one gain perspective about the situation so that one can realize its unimportance.
3. Above all, work as hard as possible to prepare fine speeches. One good speech given by a traumatized student may reassure him more

than kind words from the class or from the instructor. As the student continues to give good speeches, his successes will nullify the old experience and begin to build strong feelings of confidence that will do more than merely heal the old scar.

The methods of reducing conflict suggested so far have been limited to a discussion of ways to reduce the fear of speaking. There are, however, ways to *increase the desire to speak*. These ways may be more important, for they tend to develop that kind of confidence that contributes to success, and that make the speaker, when he *should* speak, *want to* speak.

RESOLVING CONFLICT: CHOICE OF SUBJECT

A speaker can reinforce his desire to speak by choosing a subject that makes him want to speak. If he has a subject that he knows is interesting, important, or unusual, that subject will reinforce his desire to speak. However, if the speaker has chosen a banal, trite, superficial, or otherwise insignificant, subject, he will feel less impelled to speak; instead, he may be reluctant, fearing that the audience will recognize the shallowness of his ideas. Having reinforced his desire not to speak by choosing a poor subject, he will be more prone to suffer conflict.

RESOLVING CONFLICT: PREPARATION OF THE MATERIALS OF THE SPEECH

Careful preparation can powerfully reinforce the desire to speak; lack of preparation will increase the fear of speaking. A speaker who has prepared his speech materials carefully, that is, who knows his subject well, who has vivid and valid supporting material which he knows will intrigue the audience, who knows that his speech is clear, and who has an introduction that is "sure fire" and a good conclusion, knows that he has little to fear. He will want to speak and can plunge into his speech wholeheartedly, with a minimum of conflict to disrupt him. But the speaker who suspects that his materials are dull, unclear, and who fears he knows less about the subject than he should, cannot help but be worried, and perhaps he should be. Unlike the speaker who is prepared, he cannot anticipate success; the unprepared speaker anticipates failure, and because he must speak, he will experience conflict and accompanying stage fright.

Confidence comes from competence. The well-prepared surgeon does not disintegrate at the sight of the operating table, nor does the competent boxer at the sight of his opponent. Nor does the speaker who has prepared his speech carefully disintegrate at the sight of his audience. None of these men need tricks of auto-suggestion or the other somewhat fraudulent devices sometimes advocated as "cures" for stage fright. Nor will these "cures" help those whose preparation is so poor that they are incompetent. If one thinks the speech is not worth listening to, reassurance will be hard to find. Even the beginning speaker, if he prepares his speech materials carefully, can feel competent when he gives the speech; more likely, his speech will be successful and his success will breed further confidence. Careful preparation will increase the comfort of the beginning —or advanced—speaker so that he will perceive the audience situation less fearfully and will be more comfortable than the unprepared speaker. Eventually, the speaker who prepares each speech thoroughly will begin to find an audience stimulating rather than frightening.

REDUCING CONFLICT IN THE
MOMENTS BEFORE SPEAKING

An inexperienced speaker may "work up" an unnecessarily strong case of stage fright by contemplating the blithering idiot that he thinks he is and by imagining the spectacle that he might make when he arrives at the platform. The student must avoid these thoughts. The moments just before the speech are not the moments to rehash the ideas of the speech nor to dwell upon one's ineptness. Rather, think about something else.

But it is not easy to "think about something else." One suggestion, however, may help. If you force yourself to concentrate intensely on whatever is being said just before you speak, you will probably be able to keep your mind off thoughts that are alarming. The more intensely you concentrate on the speeches that precede yours the less you can think about your plight. Moreover, you may find, in one or more of these speeches, some idea or fact to which you can refer in your own speech. (Classroom audiences listen closely when a student speaker refers to another student's speech.) Before you speak avoid thoughts about yourself and about your speech by listening carefully to whoever is speaking; try to find a way of referring to this speech when you give yours, and you will not only be more calm for having avoided unnecessary fears but will probably increase the attention the audience pays to your speech.

RESOLVING CONFLICT BY COMMITMENT
TO THE SIGNIFICANCE OF ONE'S IDEAS

A beginning speaker may reduce the fear of speaking and reinforce the desire to speak by contemplating matters that are extrinsic to what he says: He may, for example, wish to give the speech "to get it over with." Or he may reinforce the desire to speak by remembering that by speaking he will have completed another requirement of the course, or by recognizing that he will gain more experience and expertise, or by contemplating that not to speak would be embarrassing. Although such reasons are extrinsic to the ideas and materials of the speech, they make a contribution to the wholeheartedness of the speaker. One should use these extrinsic reasons if they help.

One can better develop confidence, however, by reinforcing the desire to speak for reasons that are *intrinsic*, rather than extrinsic, to one's ideas. One should speak because one is committed to one's ideas, because one is alive with a crucial idea, because one feels he knows something that is important to the audience, because he understands or has clarified a significant problem, because he has found the right answers, or even the right questions.

To be driven to speak because of the importance of one's ideas is probably the best way to develop confidence. One who suffers stage fright is, literally, self-conscious, self-aware. "True neuroses are best defined," Gordon Allport says, "as stubborn self-centeredness."[7] The speaker, on the other hand, who speaks because he is committed to an idea, is not *self*-centered, but *idea*-centered. When a man is so committed to an idea that he has caught its fire, he will want to speak, and can do so wholeheartedly.

Most beginning speakers do not grasp the significance of their ideas, and their delivery reflects this lack by its timorousness, its lifelessness, and its ineffectiveness. The best reason to speak is for the intrinsic reason that one has found something worthwhile to say. Unless one's delivery reflects this perception of worth, it will be poor delivery. Good delivery has a lively reflection of the significance of one's ideas, and this reflection is the starting point of all good delivery. Without this reflection, instruction in delivery is of little avail, and with it most speakers have little need for further instruction. Moreover, the intensity that springs from speaking because one has a sense of the value of one's ideas is one of the roads to individuality in speaking. The speaker who reflects the spirit of his ideas will not be an imitation of his instructor or of any other speaker. He is more apt to be so immersed in his ideas that he is uniquely and fully himself. Therefore, one must work to grasp and reflect the significance of his ideas not only because such a grasp will help develop confidence, but because it will develop effective, individual delivery.

But how does one grasp the intrinsic significance of one's ideas? This

---

[7] *Personality and Social Encounter*, Boston, Beacon Press, 1960, p. 173.

grasp stems from depth of knowledge about one's ideas. In particular, the person who in a mature way recognizes this significance is one who has certain kinds of knowledge about his idea, suggested by answers to the following kinds of questions:

1. In what way are these ideas important today?
2. How do these ideas relate to the material needs of my audience? To their psychological needs? To their philosophic or spiritual needs?
3. In what ways might my ideas influence the attitudes and behavior of the audience?
4. Are there times in the past when these ideas have performed an especially useful service?
5. If these ideas are accepted, how might they change the course of events?

When one is vividly aware of answers to these questions about his subject, one will *want* to speak; moreover, he will have a deeper understanding of his subject, as well as of its importance, and will begin to develop the kind of attitude toward his ideas, toward himself and toward his audience that is in itself persuasive. The reflection of these ideas in his delivery will encourage the natural development of directness, variety, vitality, intensity, and poise that dedication to ideas brings. Thus, one will, through developing a deeper understanding of the significance of one's ideas, have also developed many of the skills of delivery.

The speaker who cannot answer at least some of these questions in such a way as to provide ideas that increase his desire to speak may have either a superficial understanding of his subject or may have chosen a poor subject. But if he has chosen a worthy subject, he must not fail to grasp its importance. To miss the power that can be derived from a significant idea is to miss one of the speaker's sources of strength. The power of a great idea is the source of strength that gave confidence—and much more—to men such as Socrates, Lincoln, Churchill, and others. Great ideas have inspired people and nations to wholehearted effort during times of danger. Men possessed by a great ideal seldom fear. Many such men have endured hunger, pain, persecution, and even torture or the threat of death with less terror than the neophyte giving his first speech. If the perception of a great truth can do so much to alleviate real tortures, it is not too much to expect that when a speaker begins to grasp the significance of an idea, he will reduce his weak-in-the-knees feeling on the occasion of a short speech in a beginning class.

There are some limits, however, that one should place upon commitment, inspiration, and the drive to accomplish. The person who seems to raise his aspirations too high may fall victim, by the very strength of his desire, to stage fright. The neurotic is often one whose aspirations are too great for his capacities. The student who expects to save the world by one speech is out of touch with both his own limitations and those of the classroom situation. But what constitutes too much commitment and what is too little is never easy to determine. The student himself is probably the best judge. Nevertheless, he should keep in mind that most students reflect the kind of delivery that is characterized too little by the life and fire of commitment, and that the student's spark would be increased by a deeper understanding of the significance of his ideas.

Because overcoming stage fright requires one to be idea-centered instead of self-centered, the real challenge to the student is one that calls him to stretch his mind. It is a challenge to recognize, appreciate, understand, and commit himself to ideas. The challenge calls one to discover ideas of worth and to turn his mind toward the significant. It calls one to bury self-centered ideas and to fix attention outside one's self. When one answers the challenge to stretch his mind around a great idea, he not only gains confidence, lays the foundation for good delivery, and begins to develop his own individuality, but he becomes a speaker deserving of the attention of the audience. Such a man is not only a more effective human being; he is likewise a more worthwhile one.

RESOLVING CONFLICT: HABIT FORMATION[8]

Emotionally charged situations—those in which the rewards for success or the penalties for failure are great—do not always produce anxiety or breakdown *unless the situations are too complicated to be met skillfully.* Remember, for example, the first time you drove an automobile. Because you could have had an accident, the event was not only emotionally charged, but it was also too complicated for you: you had to manipulate the steering wheel, push down or let up on the accelerator and brake (and perhaps operate the gear shift and clutch pedal), and do these things not only in coordination with each other, but also in correspondence with what you saw through the windshield. You probably had anxiety—stage fright—and if a real emergency had occurred, you might have experienced breakdown, e.g., stepped on the accelerator when you

---

[8] The writer is indebted to Professor Clarence T. Simon for his article, "Complexity and Breakdown in Speech Situations," *Journal of Speech Disorders*, X (September, 1941), pp. 199–203, and especially for the writer's interest in the psychological means of preventing stage fright, which received its first and greatest stimulus in Professor Simon's classes over a quarter of a century ago.

intended to stop the car, or thrown up your hands in horror. One experiences anxiety and breakdown in an emotionally charged situation that is too complicated for one to respond to ably.

Complexity produces a special form of conflict situation. The responses a beginning driver can make are, perhaps, infinite, and he doesn't quite know which response to make at a given time. He can speed up, remain at constant speed, lift his foot from the accelerator and slow down, touch the brake lightly or firmly, and make innumerable adjustments with the steering wheel (and perhaps add the clutch and gear shift or gear selector). These possibilities provide him with a multi-conflict situation; at the right time, each of these things must be done. The poor novice lacks the skill either to do these things well or to recognize when the right time is. He is, therefore, in a multi-conflict situation, and is apt to behave as many do in conflict: sometimes he will over-respond, sometimes under-respond, sometimes not respond at all and often respond the wrong way—and he is anxious most of the time.

But notice what happens to him: At first, these complexities required all of his attention, but he soon learned to make appropriate responses so that he could speed up or slow down with ease, turn corners without even slight difficulty, back up, park the car, and at the same time listen to the radio or carry on a conversation. He made *habits* of the skills of driving and therefore could respond easily and appropriately in a variety of situations. *Habits converted the previously complex situation into a simple one.*

Habits convert complex situations into simple ones because *habits are relatively independent of one's attention.* Note how habits are performed without much awareness: Putting on shoes is habitual; can you remember which shoe you put on first this morning? Or remember tying the shoes? Unless something unusual happened, unless one shoe was missing or you found a knotted shoe lace, the act was independent enough of your attention so that memory of it will be dim or, perhaps, nonexistent. Because habits do not require your full attention, they simplify complex situations for you. *The development of skills that are habitual may reduce the discomfort of anxiety-producing situations.*

Here are some examples of how habits may reduce anxiety. The good football player responds on the field (in front of perhaps a hundred thousand spectators) without disintegration because he has habituated techniques of passing, dodging, and running; because these techniques are habits, he is free to expend his attention and his energy searching for the pass-receiver or finding the hole through which he can plunge with all his strength. The complicated techniques of playing are made simple because they are independent of his attention, permitting him to play with courage and to put his full strength behind his skills. In the same way, the surgeon remains calm and in possession of his skills because he knows what to expect, and through practice knows what to do as he makes an incision. But place the surgeon, for a moment, in the huddle, or give the football star a scalpel, at the side of a patient, and neither star nor surgeon would display coolness or deftness. Confidence is born of competence. When one faces an emotionally charged situation for which he does not have habituated skills, he will lack the calm assurance of the star or the swift and quiet skill of the expert. To take another example, basic training in the armed forces, in some of its more worthwhile aspects, is an attempt to habituate certain skills of fighting. The soldier, properly trained, will know how to react when he faces the enemy, and instead of disintegrating, he will use his habitual fighting know-how. Because his habits of fighting will be semiautomatic, the soldier, instead of breaking down, fights. The seasoned Marine probably has an abundance of raw courage, but he also has habituated, through training, superior skills of combat; what would disintegrate other strong men will not do so to him. When the good airplane pilot is faced with an emergency he has a repertory of skills which he uses semiautomatically, and remains effective in a situation that would terrorize us. Teach us the same skills, and we might behave as well as he. Because habits can simplify a complex situation, they can help reduce anxiety and prevent breakdown. Confidence and courage are compounded, in part, out of knowing what to do.

The same principles apply to the speech situation. It, too, is a complicated situation: The beginning speaker must walk to the platform with ease and dignity, wonders how to stand when he gets there, worries about what to do with his hands, would like to loosen his collar, can't seem to use his voice normally, occasionally forgets items he intended to include, and cannot think well, or respond fully to communicating his thoughts. He has not yet formed habits that will free his attention from the more petty skills of delivery.

One reduces complexity in an audience situation in the same way that one does in driving, surgery, or fighting, for wherever complexity causes anxiety, habituating the required skills reduces that complexity. We can now see one reason that students who take a speech course experience a reduction in stage fright: In the process of giving several speeches they form habit patterns of the skills of delivery. (Some reductions in stage fright come from a different source: the student who speaks frequently before an audience not only forms habit patterns that reduce the complexity of speaking, but he also learns what to expect from an audience. Knowing what to expect often can help reduce anxiety; when the student finds the audience does not respond with catcalls or rotten eggs, but is mildly sympathetic, his anxiety lessens.) Experience not only builds habits

that simplify the speech situation, but also gives one a healthy set of expectations that also help reduce anxiety.

The student should not rely only on the slow progress of the term to
form habits that will build his confidence. He can speed the process of
forming habits by practicing his speeches. Practice, however, does not
make perfect; practice only makes more permanent. The wrong kind of
practice may intensify the complexity. Therefore, the student should
practice so as to incorporate the best skills of speaking in the easiest way.
The following suggestions will help form habits of good speaking:

1. After the speech has been carefully outlined to include the best
main points, subheads, supporting material and the like, memorize the
outline. Memorize the outline so well that you *overlearn* it, for things that
we overlearn are not forgotten, even under stress. (You have overlearned
your name and address, and are not likely to forget them even before an
audience.) A good test of a sufficient degree of overlearning is to see if,
without reference to your outline, you can repeat it from the last line to
the first. When you can recall it line by line from the bottom to the top,
you know it so well that no audience will cause you to forget. Moreover,
because your outline is well stamped in, you will feel more confident.

2. Practice the speech from this memorized image of the outline, until you can give the speech reasonably well. When a speech is delivered
from the memorized image of an outline—without notes or a manuscript
—it is called *extemporaneous* delivery. This sort of delivery is best for the
beginner because it will help him learn to think before an audience. The
speaker must think to recall his outline, and then must think to put it
into words so that the thoughts are fuller than his sketchy outline. If, instead of delivering the speech extemporaneously, one memorizes the
speech, he is not forced to think. Nor is he if he practices reading from
a manuscript. Extemporaneous speaking, therefore, is preferable because
it helps force a person to think while speaking.

3. Practice the speech as if presenting it to your class, imagining that
you are standing before it and looking at it. Such practice best habituates
the skills you will use when you give the final presentation. If you
practice sitting down, for example, you will reinforce habits that you can't
use on the platform; such reinforcement may increase the complexity of
your final performance, because the *wrong* rather than the *right* habits, are
stamped in. Practice, therefore, as nearly as possible, in the same circumstances as those in which you will give the speech.

4. Practice the speech reflecting the significance of your ideas. It is
especially important that the beginning speaker remind himself of the
significance of his subject before he begins to practice the speech, and that
he keep that significance before his mind throughout the speech. Espe-

cially, he should try to reflect the significance of each sentence and each idea. He should check himself occasionally and ask himself: "Did I say that so as to reflect its importance?" If he practices being idea-centered, he will be more apt to give the speech in such a way as to preserve the idea-centered attitudes of his practice session and be less self-centered in front of the audience.

With abundant extemporaneous practice, you will find that, inadvertently, you will memorize parts of the speech. But you will also, inadvertently, make habits of some of the skills of delivery. With practice, you can habituate good posture, responsive use of voice and body, and a strong spirit of communication. If you can stamp in these skills before you deliver the speech, the speech situation will be all the more simple. Because you know your speech and know that you can deliver it well, and you are quite certain to face the speech situation with less anxiety. You will be freer to think, to respond to your thoughts, and to speak in such a way that the audience catches and feels the same thoughts.

On the Nature of Confidence

Confidence springs not from a bag of tricks, but from two more difficult although more certain remedies: *competence* and *commitment*. To the extent that confidence and courage can be developed, they come from knowing what to do and from being dedicated. The speaker who knows how to prepare a speech, how to design it for his audience, and how to deliver it will feel the confidence that comes from competence. The speaker who, moreover, is committed to his ideas will feel the courage of one who is idea-centered instead of self-centered. Just as the surgeon whose skill enables him to operate without a tremor and the martyr whose commitment drives him on with no concern for himself, the speaker who is competent and committed possesses the confidence that enhances his success.

The problem in developing confidence is, first, to develop skill; that development is a function of the study of speech and of practice. Developing commitment is a longer process, involving a search for the ideas, movements, problems, and values. The study of speech, especially as it is presented in this book, will be of some help. Nevertheless, the student must search his heart, and look for help from whatever sustaining forces he can find. Perhaps his search through literature, history, philosophy, religion, science, or art will help him discover those things that merit dedication. Perhaps in one or more of the problems of the present age or the high values of the past he will find that which is worthy of commitment. At any rate, the kind of confidence that stems from competence and commitment is the kind that not only enhances success, but also makes one worth hearing and worthy to influence the lives of those who listen to him. Although there is no short way to develop competence and commitment, one can begin at any time, and in some ways, the college speech class is the best of places.

What suggestions to lessen stage fright have you tried? Which seems best? What happens when we become seriously and emotionally involved in the subject matter? Can we hope to completely eliminate stage fright? Do we want to remove totally the anxiety we feel when preparing to speak, or are there advantages to being nervous when presenting verbal messages?

Asking and Answering Questions

Wayne E. Hoogestraat

Forum periods following speeches are quite common, and these periods of questions and answers may be as important to obtaining a speaker's purpose as the speech itself. Wayne E. Hoogestraat, professor of speech at South Dakota State University, deals with both the speaker (respondent) and the questioner. Types of questions, limitations on the speaker, demands of the questioner, and steps in answering questions are his main considerations. Pay particular attention to requirements of both questioner and questioned.

The question and answer process is a much used communicative device in public speaking. It is one of the more obvious procedures for providing direct "feedback" to the speaker concerning the degree to which he communicated his ideas, and it is an equally obvious method for the auditor to recheck, verify, clarify, or refute the ideas presented by the speaker. Clearly phrased relevant questions and answers can greatly enhance commonality of understanding between the speaker and his audience.

A survey of related speech literature reveals that a considerable body of theory, and some evidence, has been compiled concerning the asking and answering of questions. This information is found under such headings as interviewing, conducting surveys, dialectic, the use of rhetorical questions, questions used in teaching, etc. However, we are here concerned with the questions asked of public speakers, their understanding of these questions, and their responses to these questions. And this is markedly different from the interview, survey, pedagogical, or dialectic questions, though some of the information available regarding these skills is also applicable to the audience-speaker question and answer situation.

Reprinted with permission from Today's Speech, XII, No. 4 (November, 1964), pp. 7-9.

REGARDING RESPONSE SOUGHT

Questions can be classified with regard to response sought. In this respect two general categories suffice—information-seeking questions and argumentative questions. In the former case the questioner is simply asking an "honest" question. He truly seeks information regardless of the outcome of the question or the type of information. In asking an argumentative question the questioner not only wants an answer, but he also knows what he wants the answer to be. The argumentative questioner seeks to trap the speaker, to reveal shams and specious reasoning, or generalizations based on insufficient evidence. We have all heard this type of question, often prefaced with the remark: "Is it not true that . . . ?" The argumentative question may also take the form of a dilemma, in that regardless of the manner in which the question is answered it will work to the detriment of the speaker's point of view. A classic example of this technique is, of course, found in Lincoln's question to Douglas in their Freeport (Ill.) debate. Lincoln asked Douglas:

> Can the people of a United States Territory, in any lawful way, against the wish of any citizen of the United States, exclude slavery from its limits prior to the formation of a State constitution?

If Douglas answered in the affirmative he would suffer a loss of political favor in the South. If he answered negatively he would suffer a similar loss in the North.

It should not, however, be assumed that information-seeking questions are necessarily good questions and that argumentative questions are bad questions. Occasions do arise where refutation of a speaker is proper and necessary. And in such instances the questioner is obligated to honestly reveal erroneous conclusions on the part of the speaker. Obvious distortions, fallacious deductions, or hasty generalizations simply cannot be allowed to stand unchallenged. Nevertheless, the questioner must be guided by prudence and mature judgment in raising argumentative questions. Too often such questions arise out of a predisposition held by the questioner, which has been challenged by the speaker, rather than arising out of an apparent and observable inductive or deductive error.

REGARDING EXPECTED MANNER OF RESPONSE

Questions can be further classified according to limitations imposed on the respondent (speaker). That is, the person answering the question may be able to choose between two alternatives, in which case it is a two-valued question. An example of such a question would be, "In your travel did you get behind the Iron Curtain?" Such questions are expected to be answered with "yes" or "no."

A second category of questions, regarding limitations imposed on the speaker, is made up of those calling for a choice among several alternatives. These questions cannot be answered with a simple "yes" or "no," nor are they unlimited regarding the range of possible answers. Typical of these questions is the following: "Of the present and suggested means of paying for our hospital and medical expenses, which would be most advantageous to the majority of the United States citizens?" In answering this question the speaker must choose among the various private medical-hospital insurance plans, the various governmentally sponsored or proposed plans, direct personal payment, etc. His alternatives in answering are clearly limited.

The third category of questions classified according to degree of limitation imposed on the speaker are those which impose no, or at least very little, restriction on the range of possible answers. Such questions are sometimes called "open-end" questions. An example of a question falling in this category would be, "What should be the role of the government in providing for the medical-hospital expenses of its citizens?" The range of possible answers to this question is limited only by the breadth of imagination of the person answering the question and the matter of relevance to the problem.

ASKING QUESTIONS OF THE SPEAKER

At various times during a public speaking occasion the roles become reversed. That is, the speaker momentarily becomes, along with the rest of the audience, an auditor, while a single member of the audience becomes the speaker. Such occasions arise when a forum is conducted following a public speech, when the speaker invites interruptions in the form of questions, or when any informal exchange between speaker and audience takes place either during or after the formal presentation of a speech. It becomes necessary, therefore, for the questioner to adhere to certain basic standards required of all speakers. Among the specialized demands on the questioner are the following: (1) Get the "speaker's" and audience's attention. (2) Orient the respondent to the basic assumptions upon which the question rests. (3) Ask and define the question. (4) State the limitations imposed on the range of possible answers if it is to be limited.

1. Like any other speaker the questioner cannot communicate his question to his audience (speaker included) until he has access to the channels of communication. The original speaker and the audience must

first have their attention directed toward the questioner and, momentarily at least, away from the previous prime source of stimuli—the speaker, chairman, previous questioner, etc. It is axiomatic that a question cannot be clearly communicated to an inattentive audience. Procedures for capturing the needed attention are similar to those used in any speaking situation such as a pause, an attention getting phrase such as "Yes, I have a question," "I'd like to ask a question," etc.; rising, and raising one's hand. In many situations recognition is granted by a chairman or moderator which in itself tends to direct attention to the questioner. Closely allied with capturing and holding attention, if not a part of it, the questioner must be certain to communicate with sufficient loudness and clearness of articulation so as to be easily heard by both the "speaker" and the regular audience.

2. Having captured initial attention the next task of the questioner is to orient the respondent to the basic assumptions on which the question rests. This is illustrated as follows: "You stated that 'the economy of Cuba is more depressed at the present time than at any time since the Spanish-American War.' Yet trade between Cuba and the U.S.S.R., between Cuba and Communist China, and between Cuba and other Iron Curtain countries is reported to have greatly increased. Why have these new and increased foreign markets not resulted in a stimulation of the Cuban Economy?" Very often certain premises and details need to be commonly understood by both questioner and respondent if the specific question is to be understood.

3. Asking and defining the question comprises the third major step. Ambiguity in the question itself can often be avoided by careful phrasing, thus allowing the respondent to give a more relevant answer to the specific question. Observe the following questions arranged in descending order of ambiguity:

(a) "Can you tell us something about the Indian's problem in South Dakota?"

(b) "Could you give us some information concerning the financial and economic resources of South Dakota's Indians?"

(c) "Aside from governmental assistance, what is the average annual income of the adult male Indians living on government reservations in South Dakota?"

It will be quickly noted that question "c" calls for an answer narrowly confined by the phrasing of the question. Consequently, the person answering the question is much less likely to misinterpret the question and more likely to give an exacting answer.

Despite careful phrasing, however, many questions need further narrowing by the process of definition. In these instances the questioner needs to specifically define vague terms in the question. In the question, "What can we do to reduce traffic accidents?" the terms "we" and "traffic accidents" could be further clarified by careful definition. If the question were asked as follows the intent of the question becomes more clear: "What can we do to reduce traffic accidents? By that I mean what can 'we' as licensed automobile operators do to reduce 'traffic accidents' in our own communities and in the areas where we operate our cars?"

4. The questioner may wish to further limit the scope of the question by requesting a limitation on the range of possible answers. While the asking of the question itself imposes a limitation on the range of relevant answers, occasionally the nature of the desired information can be made even more explicit by imposing a restriction on the possible range of answers. As was indicated in the section classifying questions according to manner of response, the questioner may request a two-valued answer ("Could you please answer 'yes' or 'no'?"). He may specify the several alternatives among which the respondent is to choose. Such an example follows: "Which farm plan do you feel holds the most promise for the financial security of the small farmer? By 'small farmer' I refer to those farming 160 acres or less. And could you limit your answer to the specific plans currently offered—the Secretary of Agriculture's plan, the Administration's plan, the plan advanced by Senator Thurber, and the plan now in operation." Or the questioner may ask the question and impose no further limitation on the respondent with regard to the scope of available answers. In any case, the respondent should be allowed to state and elaborate his reasons for choosing his particular response.

ANSWERING QUESTIONS

In answering a question to his speech the respondent assumes additional responsibilities. Not only must he meet the demands of a soundly supported, logical, organized, understandable communication, but he must do so in terms of the questioner's definitions and limitations. In meeting these specialized requirements the following three procedures, to be completed in chronological order, have been demonstrated to be effective: (1) Identify the question as to response sought. (2) Restate the question, verify definitions and limitations. (3) Answer the question, provide elaboration if necessary, restate the answer.

1. In answering a question from the audience the speaker would do well to quickly identify, in his own mind, and to the best of his ability, whether the question is information-seeking or argumentative. In the interest of courtesy and tact, caution should be exercised to keep answers to information-seeking questions as informative as possible and not to give argumentative answers. The questioner who is not taking issue with the

speaker should not be made to appear argumentative. It is a tactless speaker, indeed, who encourages needless antagonism.

If the question is clearly argumentative in nature the speaker might do well to point this out to the audience. The basis of the difference of opinion should be made clear ("Mr. May has questioned the validity of my source of information which I stated in my speech as . . .") so that the dispute can be confined to the specific item raised. It is nearly always good judgment to narrow the basis of disagreement to the smallest possible scope.

2. Before giving his answer the speaker should seek clarity of understanding concerning the question itself. First, he should restate the question to be sure all have heard. Second, he should repeat the definitions and limitations imposed on the question by the questioner; or he should provide his own definitions and limitations if the questioner has failed to do so; and in this case he should, if possible, verify his definitions and limitations with the questioner ("Have I given your question the proper interpretation?") though in very large formal groups this may not be possible.

3. Proceeding, then, with the greatest possible commonality of understanding concerning the specific question, the respondent should state his answer as clearly and succinctly as he can ("No," or "I favor the Brannon Plan," or "I think the greatest need is economic, because . . ."). Then if elaboration and further evidence is needed to clarify the answer this should be presented. If further elaboration and/or evidence is presented, it should be concluded with the answer stated at the outset ("Therefore, I favor the Brannon Plan," etc.).

Questions raised during public speaking occasions take many forms and cover a wide range of subjects, few of which can be anticipated since two personalities are involved—the speaker and the questioner. Nevertheless, both the questioner and the respondent can improve their communication by following the procedures suggested above.

Hoogestraat discusses three limitations a questioner might place on the answer desired: a yes or no response, a choice among several suggested alternatives, and an open-ended response. When should we impose such limitations? What problems might an "open-ended" response create? How much can we limit the response desired and still be fair to the speaker (respondent)? The author believes that the questioner should "orient the respondent to the basic assumptions on which the question rests." How would this suggestion affect two problems of forum periods: questioners making short speeches instead of asking questions, and questioners asking such involved questions that clarity is hopelessly lost?

IV

MESSAGE

The Euphemism: Telling It Like It Isn't

This Time essay deals with an increasing problem of our modern, complicated society. We attempt to find pleasant terms or labels for the innumerable happenings, theories, concepts, functions, factions, inventions, and reactions that surround our every move in an effort, perhaps, to maintain peace of mind or some kind of order. The result is an avalanche of euphemisms and accompanying jargon.

Modern American speech, while not always clear or correct or turned with much style, is supposed to be uncommonly frank. Witness the current explosion of four-letter words and the explicit discussion of sexual topics. In fact, gobbledygook and nice-Nellyism still extend as far as the ear can hear. Housewives on television may chat about their sex lives in terms that a decade ago would have made gynecologists blush; more often than not, these emancipated women still speak about their children's "going to the potty." Government spokesmen talk about "redeployment" of American troops; they mean withdrawal. When sociologists refer to blacks living in slums, they are likely to mumble about "nonwhites" in a "culturally deprived environment." The CIA may never have used the expression "to terminate with extreme prejudice" when it wanted a spy rubbed out. But in the context of a war in which "pacification of the enemy infrastructure" is the military mode of reference to blasting the Viet Cong out of a village, the phrase sounded so plausible that millions readily accepted it as accurate.

The image of a generation blessed with a swinging, liberated language is largely an illusion. Despite its swaggering sexual candor, much contemporary speech still hides behind that traditional enemy of plain talk, the euphemism.

NECESSARY EVIL

From a Greek word meaning "to use words of good omen," euphemism is the substitution of a pleasant term for a blunt one—telling it like it isn't. Euphemism has probably existed since the beginning of language. As long as there have been things of which men thought the less said the better, there have been better ways of saying less. In everyday conversation the euphemism is, at worst, a necessary evil; at its best, it is a handy verbal tool to avoid making enemies needlessly, or shocking friends. Language purists and the blunt-spoken may wince when a young woman at a party coyly asks for directions to "the powder room," but to most people this kind of familiar euphemism is probably no more harmful or annoying than, say, a split infinitive.

On a larger scale, though, the persistent growth of euphemism in a language represents a danger to thought and action, since its fundamental intent is to deceive. As Linguist Benjamin Lee Whorf has pointed out, the structure of a given language determines, in part, how the society that speaks it views reality. If "substandard housing" makes rotting slums appear more livable or inevitable to some people, then their view of American cities has been distorted and their ability to assess the significance of poverty has been reduced. Perhaps the most chilling example of euphemism's destructive power took place in Hitler's Germany. The wholesale corruption of the language under Nazism, notes Critic George Steiner, is symbolized by the phrase *endgültige Lösung* (final solution), which "came to signify the death of 6,000,000 human beings in gas ovens."

ROSES BY OTHER NAMES

No one could argue that American English is under siege from linguistic falsehood, but euphemisms today have the nagging persistence of a headache. Despite the increasing use of nudity and sexual innuendo in advertising, Madison Avenue is still the great exponent of talking to "the average person of good upbringing"—as one TV executive has euphemistically described the ordinary American—in ways that won't offend him. Although this is like fooling half the people none of the time, it has produced a handsome bouquet of roses by other names. Thus there is "facial-quality tissue" that is not intended for use on faces, and "rinses" or "tints" for women who might be unsettled to think they dye their hair. In the world of deodorants, people never sweat or smell; they simply "offend." False teeth sound truer when known as "dentures."

Admen and packagers, of course, are not the only euphemizers. Almost any way of earning a salary above the level of ditchdigging is known as a profession rather than a job. Janitors for several years have been elevated by image-conscious unions to the status of "custodians"; nowadays, a teen-age rock guitarist with three chords to his credit can class himself with Horowitz as a "recording artist." Cadillac dealers refer to autos as "pre-owned" rather than "secondhand." Government researchers concerned with old people call them "senior citizens." Ads for bank credit cards and department stores refer to "convenient terms"—meaning 18% annual interest rates payable at the convenience of the creditor.

Jargon, the sublanguage peculiar to any trade, contributes to euphemism when its terms seep into general use. The stock market, for example, rarely "falls" in the words of Wall Street analysts. Instead it is discovered to be "easing" or found to have made a "technical correction" or "adjustment." As one financial writer notes: "It never seems to 'technically adjust' upward." The student New Left, which shares a taste for six-syllable words with Government bureaucracy, has concocted a collection of substitute terms for use in politics. To "liberate," in the context of campus uproars, means to capture and occupy. Four people in agreement form a "coalition." In addition to "participatory democracy," which in practice is often a description of anarchy, the university radicals have half seriously given the world "anticipatory Communism," which means to steal. The New Left, though, still has a long way to go before it can equal the euphemism-creating ability of Government officials. Who else but a Washington economist would invent the phrase "negative saver" to describe someone who spends more money than he makes?

A persistent source of modern euphemisms is the feeling, inspired by the prestige of science, that certain words contain implicit subjective judgments, and thus ought to be replaced with more "objective" terms. To speak of "morals" sounds both superior and arbitrary, as though the speaker were indirectly questioning those of the listener. By substituting "values," the concept is miraculously turned into a condition, like humidity or mass, that can be safely measured from a distance. To call someone "poor," in the modern way of thinking, is to speak pejoratively of his condition, while the substitution of "disadvantaged" or "underprivileged," indicates that poverty wasn't his fault. Indeed, writes Linguist Mario Pei in a new book called *Words in Sheep's Clothing* (Hawthorn; $6.95), by using "underprivileged," we are "made to feel that it is all our fault." The modern reluctance to judge makes it more offensive than ever before to call a man a liar; thus there is a "credibility gap" instead. No up-to-date teacher would dare refer to a child as "stupid" or a "bad student"; the D+ student is invariably an "underachiever" or a "slow learner."

FORBIDDEN WORDS

The liberalization of language in regard to sex involves the use of perhaps a dozen words. The fact of their currency in what was once known as polite conversation raises some unanswered linguistic questions. Which, really, is the rose, and which the other name? Is "lovemaking" a euphemism for the four-letter word that describes copulation? Or is this blunt Anglo-Saxonism a dysphemism for making love? Are the old forbidden obscenities really the crude bedrock on which softer and shyer expressions have been built? Or are they simply coarser ways of expressing physical actions and parts of the human anatomy that are more accurately described in less explicit terms? It remains to be seen whether the so-called forbidden words will contribute anything to the honesty and openness of sexual discussion. Perhaps their real value lies in the acidic, expletive power to shock, which is inevitably diminished by overexposure. Perhaps the Victorians, who preferred these words unspoken and unprinted, will prove to have had a point after all.

For all their prudery, the Victorians were considerably more willing than modern men to discuss ideas—such as social distinctions, morality and death—that have become almost unmentionable. Nineteenth century gentlewomen whose daughters had "limbs" instead of suggestive "legs" did not find it necessary to call their maids "housekeepers," nor did they bridle at referring to "upper" or "lower" classes within society. Rightly or wrongly, the Victorian could talk without embarrassment about "sin," a word that today few but clerics use with frequency or ease. It is even becoming difficult to find a doctor, clergyman or undertaker (known as a "mortician") who will admit that a man has died rather than "expired" or "passed away." Death has not lost its sting; the words for it have.

PSYCHOLOGICAL NECESSITY

There is little if any hope that euphemisms will ever be excised from mankind's endless struggle with words that, as T. S. Eliot lamented, bend, break and crack under pressure. For one thing, certain kinds of everyday euphemisms have proved their psychological necessity. The uncertain morale of an awkward teen-ager may be momentarily buoyed if he thinks of himself as being afflicted by facial "blemishes" rather than "pimples." The label "For motion discomfort" that airlines place on paper containers undoubtedly helps the squeamish passenger keep control of his stomach in bumpy weather better than if they were called "vomit bags." Other forms of self-deception may not be beneficial, but may still be emotionally necessary. A girl may tolerate herself more readily if she thinks of herself as a "swinger" rather than as promiscuous. Voyeurs can salve their guilt feelings when they buy tickets for certain "adult entertainments" on the ground that they are implicitly supporting "freedom of artistic expression."

Lexicographer Bergen Evans of Northwestern University believes that euphemisms persist because "lying is an indispensable part of making life tolerable." It is virtuous, but a bit beside the point, to contend that lies are deplorable. So they are; but they cannot be moralized or legislated away, any more than euphemisms can be. Verbal miasma, when it deliberately obscures truth, is an offense to reason. But the inclination to speak of certain things in uncertain terms is a reminder that there will always be areas of life that humanity considers too private, or too close to feelings of guilt, to speak about directly. Like stammers or tears, euphemisms will be created whenever men doubt, or fear, or do not know. The instinct is not wholly unhealthy; there is a measure of wisdom in the familiar saying that a man who calls a spade a spade is fit only to use one.

Does euphemism achieve the desired purposes, or does it add to the confusion and problems of our modern world? Could our society function without pleasant labels and terms? Would our communication problems be greater or less if euphemism was greatly reduced? Can you think of ways to describe the world around us that would avoid euphemism and jargon and help us to communicate more effectively? Is euphemism a threat to our society as this essay suggests?

The Sample with the Built-In Bias

Darrell Huff

We are constantly bombarded with statistics covering everything
from drunk driving to the average annual incomes of senior citizens.
Governmental, business, and educational institutions frequently base
decisions and plans on statistical findings. In this chapter from his
book, How to Lie with Statistics, Darrell Huff points out numerous
weaknesses in statistics gathered in polls and surveys. Lack of honesty, exaggeration, understatement, and interviewer bias make results,
especially precise averages, highly questionable.

"The average Yaleman, Class of '24," *Time* magazine noted once, commenting on something in the New York *Sun*, "makes $25,111 a year."

Well, good for him!

But wait a minute. What does this impressive figure mean? Is it, as
it appears to be, evidence that if you send your boy to Yale you won't have
to work in your old age and neither will he?

Two things about the figure stand out at first suspicious glance. It is
surprisingly precise. It is quite improbably salubrious.

There is small likelihood that the average income of any far-flung
group is ever going to be known down to the dollar. It is not particularly
probable that you know your own income for last year so precisely as that
unless it was all derived from salary. And $25,000 incomes are not often
all salary; people in that bracket are likely to have well-scattered investments.

Furthermore, this lovely average is undoubtedly calculated from the
amounts the Yale men *said* they earned. Even if they had the honor system in New Haven in '24, we cannot be sure that it works so well after a

quarter of a century that all these reports are honest ones. Some people when asked their incomes exaggerate out of vanity or optimism. Others minimize, especially, it is to be feared, on income-tax returns; and having done this may hesitate to contradict themselves on any other paper. Who knows what the revenuers may see? It is possible that these two tendencies, to boast and to understate, cancel each other out, but it is unlikely. One tendency may be far stronger than the other, and we do not know which one.

We have begun then to account for a figure that common sense tells us can hardly represent the truth. Now let us put our finger on the likely source of the biggest error, a source that can produce $25,111 as the "average income" of some men whose actual average may well be nearer half that amount.

This is the sampling procedure, which is the heart of the greater part of the statistics you meet on all sorts of subjects. Its basis is simple enough, although its refinements in practice have led into all sorts of by-ways, some less than respectable. If you have a barrel of beans, some red and some white, there is only one way to find out exactly how many of each color you have: Count 'em. However, you can find out approximately how many are red in much easier fashion by pulling out a handful of beans and counting just those, figuring that the proportion will be the same all through the barrel. If your sample is large enough and selected properly, it will represent the whole well enough for most purposes. If it is not, it may be far less accurate than an intelligent guess and have nothing to recommend it but a spurious air of scientific precision. It is sad truth that conclusions from such samples, biased or too small or both, lie behind much of what we read or think we know.

The report on the Yale men comes from a sample. We can be pretty sure of that because reason tells us that no one can get hold of all the living members of that class of '24. There are bound to be many whose addresses are unknown twenty-five years later.

And, of those whose addresses are known, many will not reply to a questionnaire, particularly a rather personal one. With some kinds of mail questionnaire, a five or ten per cent response is quite high. This one should have done better than that, but nothing like one hundred per cent.

So we find that the income figure is based on a sample composed of all class members whose addresses are known and who replied to the questionnaire. Is this a representative sample? That is, can this group be assumed to be equal in income to the unrepresented group, those who cannot be reached or who do not reply?

Who are the little lost sheep down in the Yale rolls as "address unknown"? Are they the big-income earners—the Wall Street men, the corporation directors, the manufacturing and utility executives? No; the addresses of the rich will not be hard to come by. Many of the most prosperous members of the class can be found through *Who's Who in America* and other reference volumes even if they have neglected to keep in touch with the alumni office. It is a good guess that the lost names are those of the men who, twenty-five years or so after becoming Yale bachelors of arts, have not fulfilled any shining promise. They are clerks, mechanics, tramps, unemployed alcoholics, barely surviving writers and artists . . . people of whom it would take half a dozen or more to add up to an income of $25,111. These men do not so often register at class reunions, if only because they cannot afford the trip.

Who are those who chucked the questionnaire into the nearest wastebasket? We cannot be so sure about these, but it is at least a fair guess that many of them are just not making enough money to brag about. They are a little like the fellow who found a note clipped to his first pay check suggesting that he consider the amount of his salary confidential and not material for the interchange of office confidences. "Don't worry," he told the boss. "I'm just as ashamed of it as you are."

It becomes pretty clear that the sample has omitted two groups most likely to depress the average. The $25,111 figure is beginning to explain itself. If it is a true figure for anything it is one merely for that special group of the class of '24 whose addresses are known and who are willing to stand up and tell how much they earn. Even that requires an assumption that the gentlemen are telling the truth.

Such an assumption is not to be made lightly. Experience from one breed of sampling study, that called market research, suggests that it can hardly ever be made at all. A house-to-house survey purporting to study magazine readership was once made in which a key question was: What magazines does your household read? When the results were tabulated and analyzed it appeared that a great many people loved *Harper's* and not very many read *True Story*. Now there were publishers' figures around at the time that showed very clearly that *True Story* had more millions of circulation than *Harper's* had hundreds of thousands. Perhaps we asked the wrong kind of people, the designers of the survey said to themselves. But no, the questions had been asked in all sorts of neighborhoods all around the country. The only reasonable conclusion then was that a good many of the respondents, as people are called when they answer such questions, had not told the truth. About all the survey had uncovered was snobbery.

In the end it was found that if you wanted to know what certain people read it was no use asking them. You could learn a good deal more by going to their houses and saying you wanted to buy old magazines and what could be had? Then all you had to do was count the *Yale Reviews* and the *Love Romances*. Even that dubious device, of course, does not tell you what people read, only what they have been exposed to.

Similarly, the next time you learn from your reading that the average American (you hear a good deal about him these days, most of it faintly improbable) brushes his teeth 1.02 times a day—a figure I have just made up, but it may be as good as anyone else's—ask yourself a question. How can anyone have found out such a thing? Is a woman who has read in countless advertisements that non-brushers are social offenders going to confess to a stranger that she does not brush her teeth regularly? The statistic may have meaning to one who wants to know only what people say about tooth-brushing but it does not tell a great deal about the frequency with which bristle is applied to incisor.

A river cannot, we are told, rise above its source. Well, it can seem to if there is a pumping station concealed somewhere about. It is equally true that the result of a sampling study is no better than the sample it is based on. By the time the data have been filtered through layers of statistical manipulation and reduced to a decimal-pointed average, the result begins to take on an aura of conviction that a closer look at the sampling would deny.

Does early discovery of cancer save lives? Probably. But of the figures commonly used to prove it the best that can be said is that they don't. These, the records of the Connecticut Tumor Registry, go back to 1935 and appear to show a substantial increase in the five-year survival rate from that year till 1941. Actually those records were begun in 1941, and everything earlier was obtained by tracing back. Many patients had left Connecticut, and whether they had lived or died could not be learned. According to the medical reporter Leonard Engel, the built-in bias thus created is "enough to account for nearly the whole of the claimed improvement in survival rate."

To be worth much, a report based on sampling must use a representative sample, which is one from which every source of bias has been removed. That is where our Yale figure shows its worthlessness. It is also where a great many of the things you can read in newspapers and magazines reveal their inherent lack of meaning.

A psychiatrist reported once that practically everybody is neurotic. Aside from the fact that such use destroys any meaning in the word "neurotic," take a look at the man's sample. That is, whom has the psychiatrist been observing? It turns out that he has reached this edifying conclusion from studying his patients, who are a long, long way from being a sample of the population. If a man were normal, our psychiatrist would never meet him.

Give that kind of second look to the things you read, and you can avoid learning a whole lot of things that are not so.

It is worth keeping in mind also that the dependability of a sample can be destroyed just as easily by invisible sources of bias as by these visible ones. That is, even if you can't find a source of demonstrable bias, allow yourself some degree of skepticism about the results as long as there is a possibility of bias somewhere. There always is. The presidential elec- tions in 1948 and 1952 were enough to prove that, if there were any doubt.

For further evidence go back to 1936 and the *Literary Digest's* famed fiasco. The ten million telephone and *Digest* subscribers who assured the editors of the doomed magazine that it would be Landon 370, Roosevelt 161 came from the list that had accurately predicted the 1932 election. How could there be bias in a list already so tested? There was a bias, of course, as college theses and other post mortems found: People who could afford telephones and magazine subscriptions in 1936 were not a cross section of voters. Economically they were a special kind of people, a sam- ple biased because it was loaded with what turned out to be Republican voters. The sample elected Landon, but the voters thought otherwise.

The basic sample is the kind called "random." It is selected by pure chance from the "universe," a word by which the statistician means the whole of which the sample is a part. Every tenth name is pulled from a file of index cards. Fifty slips of paper are taken from a hatful. Every twen- tieth person met on Market Street is interviewed. (But remember that this last is not a sample of the population of the world, or of the United States, or of San Francisco, but only of the people on Market Street at the time. One interviewer for an opinion poll said that she got her people in a railroad station because "all kinds of people can be found in a station." It had to be pointed out to her that mothers of small children, for in- stance, might be underrepresented there.)

The test of the random sample is this: Does every name or thing in the whole group have an equal chance to be in the sample?

The purely random sample is the only kind that can be examined with entire confidence by means of statistical theory, but there is one thing wrong with it. It is so difficult and expensive to obtain for many uses that sheer cost eliminates it. A more economical substitute, which is almost universally used in such fields as opinion polling and market re- search, is called stratified random sampling.

To get this stratified sample you divide your universe into several groups in proportion to their known prevalence. And right there your trouble can begin: Your information about their proportion may not be correct. You instruct your interviewers to see to it that they talk to so many Negroes and such-and-such a percentage of people in each of several income brackets, to a specified number of farmers, and so on. All the while the group must be divided equally between persons over forty and under forty years of age.

That sounds fine—but what happens? On the question of Negro or white the interviewer will judge correctly most of the time. On income he will make more mistakes. As to farmers—how do you classify a man who farms part time and works in the city too? Even the question of age can pose some problems which are most easily settled by choosing only respondents who obviously are well under or well over forty. In that case the sample will be biased by the virtual absence of the late-thirties and early-forties age groups. You can't win.

On top of all this, how do you get a random sample within the stratification? The obvious thing is to start with a list of everybody and go after names chosen from it at random; but that is too expensive. So you go into the streets—and bias your sample against stay-at-homes. You go from door to door by day—and miss most of the employed people. You switch to evening interviews—and neglect the movie-goers and night-clubbers.

The operation of a poll comes down in the end to a running battle against sources of bias, and this battle is conducted all the time by all the reputable polling organizations. What the reader of the reports must remember is that the battle is never won. No conclusion that "sixty-seven per cent of the American people are against" something or other should be read without the lingering question, Sixty-seven per cent of which American people?

So with Dr. Alfred C. Kinsey's "female volume." The problem, as with anything based on sampling, is how to read it (or a popular summary of it) without learning too much that is not necessarily so. There are at least three levels of sampling involved. Dr. Kinsey's samples of the population (one level) are far from random ones and may not be particularly representative, but they are enormous samples by comparison with anything done in his field before and his figures must be accepted as revealing and important if not necessarily on the nose. It is possibly more important to remember that any questionnaire is only a sample (another level) of the possible questions and that the answer the lady gives is no more than a sample (third level) of her attitudes and experiences on each question.

The kind of people who make up the interviewing staff can shade the result in an interesting fashion. Some years ago, during the war, the National Opinion Research Center sent out two staffs of interviewers to ask three questions of five hundred Negroes in a Southern city. White interviewers made up one staff, Negro the other.

One question was, "Would Negroes be treated better or worse here if the Japanese conquered the U.S.A.?" Negro interviewers reported that nine per cent of those they asked said "better." White interviewers found only two per cent of such responses. And while Negro interviewers found only twenty-five per cent who thought Negroes would be treated worse, white interviewers turned up forty-five per cent.

When "Nazis" was substituted for "Japanese" in the question, the results were similar.

The third question probed attitudes that might be based on feelings revealed by the first two. "Do you think it is more important to concentrate on beating the Axis, or to make democracy work better here at home?" "Beat Axis" was the reply of thirty-nine per cent, according to the Negro interviewers; of sixty-two per cent, according to the white.

Here is bias introduced by unknown factors. It seems likely that the most effective factor was a tendency that must always be allowed for in reading poll results, a desire to give a pleasing answer. Would it be any wonder if, when answering a question with connotations of disloyalty in wartime, a Southern Negro would tell a white man what sounded good rather than what he actually believed? It is also possible that the different groups of interviewers chose different kinds of people to talk to.

In any case the results are obviously so biased as to be worthless. You can judge for yourself how many other poll-based conclusions are just as biased, just as worthless—but with no check available to show them up.

You have pretty fair evidence to go on if you suspect that polls in general are biased in one specific direction, the direction of the *Literary Digest* error. This bias is toward the person with more money, more education, more information and alertness, better appearance, more conventional behavior, and more settled habits than the average of the population he is chosen to represent.

You can easily see what produces this. Let us say that you are an interviewer assigned to a street corner, with one interview to get. You spot two men who seem to fit the category you must complete: over forty, Negro, urban. One is in clean overalls, decently patched, neat. The other is dirty and he looks surly. With a job to get done, you approach the more likely-looking fellow, and your colleagues all over the country are making similar decisions.

Some of the strongest feeling against public-opinion polls is found in liberal or left wing circles, where it is rather commonly believed that polls are generally rigged. Behind this view is the fact that poll results so often fail to square with the opinions and desires of those whose thinking is not in the conservative direction. Polls, they point out, seem to elect Republicans even when voters shortly thereafter do otherwise.

Actually, as we have seen, it is not necessary that a poll be rigged— that is, that the results be deliberately twisted in order to create a false impression. The tendency of the sample to be biased in this consistent direction can rig it automatically.

What is random sampling? How does it differ from stratified random sampling? When gathering statistics, what can we do to insure honesty, to reduce exaggeration or understatement, and to eliminate interviewer bias? When hearing statistics, how can we determine their validity? Are there standard questions we should ask about all statistics?

How to Be Impressive
in the Pulpit

Charles Merrill Smith

Charles Merrill Smith, pastor of Wesley Methodist Church in Bloomington, Illinois, presents a delightful tongue-in-cheek account of how to be successful in the pulpit. The differences between preaching and public speaking are negligible; the basic problems and principles are the same. His suggestions can be made relevant for us by simply substituting the words classroom, conference room, business meeting, or lecture hall for pulpit or church. Pay particular attention to Smith's discussions of style versus content, audience adaptation, choice of subjects, humor, emotions, language, and noteless speaking.

Unless you attended a really first-rate seminary, which is unlikely since there are so few of them, probably you have been taught that a clergyman's first, primary, basic, fundamental, highest, most sacred, most precious function, duty and privilege is to preach.

Chances are you have been dunked in the doctrine that you will ultimately rise or sink in your chosen work on the basis of your performance in the pulpit. Also, if you were so unfortunate as to fall under the spell of a persuasive professor of preaching with liberal inclinations, you may even believe that you should take some longbearded Old Testament prophet as your ideal and denounce the supposed evils of our society as, for example, Amos whacked and lacerated the society of his day. This would certainly be a bad mistake. After all the only pulpit Amos ever filled was at Bethel —and he was requested to resign after one sermon.

At any rate, the interpretation of the minister's role largely in terms of his preaching function is encouraged by the laity which supposes that the delivery of a weekly homily constitutes the clergy's major work load.

You will get awfully sick of the jibe "Pretty good pay you get, Reverend, for working one hour a week." This is delivered always by the coarse, hearty type of parishioner who thinks it is original with him. It is best to smile if you can manage it.

However, if you care to achieve more than very modest success in the church, you must (1) convince yourself that all this business about preaching being your most important task isn't true and (2) convince your congregation that it is.

Let me elaborate. If you believe preaching to be first and most important in the work of a minister, you will naturally devote the largest slice of your time and energy to the preparation of your sermons, thus robbing yourself of the opportunity to address yourself to the genuinely vital and productive duties of your calling.

Any veteran cleric who has gotten anywhere at all will assure you that preaching is quite secondary in his scale of values. Yet we keep getting, year after year, floods of fresh seminary graduates who are enamored of the image of the pulpiteer. They buy an astonishing number of books. They use up the good working hours of the morning for study. They have a tendency to write out their sermons, polishing and repolishing them. And some of them even plan their sermons for the entire year ahead. This is expensive in terms of precious time and your meager supply of ready cash (books are frightfully costly these days). It is also entirely unnecessary.

However, your laymen should be allowed the illusion that preaching is your number one task because the illusion can be made to pay you rich dividends.

Fix firmly in the structure of your basic operating philosophy the fundamental fact about the ministry of the pulpit, which is: "It is ridiculously easy and requires but a negligible chunk of your time to be a popular pulpit personality."

Now if this is true (and rest in the confidence that it is), then it requires no especially gifted imagination to grasp the possibilities here. So long as your congregation is enthusiastic about you as a preacher, the following benefits will accrue to you:

1. The congregation will be inclined to charity concerning your weaknesses, and you are bound to have some. ("Well, we must remember that good pulpit men are hard to come by," they will say—a judgment which usually buries any criticism of your deficiencies.)

2. When your church members don't see you they will assume that you are sequestered in your study poring over the Scriptures, the philosophers, the post-Nicene fathers (they haven't, of course, the remotest notion of what a post-Nicene father is) adding to this intellectual sour mash the catalyst of your own reverent insights and thus distilling the

spiritual booze which will give their souls a hearty wallop when you serve it up on Sunday morning. So long as they assume all this, they will not wonder how you spend your time, which permits you a considerable amount of personal freedom.

3. Your reputation as a superior pulpit man will get around, and better paying churches will be after you.

Now is the time, then, to perfect yourself in the skills of the popular preacher. No other professional investment will return such dividends on so small a capitalization. It is a situation comparable to having gotten in on the initial stock offering of IBM or General Motors.

The first rule for the popular preacher to remember as he prepares a sermon is that style is of enormous importance while content makes little ultimate difference in the congregation's enthusiasm for one's efforts in the pulpit. About 1000 parts style to 1 part content is a good proportion.

No one cares very much what you say when you preach, so long as it is not radically controversial or disturbing. Your acceptability as a preacher depends almost wholly on how you say it. A really gifted preacher can deliver an exegesis of "Mary Had a Little Lamb" or extol the virtues of the single tax and send the congregation home in a spiritual trance, while a bumbler can bore it to death with a sensible and relevant exposition of the parable of the prodigal son.

All too few young clerics starting at the front door of their career trouble themselves to ask the question "What do my people want from a sermon?" Rather, they ask themselves "What had I ought to give my congregation when I preach?" Which is only another form of the question "What do I want to give them?"

Fundamentally, preaching at its best is one of the entertainment arts, and the successful pulpiteer will always think of himself first as an entertainer. His problem is much the same as Jack Benny's or Shelley Berman's or Mort Sahl's. He has to stand up and keep the customers interested in what he is saying or business will fall off at an alarming rate. The following chapters will examine the techniques of pulpit entertainment.

ENTERTAIN THE CUSTOMERS

The old pros of the pulpit know that they should always aim to do three things for and to the customers (congregation) in every sermon:
1. Make them laugh
2. Make them cry
3. Make them feel religious

This does not mean that people in church should be induced to guffaw like drunks in a night club. The amenities of civilized churchgoing preclude this sort of congregational behavior. A preacher should not aim to be a belly-laugh comedian—but he should be a hearty-giggle humorist or he is unlikely to be called to a major league pastorate.

This level of skill is attained by loading the sermon with funny stories. They don't need to illustrate anything (one can always contrive to make a story fit); they just need to be funny.

The wise young clergyman, then, will early begin the habit of collecting funny stories. Buy books of them, clip them out of newspapers and magazines, paste them in scrapbooks or keep them in files. You can never have too many of them.

Let us now illustrate how to go about selecting a funny story for pulpit use. Let us suppose you are preparing a sermon on Christian missions. One of your points will likely be "The joys and advantages of being a Christian." Now when you come to this point in the sermon you can say, "Of course there are disadvantages to being a Christian. Sometimes people take advantage of the Christian's spirit of benevolence. This reminds me[1] of the story of the Jewish man who was converted to Christianity. After he was baptized and received into the church, he went home and was met at the door by his son who said, 'Pop, I need $5000 for a new sports car,' and his father gave it to him. As he came into the front room, his daughter came in and said, 'Father, I'm going to Europe and the trip will cost $5000,' so he gave it to her. As he went into the kitchen to see what was cooking, his wife said to him, 'Dear, I've ordered a new mink coat and it costs $5000.' So he gave it to her.

"Then, alone for a moment, he meditated on all this.

" 'Here I've been a Christian for a half-hour,' he said to himself, 'and these damn[2] Jews have taken me for $15,000 already.' "

Here is a nearly ideal humorous sermon illustration. For one thing, it does illustrate a point more or less. (And though we have previously noted that this is by no means necessary, it is a good idea to connect up your stories to the sermon wherever possible—and it usually is.) More important, it subtly reinforces your people in one of the prejudices to which they cling with tenacity and makes them feel comfortable about it.

You can be certain that any middle-class, standard-brand Protestant congregation is anti-Semitic. Not blatantly anti-Semitic, of course. You would get the gate in no time at all if you preached the Gerald L. K. Smith line. Also, hardly any of your good people would admit to prejudice against Jews. It isn't popular to do so, and besides everyone wants to think he is tolerant. Most of your members even know and like some individual Jew-

---

[1] One is always "reminded" of a story in the pulpit, even though hours have been spent locating it and it is a part of the manuscript.

[2] In less sophisticated churches, substitute "darn" for "damn."

ish family. But to a person they think of Jews as avaricious, selfish, grasping and quick to take advantage of the other fellow. At the same time, they feel vaguely guilty about feeling this way.

So with this illustration, you have managed to imply (a) that Jews are actually like we all think they are, and (b) if Jews would only become Christians they would immediately become generous, warmhearted and unselfish like us, and (c) the Christian religion is demonstrably superior to the Jewish religion and, by implication, to all other religions.

So in this one brief story you have succeeded in extending permission to hold a prejudice, absolved the people of their guilt over holding it,[3] and have made them feel good about being Christian because Christians are superior people. And all this has been accomplished in the most entertaining of ways—through a funny story.

You cannot hope to turn up so ideal an example of the humorous story for pulpit use every week in the year. But if you keep it in mind as a model, it will help you in your selections and remind you to make the people laugh.

MAKE THEM CRY

Now we come to the art of making them cry. Of course we do not mean that actual tears must flow (although if the custodian regularly comes upon damp discarded Kleenex when he picks up after the service, it is a heartening indication that you are consistently striking the bull's-eye). A lump in the throat and a quivering sensation in the breast, however, are quite adequate.

For making them cry, so to speak, your best bets are stories about old-fashioned virtues and values, patriotism and self-sacrifice. If you tell them properly these will always do the trick.

Let us inspect a brief example of the lump-in-the-throat story.

A poor but scholarly and conscientious preacher has a little girl who desperately wants a new dress for an important party at the home of a wealthy parishioner. Her father sadly tells her there isn't any money for a new dress (build up his pain and anguish). She can't understand it, so finally her mother takes her into her father's study, points to the rows of books and says, "Darling, here is the reason there is no money for a new dress."

The point here which is calculated to open up the tear ducts is that the little girl must give up what all little girls have as an inalienable right

---

[3] Absolution of guilt has always been one of the first functions and duties of a priest.

to possess in order that her poor, struggling father may have the tools to do the Lord's work.

The story, of course, is full of logical holes. One could just as well conclude that her father sacrificed his daughter's welfare to his passion for scholarship. Why did he need all those expensive books? Why couldn't he have sacrificed a little for his daughter's sake? If his parishioners wanted a scholarly preacher, why shouldn't they pay the freight?

But be assured that your hearers will never even think of these questions. They will only feel sad and tearful over the plight of the little girl caught in the meshes of a necessary self-denial that a high and noble end may be achieved.

This story has the added advantage of a subliminal but persistent suggestion that the clergy bears the burden of great hidden expenses, which, you will discover, is all too true. It could easily produce a substantial book-allowance item for you in the next church budget.

You must not be too crude with the "cry stories," of course. Little Nell dying of malnutrition in the garret because Papa spends all the money at the saloon served her day, but the modern congregation, however plebeian, will not respond to it and might even chuckle—which would be disconcerting to you to say the least.

The untimely passing of a lovely young thing in the bloom of youth leaving behind a desolate and inconsolable lover is a theme with excellent possibilities so long as it is made clear that the love relationship has been entirely spiritual in nature. Turn the Lady of the Camellias into a church deaconess or a virgin schoolteacher and you will be amazed at the lachrymose response you will get.

MAKE THEM FEEL RELIGIOUS

Now we come to the problem of making them feel religious. This is the easiest of the three because it is mostly a matter of nomenclature. You need only employ a sufficient number of words and phrases which are loaded with "religious" meaning to accomplish the desired end.

For quick reference, the author here includes a brief lexicon of graded religious words and phrases. Roughly, a number one word or phrase has twice the religious punch of a number two and three times that of a number three.

LEXICON

Faith of our Fathers (1)

Bible-believing Christians (1)

Repentance (3) (Many people are not enthusiastic about repenting.)

Salvation (2) (A good word, but carries some overtones of the camp meeting.)

The Bible says (1) (Billy Graham's favorite phrase. Most congregations will believe anything you say if you precede it with this phrase.)

Christ-centered (1) (Use this often.)

Righteousness (3) (Given the lowest rating because it implies that Christians ought to behave themselves according to a standard stricter than many church members care to observe.)

God-fearing (1) (Your people aren't afraid of God, of course, but they enjoy thinking that they are.)

Serve the Lord with Gladness (1) (This has a fine biblical and literary ring to it, sounds as if you are calling for instant, forthright action, but is sufficiently vague as to require nothing at all from your hearers. Hard to beat.)

The Good Book (2) (Older members will like it, but it is a little dated for younger people.)

Sin (or *sinners*) (1) (Every sermon should include one or the other. These words conjure up images of bordellos and orgies and black lingerie—which images have an entertainment value in themselves. Your people will never connect the words with anything that middle-class white Protestants do, so you can flail away at sin and sinners to your heart's content.)

The Kingdom of God (1) (Your congregation has heard this phrase from every preacher that ever served them, so they consider it a true mark of a devout and stable minister.)

Holiness unto the Lord (1) (Not one member has a clue as to what this means but it is one of the most euphonious and soul-satisfying phrases in the lexicon.)

Heaven (1) (No preacher ever got fired for preaching about heaven so long as he made it clear that he thought everyone in his congregation would get there.)

Hell (3) (Just as well lay off this one or use it sparingly.)

These examples should suffice to give you the general idea of how to go about making people feel religious. As a rule of thumb, rely heavily on those words and phrases which evoke pleasant religious feelings, and use with considerable economy any word which might make people uncomfortable or fidgety (which is why we warn against preaching about hell, for you would be surprised at the members of your flock who are trying to quash the suspicion that they might end up there).

NOTES ON NOTELESS PREACHING

Let us now turn our attention to some do's and don'ts of preaching, little practical suggestions—each by itself a small thing perhaps—but put together adding up to great things for you so far as preferment in your calling is concerned.

At the top of the list of those items which you should do is this: Always preach without manuscript or notes of any kind.

Young clergymen seldom grasp the value of perfecting themselves in the "noteless" style of sermon delivery. Most of us have weak memories and feel horribly insecure without the comforting presence of a manuscript on the podium in front of us. Not one person in a thousand feels naturally inclined to this style of delivery. It is this very scarcity of noteless preachers which works to the advantage of the man who is one.

When you preach without notes, the focus of attention for the congregation is not your sermon but your performance. Since most of your listeners are paralyzed and inarticulate in front of an audience with everything they intend to say written down and before them, they are vastly amazed that anyone can stand up and talk for twenty minutes or so without visible aids to the memory, no matter what he says.

This situation obviates the need for undue concern over the content of your sermon since hardly anyone will be more than casually interested in what you say, thus lightening your preparatory labors and granting you many extra hours every week to do with what you please—hours which your less gifted brethren of the cloth will spend sweating over the manufacture of a manuscript for Sunday morning.

You may have observed already that the possession of a noteless preacher is a genuine status symbol for a church, the ecclesiastical equivalent of a chinchilla coat or recognition by the headwaiter at Le Pavillon. These confer status because they are rare, and rare status symbols cost quite a bit of money. This law operates just as surely in the ecclesiastical world as in the secular world, and a noteless preacher always commands a higher salary than even the most profound of his brethren who encumber themselves with manuscripts.

Those fortunate few congregations blessed with a noteless preacher become inordinately proud of him, and brag about him much as they brag about breaking 80 at golf or being invited to the Governor's for tea. They never comment that their preacher is learned or witty or forceful or devout or thought-provoking or inspiring. They always say, "You know, he preaches without a single note."

Also, the noteless style endears you to the extremely pious members of your flock who tend to be suspicious of written sermons on the grounds that excessive advance preparation allows insufficient opportunities for the workings of divine inspiration. The extemporaneous homily seems to them to come from the heart instead of the head, and is thus a sure sign and seal that their preacher is "spiritual."

Since the pietists are a hard-core type of group in the congregation, sticking together like scotch tape and presenting a solid front in both their enthusiasms and their dislikes, it is a group to be reckoned with. A sensitive ecclesiastical politician can always smell an impending change of pastorates by sniffing the wind near the pietists of the congregation. If the pietists are voicing criticisms of their pastors, no matter how few and mild, the cloud no larger than a man's hand has appeared on the horizon and this pastor is well advised to start looking for another job, because the pietists will eventually get him. They are as relentless as Javert. Therefore, the wise pastor will learn how to cater to this group, and noteless preaching is one of the best ways to commend himself to it. Exhaustive research by the author has failed to turn up a single case of a noteless preacher falling into disrepute with the pietists of his congregation.

A PREACHING PROGRAM WHICH CAN'T MISS

As you begin your career of labor for the Lord, you must keep in mind that, while the content matter of your sermons is not too important if your style is adequate, there are some types of sermons which are almost guaranteed to win enthusiastic reactions from your congregation.

If you will never forget that your beloved parishioners are primarily interested in themselves, their spiritual aches and pains, their desire for whatever they equate with happiness, their urge to succeed socially and financially, the preservation of their provincial prejudices, then you will do the bulk of your preaching on these subjects.

One eminent New York preacher whose name escapes us at the moment (Freud would probably have been able to account for our forgetfulness) has become the best-known Protestant clergyman of our generation, has made pots of money and acquired all the good things which come the way of the sensationally successful preacher simply by remembering this one simple fact. Buy his books, hear him at every opportunity, and imitate him insofar as it is possible for you to do so and you, too, will hit the ecclesiastical jackpot.

Your people, you will discover, have an insatiable appetite for sermons

on how to improve themselves or solve their emotional (spiritual) problems so long as the panacea you offer them does not require them to (a)
quit doing anything they like to do, (b) spend any money or (c) submit
to any very rigorous or time-consuming spiritual discipline.

What you need, then, is a formula tailored and trimmed to the
above specifications. The author suggests that whenever you preach a
"how to use the Christian Faith to get what you want" type of sermon
(and you should be preaching just such a sermon eight Sundays out of
ten) it is well to rely on a formula which varies no more than the rotation
of the earth. The formula is this: Whether the sermon deals with the
problem of loneliness, frustration, marital felicity, getting ahead in one's
business or whatever, the solution to the problem is always:

(a) a catchy, easily remembered Bible verse (variable with each sermon
according to the topic)

(b) a simple, sunny little prayer to repeat as needed (also variable, as .
above)

(c) an exhortation to have faith (this item is invariable. You don't have
to be specific about faith—in fact, it is better if you are not specific
—just urge faith. Faith in faith is the best-selling item in your line
of goods you will discover. There is very little sales resistance to it).

One obstacle you will need to overcome in training yourself to
preach Sunday after Sunday on these "helping yourself through the
Gospel" themes is the immense boredom you will suffer. Since you will
be preaching essentially the same sermon nearly every Sunday, changing
only the title, the text and the illustrations, you will find it difficult to
convince yourself that your congregation will not be bored too. But it
won't, and this you must accept as an article of your homiletical faith.
No one has yet come up with a satisfactory explanation for this phenomenon. It is just a fact of life. Trust it and act on it.

The remaining 20 per cent of your preaching can be devoted, for the
most part, to sermons for special occasions. These should be keyed to
our more important national holidays. Many youthful clergymen, inspired no doubt by the highest and most pious motives, begin their careers
by using the Christian calendar as a guide for their preaching. But the
wise ones quickly discard this antiquated practice. The only days in the
so-called church year which merit a special sermon are Christmas and
Easter—and these merit it because they have evolved into important
national, commercial holidays rather than for any vestigial religious significance still clinging to them.

Following is a month-by-month listing of the special days you will
want to observe from the pulpit along with suggested themes for the day.

JANUARY

First Sunday—New Year's Day sermon. Topic: "Twelve Joyous Months with Jesus."

FEBRUARY

Sunday nearest Washington's birthday. Topic: "Faithful to the Faith of Our Nation's Founder." (This may be changed on alternate years to the Sunday nearest Lincoln's birthday. It involves only a slight change in the topic, which might be "Faithful to the Faith of Our Greatest President." The sermon can be substantially the same.)

MARCH

No particularly important special day unless Easter falls in March.

APRIL

Easter Sunday (usually). Topic: "Looking Forward to a Good, Old-Fashioned Heaven." (Do not forget to give the Easter-only church-goers a thorough lacing for their failure to show up the rest of the year. This gives the regulars a sense of their own righteousness and spiritual superiority, and the Easter-only crowd expects to catch it from the preacher because they always have. They will not mend their ways, of course, but they hardly feel they have been to church if you fail to flay them.)

MAY

Second Sunday—Mother's Day. Topic: "Our Mother's Faith."

JUNE

Third Sunday—Father's Day. Topic: "Faith of Our Fathers."

JULY

Sunday nearest Fourth of July (might fall on last Sunday in June). Topic: "God's Chosen People." (Stressing, of course, that America and Americans are God's examples of what He expects other nations and other peoples to be like. This sermon may also be used at American Legion rallies and other patriotic occasions. It is a sure-fire hit.)

AUGUST

These are the dog days for church attendance. No special days. Better take your vacation in August.

SEPTEMBER

Sunday nearest Labor Day (could be last Sunday in August). Topic: "God's Labor Laws." (Point out that the laboring man needs to get back to the old-fashioned values of an honest day's work for an honest wage, and gratitude for the enterprising and risk-taking capitalist who makes his job possible. Express sympathy and concern for the good workmen of America caught in the evil grip of organized labor. Since you are likely to have few members of labor unions and lots of employers in your congregation, this will be one of the most popular sermons of the year.)

OCTOBER

Last Sunday—Reformation Sunday. Topic: "The Menace of an Alien Religion." (Reformation day isn't much of a special occasion in our churches, but it does afford an opportunity to whack the Roman Catholics. Since there is a mood of tolerance in the air, what with the late President Kennedy and the late Pope John, care must be taken to attack the still unpopular aspects of Roman Catholicism— the political aims of the Vatican, the mumbo-jumbo of its priestcraft, that sort of thing.)

NOVEMBER

Sunday before Thanksgiving. Topic: "God's Blessing Means God's Approval." (The theme here is that God has blessed America beyond the blessings of any other land, which means that God likes us best.)

DECEMBER

Christmas Sunday—Topic: "The Babe from Heaven." (There is simply no way to preach an unpopular sermon when you have a baby, motherhood, heaven, humble shepherds and adoring wise men to talk about. Stick to the pageantry of Christmas. Beware of exploring the meaning of the Advent very much beneath the surface aspects of the story, for this can get you into trouble.)

Had this book been written a few years ago, the author would have issued an iron-bound injunction against any preaching which attempts to relate the Gospel to contemporary social issues. Nothing subtracts from the marketability of a preacher so much as having the label "liberal" pinned on him. Not many of us invite attacks on our theological ortho-doxy these days because 99-44/100% of any modern standard-brand congregation is so theologically untutored that it wouldn't be able to recognize a heretic. It has no way of distinguishing between theological orthodoxy and heresy. But it is quick to spot any slight leaning toward liberal social views in its pastor. Heresy today is social rather than theo-logical, and every congregation has its self-appointed Torquemadas anxious to oil the rack or heat up the fires around the stake.

It would be best, therefore, if the preacher could avoid entirely any reference to any subject which has a side to it capable of being construed as "liberal." The author can remember when church life had a lovely, serene, otherworldly flavor to it because preachers did not concern them-selves with temporal problems. But this day has disappeared because we now live in unhappy times in which every newspaper brings tidings of some social problem which directly involves religion, the church and the faith and which forces us to make some kind of response.

It is, in fact, a decided advantage to you to be known as a fearless and forthright and prophetic pulpit voice—so long as you can achieve this reputation without being thought liberal. So you will have to venture out into the choppy and shoal-filled waters of preaching on social issues. There is no avoiding it, or the author would counsel you to do so.

THE DANGER OF BEING SPECIFIC

This, then, is the most dangerous part of the preaching ministry. But if you will follow three simple principles, you can mitigate the dangers of shipwreck.

The first principle is this: Never be specific as to the Christian posi-tion on any burning social issue of the day.

For example, if you feel compelled by current events to preach on racial segregation, never, repeat, never, suggest that integration is the Christian solution. In fact, eschew the term "integration" entirely. It is far too specific.

The points you will want to make in this sermon will go something like this:

1. Extremism in racial matters is the chief evil.
2. The colored people ought to reflect on the great strides forward they have made and not be too impatient for too much too soon.
3. Brotherhood and Christian love will point the way. "You can't

legislate love" is an excellent phrase to use here. (Since the congregation will define "Brotherhood" and "Christian love" to mean a kind of vague good will toward colored people so long as they stay in their place, they will take no offense at this.)

The problem here is to avoid any suggestion that white Protestant Christians have been at any point remiss in their attitudes or actions, and at the same time outline a solution which involves new attitudes and actions (since any idiot can reason that if what we have always done isn't working, we had darn well better think up something else).

This is a delicate but not insoluble dilemma for the preacher. The way out is to keep handy a set of nonspecific words and phrases which allow the members of the congregation to fill in their own meaning. "Brotherhood" and "Christian love" have already been mentioned. It is always a good idea to urge your people to employ more of "the spirit of Christ" in the solution to social tensions, since hardly any of them know what this means but practically all of them think they do.

What you have working for you here is the average American citizen's touching faith in simple solutions to vast and complex problems. And people who believe that a balanced budget or bombing Cuba or a Republican administration would solve the problems of the nation and the world will have no difficulty believing that your non-specific phrases are clear Christian answers and that you are therefore a keen and courageous preacher.

A second principle to follow in preaching on social issues is to preach on problems which are as remote as possible from your community. You can denounce the government of South Africa with all the vigor at your command, but be careful about denouncing political corruption in your own city because some of your good members might be involved. Criticize to your heart's content the Godless New York stage, but don't knock the local movie house, because someone in your congregation may be leasing it to the operator.

The third principle, and perhaps the one of pristine value to you in preaching on social issues, is to reserve your righteous indignation for those questions on which there is no substantial disagreement among your members.

As this is written, the Supreme Court ruling on prayer in the public schools is getting a lot of attention in the press. Since most of your people have been led to believe by the papers they read that the Supreme Court is systematically undermining the American way of life, they will welcome several sermons on "this atheistic decision." This issue should be good for several years yet. But by far the safest social problem on which the preacher may take an unequivocal position is the temperance question. You are aware, of course, that in the newspeak of the temperance movement temperance doesn't mean temperance. It means total abstinence from the use of beverage alcohol.

Your congregation is made up of members who advocate temperance and members who drink without apology, the proportions varying with the size, sophistication and urban or rural character of your community. But both groups expect the preacher to trot out a temperance sermon every so often in addition to frequent blasts on the subject as a subpoint in other sermons. The temperance people love to hear you lambaste booze, and the drinkers are not offended by it because they understand that this just goes along with your job. A preacher who doesn't preach temperance sermons is as unthinkable as a Frenchman who frowns on love. This is the one social issue which involves no danger whatever, no matter how violent your denunciation.[4]

If you understand your people, their hopes and fears and prides and prejudices (and every truly successful pastor does understand these things), then all you need to do to be a highly regarded pulpit man is to tell them what you know they want to hear. After all, they are badgered and buffeted by worldly cares six days a week, and they need a sanctuary from all this on Sunday. They should be able to come to the Lord's house when the sweet church bells chime secure in the knowledge that they will find it here. They should come anticipating a jolly, sprightly, positive, entertaining, non-controversial homily from their beloved man of God, aware that no discouraging or disturbing word will be spoken from your pulpit.

If your good people can count on this kind of preaching from you, you can count on their heartfelt appreciation expressed in their continuing affection, fulsome praise, a solid reputation as a fine pulpit man, and more tangible evidences of gratitude in the form of salary increases, better housing, and maybe a trip abroad for you and your wife with all expenses paid. Your true reward (apart from a perfectly legitimate joy in your professional success) will be, of course, the knowledge that you have served the Lord by comforting his people—and this is the knowledge which maketh glad the heart.

Do you agree with Smith that audiences are more interested in style and delivery than in subject and content? Should we try to provide audiences with what they want to hear rather than what we think

---

[4] The author knows of three churches which realize a considerable amount of annual income from the leasing of property on which alcoholic beverages are dispensed. Yet the pastors of these churches continue to preach anti-booze sermons with, apparently, the complete approval of their congregations.

they need to hear? Smith muses that preaching is for entertainment. How much of our speaking is essentially entertainment? What do you think of Smith's three rules for successful speaking: make an audience laugh, make them cry, and make them feel religious (patriotic, intelligent, tolerant, economy-minded, charitable)? Should we strive for noteless delivery of speeches? Should we select vague, remote, and noncontroversial topics if success is thus assured?

Speaking from Manuscript

Harold P. Zelko
Frank E.X. Dance

Frequent questions of prospective speakers, whether preparing for the classroom, lecture hall, legislative chamber, banquet room or conference room, concern the use of notes and perhaps manuscript. It appears that more speakers are using notes today, and that many are turning to the complete manuscript. Harold P. Zelko, professor emeritus at Pennsylvania State University, and Frank E.X. Dance, professor of communication at the University of Denver, discuss the advantages and disadvantages of manuscript speaking. They also suggest guidelines for preparing and delivering speeches from the written page that can eliminate many of the complaints against "reading" a speech.

Although the philosophy of this book primarily embraces the development of speech communication ability in all kinds of informal situations requiring face-to-face speaking and listening which draw on the resources of the individual to extemporize, we recognize the part played by the written manuscript. Actually, it is somewhat of a paradox that in an age which makes so many demands on the informal interacting process, speech presentation from a manuscript seems to be growing in importance in certain special settings. It is the purpose of this chapter to discuss the place of the manuscript and its relation to extempore speaking, the special problems and methods in preparing such a speech, and the necessary considerations and suggestions for presenting it effectively.

WHY SPEAK FROM MANUSCRIPT?

The speaker who prepares his own speeches and follows the principles and suggestions dealing with more informal situations should have little

From Business and Professional Speech Communication by Harold P. Zelko and Frank E.X. Dance. Copyright © 1965 by Holt, Rinehart and Winston, Inc. Reprinted by permission of the publisher.

or no concern or need to consider writing his speech out in manuscript form. We have pointed out that good speech communication in today's world is conversational, warm, direct, animated, and informal or even colloquial in choice of language. Some of this is usually lost in speaking from manuscript. To put this another way, *every principle and suggestion for manuscript speaking in this chapter is directed toward minimizing the loss in effective oral communication which is usually best achieved in the extemporaneous speech.*

The reasons for speaking from manuscript and the advantages of this method derive more from the situation rather than from the preference of the speaker. Of course, many speakers use a manuscript because they feel more secure with it, or they think that the stature of their own position or office either demands it or gives them license to use it, or that the situation calls for it. These may all be very good reasons why the manuscript should be used.

The *advantages* of manuscript speaking are sometimes very potent. Clarity and conciseness can be achieved more accurately, chiefly because the speaker has the opportunity to write and rewrite until he is sure that the idea or statement is clear. He can edit and revise paragraphs and sentences so that cumbersome language is eliminated. He can achieve both a clarity and nicety of language which may not be possible in extemporaneous speaking, unless he has an unusually large vocabulary and a facile ability to use it. In writing, he can select, consider, reject, change, and add words as he works for perfection of the written statement. The vivid and colorful prose of speakers like Winston Churchill, Franklin Roosevelt, John F. Kennedy, and Adlai Stevenson does not roll off the tongue readily. Yet the very fact that it is referred to as "prose" poses the major problem of keeping it informal and conversational in style. The homey, colloquial expressions of Harry Truman which brought him so close to his audiences were not usually in his written manuscript.

Top executives frequently give preciseness of language as the primary reason why they speak from manuscript and also want other company representatives to do so when they speak in public. They also indicate that the manuscript forms a permanent record that can be referred to or given to the press if the occasion calls for this. These reasons are probably the major ones given by professional and business speakers for the manuscript speech. This is true very much in government, and it is probably a justifiable reason at high levels. No one would question that the President of the United States has to be extremely careful of the way he expresses government policy, as hundreds of reporters and millions of listeners and readers are trying to interpret a wide variety of meanings from what he says. Similarly, other high government officials may be in the same position.

The need for uniformity of communication of decisions and policies sometimes makes the manuscript speech highly desirable. Although this is often used as an excuse for the manuscript, it tends to be a major reason for using this medium among business and industrial speakers. Some companies insist that all their speakers use manuscripts so that they can first be reviewed and edited to conform to company policy. Some go so far as to insist that a speaker not deviate one word from the prepared text. The more prevalent practice, however (and fortunately), is to allow for the speaker's ad lib and impromptu remarks to deviate from the manuscript, as long as the meaning is not distorted.

In the professions, teachers and scholars find themselves called upon to present "papers" on academic subjects at professional meetings and conventions. The traditional practice is to read these from manuscript, again to insure accuracy and an indication of precise scholarship. The researcher will usually reduce his message to manuscript for these reasons. The doctor follows this style when he is presenting his findings or views on some aspect of medicine to his peers at a medical convention. The lawyer may also do this, but more forensic speaking by lawyers in the courtroom is extempore or even impromptu.

The practice of reading papers at conventions and other meetings gave rise to this comment, in an editorial in which the writer pleaded for more courses in "public reading" rather than public speaking because of the prevalence of the manuscript presentation:

> Most public meetings are made unnecessarily dull because the so-called speakers are bad readers. . . . In every case if the man had been a good public reader he would have had audience attention instead of yawns. If everybody threw away their manuscripts and spoke from notes it would be fine. But people just won't do that. Reading speeches has become a convention convention.[1]

The *oral presentation of a report*, frequently technical in nature in today's business and professional society, is growing in importance as a situation calling for expert manuscript presentation. More often than not, it is delivered with a monotonous drone by a "reader" who puts his chin close to the pages and his eyes on the lectern and goes about his task like a mechanical robot. The technical report is sometimes chiefly a written document to be passed through channels of an organization or read by other experts without thought for its oral presentation. Since it is not written as a speech in the first place, even more care is needed to convert it into live oral communication. Sometimes it would be wise to

---

[1] C. B. Larrabee, "Why Not Some Courses in Public Reading?", *Printers' Ink* (September 16, 1955), p. 13.

rewrite it more as a speech, rather than to rely purely on oral techniques to make it come alive as communication.

All of us are occasionally in situations where we must read from the printed page to a group in a variety of settings. These would include reading minutes at a meeting, a committee report, excerpts from a book or magazine in support of a point or for clarification during an extemporaneous speech, or reading aloud to others for any purpose in a social or business situation.

PREPARING THE MANUSCRIPT SPEECH OR REPORT

There should be little difference in preparing a manuscript speech from the steps, procedures, and principles followed in any other kind of speech preparation, up to the point of writing it out. Then there is the all-important extra step of writing.

Mental attitude may well represent the crux of the success of the manuscript speech. There is a great deal of difference between the attitude of contemplating a speech through oral communication and that of preparing a written document whose primary purpose would normally be for others to read. Almost everything one writes is for this latter purpose— to be read by others, and the attitude of preparation is to develop a finished written document. A manuscript speech is an unusual exception, where the writer will himself be presenting its ideas orally.[2] He must therefore remember, at every step of the preparation, that he is preparing a speech, not a written piece of prose. This may be his most dangerous pitfall to avoid.

It should thus be obvious that the speaker should NOT start his preparation by sitting down to write a manuscript. He will be courting disaster if he does this, for he will probably end up with a formal and "prosey" document which at best may be good for others to read. And it will likely fall short of this objective too, for it may lack organization and coherence.

The preparation steps, then, for a manuscript speech should follow the same sequence as for an extemporaneous speech:

1. *Analysis of the audience and occasion* to determine their background, knowledge, interest, and attitudes toward the contemplated subject and purpose.

[2] The ghostwriter who writes a speech for someone else to read or present is of course in a different position, for he is developing ideas for another. His problem may be even more complex in that he must keep in mind the oral style of the potential speaker and other factors covered later in this chapter.

2. *Subject selection,* with all of the foregoing factors in mind as well as the speaker's interest, attitudes, and ability to handle the subject.

3. *Purpose of the speech,* in terms of an exact statement of the objective desired in terms of the audience.

4. *Gather necessary materials* that will be used to develop ideas for interest, clarity, and proof.

5. *Determine main ideas* which will become the main points of the body of the speech, to accomplish the speech purpose.

6. *Make an outline,* showing the subdevelopment of the main points and the materials and principles to be employed.

7. *Develop the Introduction* for maximum common ground and background for the main ideas to follow.

8. *Plan the Conclusion* to leave the optimum favorable attitude and understanding of the speech purpose.

9. *Practice speaking the ideas aloud,* to develop oral style and use of language.

At this point, you will now be ready to sit down and do the one extra step for the manuscript speech:

10. *Write the spoken speech* while maintaining all of the qualities of the extemporaneous speech.

One method of doing this is to start writing the body of the speech one main point at a time. Assuming that you will set down on paper the speech purpose and then an initial summary of your main points as a major transition step between your introduction and the start of the body, you are now ready to write out the development of main point I. Do this in your first draft as though you were recording what you want to say about the point. If you have a tape recorder and a facility for verbalizing in this way, speak the point through and then reduce this to writing. Go on to main point II and then III. (Remember the principle that a good speech should not have more than three or four main points.)

Now go back and write your introduction, and next the conclusion. And when you've finished this first draft, it might be best to put it away for a day or two before getting it out again for revision. For the revising process is one of the more important steps in perfecting your manuscript, remembering that your goal is a *speech on paper,* not a prose manuscript. It might be well at this point for us to indicate some of the essential qualities of oral style which characterize a speech rather than a written essay.

ORAL STYLE CHARACTERISTICS

Speech communication is warm, personal, informal, and with maximum consideration for the interacting objectives of listener response.

Written communication tends to be more impersonal, more formal, and less adapted to a specific audience. All of the principles and characteristics of oral style point up the effort to achieve these differences:

1. *Short and simple words.* There is abundant evidence from study and observation of successful speakers that they use short words. The texts of Franklin Roosevelt's speeches show that over 90 per cent of his words contained one or two syllables. Long words are a sign of stuffiness which may have its place only in the exceptional audience situation of a learned or professional society.

A word of caution must also be given regarding the use of technical or professional language which is common to the speaker's business or profession. We all tend to pick up a vocabulary of words which become "old hat" to us but are quite foreign to the average audience. If you must use such words, be sure that you explain and define them as you go along.

Concrete and specific references to dates, times, and names of places and people tend to add clarity and interest to language. Sometimes adjectives and adverbs can cause trouble, for the speaker may not realize the extent to which they may change the meaning of purely factual and informational material.

The quality of warmth and personal involvement we strive to achieve through words in oral communication is well expressed by Stanley Burnshaw in an article aptly titled "Speaking versus Writing,"

> If I seem to be belaboring the obvious, I do so deliberately. For nothing distinguishes the speech so much as this quality of aliveness and spontaneity—the sounds, gestures, of a warm, living human presence, of a human event about to happen. I stress this aliveness, unpredictableness, spontaneity, because they are the sources of all the significant differences between speaking and writing.[3]

. . . .

2. *Short, simple sentences.* This last comment leads to this noticeable characteristic of the use of short sentences and simple thought units and expressions by the speaker. Sentences should be confined to one idea. Compound sentences and complex dependent clauses should be avoided. When in doubt, break this up into two sentences. Use "vocal periods" which will be translated into pauses when speaking. While keeping sentences short and simple, it would be a mistake to have them all the same, for variety is essential. An occasional longer sentence will not hurt. Similarly, the direct declarative sentence should be replaced with the question, either rhetorical or followed by an answer, where appropriate.

[3] Stanley Burnshaw, "Speaking versus Writing," *Today's Speech*, VI, 3 (September 1958), p. 17.

3. *More use of questions.* Oral discourse makes more use of questions than does writing, partly because of the more intimate speaker-listener relationship. Raising a question about a point tends to stimulate thinking. If it is rhetorical and not answered by the speaker, it should be so worded that the answer in the listener's mind will be obviously in the direction of the speaker's point. Sometimes letting the listener answer the question in his own mind makes a more impressionable conclusion than if you tell him the answer. This is especially so when the point would be controversial if stated directly.

4. *More personal pronouns.* Since speaking is much more personal and intimate than most writing, the personal pronoun is used more. If you are representing a company, use "we" frequently and more than the singular "I," which sometimes cannot be avoided but should be used sparingly. The pronouns "you," "yours," and "ours" are most effective to bring your listeners into a more common ground and intimate relationship with your own thoughts.

5. *More contractions of words and colloquial expressions.* It is easier and more natural to contract and combine words while speaking, such as "we're" for "we are," "can't" for "cannot." Speaking also seems less stilted when we do this. But there are times when you can use emphasis better when these words are separated, such as "We can *not* do this" sounds stronger than "We can't do this."

Colloquial expressions creep into speaking, and they should also be in your written manuscript. Some of these may depend on local usage, so one would want to be sure of the appropriateness in the given situation. An expression like "We're all in the same boat" could probably be used anywhere, while the word "dope" might refer to an ice cream sundae in one section, a stupid person in another, and an illegal drug in another.

6. *Short, less complex paragraphs.* The paragraph should always be a unified whole. Many of us are guilty of making them too long even when we are writing for reader consumption. When in doubt, start a new paragraph. Sometimes it is even advisable to break up a long paragraph into two or more, even though it still contains only one thought unit. This is particularly helpful in terms of appropriate manuscript format for the purpose of easier reading, as we point out more fully in later pages.

7. *Transitions and connectives.* Listeners must understand you as you are speaking. They cannot read and reread as a reader can with a printed page in front of him, nor can they ask you to repeat what you said while you are speaking. Transitions thus become an essential tool of the speaker so that he makes meanings clear when he goes from one point to another. Pauses help accomplish this, but a vocabulary of transition

words is also necessary. These include the simple method of numbering, "first, second, third"; or expressions like "next," "now," "since," "more-over," "again," and longer transitions, such as "Now, let's look at this another way," or "Following this point, I would now like to discuss. . . ."

8. *Repetition.* Because the listener cannot ask you to repeat or to let him read your manuscript again, you must provide for this need. Speaking demands much more repetition than writing. This can be in identical language, or in similar language. Studies have proved that repetition and restatement are effective means of achieving greater understanding, ability to remember and recall, and gaining favorable attitudes.

9. *Internal summaries.* Similar to the use of repetition, frequent summaries help to keep your points before your listeners more clearly. You may wish to first summarize all your main points in your major transition between the introduction and body. Internal summaries are helpful as you proceed through the main development, pausing to summarize what you have said as you make a transition to each new main point. This will serve to keep the structure of the speech before your listeners and will help them avoid groping and wondering what you are "driving at." Then most conclusions should include another summary.

10. *More direct adaptation to the audience.* The speaker is talking to a particular group of listeners. In this, he directs his language more personally toward this audience, considering their background, education, sex, and other factors. When writing a speech for a particular audience, this must be kept in mind. If you are reading a speech which someone else has prepared for you, you should consider making the necessary adaptations in language and thought which will best suit your particular listeners, local conditions, and special features of the occasion.

Other principles of oral style include vividness and colorful language to develop imagery and concreteness, while the listener experiences as much involvement and sensory reaction as possible from the speaker's words. But basically one should strive for informality, simplicity, and directness.

MANUSCRIPT FORM

Most speakers will revise a manuscript several times before they are satisfied with the final copy. This is usually good practice, with one major word of precaution. Revising sometimes loses the original informality and spontaneity in favor of a more stilted and grammatically correct manuscript which becomes more a prose document than a speech. Since writers are usually applying more rigid standards of grammar and style, this is a natural tendency. Keep in mind that it is always a speech.

When you are content with the final version of the manuscript, it is time to consider the best format on the page for reading or learning. Here are a few principles and suggestions that may prove helpful:

—Typing in caps helps some speakers in reading. If not the whole manuscript, main points and transitions might be boldly typed.

—Spacing can be as much as triple-spaced for easy reading and following.

—Paragraphs should be short, with obvious indentations or other marks to distinguish one from another. Try to finish a paragraph on a page and not carry over to the next. This is particularly true of sentences, which definitely should be finished on the page where started.

—Main points might be numbered with Roman numerals to correspond with their numbering in your original outline.

—Additional space might be left between main points or paragraphs to insert revisions or impromptu adaptations. A wide margin should be left for the same purpose of making notes or directions.

—Use just one side of the paper. As you go from one page to another, slide the finished page behind the others with as little movement as possible. Do not turn over pages or have them fastened together in the upper corner and turn or fold the finished pages back.

The oral report is usually made from a written manuscript which should follow especially most of the foregoing suggestions. Frequently dealing with technical material, it is apt to become much too formal and stuffy and hard to follow because the main points and organizational structure do not stand out clearly. If it is this formal a document, a second version should be made for oral presentation, with particular emphasis on structure, simplicity of language, definition of terms, clear transitions, and appropriate use of visual aids. A long report should also be reduced to digest or précis form for distribution. This should contain the introduction and statement of purpose, a summary of the main points or findings, and possibly a brief indication of the facts or other development necessary to understand each point.

WRITING MANUSCRIPTS FOR OTHERS

The practice of "ghostwriting" is well established in business and government. Many companies and high government officials have persons on their staffs who spend full time developing and writing speech manuscripts. Sometimes the level of one's position in an organization may be gauged by whether he has a speech writer. The practice of writing for a particular person frequently develops into an intimate relationship wherein the writer and the speaker become one, and the former learns to think and express ideas as though he were the speaker. President John F. Kennedy, for example, was himself an able writer and speaker. His chief writer for most of his speeches was Theodore Sorenson, whose capacity to cast ideas into the language of the speaker was remarkable.

In large companies which are represented by a number of speakers both at headquarters and throughout the company, speech writers are employed both to develop speeches for top executives and for a variety of speakers who might use them in remote parts of the country. In earlier chapters we referred to the speaker's bureaus of such companies as The American Telephone and Telegraph Company and the affiliated Bell System companies, Smith Kline and French Laboratories, United States Steel, and General Motors. These companies vary in their policy with regard to the degree to which the local speaker is required to stick to the manuscript prepared for him at headquarters or the extent to which he may make his own and local adaptations. But they all strive to develop manuscripts that are speeches rather than prose documents.

The practice of writing speeches for others has become recognized to a degree that the publication *Today's Speech*, journal of the Speech Association of the Eastern States, ran a special series of articles on this subject in one of their issues.[4]

PRESENTING THE MANUSCRIPT SPEECH OR ORAL REPORT

With the manuscript in hand, you are now ready to prepare for its oral presentation, and you may have several choices as to the method: You may read the speech exactly as in the manuscript; you may read and add interpretative or other extemporaneous remarks; or you may present the speech as though it were prepared extemporaneously. These choices represent more formal to less formal methods and all would employ the following steps.

—Cast the speech into the most readable format as described above, if this has not already been done.

—Go through the manuscript and make markings which would include underlining main or important points, words, and sentences that should be emphasized; showing appropriate markings for pauses; inserting

---

[4] See such articles as "Ghostwriting before Roosevelt," "Ghostwriting in Presidential Campaigns," "Speech-Writing Team in State Campaigns," and "Ghostwriting Agencies," *Today's Speech*, IV, 3 (September, 1956).

notes for informal and extemporaneous revisions or additions; and any other personal markings that would be helpful to you.

—Assuming that you have read through the speech in doing the above, continue to read it over several times, first to yourself, then aloud, but basically at this point to familiarize yourself thoroughly with it. Become familiar with the structure, organization, and page continuity. Then concentrate more on wording and language. Do not do this at one time, but pick up the manuscript from time to time and work toward saturating yourself with it.

—Now you are ready for actual oral practice, in which you should stand up and read aloud, following this advice of a company speech guide:

> Begin reading the speech aloud, standing . . . , with or without the podium. Read for maximum vocal expressiveness: variety of inflections, proper emphasis, vocal modulation. Read for maximum physical expressiveness: movement about the platform, gesture, erect yet comfortable stance, animated facial expression, eyes up and out of the text at least 90 percent of the time.[5]

Eye contact will be your goal, but you may find it necessary to keep the eyes on the manuscript most of the time in your early practice. Gradually, you will work toward the degree of familiarity with it that will permit your eyes to remain on the audience most of the time. You must remember that you are communicating with a live audience and that the manuscript should interfere with this as little as possible. Much too frequently it appears that communication is from manuscript to listener rather than from speaker to listener. If it were to be the former, listeners might better read the speech.

—Voice monotony is one of the major hazards of the read speech, and we have all witnessed the steady drone of the mechanical even voice that all too frequently accompanies such a presentation. The usual variety and animation of the extempore speech must come through. What frequently prevents it is an attitude on the part of the speaker of *reading words* rather than *communicating thoughts*. You must feel and be alive with the ideas of the speech.

Establish a direct communicative manner by making informal remarks of greeting and common ground at the outset, without the manuscript. Then, as you start to read from the manuscript, try to keep the natural extemporaneous quality and avoid an obvious transition to a formal style. You should be so familiar with the introduction of your speech that you

---

[5] This and other principles of manuscript reading are presented in Robert Haakenson, "How to Read a Speech" (Philadelphia: Smith Kline and French Laboratories, n.d.).

can give it without reading. The value of doing this, then, is not only to make the thoughts more clear and more interesting, but to enhance the total communicative effectiveness of your presentation.

Again pointing up the common hazards of the read speech, one writer puts it this way:

> When is a public speaker not a public speaker? When he is a public reader. . . . When the material is read effectively, when the speaker truly communicates the meaning and the message contained in the words, phrases, sentences, and paragraphs of his manuscript, no harm is done. . . . It is when the reading is done ineffectively that harm results. Too many of us have suffered through occasions of alternating frustration and boredom as we have desperately struggled to understand and hopelessly resigned ourselves to a lack of understanding. More than one physician has told me that he never attends the sectional meetings of the American Medical Association at which important papers dealing with significant discoveries in medicine are being presented. . . . "I couldn't hear or understand the halting, mumbling, run-together, and undecodable sounds emanating from the lectern. . . ."[6]

If you have still further leeway to extemporize fully from the manuscript and not read it, you can probably accomplish the most effective delivery by working back from the manuscript and through the steps you might normally employ if you were preparing an extemporaneous speech. The decision to have all their speakers work toward this method of presentation was made by The American Telephone and Telegraph Company and the affiliated Bell System companies who now have thousands of company representatives making speeches for them. Almost all the speeches are prepared either in the headquarters office in New York or in the respective Bell company by expert speech writers. The speaker receives the manuscript and is trained to get it ready (and himself) through following a systematic sequence of steps. He learns and practices these steps so that he is able to apply them to any manuscript. In so doing, he is told that he might use his language or make additions as long as he presents the speech substantially as in the text. The manual is quoted at length because the suggestions represent a unique departure from the usual rules for reading a speech:

> Let's look at the steps you might go through in the learning and practicing of a speech.
> —Assuming you have a company-prepared manuscript, read it over several times to get the total "feel" of the message.

[6] Ralph N. Schmidt, "Speaking a Written Speech," *Today's Speech*, XI, 1 (February, 1963), pp. 1–5.

—If it is not shown at the head of the manuscript, write the specific purpose in a sentence.

—Go through the manuscript with the objective of picking out the main points, and underline these. Take each point, one at a time, and study all the developments under the point: the subpoints, the examples, statistics, and other development devices.

—As you do this, you should make an outline of the speech on a separate sheet (or sheets) of paper. You will thus end up with an outline which might be similar to one you might have prepared if you had started to develop the speech yourself.

—In the left side of the outline, and on the left side of the speech manuscript pages, make notes showing the methods, devices, and special instructions to yourself which will help you understand what is in the speech.

—Go back to the speech manuscript and read it through aloud several times. Then take the first main point in the body and read it through a few times. . . .

—Take the outline (and manuscript) and continue to speak from it, but gradually reduce the material to notes. These should take the form in which you may use them in the actual speech presentation. There is nothing bad per se about the use of notes; it is the way one uses them that may interfere with a good presentation.

    —Put notes on cards, using only one side so that you do not have to turn them over. Do not use large paper or thin paper that will make a noise.

    —Put key words, phrases, or sentences on the cards. Show transition points.

    —Put figures, statistics, or quotations on the cards.

    —Place them on the speaker's stand, or hold inconspicuously in one hand.

    —Don't allow the notes to be a barrier between you and your listeners. Get familiar with them. Glance at them quickly.

—Stand up, using the speaker's stand if possible; and go through the points, then the Body of the speech as a whole, until you are satisfied that you know what you want to say. Start practicing your Introduction and develop this in terms of the particular audience, then your Conclusion.

—At this stage, you should use a watch in your practice, keeping in mind the time limit of the speech.[7]

Whether your actual method of presentation will be to read the manuscript verbatim, to add extempore comment, or to extemporize the entire speech, you should practice as many times as necessary to achieve

---

[7] Harold P. Zelko, *Bell System Speaker's Manual*, Chapter IX, "Learning and Practicing the Speech" (New York: American Telephone and Telegraph Company, 1962). Quoted by permission.

maximum effectiveness. After learning what you want to say, keep striving for better ways to say it, constantly working on your directness, your voice projection, use of variety and emphasis, pauses, gesture, and a degree of natural animation that will give you most of these natural qualities.

USING VISUAL AIDS

The chief forms of visual aids supplementing the manuscript speech are usually the prepared chart with data or diagrams and sometimes the use of models, apparatus, or slides. The slide presentation can be most effective when another person helps with the mechanics of the projector and equipment thus enabling the speaker to stand in freedom at the side of the screen and use a pointer to focus attention where wanted while he speaks. The newer projectors have operating devices which permit the speaker to move the slides forward or backward himself by pressing a remote control button, thus permitting the maximum flexibility in his position. It is always well to practice with the slides and in the same room where the speech will be given. Speak to the audience—not the screen.

ANSWERING QUESTIONS

Since the manuscript speech is inclined to be more formal in its presentation, a question and answer forum period should be encouraged where the setting makes this appropriate. The speaker should strive for a degree of informality and close rapport in answering questions.

SUMMARY

1. The variety of settings in today's speech communication responsibilities occasionally requires that a speech be presented from a prepared manuscript. Such presentations need not be stiff and formal, and they should strive for an approximation of the extemporaneous speaking qualities.

2. The manuscript speech need not be delivered in a stuffy, formal, "nose in the manuscript" manner, and in a monotone. It may be read with variety, animation, and directness after much practice. It may be combined with some extemporaneous comment. Or it may be changed into an extemporaneous speech if the speaker has this leeway and spends sufficient time learning and practicing.

3. In writing the speech, care should be taken to use oral style char-

acteristics and not stiff, formal prose. Words and sentences should be short, paragraphs short and simple, more personal pronouns, questions, and contractions should be used, along with frequent use of transitions, summaries, and repetition.

4. The manuscript form should be adaptable to easiest reading, with markings made by the speaker to facilitate easy reading or recognition of the point.

5. The presentation of a manuscript speech may require considerably more practice than in the extempore method so as to insure familiarity, frequent eye contact with the audience, voice variety, emphasis, and natural use of gestures, and other good oral communication qualities.

Zelko and Dance claim that communication through manuscript speaking is not as effective as the extemporaneous speech. Do you agree with their evaluation? The authors say that clarity, conciseness, and a sharpness of language are better achieved through the manuscript. Do these advantages overcome the disadvantages of manuscript speaking? There are many circumstances listed when the manuscript speech is a necessity. Are we speaking more from manuscript now because we are speaking less for ourselves? Our messages seem to be increasingly for the company, school, organization, or church. Is extemporaneous speaking, then, becoming obsolete? If we must speak from manuscript, how can we achieve an oral style, and how does it differ from the written style?

V
AUDIENCE

Types of Audiences

H.L. Hollingworth

H.L. Hollingworth, formerly professor of psychology at Barnard College, Columbia University, attempts in this reading to categorize audiences into six types ranging from the pedestrian to the absent. The terms "polarization" and "orientation" are keys to his philosophy of designating audience types according to the relationship of audience to speaker. His final concern is the difference between considering the audience as a series of individuals or as a gestalt (total unit).

It is a matter of common experience that the ease with which one yields to the speaker's invitation depends first of all upon the type of audience which the occasion assembles. Although it is true that in some points every audience is unique, it is nevertheless possible to make out certain important features in respect to which audiences may be classified. Thus they might be classified with respect to the age of the individuals composing them, their homogeneity of interest, their education, or their economic status.

The most important of these features is perhaps what Bentley and Woolbert have called the degree and type of "polarization." Thus Woolbert writes:

> "To make an audience, there must be 'polarization,' the setting opposite of two objects. This it is that makes of a group an audience. Typically the audience and the speaker face in opposite directions; their minds take different bents: they are moving in opposing channels. Even though they be strongly of 'one mind' on some points, the very nature of the conditions is such as to place them at opposite poles.
>
> "In the psychological study of the audience we have to consider four kinds of relationship: (1) that of the whole group to itself,—the 'all-to-all'; (2) that of the group to the speaker or performer,—the 'all-to-one'; (3) that of the speaker or performer to the group before

him,—the 'one-to-all'; and (4) that of the speaker to each individual in the audience,—the 'one-to-one' relations."

Bentley, who has given special study to the various forms of human congregation, gives a detailed analysis of the various forms of integration, their conditions and results. Distinguishing between the audience and the mob, he writes as follows·

> In the audience, the meaning of the discourse tends to strengthen the individual relations of the mass to the speaker, who represents the topic; in the polarized mob, the significant conditions tend, on the other hand, to increase the relations within the mass, or the secondary pole, of the group. Strong interrelations among the members of the mass form the first and primary characteristic of the mob; strong individual relations between the speaker and the other members, the first and primary characteristic of the audience.

Classifying such congregates of human beings on the basis of their degree of integration, Bentley indicates the important differences between such levels as are represented in the following progressive stages:

> "Casual and unstudied aggregates" (the railway platform at train time being an example).
> "Temporary and spontaneous gatherings whither individuals are drawn by a common object of curiosity" (such as a fallen horse or a damaged machine).
> "Congregates which are led or governed. There is a spokesman to give expression or a leader to harangue, to initiate, and to command. Such groups are polarized."
> "The *selected and primed* audience, the meetings, e.g., of religious, fraternal, and social 'organizations.'"
> ". . . the Anglo-Saxon form of trial by jury. United for a special end, the jurors are expected to ponder until they 'are of one mind,' despite the mental differences which mark them as men. . . . We must look to organizations of this sort, presenting the greatest unity amid wide inherent diversity, for illustrations of our final grade. . . ."

As instructive as these classifications are, they do not entirely serve our present purpose, which does not extend to all these degrees of social integration. Instead we can to advantage bear chiefly in mind the resemblances between the performer and the advertisement, and classify audiences essentially on the basis of the tasks with which the performer is confronted when he faces them. But we may make good use of the descriptive term "polarization" which these writers have adopted, or of a somewhat similar term, "orientation," which has certain advantages over the term "polarization." By the term "orientation" we shall mean the establishment of a pattern of attention, when the group is considered, or a set and direction of interest, when we consider the individuals comprising the group. We may then with profit consider the following as the chief types of audiences.

1. THE PEDESTRIAN AUDIENCE

The lowest degree of orientation is represented by such a transient audience as the pedestrians on a busy street, before whom the street-corner orator sets up his box. Each individual is intent upon his special destination and business, and there exist no common ties or lines of com-munication between the members of the audience nor between the mem-bers and the speaker. The task of winning the audience in this case is similar to that of the show window. It involves the very first of the five steps,—catching or diverting the attention, and at least the second,—that of holding interest. Whether or not it goes further depends on the purpose of the speaker. If he is determined to influence votes or to dispose of wares, he must effectively perform the whole series of five tasks.

2. THE DISCUSSION GROUP AND PASSIVE AUDIENCE

With the discussion group we find the first signs of preliminary orien-tation toward a speaker. When people enter an auditorium, their first polarization is toward the room itself. If they could all be placed in the room at the same moment, we might say that the audience was oriented toward the physical environment. The size of the room, its arrangement, the location of the platform, the decorations, the exits, the seating arrange-ments and possibilities, the lighting fixtures, etc., command first attention. Ordinarily this orientation readily shifts, and is replaced by polarization of the members of the audience to one another. Each individual becomes conscious of himself as an object of regard by his neighbors, and is in turn prompted to scrutinize other individuals with curiosity and interest. The self-consciousness arising out of this rather formal social situation is indi-cated externally by the formal posture and bearing of each individual. Each chair is occupied by a self-conscious individual, sitting erect, observing the usual proprieties, glancing covertly at more conspicuous individuals, adjusting wearing apparel to its conventional position, and tending to inhibit such acts as will call attention to one's self. Gradually acquaintances are discovered, signs of recognition are given, comments are exchanged with companions, usually concerning the personnel of the audience. When this second phase of orientation ultimately gives way in favor of polarization toward the speaker, there will be equally obvious signs in the audience. Individuals will slouch in their seats, will ignore apparel that is awry, will cough more freely, and will assume a general attitude of restfulness rather than this one of alertness.

Now in the discussion group, where each member may in turn be speaker, the audience is very transient and unstable. Each member does not usually get his turn, unless special arbitrary rules are enforced to secure this result. Some members have a way of getting the audience related to them more easily, definitely, and frequently than do others. The initial task of diverting the attention is not so conspicuous as in the case of the street audience, nor the related case of the show window. The situation is more like that of the advertisements in a magazine, which are all placed together in an advertising section and segregated from the reading matter. Individuals compete with one another in determining the direction of orientation, although a loosely organized attitude favorable to speakers, in the one case, and to advertisements in the other, remains established in general throughout.

A similar type of audience, so far as its orientation is concerned, is represented by the miscellaneous group, assembled for some common but passive purpose, such as that of being entertained by music or drama, listening to a lecture or debate, or witnessing some performance or spectacle. Amateur night at a vaudeville house is a rather extreme case of this type of audience. The courtesy of the common purpose gives the speaker or performer his chance, and guarantees initial attention. The task of winning the audience does not begin with the first of the five tasks we have indicated, but begins at a point well along in the total process. Maintenance of interest is here the first step, and the process continues to a point determined only by the purpose or the success of the performer. The task here resembles that to be found in the sales letter, personally addressed to one.

3. THE SELECTED AUDIENCE

A further degree of polarization, upon which the speaker can build, is present in the selected audience, assembled for some common purpose of a more active sort, but not all sympathetic one with another or with the speaker's point of view or aim. A meeting of labor delegates, the deliberations of a jury, a session of Congress illustrate this type of orientation. The rules of order and the sincerity of the common purpose take care of the first two steps, in the main. Impression, persuasion, and direction, the last three of the five tasks, characterize the speaker's undertaking here. The task is comparable to that of the catalogue description of an article, which seeks to determine only which variety or brand of a commodity will be purchased by the individual who is already influenced to buy one or other of several competing wares.

4. THE CONCERTED AUDIENCE

When the audience assembles with a concerted, active purpose, with sympathetic interest in a mutual enterprise, but with no clear division of labor or rigid organization of authority, the degree of polarization is already almost complete but facile. A college class, intent upon the consideration of an economic, scientific, or literary point, a graduate seminar where mutual inquiry and joint contribution are the object, represent instances. Those not inclined to attend and not interested are either eliminated beforehand or are ignored. The fixing of impressions is taken care of by the device of taking notes, assembling outlines, or utilizing other varieties of memoranda. The main tasks are those of convincing and directing action or thought.

5. THE ORGANIZED AUDIENCE

Complete although perhaps superficial polarization of the audience toward a speaker is illustrated in a team or a company, a military unit or a gymnasium class, organized with a rigid division of labor and authority, supported by specific common purpose and interest, with tasks well learned, and already persuaded to the authority of the leader. A scout leader or a football captain has this perfect polarization of his immediate audience. Nothing remains but the last of the five tasks, the direction of specific action. The relation is like that sustained to a price list, a guide post, or a bill from the dentist.

The characteristics of these five types of audiences may be schematically indicated by the following outline. In each case there is shown, according to the foregoing analysis, the point at which the performer's task commonly begins, and the processes still to be undertaken if the typical tasks are carried to completion.

Pedestrian Audience	Discussion and Passive Audience	Selected Audience	Concerted Audience	Organized Audience
Attention	. . . .	. . . .	. . . .	. . . .
Interest	Interest	. . . .	. . . .	. . . .
Impression	Impression	Impression	. . . .	. . . .
Conviction	Conviction	Conviction	Conviction	. . . .
Direction	Direction	Direction	Direction	Direction

6. THE ABSENT AUDIENCE

It may be well to call attention to another use of the word "audience," to indicate a type of situation which does not properly come into our present discussion. The writer is accustomed to refer to his audience, as is also the editor, the publisher, the artist, and perhaps even the architect. In this connection the word "audience" is merely a collective term, used to indicate the absent and isolated individuals who will at some time or usually at different times be the observers of the produced work. There is of course usually no aggregation or congregation of people involved, and hence the group phenomena which an assembled audience may display will be missing. Nevertheless the existence of these "patrons," as they might better be called, exercises its influence on the performer; and to some extent the knowledge on the part of each patron that others will sometime view the product and be influenced individually by it, may have some influence on the reactions of each. But this group of patrons does not constitute an audience in our present sense of that word. It lacks the essential characteristic of a strictly *social* situation, in which the individuals must be influenced not only by a common stimulus but also by one another.

The special characteristic of such a group of patrons is the fact that the appeal is presented to them through but one of the various avenues of perception,—as the visual, the auditory, usually. The modern radio audience is a good illustration of such a group. Only the auditory sense is appealed to by the performance or even by relevant features of the surroundings. Stimuli to the other senses may be distracting and irrelevant. The listener's neighbors may be intent upon other subjects; his fellow listeners are remote in space, as is the performer also. There is therefore little of the orientation process in such a case, and although the performer may find numerous psychological problems in addressing such a scattered group, there is little to be said with respect to the audience as a phenomenon. There is indeed no essential difference between this type of audience and that of the writer, publisher, or artist.

THE ORIENTATION OF THE SPEAKER

The goal of the speaker is thus, abstracting from his specific purpose, the orientation of his audience toward himself. This necessitates his action toward each member of the group, rather than toward the group as a unit. The group, and therefore the audience, is an unreal abstraction. People in general are not general people. There is no oversoul possessed by the audience, to which the speaker may appeal; but, instead, there are particular individuals, each psychologically related to the speaker and to surrounding individuals. To be sure, the members of the audience influence one another. One member, failing in attention or interest, distracts his neighbors by his wrongly oriented behavior. The intent interest of a neighbor also restrains the flighty attention of the disturber. But if the speaker merely addresses the crowd as a whole, failing to take into account the individuals of which it is comprised, his speech can scarcely avoid the automatic and inflexible character of a reproduction. He tends to become a fixture in the landscape, competing with other inert objects for the polarization of the group. Only a frankly recitative performance or the timid speaker who appears under protest and wishes merely to survive the ordeal can afford to become such a fixture.

The speaker's orientation toward the individual members of the audience is even more necessary in our own time than it was in earlier days, when traditions inclined toward exaggerated eloquence, attitudinizing, and bombast to a degree which would not now be tolerated. Only obliviousness to the individual persons before one could enable the average speaker to indulge in these abandoned flights. Consciousness of individual auditors, while it may restrain fancy, encourages earnestness, directness, and simplicity.

THE AUDIENCE AS A GESTALT

A mystical movement in modern psychology, known as "gestalt-theorie" would take exception to the foregoing analysis. In fact this school of psychology eschews all analysis, or would like to do so. For them, discussion of the audience and performer would require first that a position be taken so far away from the facts that the details could not be clearly observed. The audience would appear as one vast blur, with which the performer would be merged. Discussion would then necessarily relate only to this vague whole or total blur. We may in fact quote an account of the psychology of the audience as given from this point of view by Wheeler.

> "The individual and the group constitute an organic unit. . . . Consider a lecturer speaking before an audience. He does not pause to scrutinize each individual face or to analyze the movements of each person; he does not hear the scuffling of individual feet. On the contrary he grasps the total situation at once, apprehending the attitude of the group as a whole toward him. . . . In any event the stimulus to which the speaker is reacting is the group, and not its individual members. It is an ensemble of noises, gesture and movements, not any isolated occurrence."

This conception of the audience as a blur is even carried to the point of designating the group, not figuratively, as we all do, but descriptively, as "it." Thus:

> "Had it not been inhibited by fear of breaking a long-established custom and thus subjecting itself to criticism, the audience would have walked out to relieve itself of this strain, but courtesy prompted it to remain in the hall and to make the best of it."

The strain (the feeling of indifference) and the walking are thus not attributed to the individual auditors but to the audience "as a whole." Since, however, the speaker and the audience have been said to be "an organic unit," we should expect the speaker also to be indifferent and to walk out with the audience; an organic unit should surely act in a unitary way.

The fact is that ideas of this kind rest merely on the question whether description is to be from a remote point of view (as the sociologist would undertake it) or from as close a station as the psychologist may adopt. Thus from a distant point of view we could describe the audience as awake or asleep. Suppose we say the audience is asleep. Coming closer we might observe individuals; most of them would be asleep as individuals, but here and there would be a wakeful one. Is the audience then asleep or not? Clearly, if we get close enough to the facts, the audience is not an organic unit, but an assemblage.

On the other hand, much the same thing may be said of the individual. Observing him as an "organic whole" we may say, "He is asleep." Yet even the soundest sleeper is not *entirely* asleep. Some of his systems are in abeyance; others, such as heart and lungs, are active enough; he may even be "talking in his sleep" or dreaming; he may respond promptly to some signals but not to others. Is he then asleep or not? Clearly enough, if we get close to the individual, we find that he is not an organic unit in the absolute sense, but an assemblage of loosely organized systems. Physiology would be able to show that even these "systems" are not clean-cut organic wholes.

The fact is that it is just these differences in remoteness of viewpoint that distinguish the various sciences, such as sociology, psychology, physiology, and chemistry. What is the lowest level of analysis for one science may appear as a mysticism to another science. Psychology is characterized by a point of view sufficiently near at hand to enable it to get a clear picture of the individual.

The line is not hard and fast, and it is not easy to draw; the position in fact varies with the interests and temperament of different psychologists, and with the nature of the problem. Discerning the individual clearly psychology is nevertheless interested in his relations with other individuals, also clearly discerned. It is also interested in a partial analysis of the individual into component activities and functions.

For our own purpose the point of view that takes the performer-and-audience as an "organic whole" and as the final unit of analysis remains mysticism. Nothing can be done about such a picture but to engage in ecstatic exclamations concerning the wonders of such "totals." We shall instead be interested in individuals and their relations one to another, and in at least the first step of analysis which makes it possible to consider the individual as in himself not wholly an "all or none" system.

For our purpose, if there are "feelings of indifference," they will be in individual observers. If any "walking out" is done, it will not be on the part of the "audience as a whole" but by those whose legs engage in the activity. The "members" of the audience are thus to be considered, in their orientation to one another and to the performer, who in turn is oriented toward the individuals comprising the audience.

Only in one whose usual experience is that of stagefright, or who removes himself from human affairs to so great a distance that he no longer discerns people but only "men as trees walking" can the "gestalt" account make any contribution at all to the psychology of the audience.

PRACTICAL CONCLUSIONS

1. Every audience is unique, yet it is possible to indicate a limited number of typical audiences, and it is important that the performer classify his audience correctly.

2. The type of an audience depends most of all upon the nature of its orientation toward the performer,—upon the phenomena of polarization.

3. Orientation depends chiefly upon the point in the series of five steps at which the performance begins and the step at which it ends.

4. With the "pedestrian audience" the very first step, catching attention, is primary; how much further the process goes varies with the purpose of the performer.

5. With the "passive audience" or "discussion group" the first task is usually already accomplished, or guaranteed by rules of order; the performer's initial problem is more likely to be the second step,—holding attention or interest; how far the process goes again depends upon the occasion or the success of the performer.

6. With the "selected audience" the primary task may well be the third one,—impressiveness; this may or may not give way to the fourth and fifth steps.

7. With the "concerted audience" the performer typically begins with

the first three steps already accomplished; conviction, and perhaps direction, are his chief responsibilities.

8. With the "organized audience" the performer has only to issue instructions; attention, interest, impression, and conviction may usually be taken for granted.

9. The primary virtue of the performer is to understand clearly which of these tasks will be confronted at the start, and how far through the succeeding stages it is his duty to carry the audience.

10. The tasks involved, as well as the initial and terminal points, are determined by the nature of the occasion, the purpose of the performer, and the preliminary preparation of the audience.

11. The first goal of the performer is to make sure that the audience is oriented effectively toward himself or his materials.

12. The audience can be treated as a unit only in impersonal performances (gymnastics, music) or in cases of exaggerated oratory and grandiloquence.

13. Explicit observation of individual members of the audience, though it may restrain fancy and inhibit rhetoric, does nevertheless promote earnestness, directness, and simplicity.

14. The audience as a whole is a mere verbal abstraction; actually there are only the separate individuals with their personal behaviors and mutual influences.

What does Hollingworth mean by "polarization," and how does it differ from "orientation?" Do you agree with Hollingworth's categorization of audiences? Would you change it by additions, deletions, or perhaps by selecting a different basis for classification? Under what circumstances should we concern ourselves with the "absent audience?" Now that you have read the conflicting philosophies of Hollingworth (the audience as separate individuals) and the gestalt theorists (the audience as a unit), which philosophy would you support? Is the best position a combination of both?

Analysis of the Audience

Wayne C. Minnick

In this reading Wayne C. Minnick, professor of communication at Florida State University, seeks to answer three questions about audiences: Who is the audience? How much can be known about an audience? How can we evaluate the probable effectiveness of communication? As you read Minnick's answers to these questions, pay particular attention to the many facets of persuasion and how they are related to audiences of different sizes and compositions.

WHO IS THE AUDIENCE?

The communicator may think of an audience in a number of ways. He may think of it first of all in relationship to himself, dividing it into the immediate audience and the peripheral audience. The immediate audience is the group of people he actually confronts during the delivery of the speech, whereas the peripheral audience is the one exposed to his message by word of mouth, by newspapers, or by radio and television. Today, the size of the peripheral or remote audience often substantially exceeds that of the immediate audience. Consequently, the communicator may wish to consider carefully to which segment his persuasive strategy should be aimed. In some cases, the immediate audience may be regarded simply as a pretext for reaching a much larger body of people.

The communicator may also consider the size of an audience. As the size of the audience increases, the factors of physical remoteness and psychological distance also increase. As size increases, so does the frequency of mechanical contrivances such as amplifiers, microphones, and cameras. The transactional nature of communication is impaired as the size of the audience increases, because feedback is less likely and the kind of feedback received is less useful.

The communicator may also think of an audience in temporal terms.

Most speakers think of audiences in a time-arrested context, *i.e.*, as a group of people who will be confronted for thirty or forty minutes and who will thereafter disperse, not to be seen again. But many audiences must be thought of as continual. The mass audience of the politician and the advertiser is a case in point. It persists as a continuing problem in persuasion because it is constantly being diminished at one end as the senescent and moribund die and being replenished at the other as children and adolescents mature. Thus the establishment of long-term attitudes, beliefs, product preferences, and behavior patterns requires constant renewal of persuasion. Many smaller audiences are continual as well. For instance, the Congress of the United States, particularly the Senate, is a continual audience; the United States Supreme Court is another; and so are other governmental boards and agencies. Membership in these audiences changes, but at an established and rather slow rate. Boards of directors of business corporations, congregations of churches, and faculties of universities also represent continual audiences that a single communicator may address dozens or hundreds of times over a period of years or decades.

HOW MUCH CAN BE KNOWN ABOUT AN AUDIENCE?

Perfect and complete information about other people is denied us. We can rely only on their public statements and behavior for cues as to their probable future behavior. The amount of information seems to vary with the size and/or the continuity of the audience. If a receiver is a member of our family or a close friend of long standing, we may have a great deal of information that will make possible highly accurate predictions of his response to a particular persuasive suggestion. At the opposite extreme, our knowledge about a radio or television audience of millions is confined to macrogeneralizations which are applicable only in a statistical sense: 20 per cent are Catholics; 51 per cent support Johnson for President; 38 per cent believe that capital punishment should be abolished. Between these two extremes are audiences that represent more or less homogeneous groups: the faculty of a junior college, the congregation of the First Baptist Church, the city commission, the Women's Club, etc. Most audiences have some interests or purposes in common or they would not band together in the first place. Many groups, as we pointed out earlier, will be continuing groups who meet again and again for the explicit purpose of communicating with one another. A communicator may approach audiences of this type with a substantial amount of highly detailed, relatively accurate information.

The amount and kind of information that can be known about an audience depends on the nature of the audience and the communicator's relationship to it. As a rule, the smaller the audience the more continuous it is; and the closer the communicator is to the group, the more detailed and accurate his information about it can be. The larger the audience, the more "one-shot" it is; and the more distant the communicator, the less likely he is to acquire substantial and accurate information. Acknowledging that there are limits to the amount of information one can have about an audience, it is still desirable to indicate all the kinds of information one would *like* to have before giving a speech. We shall refer to this kind of analysis as *prior analysis.* Among other things, a communicator wishes to know how best to get and hold the attention of a particular audience; how to be sure that he will instate the right hypothesis (*i.e.,* that he will be properly understood); how to choose supporting information of maximum cogency; how to relate his proposals to the needs and values of the audience; and how to avoid or overcome obstacles in the way of acceptance of his aims. Below, in schematic form, are numerous suggestions for discovering information which will supply probable knowledge about the unknowns listed above.

I. How can the attention and interest of this audience be arrested and maintained?

   A. Assess and control, as much as possible, the physical circumstances of the audience. Try to create an external perceptual field that will facilitate response. If it is impossible to control this factor (as in radio and television broadcasts, for example), recognize the handicap and make specific plans to offset it.

   B. What means of eliciting involuntary attention will be tolerated by this audience? Any audience will give involuntary attention to the proper stimulus, but some audiences, because they value such notions as propriety, dignity, etc., react negatively to certain efforts to secure involuntary attention. The fire-eating, Bible-thumping evangelist and the "Give 'em hell, Harry" type of politician may seriously alienate their listeners if they do not tame their antics to suit the occasion and the restraints considered appropriate by the audience.

   C. To what immediate and urgent wants of the audience can the speaker's remarks be related? Our attention tends to focus on the means of satisfying our wants. Wants induce us to give anticipatory and voluntary attention. Hence, to arrest attention, the speaker must quickly relate his subject to important audience wants. (How needs are discovered will be discussed in detail below.)

D. How much interest is there in the particular subject for discussion? Existing interest may vary from mild or no interest to a high state of tension and excitement. If little or no interest exists, the speaker must take specific measures, in the content and context of the speech, to generate it.

E. What factors in the immediate occasion and circumstances can be useful in arresting attention and interest?

II. How can the communicator be assured that this audience correctly understands him?

A. The capacity of an audience to understand a speaker correctly is affected by a number of factors.

1. *Age.* The speaker may need to adjust his vocabulary level and the complexity of his ideas because of the youth or immaturity of an audience.

2. *Experience and knowledge.* Has the audience any previous knowledge of, or experience with, this subject? Lack of knowledge or experience is an imposing barrier to understanding. When it is evident, the speaker must resort to painstaking exposition, particularly to definition and comparison with the familiar.

3. *Education.* A poorly educated audience has, with notable exceptions, of course, a limited capacity for understanding. Such an audience generally lacks the basic fund of information, the acquaintance with fundamental assumptions, and the skills of assimilation that make for accurate understanding of complex subjects.

4. *Intelligence.* Evidence is accumulating to suggest that intelligence, like muscle power, is partially a product of exercise. This fact suggests that the more education an audience has, the greater has been the exercise of the intellect. A rough correlation between profession and intelligence also exists. Thus, something of intellectual capacity may be surmised from the occupation or profession of the audience. In general, the more manual and repetitive the work done, the more limited will be the person's intellectual grasp. Expect notable exceptions, however.

B. The tolerance of an audience for deliberate ambiguity is affected by two things.

1. They will tolerate ambiguity more readily from a speaker who is highly respected.

2. They will tolerate ambiguity in inverse correlation to the urgency of solving the problem at hand.

III. The communicator can select the proper confirmation to use with this audience by answering the following questions.

A. What is the extent and nature of their experience and knowledge with respect to this problem? Will previous experience and knowledge tend to confirm or negate the speaker's purpose? If the audience is completely or largely ignorant of the subject, they tend to be gullible; knowledge and experience increase skepticism.

B. What is the extent of the speaker's prestige? Are he and his accomplishments well known? Will he receive a speech of introduction that will apprise the audience of his qualifications? What is the attitude of the audience toward his subject? If the audience is hostile to his message, they will attribute less credibility to his statements. If indications exist that the speaker's prestige is low, or that he is a relatively unknown quantity, he should deliberately adopt prestige-building methods.

C. What expressed group opinions does this audience respect? Are they conscious of these group loyalties, or should they be reminded? What group leaders do they admire and respect? Does testimony from these leaders support the speaker's thesis?

D. To what degree will this audience probably be swayed by arguments? Respect for argument and evidence tends to be related to education, intelligence, and job or professional status. Hovland, Janis, and Kelley feel there is some evidence to support two general hypotheses relating intelligence and logical arguments: (1) "Persons with high intelligence will tend—mainly because of their ability to draw valid inferences—to be more influenced than those with low intellectual ability when exposed to persuasive communications which rely primarily on impressive logical arguments"; and (2) "Persons with high intelligence will tend—mainly because of their superior critical ability—to be less influenced than those with low intelligence when exposed to persuasive communications which rely primarily on unsupported generalities or false, illogical, irrelevant argumentation."[1]

---

[1] C. Hovland, I. Janis, and H. Kelley, *Communication and Persuasion* (New Haven, Conn.: Yale University Press, 1961), p. 183.

IV. The needs and values to which the speaker must adapt his message can be guessed by answering certain questions.
    A. Needs
        1. Which of the universal basic wants are known to be unsatisfied? Which are threatened?
        2. What group loyalties exist in this audience? What are the needs which these groups were created to satisfy? Have expressions of discontent or approval concerning group action been expressed? What do these statements reveal concerning needs?
        3. What is the economic level of this audience? Are they poor enough to be motivated strongly by physiological needs? Are they well-to-do enough to be concerned, even in the satisfaction of physiological needs, with social wants such as status and power? Does professional or occupational status indicate strong needs for prestige, power, love, etc.?
        4. What needs do they express (or have they expressed)? What goals do they work toward—home ownership? civic improvement? religious betterment? prestige and influence?
        5. How many needs will be served by the speaker's proposal?
    B. Values
        1. What do members of the audience say are their values? Talk to members of audience. Lead them to express themselves on aesthetics, economics, social mores, etc.
        2. What has been written that may reveal the values of the community of which the audience is a part? Newspaper editorials, religious treatises, laws, charters, speeches, and many other written sources reveal explicitly or implicitly the values of the community.
        3. How does this audience actually behave? What does it strive for, spend time, energy, and money on? When confronted with choices of action, what decisions has it made? Values may readily be inferred from such information.

V. What possible obstacles exist that may prevent the audience from acting?
    A. *Tangible obstacles.* Is there a lack of money, space, time, or a lack of public support? Will the speaker's proposal require more effort and work than the audience is able to give?
    B. *Intangible obstacles.* Will proposed action conflict with other needs, *i.e.*, will it make difficult or impossible the attainment of other goals? Will it be incompatible with existing modes of satisfying needs? Are there other ways of meeting the

problem which may appear more attractive to the audience because they seem more potentially satisfying? Will adopting the speaker's proposals cause a man to violate existing group loyalties? Will it violate existing values?

In addition to seeking information about the audience prior to his speech, a skillful persuader develops the capacity to evaluate the probable effectiveness of his communication during the course of its presentation. In other words, he learns to interpret *feedback* from his audience in order to estimate how his communication is being received and how he can adapt it in accord with the information received. If he is speaking to a single person or to a small group of persons, feedback may come in the form of direct questions or comments, the most useful and satisfying kind of feedback. But in formal situations involving sizable audiences, feedback has to be inferred from the behavior of the audience. Below are suggested some of the things which, under these circumstances, the communicator tries to interpret in order to judge the probable effectiveness of his message.

I. The speaker should estimate the degree of attention and interest.
   A. *Implicit indicators.* Is the audience restless? A recent experimental study confirmed that gross bodily movement provides a measure of broad levels of audience interest. Much movement means lack of interest.[2] Whispered conversations, evidences of sleepiness, yawning, and the like imply boredom. The frequency and amplitude of laughter and applause may be indicative as well.
   B. *Explicit indicators.* Shouts of encouragement, booing, hissing, and the like, are obvious signs of audience reaction.

II. The speaker should estimate the probable accuracy of the audience's understanding of his message. This factor is exceedingly difficult to evaluate. Information may be derived from the following sources.
   A. *Interest level.* If attention is poor, understanding is likely to be fragmentary. Misconceptions of the speaker's meaning are almost bound to occur.
   B. *Gross physical activity.* Nodding or shaking of heads, whispering together, and certain gestures may be taken as indicating lack of understanding.
   C. *Facial expression.* Recent studies have shown that practiced observers of facial expressions are usually able to infer correctly

[2] E. Kretsinger, "An Experimental Study of Gross Bodily Movement as an Index to Audience Interest," *Speech Monographs,* XIX (1952), 248.

the emotion expressed when they know the situation which produced the expression.[3] Experienced speakers are able to infer bewilderment by keenly observing facial changes in their audience.

III. The speaker should estimate the degree of emotional involvement and suggestibility in his audience.
  A. Again, an estimate of attention level will help gauge emotionality and suggestibility. A highly emotional and suggestible audience is not easily distracted by extraneous stimuli. Furthermore, their reactions tend to be more expansive. Hence the fewer the observed responses to distractions and the greater the amplitude of reactions such as laughter and applause, the higher the probable emotionality and suggestibility.
  B. Facial expression, bodily tonus, and gesture are also ready indicators of emotion. The kind and degree of emotion can be roughly calculated by an experienced speaker.
  C. Response to direct suggestions may be observed. If cries of "No! No!" or "Yes! Yes!", or applause or other overt responses greet direct suggestions, then suggestibility can be roughly gauged by observing the number of persons so responding and the expansiveness of their response. If direct suggestions are greeted with silence, the audience may be suggestible, but probably only to a slight degree.
  D. Observation of emotional response provides a speaker with a rough way of estimating the probable effectiveness with which he has adjusted his message to the needs and wants of the audience.

IV. The speaker should estimate the degree of credibility the audience attaches to his statements.
  A. He should look for evidences of belief or disbelief in facial expression, gesture, and movement. Since things not understood are not believed, correct understanding necessarily precedes belief.
  B. The speaker should estimate the probable degree of his personal prestige. Do the members of the audience appear hostile or friendly, or are their attitudes mixed? Do they respond readily to friendly overtures, or are they cold and reserved?

[3] N. Munn, "The Effect of Knowledge of the Situation upon Judgments of Emotions from Facial Expressions," *Journal of Abnormal and Social Psychology*, XXXV (1940), 324–338.

Are they paying attention? Dullness has an adverse effect on a speaker's prestige.

C. Does this audience appear to respect the sources of the speaker's information, as well as the speaker personally?

D. Is there any apparent reaction to his train of reasoning? Does the audience lose interest during logical expositions? Loss of interest is a sure sign that argument is ineffective.

V. The speaker should estimate the degree of effectiveness with which he has adjusted his message to the needs and values of his audience. This is accomplished in III above when he estimates the degree of emotionality and suggestibility.

After the speech is over, the communicator can determine a good deal about the probable effectiveness of his information, argument, and modes of presentation by making a *post-analysis*. A post-analysis is of particular value if he is dealing with a continuing audience. He may turn to several sources for information concerning audience response.

OPINION BALLOTS AND OPINION SAMPLING DEVICES

Opinion ballots are usually marked by the immediate audience at the time the speech is made. If the audience opinion expressed before the speech is compared with opinion expressed afterward on the ballots, the speaker has a clear indication of the effectiveness of his speech in producing changes in opinion. Unfortunately, there is no way of knowing whether or not the audience fully understood the issue before the speech, or that they correctly reported their views.

Opinion sampling devices are generally used to determine the effectiveness of a speech on the peripheral audience. Sampling may be done on an informal, postcard poll basis or by the more exact measurements available through commercial opinion polling organizations.

OPEN FORUM PERIOD

From questions addressed to him by members of the audience after the speech is over, a speaker may discover (1) important evidence he does not have or did not present, (2) ideas or points which were not clearly understood, (3) objections or obstacles which he did not know existed or did not convincingly rebut, (4) attitudes of antagonism or disbelief he was unable to dispel, (5) a general notion of the degree of interest and thoughtful consideration he was able to elicit, and (6) a rough estimate of the degree to which members of the audience favored his proposition. Properly modified, such evidence may be invaluable in guiding the speaker on future occasions with similar audiences.

PERSONAL TESTIMONY

The speaker may himself solicit information on specific matters from his audience. How did the listener react to this particular argument? Would a point be more convincing if additional evidence of this sort were used? Did the listener think the audience as a whole responded favorably to the message of the speech? (This will enable him to tell what he thinks of the speech without embarrassment.) What objections does he think the audience might have? Questions of this kind will yield valuable information; it does little good to elicit merely the verdict that the speech was good, interesting, or thought-provoking. And, of course, the more people the speaker can talk to, the better.

NEWS SOURCES—PAPERS, PERIODICALS, RADIO, AND TELEVISION

Often a speech is aimed less at the immediate audience than at the peripheral audience which will hear or read reports of it. Along with these reports will appear criticisms in the form of editorials, articles, comments of interested parties, and evaluations by radio and television commentators and newspaper reporters and columnists. The bulk of such comment may vary, depending on the stature of the speaker, his message, and the occasion. Ordinary speakers may receive no notice at all most of the time, but when controversy is heated, the views of even little-known persons may be widely quoted and criticized. A well-known man may touch off volumes of criticism. After General MacArthur, for example, gave his famous "Old soldiers never die" address to Congress on April 19, 1951, the next volume of *The Reader's Guide to Periodical Literature* listed over 140 articles and printed commentaries about the speech and the issue it raised. And that did not include the innumerable newspaper articles and editorials or comment of radio and television reporters.

From such information a speaker can discover essentially the same things that come to light in a forum period, the only difference being that he has no direct opportunity to reply to objections, questions, and hostile attitudes.

BEHAVIOR OF THE AUDIENCE

If audience behavior is in line with the speaker's recommendation (e.g., the resolution or bill is passed, the dollar is given, the petition signed) and other sources of information described above corroborate the effectiveness of the speech, then the speaker is justified in assuming that the speech, to an extent that cannot be exactly measured, had an influence on the outcome.

When the converse is true, that is, when the audience acts in ways antagonistic to the speaker's recommendations, the speaker can assume without question that the speech, pragmatically considered, was a failure. It does not always follow, however, that by arguing better or by speaking with greater eloquence and fervor he could have changed the outcome. Often a speaker's conscience compels him to take a position which has little or no prospect of succeeding with the particular audience he is addressing. Even if addressed in the tongue of angels, they would not be moved. Nevertheless, even when a speech is a pragmatic failure, the speaker can profit immeasurably if he goes back over the speech and considers what he might have done to win a few more converts.

How important is the size of an audience when conducting audience analysis? Do classroom speeches, group discussions, or interviews have peripheral audiences? How accurately can we detect the effectiveness of our messages before classroom audiences? Other types of audiences? If, through careful prior audience analysis, we discover the listeners—contrary to our own views—are hostile to certain ideas and groups of people, what are the ethical limits to "adapting" our message to fit the audience?

The American Value System: Premises for Persuasion

Edward D. Steele
W. Charles Redding

Edward D. Steele, professor of speech at Humboldt State College in Arcata, California, and W. Charles Redding, professor of communication at Purdue University, discovered an American value system in two independent studies of political speaking in the 1940's and 1950's. In this article they list and explain value clusters that are common and relatively unchanging in American society. The authors contend that these clusters provide the premises for our persuasive efforts.

The concept of shared cultural values serving as premises for enthymemes, implicit in Aristotle's Rhetoric, has been developed explicitly in two recent doctoral dissertations.[1] Both dissertations dealt with contemporary American culture, both investigated the role of cultural values in presidential campaign speaking, and both included (among other things) formulations of specific values believed to be dominant in the United States during the 1940's. It is interesting to observe that these dissertations arrived at surprisingly similar conclusions concerning the role of cultural values in contemporary American public address, in spite of the fact that they were written independently and simultaneously—neither author being aware of the other's work at the time—and in spite of the fact that these conclusions emerged from diametrically opposite approaches to the data.

Steele, examining the 1952 campaign speeches of Eisenhower and

Reprinted with permission from Western Speech, XXVI (Spring, 1962), pp. 83–91.

1 Edward D. Steele, "The Rhetorical Use of the American Value System in the 1952 Campaign Speeches of Dwight D. Eisenhower and Adlai E. Stevenson," unpublished Ph.D. dissertation (Stanford University, 1957); W. Charles Redding, "A Methodological Study of 'Rhetorical Postulates,' Applied to a Content Analysis of the 1944 Campaign Speeches of Dewey and Roosevelt," unpublished Ph.D. dissertation (University of Southern California, 1957).

Stevenson, began with an inquiry, based upon social-science sources, into the value system of contemporary American culture; he then applied the results of this inquiry to the speeches. Redding, although concerned primarily with a methodological investigation, subjected the 1944 campaign speeches of Dewey and Roosevelt to an intensive content analysis in search of persuasive premises (which he labeled "rhetorical postulates"); he then compared these premises with social-science accounts of the American value system. Both writers, one looking first to the culture and the other looking first to the speeches, arrived at converging conclusions; both demonstrated, although in somewhat different ways and in different terminology, that: (1) it is possible to locate a body of relatively unchanging values shared by most contemporary Americans; (2) it is possible to formulate these values—at least approximately—in "clusters" of assertions; and (3) it is possible to observe the explicit or implicit functioning of such values as underpinning for persuasive, appealing, argument in speeches addressed to a mass audience. In other words, the evidence in these two dissertations appears to substantiate the basic contention that cultural values (in this particular case, those of the United States) provide many— not, of course, all—of the major premises from which the persuasive speaker argues for audience acceptance of his recommendations.[2] These premises constitute, for the rhetorician, the "concepts of the good" which are "in the mind" of an (American) audience; as such, they are among the numerous "predispositions" which determine how the audience perceives, comprehends, and reacts to the speaker's assertions. Values, as they exist psychologically in the mind of the audience, have been generalized from the total experience of the culture and "internalized" into the individual personalities of the listeners as guides to the "right" way to believe or act. In twentieth-century America the value system is derived from, and preserves the essential content of, those values identified with the Age of Enlightenment and the Puritan ethos, as refined in the experience of the American frontier.[3]

Many readers will no doubt perceive that this entire rationale is not only analogous to Aristotle's conception of enthymematic premises as

[2] The relationship between social values and the enthymeme is developed at length in the following sources: Edward D. Steele, "Social Values in Public Address," WS, XXII (Winter 1958), 38–42; the first paper of this symposium [refers to Edward D. Steele, "Social Values, the Enthymeme and Speech Criticism," Western Speech, XXVI (Spring 1962), 70–75]; the two doctoral dissertations cited above.

[3] See, for example, F. S. C. Northrop, The Logic of the Sciences and Humanities (New York, 1950), especially chapters 11, "The Eighteenth Century," and 12, "The Nineteenth Century"; Henry Steele Commager, The American Mind (New Haven, 1950), especially chapters I, "The Nineteenth-Century American," and XX, "The Twentieth-Century American"; Ralph H. Gabriel, The Course of American Democratic Thought (New York, 1940).

originating in the beliefs of the audience, but is also suggestive of recent psychological thinking: e.g., the "congruity" and "cognitive dissonance" concepts of Osgood and Festinger respectively.[4]

The following description of the American Value System is offered subject to certain reservations and qualifications: (1) It purports to offer only the core ideas in each value orientation and does not attempt to list every related premise.[5] (2) It is a summary of descriptions by social scientists, amplified and modified by comparative study of the content of speeches—as such is not necessarily definitive.[6] (3) It describes beliefs and values, elements of which are constantly changing, and any description of such elements must be interpreted in terms of the U.S.A., circa 1940–52. (4) There is patent conflict (or ambivalence) among many of these formulations, and the resolution of these conflicts depends upon the hierarchical relationships existing among particular premises in a specific situation, the "tinsit," to use Coutu's term.

PURITAN AND PIONEER MORALITY

Americans like to see the world in moral terms. Acts are said to be good or bad, ethical or unethical. The central themes in this ethic have been derived from the Christian religion and mores of the Puritan immigrants, as reinforced in the frontier experience. Good works promise salvation, and economic success is commonly interpreted as evidence of a benevolent God's grace. Like our Puritan ancestors, we still—at least verbally—venerate such virtues as continence, honesty, simplicity, cooperation, self-discipline, courage, orderliness, personal responsibility, and humility.

Although the American is notoriously competitive, it is also true that the idea of cooperation as a means to mutually desired ends has been reinforced since the days of frontier living; thus has developed the American's enthusiastic involvement in fraternal bodies, clubs, societies, associations, and labor unions. Hedonistic as we are, Americans have never ceased

---

[4] Charles E. Osgood, George Suci, and Percy Tannenbaum, *The Measurement of Meaning* (Urbana, Illinois, 1957); Leon Festinger, *A Theory of Cognitive Dissonance* (Evanston, Illinois, 1958). Cf., Fritz Heider, "Attitudes and Cognitive Organization," *Journal of Psychology*, XVL (April 1946), 107–112; Erwin P. Bettinghaus, "The Operation of Congruity in an Oral Communication Situation." *Speech Monographs*, XXVIII (August 1961), 131–142.

[5] For an extensive list of specific premises characteristic of a typical American community see Robert S. Lynd and Helen M. Lynd, *Middletown in Transition* (New York, 1937). Also Commager, *op. cit.*, chapter XX.

[6] The reader will find detailed documentation and a comprehensive bibliography in each of the dissertations cited above.

to regard impulse gratification with deep suspicion; we may insist upon our comforts and our gadgets, but we feel guilty and rationalize about them in the name of "moral purpose." Pursuit of power, prestige or economic success for its own sake has been considered immoral. Today the *ideal* American does not lie, cheat or dissimulate; and he practices what he preaches.

THE VALUE OF THE INDIVIDUAL

In both colonial and contemporary America every person is valued as an autonomous, unique, decision-making personality, worthy of concern and possessing intrinsic dignity. The individual's happiness and welfare (including his comfort, privacy, labor, physical integrity, property, health, etc.) are the ultimate criteria for private or governmental policy. "Using others" for personal gain is a denial of their integrity and thus of moral purpose.

ACHIEVEMENT AND SUCCESS

In an America characterized by an almost unlimited opportunity for the acquisition of material wealth, European measures of personal status soon broke down and competitive occupational achievement (evidenced by accumulation of wealth) became a crucial measure of personal merit. The modern ideal American is the competitive individual; the "self-made man who rose from rags to riches" has long been a dominant figure in the national folk lore. Although personal achievement in many activities is valued, success in business enterprise has usually been the ultimate criterion.

Living in a society which permits upward social mobility through individual acquisitiveness has encouraged the evaluation of sheer possession as evidence of achievement, without regard to the means. This expedient approach to wealth-getting is abetted by the traditional feeling about efficiency and rationality. At the same time, human values supposedly supersede property values; thus he who acquires wealth is said to be only its steward and must use his wealth for the general good. Consequently, sharp practices, gambling, and ruthlessness are often tolerated when exonerated by later acts of personal philanthropy. Usually, however, success has been equated with personal moral effort, and failure with personal inadequacy (rather than fortuitous circumstances). Being a "striver" is a compensating quality for the competitor who has not yet "acquired his pot."

CHANGE AND PROGRESS

The Enlightenment thesis that human nature can be improved and that society is inexorably moving toward a better form of life has been greatly reinforced by the American experience. Even now, to the American, the best is yet to be, and nothing is impossible. Early American experience taught that change was both necessary and beneficial; hence, the present is better than the past, and the future will be better than the present. Many Americans even try to live the future now by buying it on the installment plan. "Optimism" about the future, and derogation of the "old fashioned," of the "backward," and of the "obsolete," verbalize standardized attitudes. Technological developments have encouraged acceptance of the new as a necessity of modern industrial life. At the extreme, "change" has become a value in itself, often unrelated to "realities." And youth is valued as the "hope of the future."

ETHICAL EQUALITY

In the Christian view all individuals are spiritually, ethically equal in the sight of God, regardless of material differences. In America this ethic has been bolstered by the absence of traditional social, economic, or political sanctions, and by the existence of relatively abundant opportunity for personal achievement and status. Ethical equality with reciprocal concern is the criterion reflected in the abolition of primogeniture, indentured servitude, slavery, imprisonment for debt, and property qualification for voting. Further manifestations of this faith are found in free public education, the guaranteed right to vote, and homestead rights. The principle of equal rights before the law is at the core of our system of justice.

EQUALITY OF OPPORTUNITY

Despite the faith in *ethical* equality, America has not become the land of equality of *condition*. The ideal has been tempered in the fire of conflict with the concept of freedom, particularly freedom for economic activities. The gradual stratification of wealth and the corporate exploitation of resources have contributed to a de-emphasis of ethical equality in economic affairs. This conflict between the fact of unequal rewards and the criterion of ethical equality has been resolved by acceptance of the principle of equality of *opportunity*, the idea that each individual, regardless of circumstances of birth shall have the opportunity to rise in the economic and social system. Hence, we have free public education. The graduated income tax, interestingly enough, incorporates both aspects of this ambivalence.

EFFORT AND OPTIMISM

From the first, immigration to America came mainly from industriously ambitious members of the European working class. Moreover, the still prevailing Puritan tradition emphasized work as a means of realizing God's grace, and material rewards as evidence of receiving God's grace. The wealth accruing to individuals on the frontier who made the effort reinforced this faith in work. Action, guided by reason and an unshakeable optimism as to results, became a moral guiding principle. No problem was too complicated, no obstacle too big for determined, optimistic effort. At the extreme, work became an end in itself: "being busy," "doing something," "getting going," "hitting the ball." The gradual dissociation of "work" from the acquisition and ownership of property later brought a de-emphasis of physical labor, but the faith in optimistic action has persevered.

EFFICIENCY, PRACTICALITY, AND PRAGMATISM

Although being active is now emphasized in America, it must be a certain kind of activity. Activity, when guided by reason, tends to emphasize getting things done through the choice of the most effective means. When applied to economic activity, this premise has led to a concern for efficiency of business and industrial techniques. Closely related to this is the value placed on being a practical man, a man of broad practical experience, a mature and competent man. Solving problems as they arise, getting things done, characterize such a man. Abstract thinking and long-range planning are frequently relegated to the "dreamers" and the "eggheads."

REJECTION OF AUTHORITY

American culture has been built in a long historical process beginning with the early demands for freedom from feudal serfdom, quit rents, mercantilist restraints, the religious hierarchy, and "colonial policy." Hence, there is a deep aversion to the acceptance of any coercive restraint by established social organizations or by personal authorities. Underlying this entire syndrome of "freedom from" is the confidence in the rationality and competence of the ordinary individual and in his ability to make effective decisions in matters concerning his own affairs. The essence of "individualism" is freedom of choice, freedom to make decisions, subject only to the reciprocal obligation to respect the rights of others. Thus an American insists on freedom to choose his occupation, marriage partner, political party, place of residence, among many other things.

The emphasis on rejection of authority creates a tendency to think in terms of rights rather than duties. And, at the extreme, Americans tend to resent authoritarian relationships between employer and employee, parent and child, male and female, and citizen and governmental bureau.

Rejection of authority in economic affairs has become institutionalized in the attitude that the government should not interfere with the "free enterprise" system. Peace, to an American, often means the absence of an aggressive external authoritarian force.

SCIENCE AND SECULAR RATIONALITY

Americans assume that they live in an ordered universe in which intelligent beings can continually improve both themselves and their external conditions. This faith in human reason, along with the belief in honesty and the desire for clarity and order, support a rational approach to life. An ordered universe allows the possibility of control, calculability, and prediction. Problems can be foreseen and plans can be made for meeting them. The focus on the manipulation of the external environment in turn leads to an emphasis on practical knowledge, workable solutions, and to applied science rather than theoretical contemplation. At the extreme, the faith that rational, generalized answers can be produced leads to a simple faith that everything has an easy or quick answer.

SOCIALITY

In pioneer America, "getting along" with a group was often necessary for survival. Later experience also taught that the ability to make friends led to "making contacts," which in turn could mean financial gain. The smooth-functioning, outgoing, friendly personality has typically been rewarded by improved status in an upwardly mobile society. Conversely, however, upward mobility discouraged the formation of close personal attachment—a salesman's culture evolved a "superficial friendliness." All this placed emphasis on being loved, being worthy of love, but not necessarily of giving love. The cocktail hour, the service club, and the political campaign (with the "glad hand" of the campaigners trying to "get ahead" by being popular) have characterized much of American life. This concern about friendship leads to a fear of being alone, of "being used," of being "taken in" by "smooth talkers."

MATERIAL COMFORT

Apparently the opportunity to secure material comforts has elicited an unlimited desire for them (even though we may feel pangs of guilt about wanting them!). The American standard of living is one of the highest in the history of the world, and is broadly equated with "happiness." As new wants are satisfied they become regarded as essentials in nutrition, medical care, housing, transportation, and communication. At the extreme, emphasis on material comfort sometimes results in undiluted hedonistic gratification, in sharp conflict with the long prevailing Puritan denial of pleasure for its own sake. Prominent elements in this syndrome are spectator sports, motion pictures, consumer goods, and advertising.

QUANTIFICATION

On a continent characterized by wide and long rivers, broad plains, high mountains, and vast resources it was not surprising that the inhabitants would think in terms of bigness. Problems were big; distances were great; rewards were tremendous. Moreover Americans came to equate size with goodness, for size meant only more of what was wanted—land, gold, furs. This factor, accompanied by the growth of business and banking and the attendant measuring of achievement in amount of dollars, led to emphasis upon size in everything: bigger parties, faster automobiles, longer bridges, more powerful bombs. Moreover, with the growth of technological means, quantity tends to be stressed and quality becomes secondary.

EXTERNAL CONFORMITY

The desire to be like others and to please in order to be accepted is a universal characteristic of group life. Conformity becomes a value per se when adherence to the group pattern is routine or automatic without regard to the necessities of the situation. In America conformity as a value per se is promoted by factors other than political authority. It is manifested in many ways, by: (1) Aspirations of upward mobility, which discipline individual expression and dictate patterns of consumption; (2) social status, which in a business society demands subordination to the customs of competitive endeavor; (3) the equality theme, from which flows the principle that each has the right to criticize the other for failure to act as an equal; (4) role-specification, which in an efficient, technical economy causes personalities to be molded to fit specific roles and functions; (5) economic dependence of employees, which necessitates conformity to patterns of behavior set by their middle-class employers; (6) pressure for "human relations" in a diverse society, which makes necessary a certain standardized behavior—including that of language—for social intercourse (one does not discuss religion or politics in polite society); (7) the Puritan and Pioneer emphasis on cooperation to achieve ends, which implies acceptance of group standards of behavior; and, (8) the compulsive need to be popular, hence to behave in an acceptable, equalitarian manner.

HUMOR

That which tickles the risibilities is at least partially a matter of cultural definition. In America, humor is characteristically equalitarian in nature; "poking fun" at oneself, at the boss, at the officious, at authority, is a leveling influence.

GENEROSITY AND "CONSIDERATENESS"

Universal concern for the individual contributes to a genuine humanitarianism in America, especially in material ways. Disinterested concern and helpfulness are commonly reflected in acts of personal kindness—spontaneous contributions in mass disasters, support of relief for the "underprivileged," organized philanthropies, "service clubs," and public welfare agencies.

This American humanitarianism is perhaps linked with a "missionary spirit," the "Mission of America," the determination to bring to the rest of the world the benefits of God's benevolence as manifested in American economic, political and social institutions.

PATRIOTISM

Loyalty to the tradition and values of America, rather than undifferentiated, egocentric nationalism, has been (along with the conflicting sentiment for "isolationism") a persistent pattern. Faith in American ideals means a willingness to be a good citizen, to be proud of the United States, to defend it from external aggression. It should be noted that this basic pattern has frequently been expressed in charges of disloyalty in order to enforce conformity.

It must be stressed that the authors do not represent these descriptions as a complete inventory of all the values of American culture. These formulations are an attempt to describe the essential characteristics of the categories of value orientations as given by social scientists and as verified by the studies of the two authors. As such they are limited, perhaps dogmatic, but they should be useful hypotheses for continuous study of the nature of the value premises of the American.

Furthermore, cultural value orientations, although they may be couched arbitrarily in the form of categorical assertions, represent dynamic foci, or "clusters" of concepts rather than sharply defined, singular, atomistic entities. For example, the simple cultural premise, "It is wrong to be dishonest," involves a number of closely related but identifiable elements: "insincerity" (lack of correspondence between utterance and belief), "misrepresentation" (malicious lying, fraud, singling out unfair exceptions to a general rule, using "red herrings," etc.), and "opportunism" (lack of adherence to a fixed principle, selfishness, rabble-rousing, subordination of the means to any expedient end, etc.).[7]

Also, it is important to emphasize the fact of ambivalence. Thorough study would no doubt reveal that, for every cultural value in America there exists a contrary or conflicting value. As Lynd has pointedly illustrated, we believe firmly that "honesty is the best policy" but that "business is business"; we believe that "capital and labor are partners," but that "it's bad policy to pay higher wages than you have to"; and we believe that "women are the finest of God's creatures," but that they aren't very practical and are probably "inferior to men in reasoning power and general ability."[8]

In spite of the hazards, however, it has been found that it is feasible to cast many cultural values in a form precise enough to be perceived within the "content" of a speech, and that a reasonably quantitative "content-analysis" can be executed.[9] What we are discussing, therefore, in this paper is not some shadowy, intuitive guess. The concepts of culture and of cultural values (premises) are, indeed, intellectual abstractions, but they refer to real behavior. More to the point, they refer to a type of behavior that any rhetorical theoretician or critic cannot afford to ignore. For if both Aristotle and modern psychologists like Osgood are right, then

[7] Redding, op. cit., chapter IV.
[8] Robert S. Lynd, Knowledge for What? (New York, 1939), pp. 61–62.
[9] Redding, op. cit., chapter IV.

anything which helps to explain audience premises helps us to improve our understanding of human communication and persuasion.

Do you agree with Steele and Redding that the value clusters they discovered are common and unchanging? When our attitudes and beliefs change, such as our attitude toward the war in Vietnam, do they affect values like patriotism? Has our "loosening of morals" affected the value of puritan and pioneer morality? How much have value clusters affected your decisions and actions? For instance, why did you come to college? How did you select your major area of study?

Do We Know How to Listen? Practical Helps in a Modern Age

Ralph G. Nichols

Listening should be a subject of interest to all of us, for studies cited in this reading reveal that we spend nearly 75 per cent of our time either speaking or listening. When speaking, we want our audience to hear what we say and to remember as much of our message as possible. When listening or receiving, we want to hear accurately all that is said and then be able to recall the material at a later date. However, Ralph G. Nichols, Chairman of the Rhetoric Department at the University of Minnesota in St. Paul, found that only about 25 per cent of message content is retained by listeners. He discusses here the causes of poor listening and develops ten guides that would make listening more effective.

In 1940 Dr. Harry Goldstein completed a very important research project at Columbia University. It was underwritten by one of our educational foundations, was very carefully drawn, and two very important observations emerged from it. One, he discovered that it is perfectly possible for us to listen to speech at a rate more than three times that at which we normally hear it, without significant loss of comprehension of what we hear. Two, he suggested that America may have overlooked a very important element in her educational system, that of teaching youngsters how to listen.

Shortly after that Richard Hubbell, an important figure in the television industry, produced a new book. In it, he declared without equivocation that 98 per cent of all a man learns in his lifetime he learns through his eyes or through his ears. His book tended to throw a spotlight upon a long-neglected organ we own, our ears.

Reprinted with permission from Speech Teacher, X, No. 2 (March, 1961), pp. 118–124.

Together, the declarations of Goldstein and Hubbell put into perspective the highly significant studies of Paul Rankin, of Ohio State University. Rankin was determined to find out what proportion of our waking day we spend in verbal communication. He kept careful log on 65 white-collar folk, much like you and me, at 15-minute intervals for two months on end. Here is what he found: Seven out of every ten minutes that you and I are conscious, alive and awake we are communicating verbally in one of its forms; and our communication time is devoted 9 per cent to writing, 16 per cent to reading, 30 per cent to speaking, and 45 per cent to listening.

OUR UPSIDE-DOWN SCHOOLS

Quantitatively speaking, America has built her school system upside down. Throughout the twelve years a youngster normally spends in school, some teacher is continually trying to teach him how to write a sentence, in the hope that sometime he will be able to write a full paragraph, and then a complete report. Countless tax dollars and teacher hours of energy go into improving the *least used* channel of communication.

For some reason inexplicable to me, we usually chop off all reading improvement training at the end of the eighth grade, and from that time on the reading done is of an extensive, voluntary and general character. Then we decry, sometimes, the fact that America is a nation of sixth-grade reading ability. We should not be shocked at that fact, in view of the maximum training received. However, a lot of tax dollars are devoted to improving this *second least-used* channel of communication.

Then we come to something important—speech itself. Thirty per cent of our communication time is devoted to it; yet speech training in America is largely an extracurricular activity. In a typical school you will find an all-school play once or twice a year. There may be a debating team with a couple of lawyer's sons on it. There may be an orator, along with an extempore speaker, and that is about the size of it. You will find it very difficult to discover a single high school in America where even one semester of speech training is required of the youngsters going through. Actually, much of the speech taught in America today is provided by Dale Carnegie and his cohorts in night classes at a cost of about $125 per student for enrollment. Too expensive, and too late in life, to do many of us much good!

Then we come to listening. Forty-five per cent of our communication time is spent in it. In 1948, when I first became concerned about this field, you could hardly find anyone really concerned about refining his listening ability. I asked my University for a sabbatical leave that year, and spent twelve months doing research related to the characteristics of good and bad listeners. First, I learned that nobody knew much about effective listening. Only three researches which you could call experimental and scientific had been published in 1948 in the field of listening comprehension. By comparison, over 3,000 scientific studies had been published in the parallel learning medium, that of reading comprehension.

TEN YEARS MAKES A DIFFERENCE

Between 1950 and 1960 a very dramatic page has been turned. Many of our leading universities are now teaching listening, under that label. Today these schools are not only teaching listening—they are doing, at long last, graduate-level research in the field. Today, also, scores of businesses and industries have instituted their own listening training programs for selected management personnel. Three departments of the Federal Government and a number of units of our military service have followed suit.

Very important to the growing interest in listening training in the public schools has been the steady support given by the National Council of Teachers of English and the Speech Association of America. Under their guidance and help new "language arts guides" are being widely adopted. Typically, these guides give equal emphasis to the four communication skills of reading, writing, speaking, and listening.

TWO CENTRAL QUESTIONS

In view of this rather sudden surge of interest in effective listening, I should like to raise two questions, and very closely pursue answers to them.

Question number one: Is efficient listening a problem? For insight on this issue, let us revert to the classroom for a moment, for the first person to produce important evidence on it was H. E. Jones, a professor at Columbia University. One year he was in charge of the beginning psychology classes there, and frequently lectured to a population of some 476 freshmen.

It seemed to him, when he gave comprehension tests over his lecture content, that the students were not getting very much of what he was trying to say. He hit upon a very novel idea for an experiment. He talked 50 of his colleagues on the faculty at Columbia into cooperating with him. Each professor agreed to prepare and deliver to Jones' students a ten-minute lecture from his own subject-matter area. Each one submitted his lecture excerpt to Jones ahead of time, and Jones painstakingly built an objective test over the contents. Half of the questions in each quiz demanded a recalling of facts, and the other half required the understanding of a principle or two imbedded in the lecture excerpt.

EFFICIENCY LEVEL—25 PER CENT

Professor Number 1 came in, gave his little ten-minute lecture, disappeared, and the group was questioned on its content. Number 2 followed. At the end of the fiftieth presentation and the fiftieth quiz, Jones scored the papers and found that freshman were able to respond correctly to about half the items in each test. Then came the shock. Two months later he reassembled the 476 freshmen and gave them the battery of tests a second time. This time they were able to respond correctly to only 25 per cent of the items in the quizzes. Jones was forced to conclude, reluctantly, that without direct training, university freshmen appear to operate at a 25 per cent level of efficiency when they listen.

I could not believe it could be that bad. I decided to repeat the experiment at the University of Minnesota, and did so. I did not let two months go by before the retest, for I was pretty certain that the curve of forgetting takes a downward swoop long before two months have passed. Yet I got exactly the same statistics: 50 per cent response in the immediate test situation; 25 per cent after two weeks had passed.

Several other universities have run off essentially the same experiment, and all tend to report approximately the same statistics. I think it is accurate and conservative to say that we operate at almost precisely a 25 per cent level of efficiency when listening to a ten-minute talk.

WHAT CAN BE DONE?

Let us turn to a second major question: Is there anything that can be done about the problem? After all, if you and I listen badly, only 25 per cent efficiently, and can do nothing about it, the future holds a pretty dismal outlook. Fortunately, if we want to become better listeners, or to make our students or employees better listeners, it is a goal perfectly possible to attain.

A few years ago we screened out the 100 worst listeners and the 100 best listeners we could identify in the freshman population on my campus. Standardized listening tests and lecture-comprehension tests were used, and we soon had two widely contrasting groups. These poor suffering 200 freshmen were then subjected to about 20 different kinds of objective tests and measures.

We got scores on their reading, writing, speaking, listening; mechanical aptitude, mathematics aptitude, science aptitude, six different types of personality inventories; each one filled out a lengthy questionnaire, and I had a long personal interview with each of the 200.

TEN GUIDES TO EFFECTIVE LISTENING

At the end of nine months of rather close and inductive study of these 200 freshmen, it seemed to us that ten factors emerged, clearly differentiating good and bad listeners. We reported in a number of articles what we called "the ten worst listening habits of the American people." In recent years the elimination of these bad habits, and the replacement of them with their counterpart skills, seems to have become the central concern of most listening training programs. Thus, we have ten significant guides to effective listening.

1. FIND AREAS OF INTEREST

All studies point to the advantage in being interested in the topic under discussion. Bad listeners usually declare the subject dry after the first few sentences. Once this decision is made, it serves to rationalize any and all inattention.

Good listeners follow different tactics. True, their first thought may be that the subject sounds dry. But a second one immediately follows, based on the realization that to get up and leave might prove a bit awkward.

The final reflection is that, being trapped anyhow, perhaps it might be well to learn if anything is being said that can be put to use.

The key to the whole matter of interest in a topic is the word use. Whenever we wish to listen efficiently, we ought to say to ourselves: "What's he saying that I can use? What worthwhile ideas has he? Is he reporting any workable procedures? Anything that I can cash in, or with which I can make myself happier?" Such questions lead us to screen what we are hearing in a continual effort to sort out the elements of personal value. G. K. Chesterton spoke wisely indeed when he said, "There is no such thing as an uninteresting subject; there are only uninterested people."

2. JUDGE CONTENT, NOT DELIVERY

Many listeners alibi inattention to a speaker by thinking to themselves: "Who could listen to such a character? What an awful voice! Will he ever stop reading from his notes?"

The good listener reacts differently. He may well look at the speaker and think, "This man is inept. Seems like almost anyone ought to be able to talk better than that." But from this initial similarity he moves on to a different conclusion, thinking "But wait a minute . . . I'm not interested in his personality or delivery. I want to find out what he knows. Does this man know some things that I need to know?"

Essentially we "listen with our own experience." Is the conveyor to be held responsible because we are poorly equipped to decode his message? We cannot understand everything we hear, but one sure way to raise the level of our understanding is to assume the responsibility which is inherently ours.

3. HOLD YOUR FIRE

Overstimulation is almost as bad as understimulation, and the two together constitute the twin evils of inefficient listening. The overstimulated listener gets too excited, or excited too soon, by the speaker. Some of us are greatly addicted to this weakness. For us, a speaker can seldom talk for more than a few minutes without touching upon a pet bias or conviction. Occasionally we are roused in support of the speaker's point; usually it is the reverse. In either case overstimulation reflects the desire of the listener to enter, somehow, immediately into the argument.

The aroused person usually becomes preoccupied by trying to do three things simultaneously: calculate what hurt is being done to his own pet ideas; plot an embarrassing question to ask the speaker; enjoy mentally all the discomfiture visualized for the speaker once the devastating reply to him is launched. With these things going on, subsequent passages go unheard.

We must learn not to get too excited about a speaker's point until we are certain we thoroughly understand it. The secret is contained in the principle that we must always withhold evaluation until our comprehension is complete.

4. LISTEN FOR IDEAS

Good listeners focus on central ideas; they tend to recognize the characteristic language in which central ideas are usually stated, and they are able to discriminate between fact and principle, idea and example, evidence and argument. Poor listeners are inclined to listen for the facts in every presentation.

To understand the fault, let us assume that a man is giving us instructions made up of facts A to Z. The man begins to talk. We hear fact A and think: "We've got to remember it!" So we begin a memory exercise by repeating "Fact A, fact A, fact A   "

Meanwhile, the fellow is telling us fact B. Now we have two facts to memorize. We're so busy doing it that we miss fact C completely. And so it goes up to fact Z. We catch a few facts, garble several others and completely miss the rest.

It is a significant fact that only about 25 per cent of persons listening to a formal talk are able to grasp the speaker's central idea. To develop this skill requires an ability to recognize conventional organizational patterns, transitional language, and the speaker's use of recapitulation. Fortunately, all of these items can be readily mastered with a bit of effort.

5. BE FLEXIBLE

Our research has shown that our 100 worst listeners thought that note-taking and outlining were synonyms. They believed there was but one way to take notes—by making an outline.

Actually, no damage would be done if all talks followed some definite plan of organization. Unfortunately, less than half of even formal speeches are carefully organized. There are few things more frustrating than to try to outline an unoutlinable speech.

Note-taking may help or may become a distraction. Some persons try to take down everything in shorthand; the vast majority of us are far too voluminous even in longhand. While studies are not too clear on the point, there is some evidence to indicate that the volume of notes taken and their value to the taker are inversely related. In any case, the real issue is one of interpretation. Few of us have memories good enough to remember even the salient points we hear. If we can obtain brief, meaningful records of them for later review, we definitely improve our ability to learn and to remember.

The 100 best listeners had apparently learned early in life that if they wanted to be efficient note-takers they had to have more than one system of taking notes. They equipped themselves with four or five systems, and learned to adjust their system to the organizational pattern, or the absence of one, in each talk they heard. If we want to be good listeners, we must be flexible and adaptable note-takers.

6. WORK AT LISTENING

One of the most striking characteristics of poor listeners is their disinclination to spend any energy in a listening situation. College students, by their own testimony, frequently enter classes all worn out physically; assume postures which only seem to give attention to the speaker; and then proceed to catch up on needed rest or to reflect upon purely personal matters. This faking of attention is one of the worst habits afflicting us as a people.

Listening is hard work. It is characterized by faster heart action, quicker circulation of the blood, a small rise in bodily temperature. The overrelaxed listener is merely appearing to tune in, and then feeling conscience-free to pursue any of a thousand mental tangents.

For selfish reasons alone one of the best investments we can make is to give each speaker our conscious attention. We ought to establish eye contact and maintain it; to indicate by posture and facial expression that the occasion and the speaker's efforts are a matter of real concern to us. When we do these things we help the speaker to express himself more clearly, and we in turn profit by better understanding of the improved communication we have helped him to achieve. None of this necessarily implies acceptance of his point of view or favorable action upon his appeals. It is, rather, an expression of interest.

7. RESIST DISTRACTIONS

The good listeners tend to adjust quickly to any kind of abnormal situation; poor listeners tend to tolerate bad conditions and, in some instances, even to create distractions themselves.

We live in a noisy age. We are distracted not only by what we hear, but by what we see. Poor listeners tend to be readily influenced by all manner of distractions, even in an intimate face-to-face situation.

A good listener instinctively fights distraction. Sometimes the fight is easily won—by closing a door, shutting off the radio, moving closer to the person talking, or asking him to speak louder. If the distractions cannot be met that easily, then it becomes a matter of concentration.

8. EXERCISE YOUR MIND

Poor listeners are inexperienced in hearing difficult, expository material. Good listeners apparently develop an appetite for hearing a variety of presentations difficult enough to challenge their mental capacities.

Perhaps the one word that best describes the bad listener is "inexperienced." Although he spends 45 per cent of his communication day listening to something, he is inexperienced in hearing anything tough, technical, or expository. He has for years painstakingly sought light, recreational material. The problem he creates is deeply significant, because such a person is a poor producer in factory, office, or classroom.

Inexperience is not easily or quickly overcome. However, knowledge of our own weakness may lead us to repair it. We need never become too old to meet new challenges.

9. KEEP YOUR MIND OPEN

Parallel to the blind spots which afflict human beings are certain psychological deaf spots which impair our ability to perceive and understand. These deaf spots are the dwelling place of our most cherished notions, convictions, and complexes. Often, when a speaker invades one of these areas with a word or phrase, we turn our mind to retraveling familiar mental pathways crisscrossing our invaded area of sensitivity.

It is hard to believe in moments of cold detachment that just a word or phrase can cause such emotional eruption. Yet with poor listeners it is frequently the case; and even with very good listeners it is occasionally the case. When such emotional deafness transpires, communicative efficiency drops rapidly to zero.

Among the words known thus to serve as red flags to some listeners are: mother-in-law, landlord, redneck, sharecropper, sissy, pervert, automation, clerk, income tax, hack, dumb farmer, pink, "Greetings," antivivisectionist, evolution, square, punk, welsher.

Effective listeners try to identify and to rationalize the words or phrases most upsetting emotionally. Often the emotional impact of such words can be decreased through a free and open discussion of them with friends or associates.

10. CAPITALIZE ON THOUGHT SPEED

Most persons talk at a speed of about 125 words a minute. There is good evidence that if thought were measured in words per minute, most of us could think easily at about four times that rate. It is difficult—almost painful—to try to slow down our thinking speed. Thus we normally have about 400 words of thinking time to spare during every minute a person talks to us.

What do we do with our excess thinking time while someone is speaking? If we are poor listeners, we soon become impatient with the slow progress the speaker seems to be making. So our thoughts turn to something else for a moment, then dart back to the speaker. These brief side excursions of thought continue until our mind tarries too long on some enticing but irrelevant subject. Then, when our thoughts return to the person talking, we find he's far ahead of us. Now it's harder to follow him and increasingly easy to take off on side excursions. Finally we give up; the person is still talking, but our mind is in another world.

The good listener uses his thought speed to advantage; he constantly applies his spare thinking time to what is being said. It is not difficult once one has a definite pattern of thought to follow. To develop such a pattern we should:

A. Try to anticipate what a person is going to talk about. On the basis of what he's already said, ask ourself: "What's he trying to get at? What point is he going to make?"
B. Mentally summarize what the person has been saying. What point has he made already, if any?
C. Weigh the speaker's evidence by mentally questioning it. As he presents facts, illustrative stories and statistics, continually ask ourself: "Are they accurate? Do they come from an unprejudiced source? Am I getting the full picture, or is he telling me only what will prove his point?"
D. Listen between the lines. The speaker doesn't always put everything that's important into words. The changing tones and volume of his voice may have a meaning. So may his facial expressions, the gestures he makes with his hands, the movement of his body.

Not capitalizing on thought speed is our greatest single handicap. The differential between thought speed and speech speed breeds false feelings of security and mental tangents. Yet, through listening training, this same differential can be readily converted into our greatest single asset.

Are you a good listener, an adequate retainer of spoken messages? How do you know? Which of Nichols' ten guides for effective listening do you consciously employ? Which do you violate most often? Which are most important to listening? Does Nichols tend to place all of the responsibility for effective listening on the listener? What responsibility does the speaker have? How can speakers aid audiences in more effective listening?

VI
INTERPERSONAL COMMUNICATION: SMALL GROUPS

A Way of Thinking About Leadership and Groups

Thomas Gordon

One of the most common problems of communication in small groups is leadership. Thus, the first question of most groups tends to be, "Who will act as chairman?" Thomas Gordon, former professor of psychology and a psychological consultant, reviews the various theories of leadership and attempts to determine the characteristics of the successful leader. Leaders have been analyzed according to hereditary background, experience and training, special traits, and their relationship to a given situation. Gordon reviews these studies and looks at leadership as a complex phenomenon of group life, an integration of training, special traits, and situation.

The terms leadership and group have acquired many different meanings, and thus each of these terms is often used variously to stand for different things. To minimize misunderstandings arising from these different meanings, we shall attempt to specify at the outset what these terms shall mean when we use them here. Our definitions have not been developed with the idea of excluding other definitions, for there are several useful ways of thinking about leadership and groups. Instead, it is with the hope of improving our communication with the reader that we begin by examining closely the meanings we intend to give these terms.

HOW SHALL LEADERSHIP BE DEFINED?

The problem of selecting a useful and workable definition of leadership is a difficult one. None of the definitions employed by previous writers seems quite appropriate, but one is reluctant to offer yet another. The

Group-Centered Leadership, Copyright 1955 by Thomas Gordon. Reprinted by permission of the publisher, Houghton Mifflin Company.

writer has resolved this problem by utilizing certain elements of previous definitions, yet modifying them on the basis of his own particular experiences.

Early writers employed a definition of leadership that was based on the assumption that certain people were born to be leaders, whereas others could not possibly acquire this social role. Leadership was thought to be a set of unique traits or characteristics handed down from one person to another, chiefly through heredity. Certainly in the days when strong social class barriers made it almost impossible for just anyone to acquire the skills and knowledge required for positions of leadership, it must have appeared that leadership was inherited, simply because it emerged so frequently within the same prominent families. As social and economic class barriers gradually lost their early impenetrability and leaders began to emerge from different strata of society, it became evident that leadership was more than a matter of being born in the right family or with the right combination of genes. As a result, in recent times, this simplified notion of leadership has had few proponents. (In passing, however, attention is called to the recent re-emergence of this theory in the form of the Nazi belief in the genetic superiority of the Aryan "race.")

When the early genetic theory no longer fitted the facts of leadership in society, it underwent some modification. Whereas it was earlier believed that leadership was solely a function of *inherited* traits and characteristics, the modified theory held that leadership was a function of traits and characteristics that were *acquired* chiefly through experience, education, and special training. Even this concept of leadership left some room for the influence of heredity on such commonly accepted traits of leadership as intelligence, physical stature, energy output, and so on. While this way of conceptualizing leadership recognized the importance of environmental factors, it retained the old notion that leadership was a matter of specific traits and characteristics. A person by virtue of possessing the traits of leadership would somehow acquire the role of leader. Furthermore, a person so endowed, it was believed, would emerge as a leader in many, if not most, group situations.

As is apparent now, such a theory did not take into account the fact that group situations differ greatly with respect to the kind of leadership required or with respect to the particular needs of the members. The importance of the situational factors predisposing certain persons to positions of leadership became more widely recognized when social scientists began to search for "universal traits" of leaders—traits which were possessed in common by many different leaders. In an early study, Jennings concluded from her investigation of leadership among girls in a correctional institution that

> Both isolation and leadership were found to be products of inter-
> personal interaction and not of attributes residing within persons. . . .

Jenkins reached a similar conclusion after an extensive review of leadership
studies:

> Leadership is specific to the particular situation under investigation.
> Who becomes a leader of a given group engaging in a particular activity
> and what the leadership characteristics are in the given case are a
> function of the specific situation including the measuring instruments
> employed [by the investigator]. Related to this conclusion is the general
> finding of wide variations in the characteristics of individuals who be-
> come leaders in similar situations, and even greater divergence in leader-
> ship behavior in different situations.

A more recent study by Martin, Gross, and Darley produced findings
which led the investigators to conclude:

> The paucity of differences [between leaders and non-leaders] found
> tends to negate the trait approach to leadership and suggests the utiliza-
> tion of other frames of reference in the study of leadership phenomena.

Studies such as these all but killed those theories relying on the notion that certain traits of leadership were possessed by all leaders. Social
scientists began to see the necessity of also considering the situational
aspects of leadership. Consequently, in the wake of the initial stage of
debunking the earlier trait approach came theories emphasizing the importance of the total *situation*.

The next step in the direction of a more sophisticated concept of
leadership was the inclusion of the factor of the personality and needs of
the "follower" in the equation of leadership. Recent investigators have
suggested that the phenomenon of leadership can be understood only if
we consider factors relating to the personality of the *followers*, as well as
those relating to the *leader* and the *situation*. Thus, Sanford writes:

> It can also be strongly argued that the *follower*, too, must be
> studied if we are to see most clearly what happens in a leadership event.
> It is the follower as an individual who perceives the leader, who per-
> ceives the situation, and who, in the last analysis, accepts or rejects
> leadership. The follower's persistent motives, points of view, frames of
> reference or attitudes will have a hand in determining what he perceives
> and how he reacts to it. These psychological factors in the individual
> follower cannot be ignored in our search for a science of leadership.

Here is a point of view in which the significance of the "followers" is recognized. Leadership is seen as a complex phenomenon of group life in which different types of individuals carry out a variety of leadership functions depending upon both the qualities possessed by the different group members and the specific needs of the group at a given period of time. Cecil Gibb emphasizes this interactional aspect of leadership:

> Leadership is always relative to the situation—relative, that is, in two senses: (a) that leadership flourishes only in a problem situation and (b) that the nature of the leadership role is determined by the goal of the group; and this is, in fact, the second principle of leadership, that it is always toward some objective goal. The third principle is that leadership is a process of mutual stimulation—a social interactional phenomenon in which the attitudes, ideals and aspirations of the followers play as important a determining role as do the individuality and personality of the leader.

It appears, then, that recent theories have dropped the trait approach in favor of one that emphasizes the situational aspects of leadership. Yet, in their haste to drop the trait theory, some social scientists may have swung too far in the direction of emphasizing the situation. Conceivably, the situationists may be overlooking the possibility that at least some traits predispose their possessors to positions of leadership, or at least increase the chances of their becoming leaders in most situations. As Gouldner warns us, though the trait approach is not fashionable today and the situationists seem to have won the day, "uneasy rests the head that wears the crown of science."

A recent study, for example, confirms Gouldner's skepticism about an exclusively situational theory. Chowdhry and Newcomb, in a study of the relative ability of leaders and non-leaders to estimate group opinion, found that leaders of the groups that were studied were significantly superior to non-leaders and isolates in the ability to estimate group opinion on familiar and relevant issues. These investigators offer the following interpretation of their findings:

> This suggests that certain personality traits of the overchosen [leaders] make it possible for them to be in fuller communication with the members than can be said of the underchosen.

Chowdhry and Newcomb point out, however, that such traits may or may not be *potentially* of a general nature—that is, they may not make a person a leader in other groups. In other words, the findings of this study merely suggest that those who have developed an ability to judge the opinions and attitudes of the members of their *particular* groups are more often chosen as leaders of those groups. Nevertheless, such leaders may have the *potential* for judging the opinions of members of any groups, though this potential may not become actualized in other groups.

This leaves us with a slight suspicion that certain traits may eventually be discovered which universally bring leadership status to those possessing them, as long as the various groups have something in common—say, communication. We agree with Gouldner's analysis of this problem:

> Suppose, however, it were demonstrated that all human groups contained some elements in common, and that these could be spelled out. It should therefore be expected that there would be some leadership traits manifested commonly by all leaders. In short, there is no reason why leadership traits should constitute adaptations only to the diversities of groups; they should, too, involve adaptations to the similarities of groups. Thus, some leadership traits should be unique, specific to concrete groups and situations, while some could be common to all leaders.

This position, if sound, paves the way for an integration of the previously perceived divergent theories about leadership. Such an integration would retain the important contribution of the situationists—their emphasis on the demands of the group and the needs of the members; yet it would not close the door on the possibility of discovering some traits or characteristics of importance to leaders in most group situations. Perhaps now we can formulate a working definition of leadership based upon a theory that allows the kind of integration suggested above.

A WORKING DEFINITION OF LEADERSHIP

First of all, leadership can be conceptualized as an interaction between a person and a group, or, more accurately, between a person and the members of a group. Each participant in this interaction may be said to play a role, and these roles in some way must be differentiated from each other. The basis for this differentiation seems to be a matter of influence—that is, one person, the leader, influences, while the other persons respond. Gouldner's thinking is helpful here, for he sees the leader as

> any individual whose behavior stimulates patterning of the behavior in some group. By emitting some stimuli, he facilitates group action toward a goal or goals, whether the stimuli are verbal, written, or gestural.

Although not apparent from this definition, the determination of the kind of stimuli that will facilitate group action is a function of the nature of the group's goals and the reaction of the group to the contribution (stimuli) of the individual. Stated more simply, a potential "leader" of a group somehow must perceive what it is the group wants, he must contribute something that will move the group closer to that goal, and finally his contribution must be "accepted" before he can be said to have patterned the group's behavior. Thus a leader also must be led, in that he is influenced by the behavior of the group members to the extent that the group's norms, problems, and goals actually determine the kind of contribution that will pattern the group's behavior. In this sense, leadership is truly a process of interaction.

Thus, leadership is also relative to the situation. What will pattern group behavior in one situation may not in another. For a member of an athletic team to try to inspire in his teammates a fighting spirit may be an act of leadership when the team is losing but may invoke ridicule when the team is assured of winning by a large margin. Because a group itself is a moving, changing social system, its requirements for leadership will usually be different from time to time. This is not to deny, though, that a *particular* group may always require certain functions to be performed, so that a certain few members in a group may continuously emerge as leaders more often than others, even over a long period of time in the life of the group. The principle that "leadership is relative to the situation" also need not exclude the possibility that there may be certain "universal functions" that always facilitate change or movement in many or all kinds of groups. Perhaps it is more accurate, then, to say that the *pattern of leadership* is relative to the situation. Some specific functions may be required at all times in a single group or at various times in all groups, but the total pattern of leadership functions will be unique for each group and perhaps even for each situation confronting a group.

Probably the principal significance of such a conception of leadership is that it shifts the focus of attention from a *single* leader to a role that potentially may be occupied by *any group member* who is able to emit appropriate stimuli which facilitate group action toward a goal. True, in some groups one member during a short period may occupy that role more frequently than other members, as when a group is engaged in reaching a particular goal and the functions required to attain this end can be carried out best by one member. Yet our definition allows for the emergence of a new leader when the group selects a new goal.

A complicating factor, yet one that does not detract from the usefulness of our definition, is the common phenomenon of a group situation in which one person acquires a relatively permanent and often formal or institutionalized role of group leader. This may occur more or less informally when the group learns to depend upon one member as a reliable source of stimuli, as with a group that becomes committed to relatively unchanging and limited goals. Or it may occur formally, as in so many of our larger organizations, when a person is given a formal and designated role (and usually a title). Even when leadership roles become institutionalized in this way, a leader to be "followed" (or to continue having his actions pattern group behavior) must be perceived by the members as facilitating the group's efforts at reaching some goal.

As Knickerbocker has so clearly pointed out:

> The leader may "emerge" as a means to the achievement of objectives desired by a group. He may be selected, elected, or spontaneously accepted by the group because he possesses or controls means (skill, knowledge, money, association, property, etc.) which the group desires to utilize to attain their objectives—to obtain increased need satisfaction. . . . However, there will be no relationship with the group—no followers—except in terms of the leader's control of means for the satisfaction of the needs of the followers. Either the leader's objectives must also be those of the group (and he himself be seen by the group as a means to their attainment), or else accepting the leader's direction must be seen by the group members as the best available means to prevent reduced need satisfaction.

Thus, whether the leader is formally designated by the group (or by someone outside the group) or spontaneously emerges, his behavior still must be perceived as facilitating to the group if he is to remain the group's leader in a psychological sense.

One further element needs to be added to this conception of leadership. Often overlooked, yet of great significance, is the possibility that once a person is perceived as a leader in one situation, the members may in future situations tend to respond more readily to his behavior than to others'. This is to say that stimuli from one who has been perceived already as a leader may have a higher probability of directing the group's behavior, perhaps because of the attitude that somehow he is a more "legitimate" source of influence. Again Gouldner is helpful here, for he stresses this factor with exceptional clarity:

> In this sense a leader would be an individual who has the right to issue certain kinds of stimuli which tend to be accepted by others in the group as obligations. . . . The reasons why a leader's stimuli may be held as legitimate are varied. The leader may be viewed as being a person with unusual endowments; perhaps his stimuli are legitimated by virtue of the legal or traditional system of norms governing his appointment or election, perhaps because of his knowledge or expertise, or because he exemplifies other qualities valued by the group.

The extent to which this *generalization of leadership potential* occurs in a group has, as we shall see later, an important bearing on the overall functioning of a group. Here we call attention only to the fact that the potential for leadership behavior may not be equally distributed throughout a group, even though our conception of leadership fosters the notion that any member through his own behavior can pattern the behavior of the group.

Why is leadership a desired if not a necessary factor in small-group communication? How do we generally go about selecting a leader? Do we select the most knowledgeable person, the one who seems poised and talkative, the most experienced member, the member who suits the occasion, or simply the person who cannot "get out of it?" If you are preparing for small-group work in class, how are you selecting a leader?

The Individual in the Group: Analysis of Games

Eric Berne

Eric Berne, former lecturer at the University of California Medical School and chairman of the San Francisco Social Psychiatry Seminars, discusses the actions and responses of individuals in groups. Withdrawal, rituals, pastimes, and games account for many of these actions and responses. As you read this chapter, think of groups to which you belong and the applicability of Berne's ideas to the members of those groups—especially to yourself.

INDIVIDUAL PARTICIPATION

The analysis of single transactions may be very useful in certain situations, but for a more thorough understanding of the nature of the individual's participation in the proceedings of a group, it is necessary to consider chains of transactions. Such chains can be usefully classified into six important types, including the extreme cases of nonparticipation (withdrawal) and "total" participation (intimacy). This gives the individual six options or choices as to how he will conduct himself in a group.

1. Withdrawal. Some people may be physically present but are in effect mentally absent from the gathering. They do not participate in the proceedings, and on inquiry it is found that they are engaged in fantasies. These generally fall into one of two classes:

a. Extraneous fantasies in which the individual mentally leaves the group and imagines himself elsewhere doing something quite unrelated to the proceedings.

b. Autistic transactions in which he is interested in what is going on but for various reasons is unable to participate. He spends his time imagining things that he might say or do with various members of the group. Autistic transactions are sometimes concerned with the possibility of participating in an acceptable way and at other times are less well adapted to the situation and may be concerned with direct assaults or sexual advances which would be quite unacceptable to the other members. Thus, autistic transactions may in turn be classified as adapted or un-adapted.

2. Rituals, ceremonies and ceremonials. The preliminary and closing stages of the proceedings of any social aggregation, including groups, are often ritualistic in nature. These ritualistic phases may be abortive, con-sisting only of standard greetings and farewells, or they may be more prolonged, with formalities such as reading the minutes and votes of thanks. At formal ceremonies, such as weddings, not only the initial and terminal phases, but also the body of the meeting is ritualistic. From the point of view of social dynamics, the characteristic of ritualistic behavior is predictability. If at the beginning of a meeting one member says to another "Hello," it can be predicted with a high degree of confidence that the response will be "Hello" or one of its equivalents. If the first member then says "Hot enough for you?" it can likewise be predicted that the response will be "Yes," or some variant—similarly with the farewells at the end of a meeting. In a traditional ritual such as a church service, the stimuli and the responses are well known to all present and are com-pletely predictable under ordinary conditions.

The unit of ritualistic transactions is called a stroke. The following is an example of a typical 8-stroke American greeting ritual:

> A. "Hi!"
> B. "Hi!"
> A. "Warm enough for you?"
> B. "Sure is. How's it going?"
> A. "Fine. And you?"
> B. "Fine."
> A. "Well, so long."
> B. "I'll be seeing you. So long."

Here there is an approximately equal exchange comprising a greeting stroke, an impersonal stroke, a personal stroke and a terminal stroke. Such rituals are part of the group etiquette.

At a group meeting the first six strokes may be exchanged at the be-ginning and the last two at the end. The problem then remains how the time is filled in between these two segments.

3. Activity. Most groups come together for the ostensible purpose of engaging in some activity which, as noted, is usually mentioned at least

in a general way in the constitution. Pure activity in transactional language consists of simple, complementary, Adult transactions starting with something like "Pass the hammer!" or "What is the sum of 3 plus 3?" If there is no planned activity, as at many social parties, and in some psychotherapy groups, then the time is usually filled in with either pastimes or games.

4. Pastimes. Pastimes consist of a semi-ritualistic series of complementary transactions, usually of an agreeable nature and sometimes instructive. At formal meetings the time between the greeting rituals and the beginning of the formal proceedings is often filled in with pastimes. During this period the gathering has the structure of a party rather than that of a group. At social parties, pastimes may occupy the whole period between the greeting and the terminal rituals. In psychotherapy groups, they may continue or be initiated even after the entrance of the therapist which signals the beginning of the formal proceedings.

5. Games. As members become acquainted with each other, generally through pastimes carried on in the course of the group activity, they tend to develop more personal relationships with each other, and ulterior transactions begin to creep in. These often occur in chains, with a well-defined goal, and are actually attempts of various people to manipulate each other in a subtle way in order to produce certain desired responses. Such sets of ongoing transactions with an ulterior motive are called games.

6. Intimacy comes out transactionally in the direct expression of meaningful emotions between two individuals, without ulterior motives or reservations. Under special conditions, as in family life, more than two people may be engaged. Since such "pairing" may distract from the activity of a group, it is not encouraged in large work groups. For example, some organizations have a rule that if two members marry, one of them must resign. Because the subjective aspects are so important in true intimacy, and because it rarely comes out in groups because of external prohibitions and internal inhibitions, its characteristics are difficult to investigate. Indeed, this is one of the cases in which attempts at investigation are likely to destroy what is being investigated, since true intimacy is by nature a private matter. Few people would care to have their honeymoons tape recorded by a third person. There are certain sacrifices that should not be expected, even for the sake of science.

Pseudo-intimacy (with ulterior motives or reservations) is quite another matter and is frequently observed and erroneously described in the scientific literature as real intimacy. Some special groups are set up so that physical freedom, including sexual intercourse, is encouraged, but these are ritualistic, commercialized or rebellious and do not necessarily promote the subjective binding of two personalities. Pseudo-intimacy usually falls into the category of rituals, pastimes or games.

These six options have been listed roughly in order of the complexity of engagement and the seriousness of the commitment. The two extremes, withdrawal and intimacy, properly belong to the field of psychiatry. The two that stand out as most needful of further clarification for the student of social dynamics are pastimes and games, since these are the ones that most commonly affect the course of the internal group process.

PASTIMES

A pastime may be described as a chain of simple complementary transactions, usually dealing with the environment and basically irrelevant to the group activity. Pastimes are appropriate at parties, and they can be easily observed in such unstructured enclaves. Happy or well-organized people whose capacity for enjoyment is unimpaired may indulge in a social pastime for its own sake and for the satisfactions which it brings. Others, particularly neurotics, engage in pastimes for just what their name implies—a way of passing (i.e., structuring) the time "until": until one gets to know people better, until this hour has been sweated out, and on a larger scale, until bedtime, until vacation-time, until school starts, until the cure is forthcoming, or until a miracle, rescue or death arrives. (In therapy groups the last three are known colloquially as "waiting for Santa Claus.") Besides the immediate advantages which it offers, a pastime serves as a means of getting acquainted in the hope of achieving the longed-for intimacy with another human being. In any case, each participant tries to get whatever he can out of it. The best place to study pastimes systematically is in psychotherapy groups.

The two commonest pastimes in such groups are variations of "PTA" and "Psychiatry," and these may be used as illustrations for analysis. At an actual Parent-Teachers Association meeting "PTA," officially at least, is not a pastime, since it is the constitutionally stated activity of the group. But in a psychotherapy group it is basically irrelevant because very few people are cured of neuroses or psychoses by playing it. In that situation it occurs in two forms. The projective type of "PTA" is a Parental pastime. Its subject is delinquency in the general meaning of the word, and it may deal with delinquent juveniles, delinquent husbands, delinquent wives, delinquent tradesmen, delinquent authorities or delinquent celebrities. Introjective "PTA" is Adult and deals with one's own socially acceptable delinquencies. "Why can't I be a good mother, father, employer, worker, fellow, hostess?" The motto of the projective form is "Isn't It Awful?"; that of the introjective form is "Me Too!"

"Psychiatry" is an Adult or at least pseudo-Adult pastime. In its projective form it is known colloquially as "Here's What You're Doing"; its introjective form is called "Why Do I Do This?"

People in therapy groups are particularly apt to fall back on pastimes in three types of situations: when a new member comes in, when the members are avoiding something, or when the leader is absent. The superficial nature of these interchanges is shown in the following two examples, the analyses of which are represented in Figures 1 and 2.

I. "PTA"—PROJECTIVE TYPE

MARY: "There wouldn't be all this delinquency if it weren't for broken homes."

JANE: "It's not only that. Even in good homes nowadays the children aren't taught manners the way they used to be."

II. "PSYCHIATRY"—INTROJECTIVE TYPE

MARY: "Painting must symbolize smearing to me."

JANE: "In my case, it would be trying to please my father."

In most cases pastimes are variations of "small talk," such as "General Motors" (comparing cars) and "Who Won" (both "mantalk"); "Grocery," "Kitchen" and "Wardrobe," (all "lady talk"); "How To" (go about doing something), "How Much" (does it cost?), "Ever Been" (to some nostalgic place), "Do You Know" (so-and-so), "Whatever Became" (of good old Joe), "Morning After" (what a hangover), and "Martini" (I know a better drink).

It is evident that at any given moment when two people are engaged in one of these pastimes, there are thousands of conversations going on throughout the world, allowing for differences in time zones, in which essentially the same exchanges are taking place, with a few differences in proper nouns and other local terms. The situation brings to mind those printed postal cards which were supplied to the soldiers in the trenches in World War I, in which the terms that did not apply could be crossed out; or those box-top contests that require the completion of a sentence in less than 25 words. Thus, pastimes are for the most part stereotyped sets of transactions, each element consisting of what a psychology student might call a multiple choice plus a sentence completion; e.g., in "General Motors": "I like a (Ford, Plymouth, Chevrolet) better than a (Ford, Plymouth, Chevrolet) because . . ."

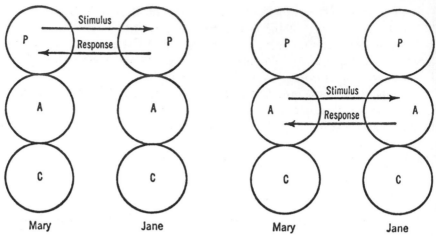

Fɪɢ. 1. "PTA"—projective type.   Fɪɢ. 2. "Psychiatry"—introjective type.

PASTIMES

The social value of pastimes is that they offer a harmless way for people to feel each other out. They provide a preliminary period of non-committal observation during which the players can line each other up before the games begin. Many people are grateful for such a trial period, because once he is committed to a game, the individual must take the consequences.

GAMES

The game called "If It Weren't For You," which is the commonest game played between husbands and wives, can be used to illustrate the characteristics of games in general.

Mrs. White complained that her husband would not allow her to indulge in any athletic or social activities. As she improved with psychiatric treatment, she became more independent and decided to do some of the things she had always wanted to do. She signed up for swimming and dancing lessons. When the courses began, she was surprised and dismayed to discover that she had abnormal fears of both swimming pools and dance-floors and had to give up both projects.

These experiences revealed some important aspects of the structure of her marriage. There were good Parental and Adult reasons why she loved her husband, but her Child had a special interest in his domineering Parent. By prohibiting outside activities, he saved her from exposing herself to situations that would frighten her. This was the psychological advantage of her marriage. At the same time, as a kind of bonus, he gave her the "justifiable" right to complain about his restrictions. These complaints were part of the social advantages of the marriage. Within the family group, she could say to him: "If it weren't for you, I could . . . etc." Outside the home, she was also in an advantageous position, since she could join her friends, with a sense of gratification and accomplishment, in their similar complaints about their husbands: "If it weren't for him, I could . . . etc."

"If It Weren't For You" was a game because it exploited her husband unfairly. In prohibiting outside activities, Mr. White was only doing what his wife's Child really wanted him to do (the psychological advantage), but instead of expressing appreciation, she took further advantage of him by enjoying herself in complaining about it (the social advantage).

But it was an even exchange, and that is what kept the marriage going; for Mr. White, on his side, was also using the situation to get questionable satisfactions out of it. As an important by-product, the White children's emotional education included an intensive field course in playing this game, so that eventually the whole family could and did indulge in this occupation skillfully and frequently. Thus, the social dynamics of this family revolved around the game of "If It Weren't For You."

In a pastime the transactions are simple and complementary. In a game they are also complementary, but they are not simple; they involve two levels simultaneously, called the social and the psychological. The transactional analysis of "If It Weren't For You" is shown in Fig. 3. At the social level, the scheme is as follows:

HUSBAND: "You stay home and take care of the house."
WIFE: "If it weren't for you I could be having fun."

Here the transactional stimulus is Parent to Child, and the response is Child to Parent.

At the psychological level (the ulterior marriage contract) the situation is quite different.

HUSBAND: "You must always be here when I get home. I am terrified of desertion."
WIFE: "I will be, if you help me to avoid situations that arouse my abnormal fears."

Here both stimulus and response are Child to Child. At neither level is there a crossing, so that the game can proceed indefinitely as long as

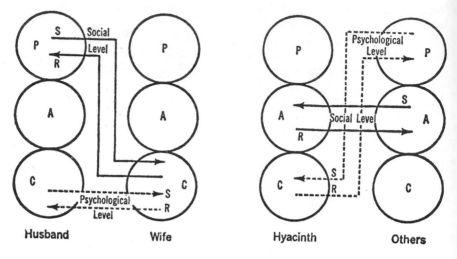

FIG. 3. "If It Weren't For You."   FIG. 4. "Why Don't You . . .
                                                    Yes, But."

GAMES

both parties are interested. Such a transaction, since it involves two complementary levels simultaneously, is a typical ulterior transaction.

A game can be defined as a set of ongoing ulterior transactions with a concealed motivation, leading to a well-defined climax. Because each player has a definite goal (of which he may not be aware), the innocent-looking transactions are really a series of moves with a snare or "gimmick" designed to bring about the climax or "pay-off."

The most common game in parties and groups of all kinds including psychotherapy groups, is "Why Don't You . . . Yes, But."

HYACINTH: "My husband never builds anything right."
CAMELLIA: "Why doesn't he take a course in carpentry?"
HYACINTH: "Yes, but he doesn't have time."
ROSITA: "Why don't you buy him some good tools?"
HYACINTH: "Yes, but he doesn't know how to use them."
HOLLY: "Why don't you have your building done by a carpenter?"
HYACINTH: "Yes, but that would cost too much."
IRIS: "Why don't you just accept what he does the way he does it?"
HYACINTH: "Yes, but the whole thing might fall down."

"Why Don't You . . . Yes, But" can be played by any number. One player, who is "It," presents a problem. The others start to present solutions, each beginning with "Why don't you?" To each of these the one who is "It" objects with a "Yes, but . . ." A good player can stand off the rest of the group indefinitely, until they all give up, whereupon "It" wins. Hyacinth, for example, successfully objected to more than a dozen solutions before Rosita and the therapist broke up the game.

Since all the solutions, with rare exceptions, are rejected, it soon becomes evident that this game must serve some ulterior purpose. The "gimmick" in "Why Don't You . . . Yes, But" is that it is not played for its apparent purpose (an Adult quest for information or solutions) but to reassure and gratify the Child. In writing it may sound Adult, but in the living tissue it can be observed that the one who is "It" presents herself as a Child inadequate to meet the situation; whereupon the others become transformed into sage Parents anxious to dispense their wisdom for the benefit of the helpless one. This is exactly what "It" wants, since her object is to confound these Parents one after another. The analysis of that game is shown in Fig. 4. The game can proceed because, at the social level, both stimulus and response are Adult to Adult, and at the psychological level they are also complementary, a Parent-to-Child stimulus ("Why don't you . . .") bringing out a Child-to-Parent response ("Yes, but . . ."). The psychological level may be unconscious on both sides.

Some interesting features come to light by following through on Hyacinth's game.

HYACINTH: "Yes, but the whole thing might fall down."

DR. Q: "What do you all think of this?"

ROSITA: "There we go, playing 'Why Don't You . . . Yes, But' again. You'd think we'd know better by this time."

DR. Q: "Did anyone suggest anything you hadn't thought of yourself?"

HYACINTH: "No, they didn't. As a matter of fact, I've actually tried almost everything they suggested. I did buy my husband some tools, and he did take a course in carpentry."

DR. Q: "It's interesting that Hyacinth said he didn't have time to take the course."

HYACINTH: "Well, while we were talking I didn't realize what we were doing, but now I see I was playing 'Why Don't You . . . Yes, But' again, so I guess I'm still trying to prove that no Parent can tell me anything, and this time I even had to lie to do it."

One object of games is to prevent discomfort by structuring an interval of time. This was clearly brought out by another woman, Mrs. Black. As is commonly the case, Mrs. Black could switch roles in any of her favorite games. In "Why Don't You . . . Yes, But," she was equally adept at playing either "It" or one of the sages, and this was discussed with her at an individual session.

Dr. Q: "Why do you play it if you know it's a con?"

Mrs. Black: "When I'm with people, I have to keep thinking of things to say. If I don't I feel uncomfortable."

Dr. Q: "It would be an interesting experiment if you stopped playing 'Why Don't You . . .' in the group. We might all learn something."

Mrs. Black: "But I can't stand a lull. I know it and my husband knows it too, and he's always told me that."

Dr. Q: "You mean if your Adult doesn't keep busy, your Child is exposed and you feel uncomfortable?"

Mrs. Black: "That's it. So if I can keep making suggestions to somebody or get them to make suggestions to me, then I'm all right. I'm protected."

Here Mrs. Black indicates clearly enough that she fears unstructured time. Her Child can be soothed as long as her Adult can be kept busy in a social situation, and a game is a good way to keep her Adult occupied. But in order to maintain her interest, it must also offer satisfactions to her Child. Her choice of this particular game depended on the fact that, for psychiatric reasons, it suited the needs of her special kind of Child.

Other common games are "Schlemiel," "Alcoholic," "Uproar," "You Got Me Into This," "There I Go Again," and "Let's You and Him Fight." Such games have many similarities to popular contests such as chess or football. "White makes the first move," "East kicks off," each have their parallels in the first moves of social games. After a definite number of moves the game ends in a distinct climax which is the equivalent of a checkmate or touchdown. This should make it clear that a game is not just a way of grumbling or a hypocritical attitude but a goal-directed set of ulterior transactions with an unexpected twist which is often overlooked.

The sequence of moves is illustrated in the game of Schlemiel. In this game the one who is "It" breaks things, spills things and makes messes of various kinds, and each time says "I'm sorry!" The moves in a typical situation are as follows:

1. White spills a highball on the hostess's evening gown.

2. Black responds at first with anger, but he senses (often only vaguely) that if he shows it, White wins. Black therefore pulls himself together, and this gives him the illusion that he wins.

3. White says, "I'm sorry!"

4. Black mutters forgiveness, strengthening his illusion that he wins.

It can be seen that both parties gain considerable satisfaction. White's Child is exhilarated because he has enjoyed himself in the messy moves of the game and has been forgiven at the end, while Black has made a gratifying display of suffering self-control. Thus, both of them profit from an unfortunate situation, and Black is not necessarily anxious to end the apparently unpromising friendship. It should be noted that as with most games, White, the aggressor, wins either way. If Black shows his anger, White can feel "justified" in his own resentment. If Black restrains himself, White can go on enjoying his opportunities.

The "gimmick" in such games almost always has an element of surprise. For example, a careless observer might sympathize with Mrs. White because of her autocratic husband, but the "gimmick" is that while she is complaining about him he is really serving a very important purpose in protecting her from her abnormal fears. In "Why Don't You . . . Yes, But" the "gimmick" has remained concealed from serious investigation through the thousands of years that this game has been played. It may have been observed facetiously that the one who is "It" rejects all the suggestions offered, but the possibility that this in itself might be a source of reassurance and pleasure has not been taken seriously enough to stimulate scientific interest. The clumsiness of the Schlemiel, and the possible secret pleasure he may derive from it, have been discussed, but this pleasure is merely a dividend; the "gimmick" and the goal of the whole procedure, which lie in the apology and the resulting forgiveness, have been overlooked.

The kinds of games, such as those mentioned above, which are of interest to the student of social dynamics, are of a serious nature, even though their descriptions may bring to mind the English humorists. They form the stuff out of which many lives are made and many personal and national destinies are decided. Any set of transactions that occurs repeatedly in a group, and that can be analyzed on two levels like the illustrations in Figures 3 and 4, is probably a game. The diagnosis is confirmed if an ulterior motive can be found which leads progressively to the same climax again and again.

What effect do rituals, pastimes, and games have on communication in groups? If you have now considered your own actions in groups, when have you withdrawn? Why? What rituals have you perceived in classroom discussions? What games? What are the values of pastimes in group deliberations? How are they detrimental?

Generalizations from Small Group Research Data

Joseph E. McGrath
Irwin Altman

Joseph E. McGrath, professor at the University of Illinois, and Irwin Altman, staff member of the Naval Medical Research Institute at Bethesda, Maryland, summarize the findings of a large sampling of small group research. First, they discuss "relationships that involve properties of group members—e.g., biographical characteristics, personality characteristics, abilities, and attitudes." Second, they generalize "about properties at the group level—e.g., group capabilities and training, interpersonal relations, and general structural properties." Third, they analyze member and group task performance in a variety of settings.

CHARACTERISTICS OF GROUP MEMBERS

MEMBER ABILITIES AND EXPERIENCE

It may appear trite to say that a consistent, positive relationship exists between the capabilities and skills of group members and their performance. However, that this apparently simple relationship is not quite so simple is suggested by the data of the review sample. It seems clear, as common sense will suggest, that member characteristics such as intelligence, aptitudes, and specific abilities have a direct and positive impact on performance, when we are dealing with *objective* measures of such capabilities. However, there is a much more ambiguous relationship between estimates of members' capabilities based on *self-reports* (either by the subject, by his peers, or by his superiors) and individual performance. Thus, use of subjective estimates of member capabilities does not lead to clear predictions of member performance. It is probable that part of the reason for the lack of a stronger relationship between subjective estimates of abilities and individual performance is the operation of a halo factor. This factor is indicated by the generally high intercorrelation between various estimates of individual task abilities and general abilities made by group members about each other.

Of equal importance is the general finding that the abilities of individual members, even in terms of objective measures, are not necessarily useful predictors of group task performance, although such measures do seem to exhibit consistent, positive relationships with member performance. Thus, it may not be possible to predict the performance of a group, as a group, from knowledge of individual abilities however measured. The differential relationship of member abilities to individual versus group performance certainly highlights the old question of whether individuals *summate* to form a group or whether the characteristics of individual members combine in some nonadditive but otherwise unknown way. . . .

It is also interesting to note that there is a very consistent and positive relationship between member abilities and manifestation of leadership performance, as judged by observers or superiors. What is especially striking about this relationship is that it holds when one uses either objective or subjective (peer) measures of abilities as predictors of leadership performance. Most of these strong relationships occur for relationships between judgments of leadership potential and measures of leadership performance, suggesting that a characteristic such as leadership potential is a fairly visible, though global, property of the individual. Recall that there was no such relationship between peer estimates of ability and task performance.

To recapitulate: research on group member abilities does not fully support the adage that the more capabilities members possess, the better group performance will be. It seems clear that *member* performance is enhanced by high *member* capabilities, but this does not seem to be the case, generally, with respect to group performance. Moreover, even the member capability versus member performance relationship applies only where we are dealing with objective measures of member capabilities; when peers make subjective judgments of capabilities, the relationship is much less clear-cut. Apparently, members are not good judges of one another's capabilities, except with respect to judgments of leadership potential.

This discrepancy between the predictive value of peer ratings of ability versus peer ratings of leadership potential also holds for relationships with various aspects of interaction process. For example, there are very weak relationships between group members' perceptions of one another's skills and objective ratings of morale, cooperation, and various other indexes of interaction process. On the other hand, people rated high on leadership potential are also seen by others as exhibiting more power and receiving deference from others, which, in turn, is related to the effectiveness of their leadership performances (as determined by both objective and subjective measures). It would seem that leadership antecedents, behavioral manifestations of leadership, and leadership effectiveness may all be visible to group members and be empirically related to one another.

PERSONALITY AND BIOGRAPHICAL CHARACTERISTICS OF MEMBERS

Surprising as it may seem, biographical and personality characteristics have not been studied very extensively in the small group literature, at least within the sample of studies reviewed. For those cases in which such variables have been studied, there do not seem to be any pervasive or general propositions that emerge. Clichés to the effect that the more stable the person is, the better he is as a leader or the more effective he is as a task performer are substantiated to some extent, but by no means are they firmly established conclusions. Actually very few data are available about the role of personality characteristics of members on various group phenomena. . . .

MEMBER ATTITUDES

One generally clear proposition is that favorable member attitudes toward the group task and toward the situation seem to be partly a consequence of high social or task status in the group, job autonomy, cooperative group conditions, and induced perceptions of task success. These relationships suggest that attitudes toward the task and toward the situation are associated with or reflect an over-all personal success in the situation. It is very interesting to note, however, that there is no indication that such attitudes enhance the individual's performance on the task or bear any definitive relationship to the quality of interpersonal relations in the group. . . .

AUTHORITARIAN ATTITUDES

One of the most popular variables in small group research is authoritarian attitudes. A distinction should be made between authoritarian attitudes of one or more members of the group, as measured by the F-scale or a similar instrument, and authoritarian role behavior by a leader who is deliberately implementing an experimental condition, as in the classic Lewin, Lippitt, and White (1939) study. For authoritarian attitudes, there has been a decided lack of consistent relationship with other variables. It should be noted that authoritarian attitudes have shown high *negative* relationships with sociometric choices as friend or as leader, and positive relationships with striving for high status and with several types of inter-action behavior. However, in general, authoritarian attitudes show very little relationship to most interaction behaviors and inconsistent relation-ships with performance on tasks of various types. . . .

POSITIONS OF MEMBERS IN THE GROUP

A general proposition that can be induced from the accumulated data is that group members who have high social or task status in the group are likely to have high power and use it, and to react favorably to the group. Specifically, in comparison with low-status members, those with high status are likely to be seen as having high task skills; to more frequently exhibit diagnosing behavior, action initiation, information giving, and at-tempts to lead; to perceive themselves as having high influence and high authority, and as delegating responsibility; to exhibit leadership behavior in leaderless situations; to have higher task satisfaction and involvement; and to perceive the group as doing well on its task. Although these gen-eral propositions may seem obvious when viewed superficially, it should be recognized that it is not conceptually necessary that those with high status have high power. The fact that this relationship appears to be con-sistent bears on the fundamental nature of interpersonal relations in small groups. Furthermore, the fact that high-status persons are more involved in the group's task and perceive group success is by no means a necessary empirical outcome. Its consistency implies that status is not only related to power, but also to the individual's commitment to the group and his motivation toward group achievement.

With respect to task performance, it is interesting to note that there is very little relationship between the task performance of individual mem-bers and their social or task position in the group. Although the absence of a positive relationship is based on a fairly small number of cases, it does suggest that an understanding of an individual's performance cannot be gained solely from knowledge of his position in the group. This type of relationship requires more study, as does the relationship between the position of members in the group and the performance of the group as a whole. It would seem important to an understanding of group behavior in general, and group performance in particular, to know how various task or social positions that members occupy contribute to over-all group performance. . . .

CHARACTERISTICS OF THE GROUP

GROUP CAPABILITIES AND EXPERIENCE

The adage "practice makes perfect" seems to be fairly well substantiated by small group research. The more task training and experience groups and group members have, the better they perform as individuals and groups. This generalization holds for ad hoc laboratory groups and for operational (e.g., military) task groups. However, if we attempt to predict performance from knowledge of group abilities, the situation is much less clear. Results of the very limited data on this issue suggest that knowledge of group capabilities alone is not sufficient to predict level of group performance. It is likely that group capabilities set an upper limit on performance potential of the group, which is achieved to the extent that the group and its members have the opportunity to practice and to gain experience as individuals and as a team. . . .

GROUP SIZE

Variation in group size, including the difference between working alone and working with others, has been much studied in group research. Unfortunately, variations in size have ranged widely but not necessarily systematically. The review sample included studies using groups with up to 50 members. Results of different studies pertain to different ranges of group size. Nevertheless, a few apparently consistent relationships have been accrued. Relatively small group size is likely to be accompanied by the following:

1. Less perceived need for guidance and for a definite leader but less perceived competence and ability of the group as a whole
2. Fewer expressed ideas and less change in attitudes or other responses by members
3. Less-frequent perceptions of the leader as exhibiting coordinating behavior, clarifying rules, or wisely delegating authority
4. Greater perception of group task success

Although the general proposition that the smaller the group, the more effective its performance is often substantiated, the situation is very ambiguous. There are cases where the proposition holds but also cases where it does not, and it is very difficult to identify the factors that contribute to this difference. From study to study, different types of tasks are used, members differ in personal characteristics, and group sizes range from 2–3 persons to 30–50—not to mention social facilitation situations where people work alone but in the presence of others. A comprehensive and systematic exploration of the effects of a broad range of differences in group size, for a range of member, group, and task characteristics, is definitely needed. . . .

THE COMPOSITION OF GROUPS

Historically one of the main arguments for the study of groups has been that groups are not mere summations of individuals but a different system level, with properties arising from the pattern of member characteristics in interaction with the situation. In spite of this much-honored credo, there is very little research on group composition, and what little there is gives an unclear picture of the role of composition. The range of variables that are potentially important for group composition is very broad—interests, values, personality characteristics, biographical properties, abilities, and so on. Moreover, hypotheses about directions of effect have little theoretical underpinning, and are often little more than formalizations of such contradictory premises as "birds of a feather flock together," "opposites attract," or "one bad apple ruins the barrel." For some variables, it is likely that need complementarity (some members high on a given property, some low on the property) is required for good group perfor mance or adequate interpersonal relationships. For other variables, it may be important that all group members exhibit a high (or low) amount of the property. . . .

INTERPERSONAL RELATIONS IN THE GROUP

Interpersonal attraction among members of a group seems to be consistently and positively associated with, and perhaps derived from, member perceptions of their own and each other's status, power, and attitudes. For example, perceptions of others' task-related abilities and others' social and task status bear a positive relationship to liking others. This finding suggests that one of the bases of interpersonal attraction may be identification with those in favored positions or with those who possess desirable task- and situation-related characteristics. The phenomenon also appears to be two-way, for those who are liked by others (and who are in the favored positions or have the desired skills) are also highly attracted to their group. It might be hypothesized that this cycle is self-supporting, with members being attracted to those in favored positions or with relevant skills, who in consequence are more strongly attracted to the group. However, it is also likely that such a mutuality occurs only in groups where the members have consensually adopted a goal to pursue and in transient groups such as we find in a laboratory situation. In real groups, where motivations and aims are more complex, it is not likely that the simple picture presented here applies.

To pursue this question further, it appears that *mutuality* of perceptions, with respect to the situation or task and to each other, is associated with member attraction to one another and to the group. People are attracted to those who they think like them, who they think have the same task orientations as they do, who they are told like them (via any of a host of induced congeniality manipulations), who they are told to cooperate with rather than compete with, and so forth.

The bases of interpersonal attraction seem fairly clear. What implications for group functioning do variations in intermember and member-group attraction have? One of the results of high member attraction toward one another or toward the group is an increased communication rate. People communicate with those they like, and in doing so they show less aggressiveness and defensiveness, fewer communication difficulties, and more attentiveness to others. Furthermore, positive interpersonal relations in the group are also associated with member perceptions that other members and the group as a whole are performing well on the task. Thus, at this juncture, the picture indicates that group members are attracted to others who are in desired positions or who have desired skills, and these favored persons likewise are attracted to the group; that individuals like those who like them, are attracted to cooperative conditions, and see congenial groups and their members as doing well on their jobs.

Unfortunately, the sequence ends at this point. The relationship between interpersonal attraction per se and performance is quite unclear. Although there have been few direct tests of this relationship, what data do exist suggest an equivocal relationship. High member congeniality, cooperativeness, mutuality of liking, and other similar indicators of high cohesion do not appear to bear a universally positive relationship to performance. . . .

In summary, the over-all picture suggests that interpersonal attractions, interpersonal communication, and perceptions of task success may vary interdependently, so that a manipulation of any one of them will lead to correlated changes in the other two. Successful induction of greater interpersonal attraction produces greater communication and increased perceptions of group task success. Similarly, successful manipulation of perceptions of group success produces greater interpersonal attraction and communication. Finally, it is possible that increasing the amount of communication among group members will lead to more favorable perceptions of other members and of the group's performance effectiveness, although the latter point is not established in the present body of research information. . . .

LEADERSHIP

A distinction is made here between measures of the effectiveness of performance of a leader *as a leader* and measures of the effectiveness of performance of the group he leads. . . .

Most of the research information about leadership performance comes from studies of leaderless group situations, although some also comes from studies using superiors' ratings of leadership performance in operational settings. Effective leadership behavior seems to be a function of a number of characteristics and conditions:

1. Individual personality characteristics such as extroversion, assertiveness, and social maturity, but not a host of other, seemingly similar, characteristics
2. Education, but not age or other biographical characteristics
3. Intelligence, general ability, and task ability
4. High group status
5. Training in leader techniques

In turn, groups with effective leaders tended to be characterized by good work relations with other groups, care of equipment, orderliness, and a range of indexes of morale. As to behavior, effective leaders tended to be characterized by a high frequency of problem proposing, information seeking, and ego-involvement, in addition to the actions used to define their leadership effectiveness. However, they were not distinguishable from nonleaders, or ineffective leaders, on a number of other behavioral indexes.

Thus, there seems to be a fairly clear picture of who will emerge as leader, or be an effective leader; in essence, the member with highest status, skills, and training. There is a far less clear picture of just what behaviors characterize an effective leader or distinguish leaders from nonleaders. . . .

TASK PERFORMANCE OF GROUP MEMBERS

. . . . Generally, the discussion to follow focuses on the performance of groups or their members, where performance is defined in terms of relatively objective measures, including ratings by supervisors. It should be noted that much of the discussion involves a synthesis of data gathered in many different settings—from highly artificial laboratory environments to real teams operating in industrial or military situations. . . .

THE ROLE OF MEMBER CHARACTERISTICS

Research results support some common-sense suppositions about the impact of member-level properties on individual task performance in groups. For example, the higher a person's general abilities or intelligence and the greater his task aptitude, the better is his performance in a group. Moreover, there is a positive relationship between job performance and actual job knowledge, training, and experience. Thus, if we are aiming to increase the performance of individuals in a group situation we should select bright people who have relevant aptitudes and knowledge of the job, and who are trained and possess experience. Although not seemingly profound findings, they do lend objective credence to institutional wisdom; and they also contrast somewhat with the factors that enhance group performance, to be discussed later.

It appears that personal-social factors, such as member personalities, attitudes, and subjective perceptions, do not have consistently clear-cut relationships to individual performance. In some situations, such personal variables are important correlates of performance, but not in other cases. Interestingly, this ambiguity, if further research continues to yield such results, may suggest re-examination of the extreme "human relations" approach to management which has been in vogue in recent years. Some possible reasons for the confusing role of these more "romantic" variables are discussed in the next section. In any case, we can predict member performance in group situations more consistently from knowledge of intelligence and job-related characteristics than from personal-social properties. . . .

THE ROLE OF ENVIRONMENTAL FACTORS

In examining the role of "outside" influences on individual performance we again obtain some expected findings. Individual autonomy seems to have a positive effect on performance. In addition, feelings of participation in decision making about various aspects of the job (whether it actually takes place or not) and feedback in the form of reward and knowledge of performance enhance member performance. Moreover, imposing the requirement to make a (task-relevant) decision upon individuals affects their performance favorably. Thus, freedom, a sense of involvement, the requirement to act, and feedback all enhance member performance. This generalization is certainly compatible with common-sense notions, substantiated by a scientific approach to behavior.

TASK PERFORMANCE OF THE GROUP

THE ROLE OF MEMBER CHARACTERISTICS

When we examine factors that bear on over-all group performance rather than individual member performance, some interesting findings appear. Results suggest that member intellectual and task-relevant abilities (e.g., mechanical aptitude) are not consistently good predictors of group performance; individual job experience is. Thus, merely having intelligent, high-potential people in a group does not necessarily produce an effective team.

The data also suggest that personality and attitudinal characteristics are not consistently related to group performance, except that the absence of extreme personality characteristics enhances group functioning. In addition, subjective perceptions of various types (e.g., personal skill estimates or estimates of the skills of others) are not always associated with good group performance.

THE ROLE OF GROUP CHARACTERISTICS

Results at the group level appear to tie in with the preceding discussions. Experience as a group (working together for a period of time) has a positive relationship with group performance, as does relatively small size of the group. However, favorable interpersonal relations in the group (e.g., high cohesion, high morale) show unclear effects, although the trend is for high morale and cohesion to be accompanied by better performance. Such results are compatible with those for individual member performance, where job-related factors have a definite impact on productivity whereas the more "romantic," social-personal variables play a less precise role.

THE ROLE OF ENVIRONMENTAL FACTORS

Outside influences play a similar role for group and individual productivity, with reward and punishment, rather than explanation and illustration alone, tending to enhance performance. In addition, there are differential effects of types of feedback on group performance (e.g., structured critiques have a more enhancing effect than completely unstructured ones). Further, several work conditions (such as efficient routing of necessary information or direct and rapid access to information) have a positive effect on group performance. Clarity of role definition (i.e., jobs each person is to do and relationships between various jobs) also aids group performance.

THE ROLE OF PERSONALITY AND SOCIAL
FACTORS ON PERFORMANCE

As indicated, results are equivocal regarding the effects of personal-social factors on individual and group performance; this equivocation is somewhat in contrast to the attention such variables have received by researchers and consumers. How can we account for such findings and what potential role do the variables play?

It may be that the confused results are due to a methodological problem. For example, in aptitude and ability measurement, psychologists have well-developed tools whereas in the measurement of personality, attitudes, and group cohesion our measurement technology is less advanced.

On the other hand, consider the role of these variables from a conceptual point of view. When we speak of abilities and experience as determinants of performance, we are usually presuming that the more of the characteristic the better, and this usually is true. However, for personal-social variables this monotonic principle may not apply; rather, we may be in a realm where either *too much* or *too little* of a characteristic interferes with performance, with some optimum, in-between point enhancing performance.

Another hypothesis related to the role of these variables is that they are *mobilizers* of individual and group productivity potential. Perhaps individual and group abilities and experience tend to set limits within which the group can function just as intelligence may have limits set by heredity. In the same way that the environment may only exert an influence within the fixed bounds of intellectual capacity, so may it be that social-personal variables can enhance group performance only within limits set by abilities, training, and experience. Thus, if sufficient ability and experience are present, then favorable interpersonal relations will allow the group to achieve its potential. If they are not present to a sufficient degree, then the member or group may not perform up to its performance potential. Steiner and Rajaratnam (1961) have presented a model of group productivity that builds upon this basic premise.

Without attempting to resolve the possibilities raised here, we may say that personal-social variables cannot be simply viewed within the common-sense adage that "the happy, well-adjusted worker is the good worker." . . .

If, as McGrath and Altman suggest, we cannot predict who will be successful in small groups, how can we best select members for small groups? Why is it easier to detect leadership ability than ability to work in a group? Why does high individual member performance not signal high group performance? Of what importance are past communications among members to group performance? If you were asked to create a small group to study the teaching on your campus, how many participants would you choose? Who might they be? Who would be the leader? Where would they meet?

VII

INTERPERSONAL COMMUNICATION: DYADS

Interviewing: A Definition and Description

Ellis R. Hays
Jerry E. Mandel

Ellis R. Hays, associate professor of speech communication at California State College at Long Beach, and Jerry E. Mandel, associate professor of communication at Kent State University, attempt to define and describe the interview or dyadic communication. We are involved in "interviews" far more often than debates, panel discussions, and public speaking settings, but until recently few colleges have offered training in the interview or dyad. Hays and Mandel disagree with the assumption that knowledge of public speaking is applicable to one-to-one stiuations—that no additional training is necessary.

Interviewing may be one of the most relevant communication events a student, whether a major in speech communication or one who is merely engaged in the basic course in speech communication, can study. This statement can be demonstrated by noting the role that interviewing plays and will continue to play in the lives and careers of most college graduates.[1]

From the beginning of a college graduate's career in a business, industrial, governmental, or educational institution, interviewing plays an important role. In fact whether or not an individual receives a position at all with a particular organization depends many times upon an interview. The interview is employed by large and small business, industrial, governmental, military, and educational organizations in decisions concerning the retention and promotion of an employee as his career progresses in an organization.

In many organizations, the college trained person will be required to

Reprinted with permission from Central States Speech Journal, XXI (Summer, 1970), pp. 126–129. This article is slightly condensed.

[1] *Making the Most of Your Job Interview* (New York: Life Insurance Company of New York).

engage in the decision making process of that organization. One of the most important aspects of decision making is the gathering of information through the vehicle of the interview. In short, the college graduate of today probably will be effected by the use of the interview in his hiring, firing, retention, promotion, and in much of the activity in his professional life.

Because of the importance of the interview, it seems almost paradoxical that the field of speech has generally failed to present a clear definition and discussion of interviewing. The objective of this article is to begin to eliminate the poverty of information in speech journals on interviewing by presenting a definition of interviewing, by noting the major components of interviewing, and by indicating just how interviewing differs from other forms of oral communication.

Interviewing has been defined in many ways by writers in the behavioral and social sciences.[2] It is important in an article of this nature, which attempts to describe the process of interviewing, to define interviewing in terms of its components or elements. The process of interviewing takes place when two people engage in a conversation utilizing verbal and nonverbal interaction for the purpose of accomplishing a previously defined goal, other than the satisfaction or "phatic" enjoyment of conversation itself.[3] The fundamental components of the interviewing process are: (1) the dyad (two persons interacting), (2) the use of face to face verbal and nonverbal communication, (3) the total situational, symbolic, ego-involved interaction between the two members of the interview, and (4) the fact that an interview has a goal or an objective which one or both of the participants are seeking to achieve.

Etymologically the term interview means a viewing between people. It is "bipolar" or "dyadic" in that there are only two parties involved in the interaction which takes place in the interviewing process. It is important to emphasize that both participants are simultaneously involved in sending and receiving messages. This means that both the interviewer and interviewees are responsible for listening and speaking during the course of an interview.

These important distinctions eliminate many modes of communica-

    [2] A less complex but interesting definition of interviewing appears in the classic work on this subject by Walter Van Dyke Bingham, Bruce Victor Moore, and John W. Gustad, *How to Interview* (New York: Harper & Brothers, 1959), Chapter One. A more sophisticated approach to this topic is provided by the psychologists Robert L. Kahn and Charles F. Cannell, *The Dynamics of Interviewing* (New York: John Wiley, 1960), Chapters One and Two.

    [3] In some situations communication events involving more than two people are termed interviews. These group interviews bring in the dimensions of group dynamics, group interaction, and the process of group communication. These variables are not prominent in the two-person interview and are not the focus of this particular article.

tion from being classified as part of the interviewing process. Communication modes such as letters, memoranda, staff meetings, telephone conversation and forms of public speaking such as oral interpretation, discussion and debating are not part of the interviewing process.

A number of conclusions can be made from the definition of interviewing thus far presented. First, since there is no majority in the dyad, the traditional rhetorical appeals used in public speaking or rhetorical analysis are simply not applicable to the interviewing situation. There is no audience such as is present in a public speaking situation. This lack of an audience in the interviewing situation means that there is no third party to act as mediator or arbitrator to soften the impact of clash over differing positions. In the dyad there is only consensus or conflict; therefore, there is a high degree of ego-involvement present. The participants in an interview cannot utilize supporters or collaborators to rally around band wagon appeals. It is strongly emphasized that speaking in the interview is unlike speaking in public. Traditional approaches to training, preparation and frames of reference used in public speaking are simply not applicable to the interview. Modern communication theory seems to have more relevance to the interview than theories of rhetoric and public address. The most frequent source for considerations of speaking and communication by traditionally oriented scholars in the field of speech are the writings of Aristotle.[4] His fundamental view that rhetorical arguments are the substance of modes of persuasion seems strangely out of place in the face to face interview.[5] Even hallowed public speaking devices such as eye contact, if continued, can become threatening and a barrier to communication in the interview. Long introductions or elaborations, used in public speaking, tend to sound "phony" in the interview, and again tend to be barriers to communication rather than supporting communication in the interview. Even the use of language and stylistic considerations, so important to public speakers, philosophers and grammarians, are not applicable to the interview. In fact, anyone sounding like an orator in an interviewing situation is probably setting up an insurmountable barrier to real communication in the interview situation.

The term "sequential programing" perhaps best describes the communicative environment of an interview. This term refers to the fact that as an interview takes place, each sequence or movement of communication which takes place between the interviewer and the interviewee, from the beginning of the interview until its termination, is directly dependent upon what has happened before. This means that an interview cannot be

[4] *The Rhetoric of Aristotle* (trans.) Lane Cooper (New York: D. Appleton & Company, 1932).
[5] Harry Stack Sullivan, *The Psychiatric Interview* (New York: W. W. Norton, 1954), p. 60.

preplanned like a speech or an acting scene. The communication in the interview is constantly being changed and altered as both the interviewer and interviewee react to actual or assumed feedback. Both participants constantly react to each other and constantly alter communication as a result of each other. This does not mean that some types of interviews cannot be planned to achieve specific goals. Questions in poll-type interviews can be standardized, but the interviewer still has to modify his probes in order to achieve the interview goals.

Because of the dyadic nature of the interviewing situation, feedback is a pervasive element of the process. Since there is no third party, coupled with the fact that the participants are usually fairly close to one another, the process of feedback is *continuous*. The usual subtleties of verbal and nonverbal response are not so subtle in the face-to-face pattern. The feedback interaction process is *instantaneous*. This eliminates the delayed response so familiar in other forms of oral communication. It has the effect of magnification on responses associated with strong feeling. The feedback responses are *direct*. The responses are not aimed at third parties, and there is no great space or time interval to soften the force of the direct responses. Fortunately, the feedback responses are *detailed*. Because of the nature of the feedback, it is easier to be sensitive to the variety of differentiated responses. Responses may range across a wide gamut within a brief span of time. These differentiated responses show up in detail in the dyad. The feedback response is *massive*. There is nothing in the interview situation to dilute the feedback response. In effect, there is no society with its rules-of-the-game to hide behind. Because feedback interaction is continuous, instantaneous, direct, detailed, and massive, it can easily be a threat to the participants. Harry Stack Sullivan, after years of interviewing experience, came to the conclusion that it is difficult to get authenticity in a dyad.[6] It may be that participants in an interview develop a "facade" simply because there is no other place to hide.

As the reader forms a foundation point or a definition of the process of interviewing, he should be particularly cognizant of the major components of that process. Particularly significant to the reader should be the considerations of the nature of a dyadic communication and the resultant role played by feedback and sequential programing in the interview; the realization of both nonverbal and verbal communication in the interview; the total interaction and involvement of both participants in an interview; and finally, the realization that interviewing is purposeful communication because each interview has a goal to be achieved.

Even though interviewing is a form of speech communication, its characteristics are so different from platform speaking and speaking in

---

[6] Sullivan, 9–27.

small groups that courses in interviewing require different sets of principles. Interviewing must continue to develop its own theory, research, and teaching techniques for this same reason.

In the definition of interviewing presented by Hays and Mandel, how does interviewing differ from mere conversation? From small group discussion? What is the most significant difference(s) between public speaking and interviewing: Lack of a majority or audience? The high ego involvement? The constantly changing "scene?" How can the interviewer overcome the interviewee's construction of a facade to hide behind? How does feedback in interviewing differ from feedback in public speaking?

Types and Uses of Questions in Interviews

Charles J. Stewart

Charles J. Stewart, associate professor of communication at Purdue University, discusses the determinants of good interview questions, types of interview questions, and the structuring of interviews. Note particularly the advantages of various types of questions and structures. Although this discussion is mainly concerned with "information-getting interviews," the treatment of questions is relevant to many persuasive settings in which the persuader bases much of his approach on key questions.

We are involved in numerous dyadic situations every day, and our most frequent aim is to get information. Students ask instructors about assignments; instructors quiz students on subject matter; wives ask husbands about delayed yardwork; interviewers ask applicants about their training and qualifications; constituents ask congressmen to explain the goings-on in Washington. In all these situations interviewers share the same goal: to obtain information that is accurate, sufficient in scope, and attainable in the shortest amount of time.

Successful "informational" interviews are not accidental—they are a matter of careful planning and skillful questioning. The interviewer should begin by determining the nature and extent of the information he seeks. Then he must select the interviewee(s) who (1) has the information he needs, (2) is willing to give the information to him, and (3) is capable of giving the information accurately.

Before formulating specific questions, either in his mind or on paper, the interviewer should be aware of several determinants of good questions. For instance, a respondent may not understand the intent of a question containing words above his level of usage, but he may give some kind of answer rather than admit he does not understand the language. If the lan-

This article is printed here for the first time.

guage is below a respondent's level of usage, he may be insulted and move to terminate the interview. The aim should be a sharing of language with the interviewee. When interviewing several people, use language that communicates successfully with the least sophisticated respondent but avoids the appearance of oversimplification.

A second determinant of good questions concerns information level and is closely related to language level. Questions beyond the knowledge of the interviewee may embarrass him or make him resentful at being asked such questions. Either response decreases his motivation to communicate freely and accurately. An added danger is that the respondent may fake an answer. If you make up a name and ask several people if they know the person or have heard of him, you will be amazed how many will say "The name sounds familiar" rather than "No, I don't know him."

A third determinant of questions is frame of reference—a respondent's attitude toward a person, place, or thing based upon his past experiences. To a student, campus unrest may conjure up a picture of students marching in orderly fashion past the administration building or listening intently to student speakers. To the state legislator, campus unrest may produce visions of fire bombs, disruption of classes, and attacks on police. To a farmer, farm prices mean too little profit for too much work and investment. To a housewife in a supermarket, farm prices mean exorbitant charges for too few groceries.

A fourth determinant is relevancy. If a respondent cannot see the relevance of a question or questions to your stated purpose, he may refuse to cooperate further or he may become reluctant to communicate freely. It is wise to explain the rationale for questions that might appear to be "off the subject."

A fifth determinant is complexity of questions. Novice interviewers tend to ask several questions at once. "Tell me about your background, training, experiences, hobbies, likes and dislikes, and future plans." Few respondents could remember all of this request. As a result, little information is gained, and the interviewer will have to ask several additional questions to make sure all parts of the original question are answered.

The final determinant is possible interviewer bias. If the interviewer is not extremely careful, the interviewee will give the answer he feels the interviewer wants to hear—whether this desire is true or not. A student interviewer of police chiefs cannot hide the fact that he is a student—and this may bias the results—but he can and must phrase his questions neutrally in order that his personal feelings are not trumpeted to his respondents.

Along with an awareness of the determinants of good questions, the interviewer should be familiar with the kinds of questions: their uses and problems. Although some authors list dozens of kinds of questions, there are basically two types: open-ended and closed.[1]

Open-ended questions are very broad in nature and allow the respondent considerable freedom to determine the information he will give. The question can be as open as "Tell me about your background" or more restricted like "Tell me about your job with General Electric." The main advantage of the open-ended question is that it allows the interviewee to choose the kind and amount of information he will give. Answers to open questions tell you what the respondent thinks is important, and he may give information you might not think to ask for. Open-ended questions are frequently asked at the beginning of interviews because they are easier to answer and may help the interviewee to relax and make him more ready to communicate. The disadvantages of open-ended questions are the amount of time consumed by answers, the danger of a respondent giving too little information which will necessitate several follow-up questions, and the inherent problem of getting information that is neither needed nor wanted.

Closed questions give the interviewer more control over both area of information and length of response. Typical closed questions are "What course did you like best in college" or "What was my grade on the last test?" There are several advantages to closed questions: the interviewer can control the interview more effectively; he can ask many more questions in a shorter time; he can get to specific information he needs; and interviews are easier to replicate if one is going to conduct several. There are corresponding disadvantages to closed questions: the interviewer may get too little information; the interviewee has little chance to volunteer potentially valuable information; and the restrictiveness of closed questions may inhibit communication. Certain types of closed questions deserve specific consideration.

The bipolar or yes-no question is a highly controlled closed question. "Do you like mathematics?" or "Did I pass the test?" are examples of bipolar questions—those phrased in such a way so that they elicit a yes or no answer. There are occasions when such questions are justified—when all you want or need is a simple yes or *no.* The majority of interviews, however, are designed to probe for attitudes, feelings, beliefs, or information not attainable through bipolar questions or simple questionnaires. For example, a yes-no response to the question "Did you like college?" will not tell you about a person's reasons for liking or disliking, degrees of liking or disliking, or aspects of college he enjoyed most or least. Untrained interviewers ask many bipolar questions, only to find it necessary

[1] See Stanley L. Payne, *The Art of Asking Questions* (Princeton, New Jersey: Princeton University Press, 1951).

to ask several additional questions to obtain the same amount of information one nonbipolar question would have elicited.

The leading question is a more highly-controlled closed question. "You like close detail work, don't you?" or "Do you oppose the administration like most students I have talked with?" are examples of leading questions. Since they are likely to bias the answer he receives, the interviewer should be aware of them and use them only for special purposes. Too frequently the novice interviewer does not recognize the leading nature of his questions and gets the answers an interviewee thinks he wants—rather than honest responses. Leading questions are appropriate when the interviewer wants to sway a person toward his point of view or when he wants to observe a person under a stress situation.

The loaded question is the most highly-controlled form of closed question. It can be recognized by the trap into which it places the respondent and by its emotional and biased language. The first characteristic is embodied in the classic question, "Are you still beating your wife?" The interviewee is damned no matter which way he answers. The second characteristic is clear in the following questions: "If you were a manager of one of my stores, do you think you could handle those damn crooks from the union?" or "How do you feel about these communist-led uprisings on our campuses?" The interviewer avoids loaded questions except in an interview where one wants to observe the interviewee's handling of stress questions or wishes to provoke an unguarded reply.

In addition to open-ended and closed questions, there are two special kinds not easily classifiable. The neutral probing question is a follow-up when an answer seems incomplete, vague, superficial, or suggestible. For instance, if a respondent says that most workers seem to like him, the questioner might ask him to elaborate on the word *seem*. If an open-ended question on an interviewee's background produced only birthplace, name of high school, and father's occupation, the interviewer might probe into the nature of the respondent's family life, activities in high school, the rural or urban nature of his background, etc. If a student says he likes only relevant courses, the interviewer should ask for a definition of *relevant*. The difference between a good interviewer and a bad interviewer is the skillful use of neutral probing questions. Lack of such questions usually means a superficial interview at best and a confused, meaningless interview at worst. In a recent classroom interview, the interviewer questioned another student about the advantages and disadvantages of small vs. large colleges without offering or asking for definitions of *large* and *small*. Without these definitions the interview was meaningless.

The second special type of question is the mirror question—a question that reflects the preceding answer or answers. Its primary purposes are to summarize the idea(s) being discussed and to insure understanding of what has been stated or implied. For instance, after a respondent has answered an open-ended question about his background—in which he has elaborated on his farming experiences, rural schools, and small towns— the interviewer might ask: "Until coming to college, then, you had never experienced urban life?" This question is part probing, part clarification, and part summary. If during an interview about a recent test, a student remarks, "It was OK for its purposes," one might pose a mirror question like, "You think, then, the test determined students' knowledge and application of material in Unit II?" The interviewee might have a different notion of the test's purposes. This mirror question would make certain that the interviewer understood accurately what the interviewee had said or implied. Too many interviews fail because the interviewer assumes that he understands the respondent. Neutral probing and mirror questions help to insure accuracy of communication.

Perhaps the best way to summarize the kinds of questions we have just examined is to take a set of hypothetical interview questions about a recent championship basketball game. You will have to supply the missing responses—either before or after each question.

> *Open-ended:* "Tell me about the championship game between the Milwaukee Bucks and the Baltimore Bullets."
>
> *Closed:* "Who tried to defense Lew Alcindor?"
>
> *Bipolar:* "Did you agree with the selection of Lew Alcindor as Most Valuable Player?"
>
> *Leading:* "Don't you think the Bullet's injuries helped the Bucks win the championship in four straight games?"
>
> *Loaded:* "What effect do you think the stupid officiating had on the final game?"
>
> *Probing:* "Why do you say the ultimate outcome was certain after the first game of the series?"
>
> *Mirror:* "You think, then, the Bucks would have won the championship even if the Bullets had suffered no injuries?"

When the interviewer is aware of the requirements of good questions and the kinds available for his use, he is ready to formulate questions. The structure he selects for his interview will determine how carefully he will prepare each question. For example, a "nonscheduled" interview has little more "on paper" than a statement of purpose, such as the following:

> The purpose of this interview is to discuss the interview training, experiences, practices, and theories of selected personnel directors. I am not concerned about their day-to-day work, only their knowledge of interviewing.

For a skilled, experienced interviewer, such a statement of purpose might be adequate preparation. He will automatically phrase questions in his own mind, be careful to probe into answers, and will impose some standardization on his interviews with personnel directors. He will have to work hard to remember the information he receives because no structure is present to help him. This form of interview is difficult to replicate, but it allows maximum freedom to probe into answers and to adjust to each respondent. The untrained interviewer would be wise to develop a more structured interview.

The "moderately-scheduled" interview is perhaps the most common form of preparation. It contains the statement of purpose, major areas of questions, and some *suggested* probing questions. It might look like the following:

> The purpose of this interview is to discuss the interview training, experiences, practices, and theories of selected personnel directors. I am not concerned about their day-to-day work, only their knowledge of interviewing.
>
> 1. What kinds of training did you have in interviewing? Did you have any formal classroom training? Did you have informal on-the-job training? Did you observe interviews? Have you read books, articles, or pamphlets on interviewing?
>
> 2. What experiences have you had in interviewing? What kinds of interviews have you conducted? How many years' experience do you have? Are you still conducting interviews? If so, what percentage of your working day?
>
> 3. How do you conduct interviews? What are your preparation techniques? How do your preparation and procedures vary with different types of interviews? What kinds of structure do you impose on your interviews?
>
> 4. What are your theories of interviewing? Do you establish rapport at the beginning of each interview? Do you use stress questions? How do you employ "psychology?" What is your theory of communication?

The "moderately-scheduled" interview allows considerable freedom to probe and to adapt to particular interviewees, while at the same time imposing a degree of structure and forcing a higher degree of preparation. Such interviews are easier to replicate and easier for the novice interviewer to conduct.

The "highly-scheduled" interview is essentially an oral questionnaire. All questions as well as standardized answers are included. A section of such an interview might look like the following:

  I. Interview Training:
    A. How many college courses in interviewing have you had?
       None_____ One_____ Two_____ More than two_____
    B. How many short-courses in interviewing have you had? None
       _____ One_____ Two_____ More than two_____
    C. During the training stage, how many interviews did you observe?
       None_____ 1 to 5_____ 6 to 10_____ Over 10_____
    D. Which of the following kinds of printed materials on interview-
       ing have you read? Books_____ Pamphlets_____ Articles_____
       Other_____

 II. Interview Experiences:
    A. Which of the following types of interviews have you conducted?
       Employment_____ Personnel Counseling_____ Termination_____
       Informational_____ Other_____
    B. Which of the above have you conducted most frequently?_____
    C. How many years have you been conducting interviews? 1 to 5
       _____ 6 to 10_____ 11 to 15_____ Over 15_____

The advantages of the "highly-scheduled" interview are the ease of replication, the possibility of using unskilled interviewers, the speed with which they can be conducted, the ease of note-taking, and the ease of tabulating results. Serious disadvantages are the lack of freedom to probe and to adapt to interviewees and the narrower breadth of information received.

In addition to planning the overall structure of the interview, one should also consider the sequence of questions for the entire interview or within topics or subtopics. A "funnel sequence," for example, begins with a broad, open-ended question. Each successive question is narrower in scope. The advantage of the "funnel sequence" is that it may eliminate many closed or probing questions. It is particularly useful when one needs a detailed description of an event, and the interviewee is motivated to cooperate.

The "inverted funnel sequence" begins with a restricted or closed question and gradually works toward broad open-ended questions. It is particularly useful when one needs to motivate the interviewee to respond freely. Such a person would not offer much of an answer to an initial open-ended question. Also, if one wishes to obtain a final judgment from the interviewee, the "inverted funnel sequence" allows one to work toward the generalization.

In conclusion, I want to stress that you must use your imagination and feel free to create questions and structures; you must adapt to different situations and interviewees. No single approach is best for all occasions. As you become skilled as an interviewer, you will structure and adapt almost automatically and paper preparation will become less important.

The novice interviewer would be wise to prepare in writing the structure as well as many of the questions he intends to use. Practice will eliminate the necessity of reading these questions to the interviewee. Make the interview a planned conversation.

How would you rank the determinants of questions in order of importance? What determinants might you add to the list? Do you agree with the author's negative attitude toward bipolar, leading, and loaded questions? In your daily interpersonal relations, what type of questions do you encounter most often? When are you most likely to employ nonscheduled interviews? Moderately-scheduled interviews? Highly-scheduled interviews?

Student Evaluation of Instructors: An Interview and Commentary

Charles J. Stewart

This interview and commentary are designed to illustrate good and bad practices in interviewing, types and uses of questions, and verbal and nonverbal communication. As you read this interview, look for instances of good communication as well as communication breakdowns. If you were conducting this interview, how might you alter the opening and closing? What questions would you alter? How? What are the two best questions in the interview? Is there adequate feedback from the interviewee? What was the interviewer's purpose? Did he fulfill it?

STUDENT: Good afternoon, Professor Smith. As I mentioned on the phone yesterday, I am a member of the committee evaluating the recent instructor evaluation conducted by the Student Government.

Good opening. Interviewer orients the interviewee.

PROFESSOR: (frowning) Hi. Come in and sit down.

Frowning may signal anger at the instructor evaluation, bad mood, or his usual mood. Interviewer would be wise to establish rapport.

STUDENT: Let me begin by asking for your reactions to this year's evaluation.

A common type of open-ended question to get into the body of an interview. No rapport established, and the question invites a possible unpleasant response from a frowning respondent.

PROFESSOR: (serious tone of voice) I personally felt that the evaluation was a waste of time and very poorly handled.

Typical vague response to a very open-ended question. Negative answer and tone requires some careful adaptation by the interviewee.

This article is printed here for the first time.

236

STUDENT: This is why Student Government appointed my committee. We want to discover the problems and weaknesses in our instructor evaluation program so we can avoid these in future years. We do appreciate faculty members, like yourself, taking the time to discuss the problems with us.

Good attempt to smooth the feelings of the interviewee. A probing question at the end might have discovered why the professor feels antagonistic.

PROFESSOR: Well (pause), I am generally in favor of the program, but only if it can be improved.

The student's response seems to have defused the professor's anger. This response may contain a clue to the professor's whole attitude toward the evaluation.

STUDENT: How did the evaluation go in your class?

This is an open-ended question with vague go as a vital word. A better question might have been a probe into the improvements needed, in the professor's view.

PROFESSOR: Do you mean how was I graded, or what?

Good mirror question to discover the meaning of the question. Apparently the two had different ideas as to what was wanted.

STUDENT: No. I would like your general reactions to procedures, forms, class time used, etc.

Suggests too many areas for response. Etc. is meaningless.

PROFESSOR: The student from the instructor evaluation committee was 10 minutes late, and this took more class time than was necessary. The general procedures were OK.

The answer covers only part of the suggested areas. Is procedures being used similarly by interviewer and interviewee?

STUDENT: Did the student give an explanation for his tardy arrival?

Good probing question.

PROFESSOR: He mumbled something about a wrong room number.

Is the professor angry with the student who conducted the evaluation rather than with the evaluation?

STUDENT: What about the evaluation forms?

A probing question to get information left unanswered in a previous response.

PROFESSOR: The wording was vague on one, and there were misspellings on another.

What does the professor mean by vague? What were the misspellings?

STUDENT: Which forms were these?

Good probe. Would have been helpful to have the forms available for checking during the interview.

PROFESSOR: (rather gruff) I can't remember the numbers now!

Seems irritated; perhaps he feels pushed. Could he be expected to remember the forms?

STUDENT: Did you make note of these problems to the committee member who was late for your class?

Probing question, but does not define problems. Use of word late could remind the professor of his major irritation.

PROFESSOR: Yes, but I doubt that it did any good.

Reveals continuing mood. Further evidence of professor's antagonism toward committee member and not the evaluation program?

STUDENT: Why do you say this?

A probing that might irritate the interviewee if he feels he is being pushed too far.

PROFESSOR: (gruff) He didn't take any notes, and seemed to care less.

Professor being pushed too far?

STUDENT: You feel, then, that procedures and forms were generally satisfactory?

Mirror question. Perhaps the interviewer should have tried to soothe the interviewee's ruffled feelings.

PROFESSOR: Yes, if tardiness, vagueness, and misspellings are signs of satisfaction. (brief smile at the end)

Hint of thawing in the cold reactions of the professor, or note of sarcasm? How can the student determine which is the true reaction?

STUDENT: How did your students react to the evaluation?

Open-ended question introducing new area. Did interviewer get enough information on the professor's reaction to the evaluation?

PROFESSOR: There were no overt reactions.

Is the meaning of overt clear?

STUDENT: You didn't talk to them about the evaluation program?

Bipolar or probing question—depending upon interviewer's intent. Are talk and overt synonymous?

PROFESSOR: No, we were busy with a new unit.

Was the timing of the evaluation wrong?

STUDENT: How do you think the published report of the evaluations will be used around campus?

Open-ended question. "Around campus" is vague. Is this a new area of questioning?

PROFESSOR: I suppose students will use them the most.

How, why, and which students are areas that need probing.

STUDENT: In what ways?

Good probing question.

PROFESSOR: Oh, some students will avoid instructors with low ratings.

Does phrase gossip piece suggest the professor's true attitude toward the

The report will be a great gossip piece.

STUDENT: You don't seem to take the report very seriously.

PROFESSOR: Well (pause), yes and no.

STUDENT: Does your feeling stem from your poor rating this year?

PROFESSOR: I'm not in a popularity contest! Such evaluations give some students a golden opportunity to knife an instructor.

STUDENT: You mean you think some students were out to get you?

PROFESSOR: Yes, in a couple of cases. Just a few low ratings can lower the whole scale.

STUDENT: How can we correct this in future instructor evaluations?

PROFESSOR: I really don't know unless you would evaluate only large classes. There is no way to determine student motives.

STUDENT: Do you have other suggestions for next year?

PROFESSOR: No, not really. Perhaps more control over evaluation committeemen—(cut off).

STUDENT: Well, thank you for your time and suggestions, Professor Smith, and thank you again for allowing us to evaluate your class.

---

evaluation program? What is it?

Mirror question. Question is to the point but very dangerous if rapport is not strong.

Means what? Is the pause significant?

Very questionable probe. The professor might have become angry and terminated the interview. Should have probed into the feeling expressed by "yes—no."

Does this reveal an attitude toward all instructor evaluations? If so, he might not be happy no matter what changes were made.

Mirror question. Interviewer should be careful not to seem impertinent.

Is this a procedural complaint? Perhaps the student should have done more probing earlier.

Open-ended question. Interviewer might have explained the procedures further and also the means used to prevent a few students from biasing the scale.

What does large classes mean?

Probing question.

Response is cut short by the student. Answer seemed to have good potential.

Unwise to cut off the professor in the midst of an answer, especially if it might have contained valuable information. The student might have suggested what would be done with the information gained from such interviews.

VIII

RHETORICAL CRITICISM

The Anatomy of Critical Discourse

Lawrence W. Rosenfield

In the portion of his article reproduced here, Lawrence W. Rosenfield, professor of communication at Hunter College, presents variations of four variables which are of importance to the critic of communication: source or creator of the message, message, context or environment, and critic. As you read Rosenfield's explanation of these variables, their interrelationships, and their importance, keep contemporary communicative events in mind and how you might criticize them.

If we schematize an instance of public communication encountered by the critic, we intuitively recognize four gross variables: the source(s) or creator(s) of the message, the message itself, the context or environment in which the message is received (including both the receivers and the social "landscape" which spawns the message), and the critic himself (who, especially in the study of public address of the past, is in a sense a unique receiver). For the sake of convenience, let us label the variables "S" (source), "M" (message), "E" (environment), and "C" (critic). Obviously, in a total interpretation of the communicative act all four variables are relevant. But equally obvious from past critical practice, such all-encompassing analysis will be rare if not impossible for the single critic. Perhaps the two most thoroughly examined messages in the English language are Shakespeare's *Hamlet* and Lincoln's *Gettysburg Address*; the very fact that criticism of these two is not yet exhausted attests to the impracticality of completely enveloping one verbal act with another. We are therefore forced to recognize that critics will have to concentrate on some permutation of the four variables as a means of making their critical tasks manageable.

Reprinted with permission from Speech Monographs, XXXV (March, 1968), pp. 50–69. Only a portion of the article is reprinted here.

For the rhetorical critic the one indispensable factor is M, the message. Exclusive concern for S, the source, is the biographer's business; study of E, the environment, is the historian's; studies relating speakers to audience apart from the substance of the message (as in explorations of the role of status or leadership in public affairs) are performed mainly by sociologists. The rhetorical critic sees the entire communicative transaction as somehow "suspended" from the language of the message under examination. For the rhetorical critic the verbal utterance constitutes a kind of linguistic architecture which supports and gives form to the total rhetorical act. In this belief the critic differs from the historian and sociologist, who may choose to treat the verbal factors as mere artifacts of the event. The rhetorical critic not only fastens his observation to M; he does so in the conviction that the message is fundamental to an appreciation of the entire event.[1]

The critic therefore occupies himself with some combination of variables which focus on the message: S-M, M-E, M-C, S-M-E, S-M-C, or M-E-C. These are combinations which constitute genuine critical options. It is not the critic's task to inspect these variables in isolation; neither is it sufficient for him to report that they all converged in a particular instance of public discourse.

Consider first the nature of the M-C focus, which represents an unashamedly introspectionist stance. This focus seeks to gauge the critic's personal response to the aesthetic object.[2] The critic who directs his attention to the M-C relationship will conceive of himself as a kind of sensitive instrument, and his analysis will be comprised primarily of reports of his own reactions to the work apart from any impact the work may have had on any particular "public." In this vein, Anatole France remarked that the good critic:

> . . . is he who relates the adventures of his soul among masterpieces. . . . The truth is that one never gets out of oneself.[3]

[1] Cf. T. Cleavenger, Jr., "Research Opportunities in Speech," *Introduction to the Field of Speech*, ed. R. F. Reid (Chicago, 1965), pp. 222–224.

[2] Cf. Heyl, p. 170; R. Wellek and A. Warren, *The Theory of Literature* (New York, 1949); W. Embler, "The Language of Criticism," *Etc.*, XXII (September 1965), 261–277. This cryptic account is obviously not the entire story. The critic is not privileged simply to report his pleasure and/or pain on confronting the discourse. He is in some manner obligated to explain how and why the work *justifies* his particular response. It is also important to note that contemporary literary critics who claim to focus entirely on the work itself are in fact often employing the M-C paradigm; their failure to recognize the implications of their critical orientation results occasionally in rather odd exigeses.

[3] Anatole France, "The Literary Life," *The Book of Modern Criticism*, trans. and ed. L. Lewisohn (New York, 1919), pp. 1–3. Cf. I. A. Richards, *Principles of Literary Criticism* (New York, 1925), pp. 5–24.

The M-C orientation grounds its validation on the premise that communication is essentially a unique event, a private transaction between message and receiver which can never be known to a third party. The critic is simply one more receiver of the message, albeit more sensitive than the typical, untrained receiver. If one accepts the notion that critical interpretation is so uniquely personal, it then follows that no interpretation can expect to be more than a justification of the critic's own state of mind as he responds to the aesthetic object.

And if communication is inherently a private matter, then one's faith in the critic's explication and overall taste constitutes at least as important a means of support for the verdicts offered as do the critic's stated reasons for his evaluation. Hence . . . we need to trust his sensitivity as much as we need to be persuaded by his analysis of the prose. It is even possible to imagine that the primary function served by reasons submitted by an observer with the M-C focus is to demonstrate to a reader the observer's competence as a critic, to "exhibit his credentials," to make authoritative judgments.[4] Such a conception of M-C analysis may account for the propensity of prominent critics to set forth lists of their favorite books, or of the best plays or speeches of all time. Having achieved eminence, they need no longer justify their selections, but are able to telescope or even abort their arguments in favor of short explications of why a particular book, play, or novel pleased them personally.

The next three foci are related to each other in their denial of an introspectionist critical stance and their advocacy of greater detachment. The S-M focus concentrates on understanding discourse as an expression of its creator. Most often the critic attempts to trace out the creative process by which the speaker externalized and structured the feelings, thoughts, and experiences contained within himself. The relation of source to message has prompted two general schools of criticism. One (which actually concentrates on the S → M relationship) seeks to account for the rhetor's behavior as a function of the factors which influenced him: his education, the books he read, the persons who inspired him, and the like.[5] The other variation of the S-M focus, S ← M, is best typified by neo-Freudian critics who treat the aesthetic event as symptomatic of the artist's personal life and psychodynamics. The critic, in other words, acts as a kind

---

[4] Embler, p. 265; M. Beardsley, *Aesthetics: Problems in the Philosophy of Criticism* (New York, 1958), pp. 129–134.

[5] Cf. M. H. Abrams, *The Mirror and the Lamp: Romantic Tradition* (New York, 1953), pp. 21–25; J. Thorp, "The Aesthetics of Textual Criticism," *PMLA*, LXXX (December 1965), 465–482; L. D. Reid, "Gladstone's Training as a Speaker," *The Quarterly Journal of Speech*, XL (December 1954), 373–380; L. Crocker, "The Rhetorical Training of Henry Ward Beecher," *The Quarterly Journal of Speech*, XIX (February 1933), 18–24.

of lay psychoanalyst, using the message as a key to understanding and evaluating the creator of the message.[6]

The M-E focus also incorporates two divergent streams of critical practice. In the one instance (M ← E), "environment" is interpreted broadly (as by historians and literary critics) to encompass the age and the civilization in which the message originated. The historian of ideas attempts to set the historical background in which particular works or clusters of works were produced, showing how the messages are themselves a reflection of their era. This emphasis finds its rationale in the assumption that to the extent that an aesthetic event can be considered typical of its age it will provide valuable insight into the intellectual and social trends of that age.[7] Another direction which critics with an M-E focus have chosen to follow, one which has gained its widest acceptance among critics with a bent toward social science, interprets "environment" in a more prescribed sense, referring to the specific audience which the message had. These critics consider the "functional" relationship which existed between the discourse and its receivers. They seek to determine how the receivers used the messages presented to them as stimuli. The assumption underlying the functional (M → E) approach to the M-E relationship is that, whatever the speaker's intention, the auditor attends to a speech in a manner which fulfills his own personal needs. An old man may attend a July 4th celebration, not prepared to be persuaded or inspired to increased patriotism, but simply because the ceremonial oratory reminds him of the speeches he heard on similar occasions in his youth. Similarly, the daily newspaper may function for some readers as a means by which they maintain an intimate contact with their favorite celebrities. For such readers, news of a Hollywood scandal is as welcome as a letter from home. In cases such as these, the M-E critic might concern himself with determining expectations of

[6] Cf. H. D. Duncan, Communication and Social Order (New York, 1962), pp. 3–16; M. Maloney, "Clarence Darrow," in A History and Criticism of American Public Address, ed. M. K. Hochmuth, III (New York, 1955), 262–312; H. M. Ruitenbeek (ed.), Psychoanalysis and Literature (New York, 1964); N. Kiell (ed.), Psychological Studies of Famous Americans (New York, 1964); W. S. Scott, Five Approaches of Literary Criticism (New York, 1962), pp. 69–73; R. L. Bushman, "On the Uses of Psychology: Conflict and Conciliation in Benjamin Franklin," History and Theory, V (#3, 1966), 225–240.

[7] For example, V. L. Parrington, Main Currents in American Thought (New York, 1927), 3 vols.; R. T. Oliver, History of Public Address in America (Boston, 1965); M. Meyers, The Jacksonian Persuasion (New York, 1960); A. O. Lovejoy, The Great Chain of Being (Cambridge, Mass., 1936); D. M. Chalmers, The Social and Political Ideas of the Muckrakers (New York, 1964); G. Orwell, "Boys' Weeklies," in A Collection of Essays by George Orwell (Garden City, N.Y., 1954), pp. 284–313; Scott, pp. 123–126.

the audience as well as the extent to which those expectations were fulfilled by the discourse.[8]

Although it is possible for a rhetorical critic to employ any of the three foci so far mentioned, the bulk of traditional speech criticisms has not explored dyadic relationships but the triadic formulations of S-M-E. Essentially, this "pragmatic" orientation treats the message as an effort at persuasion and ventures to assess the artistic skill of the speaker in achieving his persuasive goals with his audience.[9] The extensive use of the S-M-E framework can be justified if we accept the notion that public address is, literally, discourse addressed to a public by a speaker who is carrying on public business by his act of communication. Because the critic takes for granted the Janus-like quality of public address, revealing simultaneously the communicator and the social environment to which he seeks to adapt himself, the S-M-E critic emphasizes in his study the mediating nature of the message in moving (or failing to move) the audience toward the speaker's vision of how the demands of occasion ought to be met and resolved.[10]

The three foci—S-M, M-E and S-M-E—comprise a set because they share one quality which distinguishes them from the introspectionist reports of the M-C focus. This shared quality is a stress on objective, verifiable critical statements. By placing the spectator outside the critical equation, each method attempts to make of criticism a dispassionate report of what actually "is," a judicious, unbiased account of properties which inhere in the communicative event itself. In so doing they imply that the critic should strive to produce an analysis of the essential nature of the phenomenon apart from any idiosyncrasies in his personal responses.[11]

None of the three "impersonal" approaches so far mentioned can serve the ends of the introspectionist, and hence, none of the three finds encourages critical reasons employed mainly to establish the critic's own credentials as a sensitive observer. Instead, the critic who strives for a dis-

[8] Cf. Heyl, p. 169; D. Katz, "The Functional Approach to the Study of Attitudes," *Public Opinion Quarterly*, XXIV (Summer 1960), 163–204; J. K. Galbraith, *Economics and the Art of Controversy* (New York, 1955), pp. 3–31; L. W. Lichty, "The Real McCoys and It's (sic) Audience: A Functional Analysis," *Journal of Broadcasting*, IX (Spring 1965), 157–165; B. DeMott, "The Anatomy of Playboy," *Commentary*, XXIV (August 1962), 111–119.

[9] Abrams, pp. 16–21; W. N. Brigance, "What is a Successful Speech?" *The Quarterly Journal of Speech Education*, XI (April 1925), 272–277; Black, *Rhetorical Criticism*, pp. 36–58; Thonssen and Baird, pp. 448–461.

[10] D. C. Bryant, "Rhetoric: Its Scope and Function," *Quarterly Journal of Speech*, XXXIX (December 1953), 401–424.

[11] B. Harrison, "Some Uses of 'Good' in Criticism," *Mind*, LXIX (April 1960), 206; A. H. Hanney, "Symposium: Distinctive Features of Arguments Used in Criticism of the Arts," p. 169.

passionate and reliable report of the rhetorical act will find that the reasons he gives in support of his verdicts function primarily to call to the attention of others those characteristics of the original communication which merit their further contemplation. The method is similar to that of the football announcer who uses an instant replay camera. A team scores a touchdown, and seconds later the television commentator says, "As we play back the scoring play, notice the excellent footwork of the man with the ball." The listener-viewer is thus primed to observe for himself a feature of the event which the expert-commentator feels merits attention. The same ostensive function applies to the selection of reasons by the impersonal, rhetorical critic; his reasons do not report, nor do they simply support a conclusion— they call on the reader to observe for himself.

The last two foci available to the critic, S-M-C and M-E-C, reject the cleavage between introspection and impersonal functions of critical discourse. Justification for these two foci stems from the recognition of contemporary science that the very act of observation alters the event observed and so distorts the information one is able to obtain about the event. The distortions can never be overcome by more precise observations or measurements, but can only be acknowledged by specifying a degree of uncertainty and looseness in one's formulations.

As applied to the critical act, such a position holds that criticism is inevitably the product of the critic's encounter with the rhetorical event, that the locus of criticism is neither critic nor ontic event but the critic's intrusion upon the event. Such an intrusion may not directly influence the agents involved in the communication; we may wish to admit, for instance, that as he prepared his first inaugural address Thomas Jefferson probably did not significantly alter his behavior in conscious anticipation of twentieth-century rhetorical critics. But neither should we misconstrue the dilemma faced by the critic who would do more than resurrect the data of the past. His problem is less one of succumbing to personal bias than it is of taking and formulating precise measurements on the event under investigation.[12] Our final two foci suit the critic who has reconciled himself to the inevitable impossibility of making meticulously accurate statements

[12] A. G. Van Melsen, The Philosophy of Nature (New York, 1953), p. 226; L. Brillouin, Science and Information Theory (New York, 1962), p. 232; F. C. Frick, "Some Perceptual Problems from the Point of View of Information Theory," Psychology: A Study of a Science, II (New York, 1959), 77; J. Rothstein, "Information and Organization as the Language of the Operational Viewpoint," Philosophy of Science, XXIX (October 1962), 406–411; J. Ruesch, "The Observer and the Observed: Human Communication Theory," Toward a Unified Theory of Human Behavior, ed. R. R. Grinker (New York, 1956), pp. 36–54; M. Bunge, Causality: The Place of the Causal Principles in Modern Science (New York, 1963), pp. 348–349; P. Frank, Philosophy of Science (Englewood Cliffs, N.J., 1957), pp. 207–231; A. Moles, Information Theory and Esthetic Perception (London, 1958).

about the events he observes, who wishes instead the maximum fidelity possible within the limits imposed on his by the nature of perception and critical language. His framework for observation indexes neither the event *in vacuo* nor his own response to the event, but the relation which joins him to the rhetorical act.

The critic who adopts the S-M-C focus assumes that a speech will no more exist "out there" in some ontic world than does a symphony reside "in" a musical score or a drama "in" a manuscript.[13] Instead, he believes that we can discern an artistic intention in a work of art; and the aesthetic experience, be it to speech or symphony, is the experiencing and articula- tion of that artistic intention. Artistic intention is understood as the peculiar way in which the elements of the message cohere in the moment of confrontation with the observer-critic.

There are objective clues in the messages as to the meaning which will be actualized by the interaction of observer and thing observed. It becomes the critic's task to investigate that cooperation of elements and ratios in the message which give rise to the artistic meaning-as-experienced. In other words, speaker, speech, and observer momentarily coalesce as the elements of the rhetorical event unite to move toward some terminal condition. The critic's objective is to explicate that condition and the communication factors which contribute to or retard the transaction. The critic seeks to determine the nature of the demands made by the rhetorical event upon the beholder of the event. He is of course obligated to be alert to his own predilections as an instrument of observation, but his attention is focused outward upon artistic intention rather than inward as with introspection.[14]

The source enters into this equation because it is posited that the artist's intention(s) in creating the message may provide a key to under- standing the artistic intention embodied in the message. The critic assumes that the speaker, by virtue of his close connection with the message, is something of an authority on the event; that is, the speaker often possesses special knowledge about the speech which adds depth to the critic's own interpretation. Hence, a comparison of artist's intentions with artistic intentions may prove a valuable aid in centering interest on the decisive qualities of the work of art.

Consider, for example, John Kennedy's television address to the nation on the Cuban missile crisis in 1962: we might regard the policy enunciated on that occasion as rhetorically inappropriate. However, if we knew that

[13] Cf. A. G. Pleydell Pearce, "On the Limits and Use of 'Aesthetic Criteria,' " *Philosophical Quarterly*, IX (January 1959), 29–30.

[14] Cf. E. Berne, *Transactional Analysis in Psychotherapy* (New York, 1961); Ch. Perelman and L. Olbrechts-Tyteca, "Act and Person in Argument," *Philosophy, Rhet- oric and Argumentation*, ed. M. Natanson and H. W. Johnstone, Jr. (University Park, Pa., 1965), pp. 102–125.

Kennedy was privy to secret information indicating that the Russians would withdraw their missiles if we took a strong line, this knowledge would help clarify the forceful posture Kennedy chose to adopt and possibly alter our critical assessment of the artistic intention evidenced in the discourse. We might now see the message as primarily a warning to Russia rather than as a report to the nation.

Notice that the S-M-C focus does not obligate the critic to accept the artist's personal conception of his creation; the purpose of uncovering Kennedy's purpose in speaking is not to whitewash Kennedy but to understand the parameters within which his verbal behavior operated. We might still find that Kennedy chose an inappropriate rhetorical strategy. Or we might conclude that Kennedy was himself not fully aware of the real significance of the discourse he produced. Our search does not necessarily tell us anything about the ultimate character of the message for the artist's intentions are ancillary to our primary concern, which is artistic intention.[15] We seek to discover the speaker's point of view; the symptoms of artistic and intellectual choice thereby revealed may lend depth to our apprehension of the design of the message.

Like its S-M-C counterpart, M-E-C rests on a conception of the critical act as an encounter. And it also recognizes the importance of artistic intention, of the demands made by the work upon the recipient of the message. The primary distinction between the two frameworks is the emphasis that the M-E-C focus places on the rhetorical event as an act, a performance which is only fully consummated in that instant when message is apprehended by receiver. Just as a play is not theatre until it is being performed for an audience, so the rhetorical artifact (such as a speech manuscript) becomes discourse only when it is experienced in a public "arena" or forum.[16] The rhetorical critic therefore necessarily fastens his attention not on the moment of creation but upon the moment of reception, realizing all the while that by his intrusion he is mutilating the confrontation of message and audience.

---

[15] Cf. R. Kuhns, "Criticism and the Problem of Intention," *Journal of Philosophy*, LVII (January 7, 1960), 5–23; S. Gendin, "The Artist's Intentions," *Journal of Aesthetics and Art Criticism*, XXIII (Winter 1964), 193–196; E. Roma III, "The Scope of the Intentional Fallacy," *The Monist*, L (April 1966), 250–266.

[16] M. O. Sillars, "Rhetoric as Act," *The Quarterly Journal of Speech*, L (October 1964), 277–284; H. Arendt, *Between Past and Future* (Cleveland, 1963), pp. 143–172; S. K. Langer, *Problems of Art* (New York, 1957), pp. 1–58; S. C. Petter, *The Work of Art* (Bloomington, Indiana, 1955); M. Natanson, "The Claims of Immediacy," in *Philosophy, Rhetoric and Argumentation*, ed. M. Natanson and H. W. Johnstone, Jr. (University Park, Pa., 1965), pp. 10–19; W. Sacksteder, "Elements of the Dramatic Model," *Diogenes*, LII (Winter 1965), 26–54; P. K. Tompkins, "Rhetorical Criticism: Wrong Medium?" *Central States Speech Journal*, XIII (Winter 1962), 90–95.

One consequence of this shift in emphasis is that the M-E-C critic is less concerned with the speaker's influence on the message than is the S-M-C critic. As the French symbolist Paul Valéry has contended:

> There is no true meaning to a text—no author's authority. Whatever he may have wanted to say, he has written what he has written. Once published, a text is like an apparatus that anyone may use as he will and according to his ability: it is not certain that the one who constructed it can use it better than another.[17]

Although there are important differences between symbolist literary criticism and the traits of M-E-C rhetorical analysis, they are in this respect similar.

Whereas the S-M-C focus concentrates on the aesthetic demands of the event upon an auditor (the potential interpretation which any sensitive recipient might make), M-E-C considers the aesthetic demands made by the event upon the auditors (the likely meaning of the message for a given public). To illustrate, the S-M-C critic would seek to assess the enduring worth of medieval morality plays, taking account of their original cast as inculcators of religious faith; the M-E-C critic, on the other hand, would distinguish between the meaning of a morality play for its original audience and its meaning (perhaps totally different) for a typical contemporary auditor. Constrained thus by context, the M-E-C critical focus is more particularized, with the critic acting as a kind of surrogate for the audience he projects into the communicative event.[18]

Nor is the M-E-C frame simply a variation of the more objective message-environment focus. M-E analysis offers a predominantly historical interpretation of "how it was" when the public confronted the speech. The M-E critic seeks to understand the nature of the transaction as it in fact originally occurred. He may even go so far as to evaluate the speech using the rhetorical norms of the period and society in which the speech was delivered. He has a tendency to work back from the context to the message as he engages in assessment.

In contrast, an historistic interpretation might be more appropriate to an M-E-C focus. The M-E-C critic would try to go beyond understanding the message as the original participants understood it and attempt also to understand it better than they did.[19] He would seek to determine "how it

---

[17] Paul Valery, *The Art of Poetry* (New York, 1958), p. 152.

[18] The problem of a possible shift in meaning for morality plays is raised in F. J. Coleman, "A Phenomenology of Aesthetic Reasoning," *Journal of Aesthetics and Art Criticism*, XXV (Winter 1966), 197–203.

[19] The distinction has been alluded to by R. L. Scott in his review of E. Black's *Rhetorical Criticism* (*The Quarterly Journal of Speech*, LI (October 1965), 336). Scott

would have to be" if one were to derive the fullest significance implicit in the rhetorical event. It is likely that an observer with an M-E-C orientation would follow a course of action in which he first analyzed the message, then projected from his analysis a description of the public for whom the message would be most appealing, and finally compared the bulk of the actual audience with his composite ideal auditor.

It is suggestive for us to bear in mind that both frames originate in the physicist's efforts to accommodate his formulations to the inherent uncertainty of the cosmos. We might therefore expect S-M-C and M-E-C critics to be somewhat more heedful of the limitations of their investigations and less inclined to construct a brief for a particular interpretation. They might be somewhat more prone to employ their reasons as part of a calculation of the validity of particular rhetorical concepts. Their primary objective would then be to modify rhetorical theory to accommodate their clinical observations rather than to establish their own credibility or assist readers to derive increased satisfaction from the rhetorical event under discussion. We would expect critics with this cast to be more tentative in their reason-giving, since their comments would operate less in an advocative capacity and more as a special kind of scientific discourse. Such a critic might very well take the view that if his reasons are sound those to whom he reports will *probably* attach greater value to his judgments. He would therefore seek to determine the strength of his reasons.

Let us conclude consideration of alternative critical foci by reminding ourselves that the focus adopted by the critic determines what kind of questions he will find most interesting. Insofar as the critic chooses to relate the rhetorical event to its creator he will ask: How did the message come to be? Is it symptomatic of the speaker? What are the capacities of the rhetor as an artist? How does the man shape the message? The critic who regards the message as the initial stimulus in his formula will ask himself a complementary set of questions: How does the message reflect its context? What evidence is there that the message as created was appropriate to the climate in which it was employed? How did the message serve to influence its environment? How and why does my experience with this message differ from the likely experiences of other recipients? These are all legitimate questions for a critic to ask; but his decision as to which shall occupy his attention will be at least partially influenced by the focus he has chosen to adopt. . . .

---

suggests that one may go to extremes in appealing to the immediate audience as a decisive measure of rhetorical merit, that in such instances the critic may be more concerned with direct measures of audience response such as shift-of-opinion ballots than with the speech itself. An extremist M-E critic might indeed tend to fit such a description, but an M-E-C critic would be unlikely to find himself in such a posture.

Which of the four variables—source, message, environment, critic—cannot be left out of a critical formula? Why not? Which of the many variations of critical emphasis offered by Rosenfield do you prefer? If the President of the United States were scheduled to speak on your campus, and you were assigned the task of criticizing his speech, which formula would you choose—M-C, S-M, M-E, S-M-E, S-M-C, or M-E-C?

The Criticism of Rhetoric and the Act of Communication

James T. Boulton

James T. Boulton, professor of English literature at Nottingham University, suggests that the critic study an act of communication by asking "Why does who say what to whom and with what effect?" Above all, he wants the critic to consider communication in all its complexities and ramifications. Boulton illustrates his ideas with English history; you might profit more by keeping a contemporary American event in mind as you read this chapter.

An extract from a recent essay by Raymond Williams provides a valuable starting point:

> One of the marks of a conservative society is that it regards style as an absolute. A style of writing and speaking is judged as a question of manners, and appreciation of this style as a question of taste. In important literary criticism, since the time of Coleridge, this merely conventional judgment has in fact been set aside: style is not an abstract quality, but is inseparable from the substance of the ideas and feelings expressed. In modern communication theory, a new dimension has been added: style is also inseparable from the precise relationship, whether explicit or assumed, between a writer or speaker and his expected reader or audience. This is never a mechanical relationship; the ordinary formula for communication—"who says what to whom with what effect?"— characteristically neglects the real sources of communication. A more adequate formula—would be "why does who say what to whom with what effect?" It is clear, also, that the precise relationship, in any act of communication, is not finally separable from the substantial ideas and

Reprinted with permission from Essays on Rhetorical Criticism (New York: Random House, Inc., 1968). *Only a portion of the original chapter is reprinted here.*

feelings. In almost all speech and writing, this substance includes, though often unconsciously, the real relationship, of the writer or speaker and other men.

It is remarkable how often, in literary criticism but especially in ephemeral commentary, the mechanical version of style as an abstract quality, supported of course by the unnoticed conventions and traditions of particular groups, is still in practice assumed. But when the writing or speaking in question is not literary, the assumption is almost universal. Style is regarded as a decoration, a merely tasteful or mannered addition to substance, even in politics, where the kind of experience being drawn on and the version of other men indicated by a particular way of talking to them, are not only substantial but are even crucial to the precise nature of a political act.[1]

In this statement Williams stresses the central and complex nature of the relationship that exists between a writer or speaker and his audience whenever an act of communication takes place. He rightly emphasizes that, whatever the subject or occasion of the discourse, criticism cannot properly function unless this relationship is explored. He might also have explicitly affirmed the importance of "situation," the context in which communication is established, of which both writer and audience are a part, and on which they exert influence. In the case of private correspondence the situation will be personal and intimate; on the other hand it may be public, as with Burke's speeches on Economical Reform or Conciliation with America, but created by specific events which called for equally specific action; or yet again, it may have the complexity of the political or religious controversies which gave rise, for example, to Paine's *Rights of Man* or Newman's *Apologia pro Vita Sua*. In these last instances the situation is fluid and, though having a recognizable dialectical center, is constantly being reshaped by the efforts of each participant. None of these categories is exclusive—clearly Burke's response to the parliamentary situation was not only to the words on the order paper but also to what previous speakers in the debate had made of them; Milton in his *Areopagitica* does not confine his attention to the licensing system but dilates on the broad issues of the nation's moral and political health. Nevertheless, in each case the situation is a decisive factor. Unless we explore it fully we cannot answer William's question, "why does who say what to whom?"

The final words in his question—"with what effect?"—form a relevant though a potentially hazardous criterion unless certain safeguards are defined. Hitler's speeches had massive effect; other demagogues have been highly successful in persuading their audiences to action of a more or less desirable kind; whereas several speeches by Fox or Burke, recognized by

---

[1] Raymond Williams, *History and Theory*, IV (1965), pp. 380-381.

posterity as masterly orations, were ineffectual. Defoe's *Shortest-Way with the Dissenters* produced, initially at any rate, the reverse of the effect aimed at. Indeed if Williams' question regarding "effect" is to prompt qualitative judgments and not merely description, it needs delicate handling. Perhaps we should be honest enough to state that effect is sometimes not measurable, that it may not be a mark of oratorical or literary excellence, and that in most cases it should be judged in the long term: what degree of permanent interest or pleasure has the discourse given to mankind, whether or not they were part of the original audience? By this measure we recognize the excellence of Burke's speeches and the shoddiness of Hitler's.

From what has been said so far it might appear superficially that the business of the rhetorical critic is exhausting but relatively straightforward: establish all the discoverable facts about the situation, audience and speaker or writer, and then decide "why does who say what to whom." If this were true then the historical or "extrinsic" critic might appear supreme, his timorous trust in verifiable facts justified. Certainly without the information he can supply, rhetorical criticism cannot function satisfactorily. For example, unless the original situation is thoroughly known, one can make the wrong assumptions about a writer's or speaker's purpose, misunderstand his tone of voice, misinterpret his allusions, or be ignorant of extrinsic circumstances which were of cardinal importance in shaping his discourse. Information which prevents such blunders is vital; it provides a foundation for the critical act; but it must not be confused with the superstructure to be built on it. Extrinsic criticism by itself is barren; in association with the intrinsic it is essential. The ideal critic—of rhetorical as of all literary discourse—must concern himself not only with the "facts" alluded to, but also with the orator's primary meaning and the subtle suggestiveness communicated by his tone; the patterns of thought and argument which sometimes reveal themselves in clearly definable ways but sometimes in a manner of which the speaker himself may have been only dimly aware; his idiom and imagery; his sense of the rhythm and sound of language; and with his understanding of the character—in the fullest sense—of his intended audience. This is, of course, merely to hint at the kind of approach that would seem normal to a critic of "literature"; only—as Williams remarks— where "the writing or speaking in question is not literary," but rather "political" or in some sense an "occasional" act of public communication, do these critical methods unaccountably seem to some to be out of place or irrelevant.

A single question will illustrate this general reluctance to grapple with the critical issues raised by publications which, in their day, were of vital consequence to their authors and public, and which remain of continuing interest. Wilkes' *North Briton* No. 45 is mentioned countless times in studies of the eighteenth century: how often has it been examined by a rhetorical critic? It surely is important to decide how far governmental reaction to the "No. 45" can be attributed to extrinsic reasons—fear of the power of the press, Wilkes' public "image," or a nervous administration—and how far the author's literary manner was responsible. The question has obvious significance for the historian, but the rhetorical critic must clearly be involved in resolving it. One approach open to him might be to compare Wilkes' paper with Defoe's *Legion's Memorial*. The work of experienced journalists and political writers, both pieces proclaim "the spirit of liberty"; both are addressed partly to Parliament, partly to the general public; both are threatening and defiant—"*Englishmen* are no more to be Slaves to *Parliaments*, than to a King" (Defoe) might be from either publication; both protest against the encroachment on "the ancient liberties of this kingdom"; and both achieved an effect that can in part be assessed. Yet there are differences between them, the examination of which would help to define the essential character of both publications. To select one point of similarity which also points to an important distinction, both pieces end with a quotation:

> WILKES: The Prerogative of the Crown is to exert the Constitutional powers entrusted to it in a way not of blind favour and partiality, but of wisdom and judgment. This is the spirit of our Constitution. The people, too, have their prerogative, and I hope the fine words of Dryden will be engraven on our hearts:
> *Freedom is the English subject's Prerogative.*
>
> DEFOE: Thus, Gentlemen, you have your Duty laid before you, which it is hoped you will think of; but if you continue to neglect it, you may expect to be treated according to the Resentments of an *injur'd Nation; for Englishmen* are no more to be Slaves to *Parliaments*, than to a King.
> *Our Name is Legion, and we are many.*

Both writers sought an impressive close which would be memorable, easily quoted by their supporters. Wilkes chose a high-sounding line relevant to his subject—though selecting it, oddly enough, from Dryden's "Poem Sacred to the Happy Memory of King Charles II" and, perhaps to avoid ambiguity, omitting Dryden's penultimate word, "sole"—whereas Defoe's choice was the familiar biblical sentence. The latter is the more effective, not only because it was better known, but also because it confirms the feeling given by the whole *Memorial* that this is no casual remonstrance; rather is it the voice of a mission undertaken in the name of the whole nation. As a result the well-known quotation is transformed from a cliché into a statement of menacing power. Wilkes, for his part, protests too stridently and volubly throughout his paper that he is the mouthpiece of the whole people; he makes overt threats; his anger is on the surface and superlatives abound; and he gives the impression of a man barely in control of his prose medium. The consequence is that the words from Dryden, expressed with the formality of verse and lacking the extreme intensity of Wilkes' own language, come as an anticlimax. They do not sustain the vehemence of the preceding paragraphs; they are not so finely phrased as to be inevitably remembered; indeed one suspects that they were the choice of a demagogue in search of dignity. But it is a false dignity.

Much more could be added about the famous *North Briton* if space allowed; all I have done is to begin to place it critically. However, some tentative conclusions can be suggested. While men of all cultural classes would undoubtedly read Wilkes out of a delight in scandal or in swingeing attacks on the Ministry, few outside the "mob" (to use Fielding's non-social term)[2] would be influenced by him. Stylistic analysis suggests that Wilkes fell foul of the government for extrinsic as much as intrinsic reasons; his was a bombastic rather than a fundamental threat; he was in fact a demagogue who was dangerous because of his appeal to men discontented from other causes.

If, then, rhetorical criticism is to be fully effective it must examine the nature of the act of communication in persuasive discourse, in all its complexity and ramifications. To achieve this end the skills of the literary critic must, ideally, be associated with those of the historian of politics, culture, and society, the philosopher, and the specialist in the particular field of a specific speech or writing. The scope for joint and fruitful endeavor is unlimited. There is, for example, a vast opportunity for collaborative inquiry into what might be called the "image" of George III. How much was it the result of the King's own maneuverings and how much of the political situation of which he was only a part? To what extent was it created by political writers, satirists, and orators: Wilkes, Junius, Pindar, or Burke? To what extent was Byron's attitude to George in "The Vision of Judgment" or Fonblanque's in the *Examiner* generally shared? Did such writers merely perpetuate the image which had been previously established? Answers to such questions would certainly affect our view of the writers mentioned; they would increase our understanding of the reign; and central to much of the inquiry would be the work of the rhetorical critic. Whenever men publicly communicate with their fellows in an effort to secure *persuasion*, whether by the spoken or written word, he should feel involved.

Newman's *Apologia* is a case in point. It seems fairly simple, in answer to Williams' question, "why does who say what . . . ?", to reply that Newman wished to justify his own course of action and to refute Kings-

---

[2] "It intends persons without virtue or sense, in all stations; and many of the highest rank are often meant by it" (*Tom Jones*).

ley's charges against him. It can be shown that for this purpose Newman produces a narrative of his spiritual and intellectual development; he gives evidence of the stages by which he accepted the superior claims of Roman Catholicism; and he undoubtedly tries to convince the reader of the propriety of his final choice. But to say this is certainly not to account for the contemporary or the permanent impact made by the *Apologia*. It is a persuasive work of a subtle kind; it requires all the skill of the rhetorical critic to assess it. He will not wholly succeed alone; the theologian and historian should also be involved, but primarily the challenge is his.

Though, for instance, Newman claimed that he wishes "simply to state facts," his tone at the outset is immensely important:

> It is not at all pleasant for me to be egotistical; nor to be criticized for being so. It is not pleasant to reveal to high and low, young and old, what has gone on within me from my early years. It is not pleasant to be giving to every shallow or flippant disputant the advantage over me of knowing my most private thoughts. . . .

At once the reader is induced to participate in the self-analysis of a man reluctantly compelled to publicize "the intercourse between [himself] and [his] Maker"; compelled to do so by Kingsley who "has no personal knowledge of [him] to set right his misconceptions," and whom Newman has never seen. The reader, then, is to obtain insights not available to Newman's adversary, and immediately an intimate relationship is established between writer and audience. Again, when Newman begins his account of the influences affecting him in his earlier years—ranging from Paine and the Gothic novelists to Scott and the Romantic poets—he is assuring his readers that there is common ground between them, that—initially at any rate—the *Apologia* will not cover territory completely foreign to them. But these ordinary and diverse experiences cumulatively prove to be part of the inescapable forces which direct Newman towards the decision taken on October 8, 1845. The inevitability of this development is his central theme; that it involves experiences shared with Newman's readers carries implications too plain to be missed. Associated with this theme are the numerous hints that Newman felt himself an agent under the direction of a ruling Providence; they not only dignify his career but also undermine the kind of criticism that impugned the honesty of his final decision; and cumulatively they win the reader's assent. To further strengthen this theme, Newman gives the impression of extreme urgency. He uses, for example, a variety of prose media—narrative, sermons, letters, quotations from pamphlets, or snatches of direct conversation—all, taken together, communicating the excitement of a mind recollecting significant evidence. The inference is that an unlimited reservoir of evidence existed, all of it bearing on the crucial decision. Then there is the vivid imagery suggesting action that was courageous, continuous, or urgent: Hurrell Froude was "a bold rider, as on horseback, so also in his speculations"; the trial to be made of the English Church was "like proving cannon"; or the frequently recurring sea imagery, instinct with unceasing and irresistible energy. Such qualities reinforce on the level of suggestion or "submerged" persuasiveness what is urged on the surface by logical argument: that Newman was right to reject a "paper system" in favor of a religion which "would work."

What is implied by this glance at the *Apologia* is that the rhetorical critic cannot remain satisfied with an analysis of purely formal or structural features; he must—if he is to account for other, less tangible but permanently affecting characteristics—examine what might be called the "imaginative logic" of a work. Rhetorical discourse, operating on two main levels —the logical and argumentative, and the imaginative or emotive—provides for the listener or reader an experience that is highly complex and not solely intellectual. Newman does not merely refute Kingsley or prove through argument the rightness of his secession; by means touched on earlier, he communicates a wide range of emotions, imaginative insights, a sense of personal dignity and honesty, and a sympathetic personality, all of which are combined with intellectual penetration to form a total rhetorical experience.

What are the differences between extrinsic and intrinsic criticism? What are the dangers of trying to determine effect of communication or rhetoric? In the question "Why does who say what to whom and with what effect?" how do you discover the why, who, what, whom, and effect? Which is the most important? In studying a typical instance of communication, how much attention should be given to the "emotional" versus the "logical" aspects of the message?

PART TWO MESSAGES

I

NATIONAL
GOALS/PROBLEMS

Election Eve Address

Edmund S. Muskie

Senator Edmund Muskie of Maine delivered this speech over national television on November 2, 1970—election eve. Seldom had
off-year elections been so important to both political parties, and
the campaign had been loud and mud-filled. The use of television
spot commercials—many of which had been suggestive and outright
vicious—had become a national issue. Senator Muskie's speech pur-
posely was designed to contrast sharply with last-minute Republican
efforts—mainly a bare fisted attack by President Nixon. Note the
calm, dispassionate, and conversational quality of the speech, its
appeal to American middle class voters, and its attempt to reduce
the impact of the law and order issue.

[1] Fellow Americans, I am speaking from Cape Elizabeth, Maine,
to discuss with you the election campaign which is coming to a close. In
the heat of our campaigns, we have all become accustomed to a little
anger and exaggeration. Yet, on the whole, our political process has served
us well, presenting for your judgment a range of answers to the country's
problems, and a choice between men who seek the honor of public
service. That is our system. It has worked for almost two hundred years,
longer than any other political system in the world. And it still works.
But in these elections of 1970, something has gone wrong. There has
been name-calling and deception of almost unprecedented volume. Honor-
able men have been slandered. Faithful servants of the country have had
their motives questioned and their patriotism doubted. This attack is not
simply the overzealousness of a few local leaders. It has been led, inspired,
and guided from the highest offices in the land. The danger from this
assault is not that a few more Democrats might be defeated; the country
can survive that. The true danger is that the American people will have
been deprived of that public debate—that opportunity for fair judgment
—which is the heartbeat of the democratic process. And that is something
the country cannot afford.

Reprinted with permission from Senator Edmund S. Muskie.

[2] Let me try to bring some clarity to this deliberate confusion. Let me begin with those issues of law and order, of violence and unrest, which have pervaded the rhetoric of this campaign. I believe that any person who violates the law should be apprehended, prosecuted, and punished, if found guilty. So does every candidate for office of both parties. And nearly all Americans agree. I believe everyone has a right to feel secure on the streets of his city and in the buildings where he works or studies. So does every candidate for office, of both parties. And nearly all Americans agree. Therefore, there is no issue of law and order or of violence. There is only a problem. There is no disagreement about what we want. There are only different approaches to getting it. And the harsh and uncomfortable fact is that no one, in either party, has the final answer. For four years, a conservative Republican has been Governor of California. Yet there is no more law and order in California today than when he took office. President Nixon, like President Johnson before him, has taken a firm stand. A Democratic Congress has passed sweeping legislation. Yet America is no more orderly or lawful nor its streets more safe than was the case two years ago, or four, or six. We must deal with symptoms, strive to prevent crime, halt violence, and punish the wrongdoer. But we must also look for the deeper causes in the structure of our society. If one of your loved ones is sick, you do not think it is soft or undisciplined of a doctor to try and discover the agents of illness. But you would soon discard a doctor who thought it enough to stand by the bed and righteously curse the disease. Yet there are those who seek to turn our common distress to partisan advantage; not by offering better solutions, but with empty threat and malicious slander. They imply that Democratic candidates for high office in Texas and California, in Illinois and Tennessee, in Utah and Maryland, and *among my New England neighbors* from Vermont and Connecticut, men who have courageously pursued their convictions *in the service of the Republic in war and in peace*, that these men actually favor violence and champion the wrongdoer. That is a lie. And the American people know it is a lie.

[3] And what are we to think when men in positions of public trust openly declare that the party of Franklin Roosevelt and Harry Truman, which led us out of depression and to victory over international barbarism; the party of John Kennedy, who was slain in the service of the country he inspired; the party of Lyndon Johnson, who withstood the fury of countless demonstrations in order to pursue a course he believed in; the party of Robert Kennedy, murdered on the eve of his greatest triumphs; how dare they tell us that this party is less devoted or less courageous in maintaining American principles and values than are they themselves. This is nonsense. And we all know it is nonsense.

[4] And what contempt they must have for the decency and sense of the American people to talk to them that way and to *think they can make them believe.* There is not time tonight to analyze and expose the torrent of falsehood and insinuation which has flooded this unfortunate campaign. There is a *parallel* in the campaigns of the early fifties, when the turbulent difficulties of the post war world were attributed to the softness and lack of patriotism of a few, including some of our most respected leaders such as General George Marshall. It was the same technique. These attacks are dangerous in a more important sense for they keep us from dealing with our problems. Names and threats will not end the shame of ghettos and racial injustice, restore a degraded environment, or end a long and bloody war. Slogans and television commercials will not bring the working man that assurance of a constantly rising standard of life which was his only a few years ago and which has been cruelly snatched away.

[5] *No administration can be expected to solve the difficulties of America in two* years. But we can *fairly ask two things:* that a start be made, and that the nation be instilled with a sense of forward movement, of high purpose. This has not been done. Let us look, for example, at the effort to halt inflation. We all agree that inflation must be arrested. This administration has decided it could keep prices down by withdrawing money from the economy. Now I do not think they will ever control inflation this way. But even if their policy was sound, the money had to come from someone. And who did *they pick to pay?* It was the *working man,* the consumer, the *middle class American.* For example, high interest rates are a part of this policy. Yet they do not damage the banks which collect them. They hardly touch the very wealthy who can deduct interest payments from their taxes. Rather, they strike at every consumer who must pay exorbitant charges on his new car or house. And they can cripple the small businessman. Their policy against inflation also requires that unemployment go up. Again, it is the working man who pays the price. In other fields the story is the same. They have cut back on health and education for the *many* while *expanding subsidies* and *special favors for a few.* They call upon you, the working majority of Americans, to support them while they oppose your interests. They really *believe* that if they can make you *afraid enough* or angry enough, you can be tricked into voting against yourself. It is all part of the same contempt, and tomorrow *you can show them the mistake they have made.*

[6] Our difficulties as a nation are *immense, confused and changing.* But our history shows, and I think most of you suspect, that if we are ever to restore progress it will be under the *leadership of the Democratic party.* Not that we are smarter or more expert, but we *respect the people.* We *believe* in the people. And indeed we must, for we are of the people.

[7] Today the air of my native Maine was touched with winter, and

hunters filled the woods. I have spent my life in this state, which is both part of our oldest traditions and a place of wild and almost untouched forests. It is rugged country, cold in the winters, but it is a good place to live. There are friends, and there are also places to be alone, places where a man can walk all day, and fish, and see nothing but woods and water. We in Maine share many of the problems of America, and, I am sure, others are coming to us. But we have had no riots or bombings, and speakers are not kept from talking. This is not because I am Senator or because the Governor is a Democrat. Partly, of course, it is because we are a small state with no huge cities, but partly it is because the people here have a *sense of place.* They are *part of a community* with common concerns and problems and hopes for the future. We cannot make America small. But we can work to restore a sense of shared purpose, and of great enterprise. We can bring back the belief, not only in a better and more noble future, but in our own power to make it so.

[8] Our country is *wounded* and *confused,* but it is charged with greatness and with the possibility of greatness. We cannot realize that possibility if we are afraid, or if we consume our energies in hostility and accusation. We must maintain justice, but we must also believe in ourselves and each other, and we must get about the work of the future.

[9] There are only two kinds of politics. They are not radical and reactionary or conservative and liberal. Or even Democratic and Republican. There are only the politics of fear and the politics of trust. One says: "You are encircled by monstrous dangers. Give us power over your freedom so we may protect you." The other says: "The world is a baffling and hazardous place, but it can be shaped to the will of men." Ordinarily that division is not between parties, but between men and ideas. But this year the leaders of the Republican party have intentionally made that line a party line. They have confronted you with exactly that choice. Thus, in voting for the Democratic party tomorrow, you cast your vote for trust, not just in leaders or policies, but for trust in your fellow citizens, in the ancient traditions of this home for freedom, and most of all, trust in yourself.

On the Banks of the Wabash

Bill Campbell

Bill Campbell delivered this speech as a freshman at Purdue University in May, 1966. The topic of water pollution is a growing national problem. The chief form of supporting material in this speech is the use of specific instances, showing where the problem exists and how a solution has been achieved. Notice the use of proximity and familiarity as interest-gaining devices in the introduction to the speech. If you were going to improve this speech, what revisions would you suggest? How might you update it?

[1] When Paul Dresser wrote "On the Banks of the Wabash, Far Away," I am reasonably sure that he was not talking about that sluggish, stagnant river that today confronts citizens of Peru, Logansport, Terre Haute, and Lafayette, Indiana. If he was speaking of today's Wabash River, he correctly entitled his song, for here is one river whose banks most people would prefer to stay far away from.

[2] The Wabash River has become one more dumping area for industry, one more sacrifice to the dollar sign, one more proud waterway plagued with water pollution.

[3] Today, the names that once denoted crystal-clear mountain brooks, meandering low-land streams, great rolling rivers, huge fresh-water lakes and salt-water bays, are only more entries in a ledger of national disgrace.

[4] Let us examine a few of these names. The Potomac River—an aquatic history tour that passes such places as Arlington, Washington, and Mount Vernon. Today, if one visits Mount Vernon he will find a sign posted at the water's edge, just below George Washington's home. It reads "Do Not Come into Contact with the Polluted Water."

[5] Then there is Lake Tahoe, one of the three clearest bodies of water in the world. Presently, Tahoe is threatened with silt and sewage that will turn its crystalline waters a murky green. Things haven't reached

Reprinted with permission from Bill Campbell.

the critical stage yet. As one local citizen proudly boasts, "You can still see a beer can, thirty or forty feet down."

[6] Consider also Chesapeake Bay, where oyster production has fallen off from fifteen million to one and a half million bushels per year because of water pollution. The oysters are still there, but they are now judged "unfit for human consumption." Then there's the Hudson River, which receives all the waste that a slovenly society can pour into it, before it gets to New York City, which gives it similar abuse. Senator Robert Kennedy has said that if you fall into the Hudson River, you don't drown—you decay. Just how dangerous the Hudson is was demonstrated only last year when a group of small children found a watermelon floating downstream at 125th street. They took it home, washed it, ate it, and contracted typhoid fever.

[7] The once proud Mississippi River is today called "the colon of mid-America." I could also cite examples of the Detroit River, Lakes Erie and Michigan, the Missouri River, the Delaware River, and Niagara Falls. The list is virtually endless, and includes every major water system in the United States today.

[8] From this deluge of pollution comes the following results: water shortages, with actually unsafe water being drunk in many areas; disease breeding in, and being spread by our water system; the death of fish and wildlife; and the destruction of many valuable recreational areas.

[9] There are, of course, antipollution laws with fines and penalties, but local authorities have so far succumbed to the pressure of industry. Industry has, in fact, been most uncooperative in the problem of water pollution. As one official complained, "They won't even tell us how much of what they are dumping into the river." If the local authorities can't stop water pollution, it would seem that they could at least effectively treat the water that they use, but this is not the case. Multistage water treatment plants, the kind absolutely necessary with today's level of pollution, are expensive to build and maintain, and they don't bring in one additional cent of profit. In fact, they are of more benefit to the next town down river. The federal government has a law but it is restricted, as you might expect, to interstate pollution, and so far has proved to be slow and confusing.

[10] What is needed is federal regulation that would enable the government to take action on any waterway, interstate or intrastate. The long, legal preliminaries must be done away with, and polluters must be prosecuted quickly, especially the ones who now regard their waste as a trade secret.

[11] It is possible to control water pollution. This has been shown several times, most notably by the Kimberly-Clark Corporation, which built a huge pulp-and-paper mill in Northern California. One of the state's

specifications was that young salmon be able to swim in the same water into which Kimberly-Clark was to dump their waste. Young salmon are notoriously susceptible to water pollution, and pulp-and-paper mills are notorious polluters, but a special two million dollar water treatment plant was built in conjunction with the mill, and today, Kimberly-Clark and the salmon industry are the best of friends.

[12] The fight against water pollution was begun by individuals, such as Dr. David Blaushild of Shaker Heights, Ohio, who was enraged over the pollution of Lake Erie, and took out ads in the Cleveland papers to tell the citizens so. Today, people in higher places, including President Johnson, are becoming more interested in the problem. A new agency, the Federal Water Pollution Control Administration, has been authorized, but it is still in an advisory position, for the legislation it is to oversee has yet to be passed. What yet has to be done is the persuasion of Congressmen now in the grips of industry that water pollution, with its disease, being spread by our waterways, its destruction of our fish and wildlife, and its desecration of a national heritage, must stop.

The Day Before Christmas

Jack Rogers

Jack Rogers delivered this speech as a student at the University of Nebraska in 1953. The issue is very much with us in the 1970's; only the date of delivery needs changing. As you read this speech, note the manner in which suspense is built before the problem is stated; the vivid detail of the introductory illustration; the way in which statistics are brought to life in the analysis of the problem; and the emotional appeal of the peroration in which Rogers returns to his opening illustration.

[1] It was the morning of December the 24th, 1952. The day before Christmas. Outside the courthouse the lawn was hidden by a thick coverlet of snow. The branches of the trees were heavy and white. Somewhere down the hall from the courtroom where I was sitting, a radio was sending forth the voices of singers, telling of a "Silent Night, Holy Night," reminding us that this evening we would commemorate the birth of Christ, who taught us of peace on earth, and good will toward men.

[2] It would be a family night. Parents and children would gather in spacious living rooms and cozy parlors, drawn closer together by the warmth of the Holy Season; singing hymns, giving gifts, and rejoicing in the Savior's birth.

[3] But now it was morning. I was sitting on a hard, straight-backed chair, and there were five other people in the big, bare room. The woman who was sitting near the center of the room was wearing a Christmasy red dress, but it was completely incongruous with the drab atmosphere of the court. The judge listened quietly as the woman told of her nervousness and loss of weight. In a few moments, the plaintiff's sister followed her to the stand and answered a few simple questions. The lawyer then dropped his papers into his briefcase and walked across the courtroom and into the hall. The two women followed, the woman in the red dress dabbing at her eyes with a much wrinkled handkerchief she held clutched in her hand.

Reprinted with permission from Jack Rogers.

[4] There was no sound but the voices of the carolers as they finished the last verse of "Silent Night." And there was no movement except that of the judge's hand as he signed the decree.

[5] What had happened? Nothing very unusual. A woman had received a divorce. A family had been separated. It happens every day, even the day before Christmas, that special day when a family wishes to be together.

[6] The morning paper the day after the trial gave the names of the parties in the action. The names don't matter, but some other things are significant. The couple was married in 1930. They have one 14-year-old boy. And a union which had lasted for 22 years was broken in about 3 minutes. I asked the court reporter after the trial approximately how long it had taken. With a note of admiration in his voice he told me, "They hardly ever take more than five minutes, but that lawyer really runs them through. He couldn't have taken more than three." I was startled to realize that a partnership which was supposed to last for life, had been terminated while a choir was singing three verses of a Christmas hymn. And for one 14-year-old boy, "Silent Night" would mean much less this Christmas.

[7] Fifty-two years ago, when our grandparents were driving a horse and buggy, one out of every twelve marriages ended in divorce. In 1945, when our older brothers and sisters were coming back from World War II to begin building a new life, one out of five of their friends' homes was breaking up. In 1950, a generation which had harnessed the power of the atom was unable to prevent one marriage in every three from being a failure. The morning paper on December the 25th, 1952, listed five marriage licenses and three divorce decrees granted the day before Christmas.

[8] What's disturbing about such a high divorce rate? Nothing! Nothing, if you don't count the ruined lives of the eight million couples whose marriages have failed in the last ten years. Nothing, if you can forget the 300,000 children, every year, who find themselves with only half a home. Nothing, if you can overlook the fact that we are allowing the basic unit of society, the family, to be destroyed.

[9] What is society doing about this situation? Don't we have laws to stop the breakup of our families, and the breakdown of society? We have laws, but the sorry truth is that poor laws have made divorce easy.

[10] Grounds for divorce vary from state to state, but in nearly all states there is the catch-all of extreme cruelty, usually mental, which may mean, and has meant in actual cases, anything from one party's using vile language to eating crackers in bed.

[11] If the state in which a person lives is too particular about grounds or has too long a waiting period before divorce, things are made easier for him by the more lax laws of another state. You must live two

years in Nebraska before you can get a divorce. It's three months in Florida. In Nevada, it's six weeks.

[12] Divorce law is still based on the archaic principle that one party is completely wrong and the other completely right. The two are forced to fight it out in court to prove which is which. Or, if one party chooses not to contest the action, the divorce can be granted, as in the case I saw tried, with one party not even being represented. There is no provision of law which requires two people who have lived together and shared everything, even to meet each other face to face after one decides that he or she doesn't want the marriage to go on.

[13] That's the law. Because people are human, they let their emotions get in the way of their common sense. Many feel that whenever there is marital trouble, divorce is the only answer. And the law doesn't help them. But these people must be helped.

What then can we do?

[14] I'm not an all-wise sage. I can't give a perfect answer to the problem of divorce. I can only tell you those beliefs which I have formed by reading, by observing, and by talking with a lawyer, a judge, a clergyman, and others who have been in some way close to divorce.

[15] I could phrase my beliefs in abstractions and platitudes and possibly offend no one in this room, regardless of their views. But I would rather state my real beliefs, specifically, and rely on the fairmindedness of all of you to weigh and consider them carefully.

[16] To protect people against themselves, we must make the laws so strict that divorce is almost impossible. In a case of adultery, in which one party was actually living outside the marriage contract, a divorce could be granted. Remarriage would be possible only for the injured party. In no case would a third marriage be permitted. For those couples who no longer wished to live together, but whose circumstances were not exceptional, there would be legal separation.

[17] For such a law to be effective, it must be uniform nationally, for the family is a basic unit, not of an individual state, but of society as a whole. It must be dealt with in Florida and Nevada, the same as it is in New York or Nebraska.

[18] The fundamental concept of the legal action to be taken must be revised. The American Bar Association has proposed to change the judgment from one of where the guilt lies to what is best for the family, and hence, society. The petition would no longer read, "John Doe versus Jane Doe," but "In the interest of the Doe family." A private consultation with the judge and investigation by trained social workers would be held to try to get at the basic source of the difficulty. Welfare counseling to help with economic problems would be a part of the plan. In this way, the chances of reconciliation would be much greater. If two people were

hopelessly mismatched, the court could part their social ties and try to help them adjust to society in their new role of living separately.

[19] All of these things will help, but they alone cannot do the job, for they attack the problem after the trouble arises; the important work must be done before the marriage is begun.

[20] Is it too much to require of people who are going to be married that they see their minister and a trained marriage counselor before taking a step so full of meaning to themselves and to society?

[21] I didn't personally know the woman in the Christmasy dress who sat across the courtroom from me, on December 24th, last year. But I can well imagine how she, and the defendant, her husband, must have looked in a far different setting. In a small chapel, fresh with the fragrance of flowers just cut, the rustle of new satin and lace, and two peoples' faces flushed with happiness, as they repeat after the minister the familiar lines: ". . . for better, for worse, for richer, for poorer, in sickness and in health, till death do us part."

We must think and pray, before these vows are taken.

[22] If we realize our obligations to ourselves and to society; if we are forewarned of the dangers of carelessness; if we know what marriage really means; then, ". . . what God hath joined together," no man will put asunder.

[23] Not today, nor tomorrow, nor the day before Christmas.

II

THE NEWS MEDIA

Television News Media

Spiro T. Agnew

Vice President Spiro T. Agnew delivered this speech to the Midwest Regional Republican Committee on November 13, 1969, in Des Moines, Iowa. It was his maiden broadside in a series of attacks on the news media—television in particular. The Vice President offered a wide variety of evidence to prove his case against the television networks. Note particularly his use of comparison. Many listeners claimed the Vice President threatened censorship or control of television. What are the grounds for this charge?

[1] I want to discuss the importance of the television medium to the American people. No nation depends more on the intelligent judgment of its citizens. No medium has a more profound influence over public opinion. Nowhere in our system are there fewer checks on vast power. So, nowhere should there be more conscientious responsibility exercised than by the news media. The question is, Are we demanding enough of our television news presentations? And are the men of this medium demanding enough of themselves?

[2] Monday night, a week ago, President Nixon delivered the most important address of his administration, one of the most important of our decade. His subject was Vietnam. His hope was to rally the American people to see the conflict through to a lasting and just peace in the Pacific. For 32 minutes, he reasoned with a nation that has suffered almost a third of a million casualties in the longest war in its history.

[3] When the President completed his address—an address, incidentally, that he spent weeks in the preparation of—his words and policies were subjected to instant analysis and querulous criticism. The audience of 70 million Americans gathered to hear the President of the United States was inherited by a small band of network commentators and self-appointed analysts, the majority of whom expressed in one way or another their hostility of what he had to say. It was obvious that their minds were

Reprinted with permission from Vice President Spiro T. Agnew.

made up in advance. Those who recall the fumbling and groping that followed President Johnson's dramatic disclosure of his intention not to seek another term have seen these men in a genuine state of nonpreparedness. This was not it.

[4] One commentator twice contradicted the President's statement about the exchange of correspondence with Ho Chi Minh. Another challenged the President's abilities as a politician. A third asserted that the President was following the Pentagon line. Others, by the expression on their faces, the tone of their questions and the sarcasm of their responses, made clear their sharp disapproval.

[5] To guarantee in advance that the President's plea for national unity would be challenged, one network trotted out Averell Harriman for the occasion. Throughout the President's address, he waited in the wings. When the President concluded, Mr. Harriman recited perfectly. He attacked the Thieu Government as unrepresentative; he criticized the President's speech for various deficiencies; he twice issued a call to the Senate Foreign Relations Committee to debate Vietnam once again; he stated his belief that the Vietcong or North Vietnamese did not really want a military take-over of South Vietnam; and he told a little anecdote about a very, very responsible fellow he had met in the Vietnamese delegation. All in all, Mr. Harriman offered a broad range of gratuitous advice challenging and contradicting the policies outlined by the President of the United States. Where the President had issued a call for unity, Mr. Harriman was encouraging the country not to listen to him.

[6] A word about Mr. Harriman. For 10 months he was America's chief negotiator at the Paris peace talks—a period in which the United States swapped some of the greatest military concessions in the history of warfare for an enemy agreement on the shape of the bargaining table. Like Coleridge's Ancient Mariner, Mr. Harriman seems to be under some heavy compulsion to justify his failure to anyone who will listen. And the networks have shown themselves willing to give him all the air time he desires.

[7] Now every American has a right to disagree with the President of the United States and to express publicly that disagreement. But the President of the United States has a right to communicate directly with the people who elected him, and the people of this country have the right to make up their own minds and form their own opinions about a Presidential address without having a President's words and thoughts characterized through the prejudices of hostile critics before they can even be digested.

[8] When Winston Churchill rallied public opinion to stay the course against Hitler's Germany, he didn't have to contend with a gaggle

of commentators raising doubts about whether he was reading public opinion right, or whether Britain had the stamina to see the war through.

[9] When President Kennedy rallied the nation in the Cuban missile crisis, his address to the people was not chewed over by a roundtable of critics who disparaged the course of action he'd asked America to follow.

[10] The purpose of my remarks tonight is to focus your attention on this little group of men who not only enjoy a right of instant rebuttal to every Presidential address, but, more importantly, wield a free hand in selecting, presenting and interpreting the great issues in our nation.

[11] First, let's define that power. At least 40 million Americans every night, it's estimated, watch the network news. Seven million of them view ABC, the remainder being divided between NBC and CBS.

[12] According to Harris polls and other studies, for millions of Americans the networks are the sole source of national and world news. In Will Rogers' observation, what you knew was what you read in the newspaper. Today for growing millions of Americans, it's what they see and hear on their television sets.

[13] Now how is this network news determined? A small group of men, numbering perhaps no more than a dozen anchormen, commentators and executive producers, settle upon the 20 minutes or so of film and commentary that's to reach the public. This selection is made from the 90 to 180 minutes that may be available. Their powers of choice are broad. They decide what 40 to 50 million Americans will learn of the day's events in the nation and in the world.

[14] We cannot measure this power and influence by the traditional democratic standards, for these men can create national issues overnight. They can make or break by their coverage and commentary a moratorium on the war. They can elevate men from obscurity to national prominence within a week. They can reward some politicians with national exposure and ignore others.

[15] For millions of Americans the network reporter who covers a continuing issue—like the ABM or civil rights—becomes, in effect, the presiding judge in a national trial by jury.

[16] It must be recognized that the networks have made important contributions to the national knowledge—through news, documentaries and specials. They have often used their power constructively and creatively to awaken the public conscience to critical problems. The networks made hunger and black lung disease national issues overnight. The TV networks have done what no other medium could have done in terms of dramatizing the horrors of war. The networks have tackled our most difficult social problems with a directness and an immediacy that's the gift of their medium. They focus the nation's attention on its environmental abuses—on pollution in the Great Lakes and the threatened ecology of the Everglades.

[17] But it was also the networks that elevated Stokely Carmichael and George Lincoln Rockwell from obscurity to national prominence.

[18] Nor is their power confined to the substantive. A raised eyebrow, an inflection of the voice, a caustic remark dropped in the middle of a broadcast can raise doubts in a million minds about the veracity of a public official or the wisdom of a Government policy.

[19] One Federal Communications Commissioner considers the powers of the networks equal to that of local, state and Federal Governments all combined. Certainly it represents a concentration of power over American public opinion unknown in history.

[20] Now what do Americans know of the men who wield this power? Of the men who produce and direct the network news, the nation knows practically nothing. Of the commentators, most Americans know little other than that they reflect an urban and assured presence seemingly well-informed on every important matter. We do know that to a man these commentators and producers live and work in the geographical and intellectual confines of Washington, D.C., or New York City, the latter of which James Reston terms the most unrepresentative community in the entire United States. Both communities bask in their own provincialism, their own parochialism.

[21] We can deduce that these men read the same newspapers. They draw their political and social views from the same sources. Worse, they talk constantly to one another, thereby providing artificial reinforcement to their shared viewpoints.

[22] Do they allow their biases to influence the selection and presentation of the news? David Brinkley states objectivity is impossible to normal human behavior. Rather, he says, "we should strive for fairness." Another anchorman on a network news show contends, and I quote: "You can't expunge all your private convictions just because you sit in a seat like this and a camera starts to stare at you. I think your program has to reflect what your basic feelings are. I'll plead guilty to that."

[23] Less than a week before the 1968 election, this same commentator charged that President Nixon's campaign commitments were no more durable than campaign balloons. He claimed that, were it not for the fear of hostile reaction, Richard Nixon would be giving into, and I quote him exactly, "his natural instinct to smash the enemy with a club or go after him with a meat axe." Had this slander been made by one political candidate about another, it would have been dismissed by most commentators as a partisan attack. But this attack emanated from the privileged sanctuary of a network studio and therefore had the apparent dignity of an objective statement.

[24] The American people would rightly not tolerate this concentration of power in Government. Is it not fair and relevant to question its concentration in the hands of a tiny, enclosed fraternity of privileged men elected by no one and enjoying a monopoly sanctioned and licensed by Government?

[25] The views of the majority of this fraternity do not—and I repeat, not—represent the views of America. That is why such a great gulf existed between how the nation received the President's address and how the networks reviewed it.

[26] Not only did the country receive the President's address more warmly than the networks, but so also did the Congress of the United States.

[27] Yesterday, the President was notified that 300 individual Congressmen and 50 Senators of both parties had endorsed his efforts for peace.

[28] As with other American institutions, perhaps it is time that the networks were made more responsive to the views of the nation and more responsible to the people they serve. Now I want to make myself perfectly clear. I'm not asking for Government censorship or any other kind of censorship. I'm asking whether a form of censorship already exists when the news that 40 million Americans receive each night is determined by a handful of men responsible only to their corporate employers and is filtered through a handful of commentators who admit to their own set of biases.

[29] The questions I'm raising here tonight should have been raised by others long ago. They should have been raised by those Americans who have traditionally considered the preservation of freedom of speech and freedom of the press their special provinces of responsibility. They should have been raised by those Americans who share the view of the late Justice Learned Hand that right conclusions are more likely to be gathered out of a multitude of tongues than through any kind of authoritative selection.

[30] Advocates for the networks have claimed a First Amendment right to the same unlimited freedoms held by the great newspapers of America. But the situations are not identical. Where The New York Times reaches 800,000 people, NBC reaches 20 times that number on its evening news. Nor can the tremendous impact of seeing television film and hearing commentary be compared with reading the printed page.

[31] A decade ago, before the network news acquired such dominance over public opinion, Walter Lippman spoke to the issue. He said there's an essential and radical difference between television and printing. The three or four competing television stations control virtually all that can be received over the air by ordinary television sets. But besides the mass circulation dailies, there are weeklies, monthlies, out-of-town newspapers and books. If a man doesn't like his newspaper, he can read another from out of town or wait for a weekly news magazine. It's not ideal, but it's infinitely better than the situation in television. There if a man doesn't like what the networks are showing, all he can do is turn them off and

listen to a phonograph. Networks he stated which are few in number have a virtual monopoly of a whole media of communications.

The newspapers of mass circulation have no monopoly on the medium of print.

[32] Now a virtual monopoly of a whole medium of communication is not something that democratic people should blindly ignore. And we are not going to cut off our television sets and listen to the phonograph just because the airways belong to the networks. They don't. They belong to the people.

[33] As Justice Byron White wrote in his landmark opinion six months ago, it's the right of the viewers and listeners, not the right of the broadcasters, which is paramount.

[34] Now it's argued that this power presents no danger in the hands of those who have used it responsibly. But, as to whether or not the networks have abused the power they enjoy, let us call as our first witness former Vice President Humphrey and the city of Chicago. According to Theodore White, television's intercutting of the film from the streets of Chicago with the current proceedings on the floor of the convention created the most striking and false political picture of 1968—the nomination of a man for the American Presidency by the brutality and violence of merciless police.

[35] If we are to believe a recent report of the House of Representatives Commerce Committee, then television's presentation of the violence in the streets worked an injustice on the reputation of the Chicago police. According to the committee findings, one network in particular presented, and I quote, "a one-sided picture which in large measure exonerates the demonstrators and protesters." Film of provocations of police that was available never saw the light of day while the film of a police response which the protesters provoked was shown to millions.

[36] Another network showed virtually the same scene of violence from three separate angles without making clear it was the same scene. And, while the full report is reticent in drawing conclusions, it is not a document to inspire confidence in the fairness of the network news.

[37] Our knowledge of the impact of network news on the national mind is far from complete, but some early returns are available. Again, we have enough information to raise serious questions about its effect on a democratic society. Several years ago Fred Friendly, one of the pioneers of network news, wrote that its missing ingredients were conviction, controversy and a point of view. The networks have compensated with a vengeance.

[38] And in the networks' endless pursuit of controversy, we should ask: What is the end value—to enlighten or to profit? What is the end result—to inform or to confuse? How does the ongoing exploration for

more action, more excitement, more drama serve our national search for internal peace and stability?

[39] Gresham's Law seems to be operating in the network news. Bad news drives out good news. The irrational is more controversial than the rational. Concurrence can no longer compete with dissent.

[40] One minute of Eldridge Cleaver is worth 10 minutes of Roy Wilkins. The labor crisis settled at the negotiating table is nothing compared to the confrontation that results in a strike—or better yet, violence along the picket lines.

[41] Normality has become the nemesis of the network news. Now the upshot of all this controversy is that a narrow and distorted picture of America often emerges from the televised news.

[42] A single, dramatic piece of the mosaic becomes in the mind of millions the entire picture. The American who relies upon television for his news might conclude that the majority of American students are embittered radicals. That the majority of Black Americans feel no regard for their country. That violence and lawlessness are the rule rather than the exception on the American campus. We know that none of these conclusions is true.

[43] Perhaps the place to start looking for a credibility gap is not in the offices of the Government in Washington but in the studios of the networks in New York.

[44] Television may have destroyed the old stereotypes, but has it not created new ones in their places? What has this passionate pursuit of controversy done to the politics of progress through local compromise essential to the functioning of a democratic society? The members of Congress or the Senate who follow their principles and philosophy quietly in a spirit of compromise are unknown to many Americans, while the loudest and most extreme dissenters on every issue are known to every man in the street. How many marches and demonstrations would we have if the marchers did not know that the ever-faithful TV cameras would be there to record their antics for the next news show?

[45] We've heard demands that Senators and Congressmen and judges make known all their financial connections so that the public will know who and what influences their decisions and their votes. Strong arguments can be made for that view. But when a single commentator or producer, night after night, determines for millions of people how much of each side of a great issue they are going to see and hear, should he not first disclose his personal views on the issue as well?

[46] In this search for excitement and controversy, has more than equal time gone to the minority of Americans who specialize in attacking the United States—its institutions and its citizens?

[47] Tonight I've raised questions. I've made no attempt to suggest

the answers. The answers must come from the media men. They are challenged to turn their critical powers on themselves, to direct their energy, their talent and their conviction toward improving the quality and objectivity of news presentation. They are challenged to structure their own civic ethics to relate their feelings with the great responsibilities they hold.

[48] And the people of America are challenged, too, challenged to press for responsible news presentations. The people can let the networks know that they want their news straight and objective. The people can register their complaints on bias through mail to the networks and phone calls to local stations. This is one case where the people must defend themselves; where the citizen, not the Government, must be the reformer; where the consumer can be the most effective crusader.

[49] By way of conclusion, let me say that every elected leader in the United States depends on these men of the media. Whether what I've said to you tonight will be heard and seen at all by the nation is not my decision, it's not your decision, it's their decision.

[50] In tomorrow's edition of *The Des Moines Register*, you'll be able to read a news story detailing what I've said tonight. Editorial comment will be reserved for the editorial page where it belongs. Should not the same wall of separation exist between news and comment on the nation's networks?

[51] Now, my friends, we'd never trust such power, as I've described, over public opinion in the hands of an elected Government. It's time we questioned it in the hands of a small and unelected elite. The great networks have dominated America's airwaves for decades. The people are entitled to a full accounting of their stewardship.

Reply to the Vice President

Frank Stanton

Frank Stanton, president of CBS, delivered this reply to Vice President Agnew's Des Moines speech (and subsequent ones) on November 25, 1969, in New York to the International Radio and Television Society. Note the careful organization of Stanton's speech —essentially a point-by-point rebuttal of the Vice President. What are the strengths and weaknesses of this reply? Has Stanton exaggerated the threat of control or censorship of the television networks?

[1] I am not here to defend broadcast journalism as being beyond all criticism. No one could have worked as long as I have in radio and television without realizing that we are far from perfect in carrying out our enormous responsibilities in broadcast journalism. We have never been satisfied with the job we are doing. We are not satisfied now. It is our continuing hope and our continuing effort to do better. We are concerned with what the press says of us. We are concerned with what our audiences write us. We are concerned with what our affiliates tell us. We do strive for objectivity, although it is not always easy to achieve. While freedom of the press is meaningless without the freedom to be wrong, we do try to be right. And I think that in the vast majority of cases we have succeeded.

[2] Let me turn now to the events of the past few weeks that have commanded the attention of many of us. On November 3, the President of the United States delivered a much-publicized and eagerly-awaited speech presenting the Administration's position and plans on the war in Vietnam. That war has been the subject of one of the longest and most fervent public debates in all American history. Good, conscionable and dedicated men and women, from all sections of our society, have earnest and deeply-felt differences as to its meaning, its conduct and its prospects. Fundamental questions of rightness and wrongness have disturbed our people as no other issue has in this century.

Reprinted with permission from Frank Stanton.

[3] The President spoke for 32 minutes on all four nationwide television networks, four nationwide radio networks and scores of independent stations. Some 88 million people heard his words as they were conveyed, uninterrupted and in a place and under conditions of his own choosing. Following the President's address, each of the television networks provided comments by professionals analyzing the content of the speech. Participating were experienced newsmen, most of whom have performed similar functions for many years following the live broadcast of special events of outstanding significance. Since the participants were different on the four television networks, the comments of none of them were heard by the same huge audience that heard the President. One of the networks added to the expertise by presenting the views of a distinguished diplomat and public servant, who had held high posts in nine Presidential terms, of both parties, prior to the present Administration. Another presented the comments of two United States senators, who took divergent views of the policy advocated in the speech.

[4] In all this, nothing unprecedented had happened. Such comments have customarily been offered after most significant Presidential appearances—State of the Union, Inaugurals, United Nations addresses, press conferences, for example. And they usually have been more than mere bland recapitulations, which would serve little purpose, and have frequently called attention to emphases, omissions, unexpected matters of substance, long anticipated attitudes, changes of views, methods of advocacy or any other aspect of the speech. Such comments have been offered by enterprising news organizations since the dawn of the modern press and continued into the era of radio and television.

[5] Following the President's speech and following the relatively brief comments made directly after it, the White House was deluged with telegrams and letters approving the President's speech, the White House reported, by an overwhelming margin. Two days later, the Gallup Survey reported that nearly four out of every five of those who heard it, approved the President's speech and the course that it advocated with regard to Vietnam.

[6] Ten days after the President's speech, the second highest official in the Administration launched an attack on the television networks on the grounds that critical comments on government policy as enunciated in a Presidential address might unduly influence the American people—even though, following such comments, the President received a 77 per cent vote of confidence from those who heard him on the issue discussed.

[7] The Vice President also censured television network news for covering events and personalities that are jolting to many of us but that nevertheless document the kind of polarized society—not just here but throughout the world, whether or not there is television and whether it is controlled or free—in which, for better or worse, we are living. It is not a consensus society. It is a questioning, searching society—unsure, groping, running to extremes, abrasive, often violent even in its reactions to the violence of others. Students and faculties are challenging time-honored traditions in the universities. Young clergy are challenging ancient practices and even dogma of the churches. Labor union members are challenging their leaderships. Scientists, artists, businessmen, politicians—all are drawn into the fray. Frequently, because everyone is clamoring for attention, views are set forth in extreme terms.

[8] As we do not propose to leave unreported the voice of the Vice President, we cannot in good conscience leave unreported any other significant voice or happening—whether or not it supports government policy, whether or not it conforms with our own views, whether or not it disturbs the persuasions of any political party or bloc. But no healthy society and no governing authorities worth their salt have to fear the reporting of dissenting or even of hostile voices. What a healthy society and a self-respecting government do have to fear—at the price of their vitality if not of their life—is the suppression of such reporting.

[9] To strengthen the delusion that, as a news medium, television is plunging the nation into collapse and can be deterred only by suppressing criticisms and by either withholding bad news or contriving a formula to balance it with good news, the Vice President's speech was replete with misinformation, inaccuracies and contradictions. To deal adequately with all of these on this occasion would take us through the afternoon, but let me note some of them by way of example, then move on to consider with you the context of the Vice President's speech so far as the actions and statements of other Administration officials are concerned and, finally, make some observations on the significance of this unhappy affair.

[10] The Vice President began his indictment of November 13 with a monstrous contradiction. He asserted flatly that "no medium has a more profound influence over public opinion" than television. And yet he also claimed that the views of America have been very little affected by this "profound influence," when he said, "The views of the majority of this fraternity [i.e., television network news executives and editors] do not—and I repeat, not—represent the views of America." The Vice President can't have it both ways. If the views of the American people show "a great gulf" between how a speech is received by them and how it is treated in a broadcast, obviously the treatment of it has no material effect upon their opinion. Even the premise of the Vice President's claim is proved wrong by the Gallup findings already mentioned.

[11] The Vice President objected to the subjection of the words and policies of the President to "instant analysis and querulous criticism." The analysis, whatever its merits or failings, was hardly instant. Highly-

informed speculation about the content of the speech had gone on for days and even weeks. Copies were made available at least two hours in advance of the analysis, allowing at least as much time as most morning newspapers had before press time. If a professional reporter could not arrive at some meaningful observations under those circumstances, we would question his competence.

[12] The Vice President took care—and the point should not be lost on us—to remind us that television is "enjoying a monopoly sanctioned and licensed by government." A monopoly, by any definition I know, is the exclusive control of a product or a service by a single entity. Television news is broadcast in this country by four networks, all with different and fiercely competitive managements, producers, editors and reporters, involving hundreds of strongly individualistic people; by a dozen station groups, initiating and producing their own news broadcasts, and by hundreds of stations, producing their own news broadcasts wholly independent and distinct from those of any network they may otherwise be associated with. Moreover, it is estimated that, on the average day, 65 per cent more hours of viewing are devoted to station-originated news broadcasts than to network news broadcasts. In addition, there are 6,717 radio stations in this country—the overwhelming majority without network affiliations.

[13] All this hardly represents monopolistic control.

[14] The Vice President seems to maintain that the First Amendment applies differently to NBC from what it does to *The New York Times*, because NBC's audience is bigger and because television has more impact. That the First Amendment is quantitative in its applicability is a chilling innovation from a responsible officer of the government. By this standard the *Times* is less entitled to the protection of the Bill of Rights than the *Des Moines Register*, with a third of its circulation, and twice as entitled to it as the *New York Daily News*, which has double the *Times'* circulation. As for the impact of the television medium, it may be true that combined picture and voice give television a special force. On the other hand, print can be reread, it can be lingered over, it can be spread around, it can be consulted over and over again. Should, on the grounds of these advantages over television, the print media have less freedom?

[15] The Vice President asked how many "marches and demonstrations" there would be if there were no television cameras. An elementary textbook in American history might prove instructive. There was no television to record the demonstrations against slavery; demonstrations against the Mexican War; demonstrations against the Civil War draft; demonstrations for women's suffrage; demonstrations for Prohibition; demonstrations for the League of Nations; demonstrations against child labor; demonstra-

tions for economic justice. That there would be no disturbing news except for television is a canard as dangerous as it is egregious.

[16] Now let us turn to the crucial issue raised by the Vice President.

[17] Despite his complaints about how and what we report, the Vice President protested that he was not advocating censorship. He found it necessary, a week later, to repeat his protest three times in one paragraph. It is far more shocking to me that the utterances of the second-ranking official of the United States government require such repeated assurances that he had in mind no violation of the Constitution than it is comforting to have them at all. Of course, neither he nor any of his associates are advocating censorship—which would never survive judicial scrutiny. But it does not take overt censorship to cripple the free flow of ideas. Was the Vice President's reference to television's being "sanctioned and licensed by government" accidental and devoid of any point or meaning? Was his suggestion that "it is time that the networks were *made* [emphasis added] more responsive to the views of the nation" merely sloppy semantics and devoid of any notion of coercion?

[18] Perhaps the Vice President, in his November 20 follow-up speech, was not referring to government action, but only to a dialogue among citizens when he said, "When they [network commentators and some gentlemen of *The New York Times*] go beyond fair comment and criticism they will be called upon to defend their statements and their positions just as we must defend ours. And when their criticism becomes excessive or unjust, we shall invite them down from their ivory towers to enjoy the rough and tumble of public debate." Who, in those sentences, will do the calling of these men to defend themselves, and before whom? Who is the "we" who shall do the inviting? And by whose standards will the limits of "fair comment" and "just criticism" be judged and who shall be the judges?

[19] The ominous character of the Vice President's attack derives directly from the fact that it is made upon the journalism of a medium licensed by the government of which he is a high ranking officer. This is a new relationship in government-press relations. From George Washington on, every Administration has had disputes with the press, but the First Amendment assured the press that such disputes were between equals, with the press beyond the reach of the government. This all-important fact of the licensing power of life and death over the broadcast press brings an implicit threat to a government official's attacks on it, whether or not that is the intention and whether or not the official says he is speaking only as an individual.

[20] But the Vice President does not seem to have been walking a lonely path in the direction of suppression and harassment:

[21] Herbert G. Klein, the Administration's Director of Communi-

cations, revealed that, on November 4, the day after the President's speech, calls from White House offices went out to broadcast stations asking whether editorials were planned and, in Mr. Klein's words, "to ask them what they would say in their editorial comment."

[22] In Washington, D.C., television stations were called by a member of the Subversive Activities Control Board, Paul O'Neil, requesting logs of news coverage devoted to support of and in opposition to the Administration's Vietnam policy. His wife, a Dade County official of the Republican Party, who specified her husband's official position, made the same request of Miami, Florida stations.

[23] On November 4, the Chairman of the Federal Communications Commission, in unprecedented calls to the presidents of the three broadcasting companies with national television networks, requested transcripts of the remarks of their reporters and others who had commented on the speech, saying there had been complaints, the source of which he failed to specify—although, two weeks later on sober second thought, he seemed to reverse himself when he signed a letter adopted by the full Commission finding that the comments made on the networks after the speech in no way violated its doctrine of fairness.

[24] A special counsel to the President, Clark R. Mollenhoff, said that the speech "was developed by various White House aides," adding "if you are asking me, 'does it reflect the Administration's views,' the evidence is abundant that it does." The President's press secretary, Ronald Ziegler, agreed that a White House special assistant, Patrick J. Buchanan, "very well could have contributed some thoughts to the speech."

[25] Mr. Klein, on November 16, said, "I think that any time any industry—and I include newspapers very thoroughly in this, as well as the networks—if you look at the problems you have today and you fail to continue to examine them, you do invite the government to come in."

[26] In my judgment, the whole tone, the whole content and the whole pattern of this government intrusion into the substance and methods of the broadcast press, and indeed of all journalism, have the gravest implications. Because a Federally-licensed medium is involved, no more serious episode has occurred in government-press relationships since the dark days in the fumbling infancy of this republic when the ill-fated Alien and Sedition Acts forbade criticism of the government and its policies on pain of exile or imprisonment.

[27] In the context of this intimidation, self-serving disavowals of censorship, no matter how often repeated, are meaningless. Reprisals no less damaging to the media and no less dangerous to our fundamental freedoms than censorship are readily available to the government—economic, legal and psychological. Nor is their actual employment necessary to achieve their ends; to have them dangling like swords over the media

can do harm even more irreparable than overt action. If these threats implicit in the developments of the past week are not openly recognized, unequivocally denounced and firmly resisted, freedom of communications in this country will suffer a setback that will not be limited to checking the freedom of television or to barring critical comment on government policy. It will precipitate an erosion that will inevitably destroy the most powerful safeguard of a free society—free, unhampered and unharassed news media.

[28] This does not have to be the resolute intention of any person or group, any party or government. We can wander unintentionally—all of us—into a lethal trap if we let our dissatisfaction with the handling of specific issues, which are variable, and of events, which are transitory, compromise our adherence to basic principles, which are constant. No permanent freedom was ever wisely exchanged for temporary popularity, for the popularity can be gone with changing political or social cycles and the freedom can be regained, if ever, only at fearful cost. And this is a truth that should be remembered by those who demand that our freedoms be preserved only when they agree with us, but who have been eager to restrict them whenever they disagree with us. You cannot side with restrictions or with bullying or with recriminations when they support your views and then oppose them when they differ, for they will rise up and haunt you long after your cause is lost or won.

[29] The issue here is simple. Dwight D. Eisenhower said, "I believe the United States is strong enough to expose to the world its differing viewpoints . . . ." His successor, John F. Kennedy, said, "The men who create power make an indispensable contribution to the nation's greatness, but the men who question power make a contribution just as indispensable."

[30] Criticism is an essential ingredient in that mix. It is central, not tangential, to a free society. It is always a free society's strength and often its salvation. Television itself is not and should not be immune to such criticism. As a matter of fact, it is the most criticized medium in the history of communications. Newspapers, magazines, academic groups, learned societies—who wouldn't dream of criticizing each other—criticize us every single day. Everyone has free access to what we do, and everyone sees us do it. We are *not* unaccountable. We are *not* clandestine. We have no end product that is not seen and judged by everyone. But such open criticism is a far cry from sharp reminders from high official quarters that we are licensed or that if we don't examine ourselves, we in common with other media "invite" the government to move in.

[31] The troubled pages of this century's history are writ dark with the death of liberty in those nations where the first fatal symptom of political decay was an effort to control the news media. Seldom has it been

called censorship. Seldom is the word used except in denials. Always it has been "guidelines" in the name of national unity. And we might well ponder the fate of the unhappy roll of nations that had no regard for their freedoms or took them for granted or held them lightly.

[32] As we meet here, 39 nations in the world have a controlled press or a press that wavers uncertainly between control and freedom. This melancholy statistic might well be borne in mind by those of our countrymen who, as the Vice President descends upon one part of the country to attack the journalists of another part, are moved by their temporary irritations to applaud their own ensnarement. In his speech of November 13, the Vice President turned to Learned Hand to support a proposition that would have been total anathema to the great judge. Let me, in conclusion, invoke Hand in more revealing words:

> Our democracy rests upon the assumption that, set free, the common man can manage his own fate; that errors will cancel each other by open discussion; that the interests of each when unguided from above, will not diverge too radically from the interests of all. . . .

[33] All thoughtful people must regard this as a critical period in the life of a free society and of the free communications without which it cannot exist.

The News Media and Campus Unrest

John R. Bittner

John R. Bittner—at the time Vice President of United Press International-Broadcasters of Indiana, news director of WAZY radio in Lafayette, Indiana, and a graduate student at Purdue University— delivered this speech on October 4, 1969, to the Indiana Speech Association meeting in Indianapolis. His aim was to explain the problems faced by news reporters during occurrences of campus unrest. The speech is essentially one large factual illustration from the speaker's own experience. Note how the illustration is used to explain each major point of the speech. What effect does this approach have on the credibility of the speaker? Is it practical only for a highly credible speaker?

[1] As you know, the year 1968–69 was one of the most serious ever experienced by this nation's colleges and universities dealing with campus unrest. In Indiana, Purdue University probably felt the greatest impact, where a total of 229 persons were taken into custody in one instance as the result of a so-called "mill-in" or "lounge-in" at the Purdue University Memorial Union. Other forms of campus unrest were felt at Indiana University, Indiana State University, and Ball State University as well as regional campuses of the four state universities and even into some of Indiana's smaller private colleges such as Wabash at Crawfordsville, DePauw University at Greencastle, Valparaiso, and so on. Nineteen sixty-nine has been called the year of campus unrest. As this unrest was undoubtedly one of the most frustrating experiences for college administrators, it was a year of equal frustration for members of the news profession who covered the unrest, and the media coverage of campus unrest has been criticized by many college administrators and the public.

[2] The predicament the press finds itself in was exemplified re-

Reprinted with permission from John R. Bittner.

cently in a letter to me from Dr. Morris B. Mitchell, Chancellor of the University of Denver. He said, "I realize that many accuse the press, radio, and television of overemphasizing the dramatic and failing to underline the relatively small percentage of total student bodies engaged in violent activities. On the other hand, I do not see how alert editors can play down news of this kind, just as I would ruefully admit that the driver who doesn't have an accident isn't likely to get his picture in the paper or his name on a radio station." The big problem for the press, according to Dr. Mitchell, is to struggle to find perspective within the framework of each story. He states, "Life isn't made any easier for them by the naïveté of most university officials and public relations departments in matters of such high intensity and emotional content. Add to this fact that today's students are very press conscious and have learned to make maximum use of press, radio, and television in dramatizing their cause, and you really have a tough situation." Those tough situations bring back memories of many experiences lived by this reporter, and I am sure by other reporters in the national news media. Covering campus unrest, contrary to some popular belief that it results only in going to campuses and shooting television pictures of students in confrontations with police or vice versa, is a very involved process—a process that involves responsibility and responsibility that has not always been realized or accepted by many members of the press.

[3] What I'd like to do this morning is to relate to you some of those, as Dr. Mitchell said, "tough situations" which the press finds itself in, in the coverage of campus unrest, and, for the purposes of example, I'll refer mostly to the troubles of Purdue University in the spring of 1969. The first major protest at the university occurred on April 21 over a 75 per cent tuition hike enacted by the Purdue Board of Trustees. That afternoon over 200 students marched on the Administration Building at Purdue University. It started fast. The town and the university were unaware of what was taking place. The press converged on the area, and in an effort to report the news, perhaps irresponsibly, began to broadcast "live" reports from the Purdue Administration building. This was the first instance where one of the most common problems in press reporting made itself known—that of estimating crowd size. Now that may seem to be a relatively simple procedure for those of us who are sitting in this room, relatively unpacked, compared to an administration building with students in the halls, up the stairs, and down the stairs to a degree where it was literally difficult to breathe, let alone walk. That night in the Purdue Administration Building there were four reporters: three radio and one newspaper reporter. The crowd size reported by the different media went anywhere from 200 up to 700 students and on one occasion traced as high as 1000 students reported to be occupying the Purdue Administration

Building. A later head count showed approximately 350. There is a lot of difference between 200 and 1000, but regardless of whether it is 200 or 2000 there should be some type of cooperation and organizational leadership when more than one member of the press is covering an event such as sit-ins or demonstrations.

[4] There were other problems in estimating crowd size in the Purdue University unrest which resulted in discrepancies into the thousands. One example was a student march through West Lafayette which was estimated at 5000 students by the wire services. The agreement of three reporters, who were present, was an estimate closer to 10,000.

[5] In a 25,000 student population there is a lot of difference between 5000 students and 10,000 students. It leads to another problem in dealing with crowd size, that of determining how many of the actual students in the crowd support the cause and how many are merely there as curiosity seekers. It is a very difficult process, if not impossible.

[6] Another facet of reporting, which the public hears very little about, is university information services. The information services by their very nature are public relations arms of colleges. They are the arms which project the positive image to a public. The Purdue University Information Service, for instance, has guidelines for every one of its staff. In brief, these guidelines include a positive presentation to the public of the multicurriculum approach of the university and the cooperation of interdisciplinary programs, the achievement of students and faculty members in the university, the story of a rigorous university curriculum, and the list goes on. When a university information service finds its university torn apart by campus dissidence it becomes difficult for it to achieve objective and thorough reporting.

[7] The instance I will use as an example occurred on the morning of May 6, 1969, when 229 students were taken into custody by Purdue police. The students were alleged to have been milling-in or lounging-in the Union Building after the president of the university had issued an executive order telling them to leave. Of the 229 who were taken into custody, three were known faculty members. These figures were reported by the news media in Lafayette and subsequently used by United Press International. The story cleared the wire early that morning. Shortly thereafter the Purdue Information Service filed its version of what had taken place. They denied that any faculty members were involved in the lounge-in. UPI consequently proceeded to correct the broadcast wire in Indiana with a series stating this fact and stating the Purdue University News Service said there were no faculty members taken into custody or involved in the lounge-in that morning. Some of the press, learning of this through their own affiliate stations, had the feeling of literally being called liars. It took approximately four hours of confirmation to determine which

three faculty members were involved, the charges against them, their names, ranks, departments, and when they would appear in court. And, in an effort to save the credibility of the local Lafayette press, this information was given to the wire services and the wire subsequently changed the story. As a result, the Purdue Information Service succeeded only in losing credibility. It was later determined the conflicting report occurred because the information service reporter at the scene of the lounge-in did not have time to call the story back to his main office. It should be noted that many solutions to problems such as this are being made in the university news services themselves. They are understanding that in an era of protest, in an era of emotional impact, their best bet is to cooperate with the press in providing a balanced objective presentation of what is taking place on the campus. They are beginning to realize that at the very least they can identify the issues behind the campus unrest and make these available to reporters who come on campus.

[8] Which leads us to another problem. It's very difficult for an out-of-town reporter to get up in the morning; receive a news director's assignment to fly to a campus with cameras; take pictures; be back for a 6 P.M. television newscast, and still have time to look into many of the issues behind campus unrest. When reporters arrive on campus, they shoot their film of any action confrontation that takes place and they are on their way home. The universities and their images have been warped by reporters who have not provided a satisfactory balance between a turbulent academic community and a peaceful one. There is a great danger in the reporter who reports on campus unrest and has only been on a college campus for a Saturday football game. He does not understand the inner workings of the academic community and thus cannot report them. The reporter who comes, shoots film, and leaves gets tagged a *sensationalist.*

[9] Geography is another problem experienced in reporting campus unrest. It is a fact that many colleges and universities by their very nature grow up in small towns and small town radio and television markets. News staffs in such stations range usually from a single news reporter to the maximum of a three man staff, those being very rare. The reporters in such areas receive their biggest news assignments covering a local political gathering or a major traffic fatality—perhaps at most a visiting dignitary who issues press releases and hands out statements from which he expects the press to report. When campus unrest develops in their community they are not only understaffed but ill-equipped to handle the serious investigative reporting which is necessary on such occasions. Local reporters who have not had the experience of serious investigative reporting are placed in the turbulent atmosphere madly taking down any type of information which may be available, including, for instance, quotes that may be uttered from any obscure student's mouth, a student leader or the lowest

flunky on the academic ladder, having no association whatsoever with the campus protest.

[10] Also in many cases news media in college communities are very susceptible to hiring college students as cheap personnel to act as news reporters. Many times these are part-time reporters who are hired for the purpose of ripping and reading wire copy and making a few minor stops at local police stations or city halls. When this person becomes the sole reporter to the local news media on the unrest on a college campus, investigative jobs of reporting are not the result. Regardless of how objective a college student may be in his attempt to report activities on the college campus, his student status makes him susceptible to getting caught in the polarization which inevitably takes place on the campus, and there is the danger of this polarization being reflected in his reporting. It may not seem overly serious when one considers that perhaps the only damage that is done to the image of the university is in that local community, but it becomes far more critical when one understands that this same local reporter is also called upon to feed reports and news stories to major metropolitan stations and, in fact, to national news services. Wire services who are interested, but who do not have the staff to cover every college campus protest in the nation, rely on the local reporter. Therefore, the local reporter, lacking in ability, becomes the sole agent to disseminate news to a national public. The result in many cases is unintentional sensationalism. When one's daily work is mostly concerned with the gory details of personal injury traffic accidents or the sensationalized excitement of fire engines and police cars, one becomes intoxicated with the same type of sensational reporting regardless of the type of stories being covered.

[11] One final problem I'll touch on today is the problem of identifying student leaders. When campus unrest breaks out, student leaders are everywhere. There are the typical student government leaders who supposedly represent the majority of the student body. There are other more radical or protest leaders who represent certain unidentified segments of the student body. I have seen some reporters on a university or college campus find a student, ask him a question, then in turn quote him as a "student spokesman." This becomes the image of the issue and the student body.

[12] Solutions to these and other problems are being sought. To quote Dr. Mitchell once again, he said, "One of the things I recommended to my friends in broadcasting is that they consider running some courses in high tension press relations with the faculty and the administration of universities that are likely to be subject to campus violence. . . . Despite the fact that the events which lead to violence are known to university administrators and their staffs months in advance, very few of them ever take the time and trouble to prepare a peace kit which gives the full back-

ground of these problems and itemizes the many meetings, discussions and other efforts that have been made to deal with the situations which precipitate in ultimate incidents. When there is nothing for a newspaper man or a broadcaster to describe except a student standing on the steps of a building and brandishing a rifle, then that is what is going to get in the paper. But when editors have all the background or a great deal of it, and when they are taken into the confidence of the institution in order to inform themselves of the events that might lead to crises, the press coverage from the very beginning is likely to be better balanced." I might add, the press in Indiana and nationally must accept the responsibility as we have done in previous summers when we reported the racial confrontations in cities and then accepted the responsibility of informing the public of the condition of the ghettos and the contributions that minority groups can make to society. Colleges are certainly not to be compared with minorities, but the press has in fact reported the violence and the confrontations on college campuses, and now the press has the responsibility to renew in the American public the knowledge of the importance and contribution that colleges and universities can make to American society.

III

UNREST ON THE COLLEGE CAMPUS

Is This Your University?

Al Capp

*Al Capp, the creator of Li'l Abner cartoon, delivered this speech at
Franklin Pierce College, Rindge, New Hampshire, on April 27,
1969. Alarmed by the unrest and disorder on many college campuses,
Capp decided to conduct a speaking tour of colleges throughout the
country. This speech is a hard line reaction to overpermissiveness.
Capp uses heavy doses of satire and sarcasm and does not hesitate to
cite names, places, and events. In essence, he is giving his opponents
some of their own medicine. How wise is such an approach? Is it too
rough and too reactionary to persuade college audiences?*

[1] I live in Cambridge, Mass., a stone's throw from Harvard—but
if you duck you aren't hurt much—and I know you'll believe me when
I tell you I'd rather be speaking here today. It's safer, and it's at your sort
of college that I can use the commencement speaker's traditional phrase.
I can say you're the hope of the future without bursting out laughing, as
I would if I said it at a Harvard commencement—assuming, of course,
that there will be a commencement there this year. They haven't heard
from the Afros or the SDS yet.

[2] Three or four of the Afros may decide that commencements are
racist institutions, and then five or six SDSers may decide that commencements are a CIA plot, and then of course the entire faculty, administration
and student body of Harvard, with the courage that has made them a
legend, will replace its commencement by some sort of ceremony more
acceptable—something they know the boys will approve of—say, a book
burning; they loved that at Columbia, or a dean killing; they never quite
accomplished that at University Hall. Dean Ford let them down by having
recuperative powers they didn't count on.

[3] But the fact that you can have a commencement here without
getting down on your knees to a student wrecking crew, or without calling
up the riot squad, is mainly luck. You enjoy advantages Harvard doesn't.

Reprinted with permission from Al Capp.

For one thing, you have the advantage of not being so revered for the wisdom and courage of past generations of administrators that you haven't noticed the moral flabbiness and intellectual flatulence of the majority of your present generation of administrators and faculty. You show me any institution with such a glorious past that anyone presently employed by it is regarded as retroactively infallible, and I'll show you a collection of sanctimonious fatheads.

[4] But the greatest advantage Franklin Pierce has over Harvard is that you are not rich enough to hire three such famous professors as Rosovsky, Galbraith and Handlin and not extravagant enough to waste the wisdom of the only one of them with guts and sense—Handlin. All three are world-renowned historians. All three this week have helped make history.

[5] Prof. Henry Rosovsky was born in Danzig. When the young Nazis invaded the University of Danzig in the 30's and beat up its professors and disrupted its classes, Rosovsky's family gave up their citizenship and fled to the United States. In the 60's, Rosovsky was teaching at Berkeley. When the young Nazis invaded there, Rosovsky gave up his professorship and fled to Harvard. When the young Nazis invaded there the other day, Rosovsky gave up the chairmanship of his department and started packing.

[6] Prof. Galbraith, as national chairman of the ADA, was the intellectual leader of the Democratic Party in the last election and one of the Nation's few political thinkers over 19 who mistook Sen. McCarthy's menopausal capriciousness for high-principled statesmanship.

[7] Prof. Handlin has won the Pulitzer Prize and other honors for his histories of those groups who, so far, have risen from their ghettos by sweating blood instead of shedding it, by shaping up instead of burning down.

[8] Although Harvard is the home of these three wise men and hundreds more, it was the only bunch in town that was dumbfounded at what happened there. Everybody else in the community expected it. We had all watched Harvard for the last few years educate its young in the rewards of criminality. We had watched Harvard become an ivy-covered Fagin.

[9] We saw it begin a couple of years ago when Secretary of Defense McNamara was invited to speak at Harvard. Now, it is true that McNamara was a member of a despised minority group, the President's Cabinet, but under the law, he had the same rights as Mark Rudd. Harvard's Students for a Democratic Society howled obscenities at McNamara until he could not be heard.

[10] He attempted to leave the campus. The SDS stopped his car, milled around it, tried to tip it over. McNamara left the car. The SDS began to club him on the head with the poles on which their peace posters

were nailed. If it hadn't been for the arrival of the Cambridge police, who formed a protective cordon around McNamara and escorted him through a series of interconnecting cellars of university buildings to safety, he might have been killed.

[11] The next morning, Dean Monroe was asked if he would punish the SDS. And he said—and if you want to know where the malignancy started that has made a basket case of Harvard, it started with this—Dean Monroe said that he saw no reason to punish students for what was purely a political activity. Now, if depriving a man of his freedom to speak, if depriving him of his freedom to move, if damn nearly depriving him of his life—if that's political activity, then rape is a social event and sticking up a gas station is a financial transaction.

[12] Now, there's nothing unusual about a pack of young criminals ganging up on a stranger on their turf as the SDS ganged up on McNamara; it's called mugging. And there's nothing unusual about a respected citizen, even a dean, babbling imbecilities in an emotional crisis; it's called a breakdown.

[13] Both are curable by the proper treatment but there was something unusual, and chilling, too, about seeing the responsible authority, Harvard, treat a plain case of mugging as democracy in action and a plain case of hysterics as a dean in his right mind.

[14] Well, after Harvard taught its young that the way to settle a difference of opinion is to mug anyone who differed with them, it was no surprise that they'd soon learn that shoving a banana into an instructor's mouth is the way to win a debate and bringing a meat cleaver to a conference is the way to win a concession. Because that's what happened at Harvard in the last month.

[15] When its militants stormed into the opening class in a new course on the causes of urban unrest and stopped it because they found it ideologically offensive, the instructor attempted to discuss it with them. So one of the militants shoved a banana into his mouth. This stopped the instructor, of course, he stopped the class and then Harvard dropped the entire course.

[16] This week, the Crimson published a photograph of a black militant leaving an historic conference with the administration—historic because it was here that the administration granted black students, and only black students, hiring, firing and tenure powers equal to that of any dean. The militant was holding a meat cleaver. The next day President Pusey said that Harvard would never yield to threats. Shows how silly a man can look when he doesn't read his local paper.

[17] President Pusey said that, by the way, at a televised mass meeting advertised as one in which all sides of the question would be fairly represented. The Harvard student body was represented by a member of

the SDS (numerically, they are less than 1 per cent). The average resident of the Cambridge community was represented by a black militant graduate student who lives in Roxbury and commutes in a new Cadillac. And anyone who'd call that unfair representation would have been mean enough to say the same thing about the Chief Rabbi of Berlin being represented by Adolf Eichmann.

[18] And so when Harvard was raped last week, it had as much cause to be surprised as any tart who continued to flounce around the fellas after they'd unbuttoned her bodice and pulled down her panties.

[19] What surprised the world was Harvard's response. Nowhere in the world was Mayor Daley's response to precisely the same sort of attack by precisely the same sort of mob more loftily denounced than at Harvard. Yet in its moment of truth, Harvard responded in precisely the same way Daley did.

[20] Pusey called for the cops just as Daley did, and the cops treated the criminals at Harvard just as firmly as they treated the criminals in Chicago. The Harvard administration applauded President Pusey's action to a man. There is no record that they ever applauded Daley.

[21] That either proves that the Harvard administration believes in the divine right of kings to act in a fashion that, in a peasant, is considered pushy. Or it may prove that President Pusey is just as Neanderthal as Mayor Daley. Or it may prove that President Pusey learned how to handle Neanderthals from Mayor Daley. At any rate, if they're looking for a new president of Harvard, I suggest they teach Mayor Daley to read and write and offer him the job.

[22] Let's forgive the president of Harvard for not having the grace to thank the Mayor of Chicago for teaching him how to protect his turf; they aren't strong on graciousness at Harvard this year. But as a member of the Cambridge community, what alarms me is that Harvard doesn't have the brains to protect itself, and the community, from further, more savage and inevitably wider-ranging attacks. And I feel that I have the right to speak for some in the Cambridge community, possibly equal to that of any resident of Roxbury who parks his car there for a few hours a few days a week.

[23] I've lived in Cambridge over 30 years. My children and grandchildren were born and raised in Cambridge. I help pay the taxes that support Harvard. I help provide Harvard with the police that it will increasingly need to protect it from the once-decent kids it has corrupted into thugs and thieves, and the worse kind of thugs and thieves—the sanctimonious kind.

[24] I ask, and my neighbors in the Cambridge community are asking: If a horde of howling, half-educated, half-grown and totally dependent half-humans can attack visitors in their cars, and deans in their offices, and get away with it, how long before they'll widen their horizons a block or two and attack us in our homes?

[25] If they can use clubs and meat cleavers on the Harvard community today and get away with it, who stops them from using clubs and meat cleavers on the Cambridge community tomorrow? Certainly not the Harvard community. If it was necessary last week for Harvard to organize a round-the-clock guard to prevent the untoilet-trained pups they've made into mad dogs from blowing up the Widener Library and the Fogg Museum, must we of the Cambridge community prepare to defend ourselves from the pack Harvard has loosed among us? Or should we all pull a Rosovsky and take off to safe, sane Saigon where it's legal to shoot back at your enemy?

[26] When the president of Harvard proved that, in a crisis, he was the intellectual equal of the Mayor of Chicago and called the cops, it was his finest hour. Although it was true that he had presided over the experimental laboratory that created the Frankenstein's monster that stomped mindlessly into University Hall, fouling everything in its path, he did, at long last, recognize what he had wrought and took the steps to rid his university and our community of the filthy thing.

[27] After throwing the SDS out physically, the next sane move was obviously to keep them out officially, and expel them. And leave them to the criminal courts to educate, or to the Army, or to the gutters of Toronto, or to the rehabilitation centers and public charity of Stockholm. Their few score places at Harvard, and those of their sympathizers, could have been instantly filled by any of the tens of thousands of fine youngsters, black and white, they had been chosen instead of.

[28] And Harvard could have gone on with pride and strength as an institution of learning, as an example of the vigor of the democratic process to other universities, instead of degenerating into the pigpen and playpen it is today. But after the president of Harvard made the one move that might have saved Harvard, the Harvard faculty, in the words of San Francisco State President Hayakawa, betrayed him.

[29] And that brings us back to Rosovsky and Galbraith. And to Handlin.

[30] Rosovsky, whose family had given up and fled when the German Nazis invaded the University of Danzig, who gave up and fled when the California Nazis invaded Berkeley, gave up the chairmanship of his course and started packing when the Cambridge Nazis invaded University Hall. And all over this country—at Cornell, in New York—other professors are using the Rosovsky solution: giving up and running away. The only trouble with it is that, sooner or later, you run out of places to run away to.

[31] Now, the Galbraith solution is one that is bound to be popular with his fellow puberty-worshipers: those who have just achieved puberty,

and those who worship those who have just achieved it as sources of infinite wisdom and quite a few votes. But I'm not criticizing Galbraith's religious convictions. What I say is, in this country, any professor who is panting to get back into public life is free to worship the SDS chapter of his choice.

[32] Galbraith's solution is to promptly restructure our universities— and Harvard more promptly than any other, because, in Galbraith's opinion, those who administer Harvard have "little comprehension of the vast and complex scientific and scholarly life they presume to govern." Well, now, who does Galbraith presume to replace them with?

[33] If those who created Harvard, and made it into the vast and complex scientific and scholarly structure it became, must be restructured out of it because they have too little comprehension, who has enough? The only ones who claim they have, and who will shove a banana into the mouth of anyone who denies it, are the student militants.

[34] And so the Galbraith solution is a forth-right one: Let the lunatics run the asylum.

[35] Well, I'm going to tell Galbraith the news: they've already tried your sort of restructuring, Ken. They tried it at Berkeley; they tried it at Cornell; they tried it at Harvard all last week, and the result was that on Friday, a mob of militant students, of a Harvard frenziedly restructured to suit their wildest whims, marched into the Harvard planning offices.

[36] They shouted obscene charges at Planner Goyette. When he attempted to answer, they shouted him down with obscenities. They demolished the architectural model of Harvard's building plans, they kicked over files, they hurled telephones to the floor. And while Goyette cowered and his secretaries screamed, they marched out, uninterfered with by the six policemen who were summoned there presumably to see that they remained uninterfered with, unrebuked and, of course, unsatisfied.

[37] And they won't be satisfied until Harvard is restructured the way they restructured Hiroshima. They'll be back, on another day, to another office. Possibly Galbraith's.

[38] Well, those were the voices that prevailed at Harvard, the resigners like Rosovsky, the restructurers like Galbraith. There was another voice, however, the voice of Oscar Handlin.

[39] Prof. Handlin said he was appalled at the argument that the students' takeover of University Hall, their attack on the deans, their destruction of private property and their thefts from personal files were unwise but not criminal. It was criminal, said Handlin, by every decent standard.

[40] If Harvard had not chickened out, said Handlin, if it had had the courage to recognize the criminality on its campus over the last few years, beginning with the beating up and silencing of McNamara and con-

tinuing through innumerable other incidents of the brutal deprivation by its mad-dog students of the rights of those who dared to dissent with them, it "would not be in the position it is in today—following the road that Berkeley has followed, following the road that has destroyed other universities."

[41] Oscar Handlin urged Harvard not to go down that road. That was last week. This week, Harvard has gone so far down the road that it can never turn back. In this last frantic, fatal, foolish week, Harvard has reversed the civil rights advances of the last 20 years.

[42] Today at Harvard, any student with the currently fashionable color of skin is given rights denied to students of the currently unfashionable color. Harvard, which educated the President who brought America into the war that defeated fascism, today honors and encourages and rewards its fascists. Harvard, which once turned out scholars and gentlemen, now turns out thugs and thieves or let me put it this way: now, if you are a thug and thief, Harvard won't turn you out.

[43] Once people were attracted to the Cambridge community because Harvard was there. Today, because Harvard is there, people are fleeing the Cambridge community, even Harvard's own.

[44] Harvard's tragedy was that it was too arrogant to consider that it too might be vulnerable to the cancer that is killing other universities. And when Oscar Handlin diagnosed it as malignant, Harvard was too cowardly to endure the radical surgery that could save its life.

[45] And that's why I can say that colleges like yours, as yet too unproven to have become arrogant, and too determined to prove yourself to be anything but courageous, are the hope of the future. Because I believe that America has a future.

[46] It has become unfashionable to say this; it may be embarrassing to hear it; but I believe that America is the most lovely and liveable of all nations. I believe that Americans are the kindest and most generous of all people.

[47] I believe there are no underprivileged Americans; that even the humblest of us are born with a privilege that places us ahead of anyone else, anywhere else: the privilege of living and working in America, of repairing and renewing America; and one more privilege that no one seems to get much fun out of lately—the privilege of loving America.

IV

CIVIL AND HUMAN RIGHTS

Puerto Ricans and the Neighborhood: A Persuasive Interview

Philip Zimbardo

Philip Zimbardo, a professor at Stanford University, tape-recorded this interview in a community center in New York City. A college freshman was trying to persuade a middle-aged housewife that she was wrong in her attitudes toward Puerto Ricans who were moving into her East Bronx neighborhood. Zimbardo initiates and closes the interview, and the woman's daughter occasionally enters into the interview. Notice particularly the student's challenges of unsupported generalizations and his probing questions into why the woman feels the way she does. The woman was not persuaded in this interview. What could or should the student have done differently for better results?

[1] INTERVIEWER (P. Zimbardo): You've been living in this neighborhood quite a number of years. Do you think there's been any change in the composition of the neighborhood?

[2] WOMAN: There certainly has. I've been living in this house now for 21 years, and I daresay I'm ashamed to tell people that I live in the neighborhood I do.

[3] BOY: Why is that?

[4] WOMAN: Because of what the Puerto Ricans have done to it.

[5] BOY: What do you mean, specifically?

[6] WOMAN: Well, to start with, their filth. Second, the language they use, and third, because the teachers waste eight hours a day with them in school and find that they get nowhere the minute the children are released.

Philip Zimbardo and Ebbe B. Ebbesen, Influencing Attitudes and Changing Behavior, 1969, Addison-Wesley Publishing Company, Inc., Reading, Mass.

[7] Boy: You mean you never heard that language from anyone else but a Puerto Rican?

[8] Woman: I certainly have, but not as much as I hear it from them.

[9] Boy: Maybe you listen to it from them more often than you listen to it from others.

[10] Woman: I can't help it, because the streets are overcrowded with them.

[11] Boy: Well, why are they overcrowded with them?

[12] Woman: It doesn't have to be overcrowded, they can live somewhere else, or gather somewhere else. But I find that this is the biggest dope center, because there's nothing done about it. We pay police the salaries that we do, we pay taxes, and yet what has been done?

[13] Boy: What do you know about dope centers? You say this is the biggest dope center. Do you know of other dope centers . . . (Woman: I can't help but know, because I see it right under my window.) Do you know of other dope centers?

[14] Woman: I don't look (Boy: So how could you say . . . .) but this is something you can't help but see.

[15] Teenage Daughter (overlaps): You don't judge people all over the world, you judge people by your own neighborhood. If there are bad people right in your neighborhood, you don't say that everybody's bad or everybody's good, you judge by your own neighborhood . . . (Boy: Well, you're Jewish, right?) This happens to be a terrible neighborhood.

[16] Boy: You're Jewish, right?

[17] Daughter: Yes.

[18] Boy: You don't know any people that are Jewish that are bad or that you wouldn't associate with?

[19] Daughter: That's right, but they didn't tear down the Bronx like the Puerto Ricans did.

[20] Boy: So you're going to say . . . are you gonna say that all the Jewish people are bad just because you know a few of them that you wouldn't associate with or you don't like?

[21] Woman: I think they're the filthiest race, they're devoid of brains, and it's a disgrace with what goes on.

[22] Boy: Why do you say they're the filthiest race?

[23] Woman: They are, because I've worked with colored people, and I find that they're 50 per cent more immaculate than the Puerto Ricans.

[24] Boy: Well, why are they dirty? Isn't there a reason why they're dirty?

[25] Woman: They don't know any better, unfortunately.

[26] Boy: So then how can you condemn them because they don't know better? If you find a person that's ignorant, are you gonna condemn him?

[27] WOMAN: You can condemn people for being poor, but you can't condemn them for being filthy. [She means the opposite, or does she?] Soap and water doesn't cost much. If a person is ignorant, he knows nothing about cleanliness. And if he's devoid of brains, he certainly doesn't know.

[28] BOY: All right, look, you say they're filthy and all that. But look at the sanitation problems in Puerto Rico.

[29] WOMAN: I've never been to Puerto Rico, so I can't speak about Puerto Rico. I live in the Bronx and I can only tell you what happens there.

[30] BOY (overlaps): In New York here or even in the United States we have the highest standard of living. They don't have that in other places, if a person just comes over from a low standard of living into a high standard of living . . .

[31] WOMAN (interrupts): Why is it that most of the Puerto Ricans own the most beautiful cars, and yet 90 per cent of them are on relief?

[32] BOY: A lot of people own cars and don't have a lot of money.

[33] WOMAN: Not a lot. Puerto Ricans more than any other race.

[34] BOY: Why Puerto Ricans more than any other race?

[35] WOMAN: 'Cause I happen to know someone that works on the Home Relief Bureau [Welfare Service]; and more Puerto Ricans than any other race.

[36] DAUGHTER: Why d'ya think they live so many in a family? They can't support children, they don't know how to bring 'em up, they haven't got the money . . . .

[37] WOMAN: But they know how to make them, every nine months.

[38] BOY: So are you going to condemn them for having kids?

[39] DAUGHTER: No, you don't condemn 'em, but if they don't know how to bring them up . . . .

[40] WOMAN: Why do they have so many of them? *You could condemn them for having kids.* They should go out and look for jobs! The hospitals are flooded with them today. Do they know about going to pediatricians? No! What do they bring them up on? When the child's seven months old, it learns to drink beer from a can!

[41] BOY (interrupts): My God, the people . . . the people just came over here, how long have they been in the United States? What chance have they had?

[42] WOMAN: They've been here much too long to suit me.

[43] DAUGHTER: There are girls we have right here on our own block, little snot-noses, ten to twelve years old, hang out with these boys, they go in . . . they go up the schoolyards, they're, uh [becomes emotionally agitated] . . . at night when they should be home getting ready for school, gettin' ready for, uh, the next day . . . .

[44] BOY: That's only Puerto Ricans, you don't know any . . . no other white girls or any thing like that?

[45] WOMAN: It was never as obvious as it is now.

[46] DAUGHTER: No, all these girls are Puerto Ricans.

[47] BOY: So you blame them for being *obvious* instead of hiding it . . . right? Instead of being sneaks about it?

[48] WOMAN: *Yes,* because their parents don't know enough to take care of them.

[49] BOY: How do you know their parents don't know?

[50] WOMAN: Because if you go to dance halls, who do you find there? More Puerto Ricans.

[51] BOY: You find anybody at dance halls . . . (Girl: Wait a minute, don't you think at the age of . . . .) You mean before the Puerto Ricans came there were no dance halls?

[52] WOMAN: Refined, but not like now.

[53] BOY: Why refined? What do you mean by . . . . You never read in the papers or anything like where there were fights in dance halls where there wasn't Puerto Ricans?

[54] WOMAN (interrupts): I lived in a building that was the most upstanding house on the block. Today it's disgraceful, because it's surrounded with Puerto Ricans.

[55] BOY: Surrounded with . . . . Why? Do you think just because a person's Puerto Rican, right away he's filthy and he's dirty and he's dumb? You think just because a person's a Puerto Rican or something like that, that you call him dumb and ignorant because he's born Puerto Rican? A few years ago there was prejudice against the Jewish people. They weren't allowed in colleges, they're not allowed in colleges, they're not allowed in, uh . . .

[56] DAUGHTER (interrupting): And you have to be afraid to let, to let your children go . . .

[57] WOMAN: Why is it that a family of ten moves into a three-room apartment?

[58] DAUGHTER: Because they're Puerto Ricans.

[59] BOY (overlaps daughter): Answer me why. Because they like it?

[60] DAUGHTER (overlaps boy): Because they like to save money to buy cars.

[61] BOY: They like to save money. Maybe they can't afford larger apartments.

[62] WOMAN: Then they shouldn't come here. They should stay in Puerto Rico.

[63] Boy: Is it so easy to find apartments now that you can go out and get all the apartments you want? So then why are you condemning?

[64] Woman: It isn't easy, because I'm a little fussy. I want to stay away from them. I want to go to a neighborhood that *restricts them.*

[65] Boy: But you still didn't answer a question I asked before. Just because the . . . they're Puerto Ricans or something like that, they're . . . that they're filthy, they're dirty. How many years ago was it before the Jewish people were, uh, discriminated against?

[66] Woman: Not that I know of.

[67] Boy: Not that you know of! How . . . a Jewish people . . . A Jewish person couldn't get into law school or anything like that then, you couldn't get into the Bell Telephone Company, you couldn't get into . . . to millions of jobs.

[68] Woman: That's only hearsay. But can you prove it?

[69] Boy: It isn't, yes, I can prove it. I have relatives that tried out for the Bell Telephone Company and they couldn't get in because they were Jewish. I had a . . . one of my relatives graduated from law school. He was one of the first people who graduated like that.

[70] Daughter: So tell us why has the Bronx come down so much?

[71] Boy: Because it's overpopulated.

[72] Daughter: With dirty Spics!

[73] Boy: So what reason do you have to call them dirty Spics?

[74] Daughter: What reason!

[75] Woman: One, because they don't know how to bring up children. Second, because their morale [she means morals] is so low. Third, because they're known to consume more alcohol than any other race in this world.

[76] Boy: Aw, that's ridiculous. You never heard of Irish people drinking beer? Who drinks more beer than Irish people?

[77] Woman: And fourth, they're the biggest marijuana smokers.

[78] Boy: Who drinks more beer than Irish people?

[79] Daughter: Yeah, but, uh . . . most Irish people can afford it. You walk into the house of Puerto Ricans and you find that under the bed people are dying, uh . . . their children haven't got clothes. Their children have no food . . . but you'll find beer cans under the bed.

[80] Boy: Where did you ever walk into a house and see somebody under a bed? (*laughing*)

[81] Woman: Who wanted to shoot the President, if not the Puerto Ricans? [reference to assassination attempt on President Truman by Puerto Rican Nationalists]

[82] Boy: What about John Wilkes Booth, who tried to shoot Abraham Lincoln, what was he?

[83] WOMAN: You're going back so many years!

[84] BOY: All right, so what does that mean?

[85] WOMAN: You pick up the paper and read about prostitutes. Who's involved? Puerto Ricans.

[86] INTERVIEWER: We seem to be going off on a tangent, so let's wind up the discussion with your views on how the problem could be solved.

[87] BOY: About ten years ago we were the minority group, the Jews, and when we went to Jewish school the Irish used to pick on us. People find faults with the Puerto Ricans because they are the lowest and newest minority group now, and there's no real reason for that, actually it's ignorance, that's all prejudice really is, and it must be changed by getting to know them.

[88] WOMAN: It could be solved by dropping a token in the subway and sending them all back where they came from!

Women's Liberation: Where the Movement Is Today and Where It's Going

Roxanne Dunbar

Roxanne Dunbar, a staff member of the Southern Female Rights Union, granted this interview with NOW (National Organization for Women) in May 1970 during a speaking tour of the West Coast. She is small physically, wears her hair short and straight, and wears jeans. Her appearance is intentionally designed to reduce the sexuality of her image. This interview contains many insights into the nature of persuasion in our society, the problems of creating a movement for social change (especially for women's rights). Note the questioning techniques of a sympathetic, skilled interviewer. How does presenting one's views in an interview format differ from a persuasive speech?

[1] *Where is the women's movement today?*

[2] ROXANNE: It seems to me that even though the women's movement is building, it's also beginning to die. There are so many aspects of women's oppression, so many symbolic and real secondary symptoms of women's oppression, that it's easy to get off the track, go in a million different directions and never really get to the core of what is the problem.

[3] We have been constantly responding to everything that comes up, but it dissipates a lot of energy. We have been thinking in terms of action, losing people constantly, gaining a great number of people and then losing them. Then we start to think, sort of manipulatively: how can we get more people, how can we hang on to them, how can we get Black women and how can we do this and that—without really even knowing

Reprinted from Handbook of Woman's Liberation by Joan Robbins by permission of American Art Enterprises, Inc. Copyright 1970 by Now Library Press.

what you're getting 'em for. It's been a very spontaneous movement and its being so has been inevitable up to this time.

[4] *By spontaneous, do you mean disorganized and chaotic—as it certainly has been—or are you condemning a lack of regimentation?*

[5] ROXANNE: The movement was just not off the ground or going anywhere, but just reacting to immediate things. You can't go on and say 'Well, this was all wrong because it was spontaneous.' I feel spontaneity is a defect, a necessary defect until one learns something from the experience and then they can go in a certain direction.

[6] We need to pool our political experience so that we know the very best way of doing things, as well as we know it, rather than each person or every group going through a lot of bad experiences and all making the same mistakes.

[7] *Was your own group, Cell 16, one of these spontaneous reactors?*

[8] ROXANNE: We had an incredible task ahead of us two years ago when we started forming some women's groups. For one thing there was no literature at all available. There was nothing. So one of our first projects was to start a mass journal that we could sell in the street to get to women. We had no hope of getting articles in magazines. We called up the TV once and asked to be on and the man laughed at us. He just giggled. It was a whole year before anyone ever asked us to be on any public thing, and then it was always messed up.

[9] We had no political experience. The group was composed of working-class women. We did not use consciousness-raising as a method, but we touched on everything consciousness-raising touches on in the four months before we dissolved. We didn't get the strong bond people get from consciousness-raising, but after we split up we had no trouble getting the group back together again later on.

[10] When the group first came together, in some of our early programmatic discussions it was proposed that the group assassinate some man to make our presence known! We even made up a list but we finally decided not to because whoever we did in would become such an important person because we'd chosen him over all these other guys.

[11] *That sounds like a lesson from Valerie Solanas (author of the SCUM [Society for Cutting Up Men] Manifesto and Andy Warhol's assailant).*

[12] ROXANNE: We went down and visited her in the insane asylum a couple of times, where they put her after she'd shot Andy Warhol, assuming that any woman who shoots a man must be insane, I guess.

[13] She really is an incredible sort of anarchist-terrorist and didn't really have much to tell us and really wasn't interested in learning politically. But she's quite brilliant and interesting and I wouldn't be surprised if she shot Andy Warhol again, especially since he's making a woman's liberation film.

[14] But, I'd been very influenced by the Black Panthers of northern California. One of their first acts was going with shotguns to the State Legislature. We planned to get shotguns and go to the Boston Common to deal with the men who ogle the secretaries. We set up a committee to acquire the shotguns. When some new women came into the group they were horrified at what we were doing. The group didn't have any trouble coming apart. Unless we can pool our experience, there's the danger of messing up some people's lives, and maybe your own, floundering around and wasting energy.

[15] *Did you have any contact with the National Organization for Women?*

[16] ROXANNE: I'd never heard of it. NOW is a structure to which a lot of women come and leave. Women tend to respond to whatever organization they first have some contact with and NOW has been active since 1966, I think, and has reached an awful lot of middle-class housewifes and professional women, but it never reached me.

[17] NOW has transformed itself a lot. There are more Black women in it than in any other women's liberation organization. The Black women did caucus at the last NOW convention and they elected a Black president. The program NOW adopted at their last convention is the same as ours except for self-defense.

[18] Most of the women who go into NOW and stay believe in extreme individualism, every woman can make it. It's like a conglomerate rather than a collective—individual women making it and helping each other like the Masons—help each other along, give each other jobs, get women into all kinds of positions of power, just like men operate. They're very deformed by this and they become like caricatures of the men. They are very protective and admire masculine values.

[19] I don't know how long such a point of view will continue to exist if they really do start working on the programs that they stated because the programs really don't reflect that attitude.

[20] *And the rest of the movement, how does it differ from NOW? You say, NOW has picked up our program, so where's the movement going?*

[21] ROXANNE: I think we have gained enough understanding to begin plotting some direction. I think there are several principles we can look at and follow to begin plotting a direction. One is: there is no basic unity among women unless that unity is based on oppression of the most oppressed. You can't have a unity based upon the oppression of, say, middle-class women. There's no unity because of the many privileges in-

volved in their economic position, having access to certain goods, education, and so forth.

[22] So we're really talking about a mass woman's movement. The point is not how to get Black women in, not how to get working women, but how to change middle-class women's perception of their own condition, that is, how can middle-class women come to know the part they really play in society and truly identify with other women, struggling for the demands of the most oppressed women, and not in some sacrificial sense, but in the full understanding that there's not going to be any freedom for women unless all women are free.

[23] I think that that's a principle that we haven't yet dealt with and thought about in these terms. At the same time, if you can find this basis of unity in progress it doesn't mean that Black and white women, or working women or middle-class women will necessarily be in the same organizations.

[24] *Why do so few Black women join women's liberation?*

[25] ROXANNE: Black women have started forming caucuses within the different Black organizations in this country, and I don't think Black women feel very much of a sense of unity with the White woman for many very good reasons—not because they don't sense their oppression, or because they consider it secondary. They don't know, they haven't seen whether or not white women are serious about struggling against this society—which is racist and sexist.

[26] They cannot afford to commit themselves to a cause that has not yet shown what its basic point of view is and I don't think the white woman's movement has voiced that as a movement, but in actions they have been somewhat counter to the Black movement. I compare it to the yippee-type meaning of the youth movement being counter Black movement—that is, promoting drugs and sort of free love at a time when Black people are trying to struggle against those things which so oppress ghetto people. The white movement has made a major demand of abortion repeal at the same time that Black people are involved in a very complicated struggle against genocide, both psychological and physical, and the threat of genocide. In a very real sense they should increase their number so as not to be susceptible to genocide. A large minority is not susceptible to genocide. Those numbers make a great deal of difference. I don't think there is very much willingness on the part of the white woman's movement to deal with this and to confront it.

[27] There are other things too that Black women mistrust—the continuation of certain privileges of being sexual symbols, which have been so oppressive of Black women. White women in the white women's movement continue looking exactly like the image that society promotes, the image of the "free chick."

[28] You mean the long hair, breasts flowing in the breeze, the ultra-hip look, it's oppressive to women who can't be that way.

[29] ROXANNE: On the whole, if you step back and look at what Black women are seeing and what working women are seeing, there's not much there to trust. I feel that's the same with what I've done. There's not much I have done that would bring us a great sense of unity.

[30] What I do feel the women's movement has done so far is question that whole image—however hypocritical some of us might be in not living up to the criticism—criticizing the whole media image of what sex is, of what a sexy, desirable woman is and making a satire out of that and debunking that whole thing. It is very important for all poor women, Black and White . . . because my own memories of how oppressive that is to not be able to live up to that model, not knowing that that image is a man-made one.

[31] And it helps to have braces on your teeth and all kinds of things when you're young, the kinds of things that poor women don't have so they're just marked forever with their class. It makes for class ugliness, and for Black women, especially, it is inevitable ugliness because they can't begin to meet that image.

[32] It is also extremely important for there to be the kind of split in the ruling class, what with the women beginning to break away and simply not identify with the class of men who rule.

[33] One reason that Black women do not have the need for a very strong separate women's movement is that Black women do not suffer from the negative power differential in relation to Black men that white women suffer in relation to white men. They simply don't and that's economically based. That is, Black women are almost fully employed, are capable of supporting themselves and have already much of the psychological sense of independence and strength that we are struggling to get. You see, they're ahead of us.

[34] We're going through a struggle that Black women have been forced to go through historically. It is good that we are doing that, but there is a kind of arrogance about saying: 'Well, poor Black women, when will they ever get themselves together and struggle like we are.' I think it's just the reverse.

[35] You've mentioned the negative connotations of the movement's campaign to repeal all abortion laws. I gather you don't think abortion is an important issue.

[36] ROXANNE: Abortion keeps us passive. It's a law that gets passed and something that gets done to us. And, as a tactic, it seems to me it's absolutely analogous to, almost the same as the suffrage issue and has exactly the same potential for completely sucking in the energy of the whole women's movement and then, when it's won—and I'm convinced the government is waiting to allow women to win abortion repeal because the government wants abortion repealed and could put it through any time it wants, because there's enough consciousness raised about that—I think we will sense that we've won that after devoting a great deal of energy to it. That's a possibility. I think enough people are aware of that that it won't happen. And the people who are working on that as their major issue are going to be isolated from the mainstream of the growing women's movement. I don't care how many other issues you raise, if that's the only thing that's legal and on paper, it's going to become the strongest issue at hand.

[37] And I think that there is a way to recognize what the system wants out of abortion at the same time that you're talking about this concept of a woman's right to control her own body. When I talk about that concept, I mean the right to learn karate, get a few muscles in your body and knock a man down if he bugs you. And not just to have an abortion. To refuse to have sex is a means of birth control.

[38] I mean there's only one way to get pregnant and that's intercourse. It has nothing to do with loving human relations. It has to do with most generally oppressive human relations. To raise that whole issue of woman's passivity, if you really want to talk about women controlling their own bodies, then talk about developing some skill and aim with the fist as well as child care and good medical care and so forth.

[39] It depressed me to think about the fact that the population control issue of the government could so easily coincide with the women's movement, at just the time when women were beginning to question their sole function—of motherhood. The middle-class women's rebellion against breeding is very healthy, but that this could then be used by the government as a population control gimmick is really possible only because of the historical circumstance that we can now begin to think about limiting population. I think the last hundred years of the development of the women's movement may be attributed to the fact that there is not such a necessity in the human race to reproduce in such numbers in order to survive. In fact, some say the reverse. I think that's also nonsense that there's such a critical danger at the present time. I think it's a smokescreen for much deeper problems in the world.

[40] Clearly, the center of life in the future is not going to be reproducing great numbers of people. When the human race was very tiny, there had to be an obsession with reproduction in order to increase the population. We are no longer needed as reproducers. This contributes to the possibility of our liberation but it also has devalued our existence a very great deal. This has been gradually happening in the last two or three centuries. Certainly in the last fifty years or so women have become ridiculed and useless people.

[41] As middle-class women, or women who have access to middle-

class privileges, we tend to blame children for our oppression because they're the only people underneath us, or we in fact do what the society tells us to do, to fulfill ourselves though having children, and I think neither of these are really resolutions to the problem of attitude toward children.

[42] The abortion repeal issue is a very anti-children thing at this time because we have not yet really raised the issue of 'feminism,' of caring for children. This should be the duty of all human beings.

[43] Poor women are already strongly feminist. I identify that from the way poor women see themselves in relation to children. They see themselves in relation to children in such a way that all men and women should come to see themselves, in relation to children—as being responsible in caring for children and their not being objectively burdens, but burdens because of the conditions under which they have to be raised.

[44] *So you're saying childbearing and caring for children are not oppressing women?*

[45] ROXANNE: Childbearing is the most common form of women's experience. Child rearing is less common because the upper classes pass it onto their servants. The idea of abortion repeal programmatically becoming the basis of unity among women is absurd. I don't think pregnancy is the basis of female oppression. I think its by-product, the total responsibility for child care, especially under economic conditions of a woman not being economically capable of caring for a number of children, having to have a man to provide for her and her children—I think that that is definitely a principal source of oppression. But I don't think reproduction, per se, is.

[46] *Especially with the reduction in family size, what remains that all women share in common?*

[47] ROXANNE: The role of housewife is still a woman's function. Sixty per cent of the women are occupied with housework twenty-four hours a day, 365 days a year. With private housework that's really what we're dealing with. If we are going to deal with masses of women, we have to deal with that. That is the material basis for the oppression of women. The fact that so many of us are doing supposedly socially useless work, unpaid labor in the feudal style of private production, means of course that we can be used as a surplus labor force. There is a vast number of women in that category, sixty per cent of half the population who can be brought into the labor force and put back out again at will.

[48] *Is this the middle-class women?*

[49] ROXANNE: It seems to me that there's a false consciousness in our movement that comes to the dichotomy of there being these classes of women: middle-class women, working-class women, and that we haven't really looked at the woman's objective position in relation to the economy, the social actuality of power and control. Women are not in positions of

power because they are juxtaposed to the people in positions of power: the mistresses, prostitutes, or secretaries or wives of men who have some relative power. They are isolated from one another. Having no organized power, they tend to take whatever they can get.

[50] *And put other women down to get there.*

[51] Roxanne: Horizontal oppression is how oppressed people keep one another oppressed, the philosophy being that, 'If we're going to be oppressed, all of us are going to be oppressed, by God. No one is going to get her head out.'

[52] This shooting down one another used to occur with Black people in the Black movement and certainly with women it occurs, and there's also fear of one woman being above another in terms of male appreciation. Of course that is much stronger among us than among other oppressed people because that is our source of subsistence—having a man.

[53] Some women say: 'I'm not oppressed.' When they go into detail they quite often mean: 'I have a man, I have a family, I have a house.' There are worse positions a person could be in.

[54] Women who work in industry or clerical work, or any of the categories that women work in also serve the function of doing the housework, childcare. This has not been resolved in the socialist countries either, so that working women everywhere have the double duty of doing their job and also doing the household chores. I think that the reason there is such contempt for women is because of our powerlessness in society.

[55] *So how do we change these relations?*

[56] Roxanne: I think we have to try to establish a basis of unity that is material rather than just saying: 'We're all women.' One way I began thinking about dealing with the problems has to do with forming a union. A household workers union which would be composed of all women, essentially, because all women are potentially in the role of doing housework at whatever level. Talk about women's work, this is what we always mean. We don't even mean sex. That's part of the parcel, but it's not the dominant part. It's really the household work and childcare, making beds and always being there and being comforter and all these things—all this is considered Acts of Love, not productive labor.

[57] A union would bring women out of the private sphere of work. I started thinking about it when I was in Atlanta and there was a garbage strike going on. It was so powerful and the people were really suffering from that garbage strike. I thought a few years ago nobody used to know there were garbage collectors. I guess we knew they were Black and get paid very little. Now everyone knows there are garbage collectors and that the whole city will fall apart if the garbage is not collected.

[58] That's also true of housework. Millions of hours of love. Act after act of love.

[59] *What could women do in a union? How could you strike? What would you demand?*

[60] ROXANNE: Struggle for things that would actually destroy that type of housework. public dining halls, free childcare—taking that out of the private home. That kind of labor and the people who work in those places would get paid so that any domestic workers that would work in a public place and not under the arbitrary control of one woman or man, would have bargaining rights. And the housewife would have a completely different concept, a pride in the fact that she's a worker. Because I do think there's a kind of pride in being a worker as opposed to being a leech, which is the position women are in now. I think women who work have more dignity, more independence, more competence than women who are housewives. That's very clear even when they're very exploited. Industrialization bringing the work into the public sphere won't make the work any easier but it will be seen as productive labor.

[61] *Then the union wouldn't strike against husbands?*

[62] ROXANNE: No. It would take women away from the focus of their oppression being a husband who either doesn't bring home enough money, loses his job, leaves her or beats her or whatever, in that people are turned against each other in the family. A woman would go away from this one, single, also powerless person to make her demands for a new washing machine into a political demand for public washing facilities. For the fact that her husband doesn't give her enough money, she would make demands with other women upon the price of food. In other words, to make public these demands rather than the kind of fighting that has to go on now. And it's fruitless. It doesn't get anywhere because it's like trying to get blood out of a turnip. The man doesn't have access either to these resources. Yet the woman is totally powerless, has no access to the outside world. It's kind of a mystery to her as a housewife just where this comes from.

[63] *What about sharing childcare?*

[64] ROXANNE: Caring for someone else is a maternal concept that women learn and it's good but when it's put off onto only one segment of the people, then those people are just slaves. And that should be democracized. Everyone should be doing these kinds of things but publicly. I don't see getting men to change the baby's diapers, something that's totally repulsive to men, in a private home. I say put pressure upon them to work in childcare centers and do that publicly.

[65] *It sounds like society would be altogether different if you had your way.*

[66] ROXANNE: We want a different world, not a share in this one, and we demand that all people be a part of it. We demand that all people be humane and responsible to others and we reject the paternalism that allows us to be 'free' of responsibility.

V
THE MEANS OF
SOCIAL CHANGE

Love, Law, and Civil Disobedience

Martin Luther King, Jr.

The late Martin Luther King, Jr., delivered this speech at the annual meeting of the Fellowship of the Concerned on November 16, 1961. It was an attempt to explain "nonviolence" as a means of achieving social change. He dismissed surrender and violence as unsatisfactory means of removing oppression, and explained both the history and methods used in nonviolent protest. Note the extensive use of comparisons and definitions to clarify his ideas, practices, and goals. This speech is essentially informative in purpose and nature, but where is the line between informing and persuading? How can you as a listener determine the speaker's purpose?

[1] Members of the Fellowship of the Concerned, of the Southern Regional Council, I need not pause to say how very delighted I am to be here today, and to have the opportunity of being a little part of this very significant gathering. I certainly want to express my personal appreciation to Mrs. Tilly and the members of the Committee, for giving me this opportunity. I would also like to express just a personal word of thanks and appreciation for your vital witness in this period of transition which we are facing in our Southland, and in the nation, and I am sure that as a result of this genuine concern, and your significant work in communities all across the South, we have a better South today and I am sure will have a better South tomorrow with your continued endeavor and I do want to express my personal gratitude and appreciation to you of the Fellowship of the Concerned for your significant work and for your forthright witness.

[2] Now, I have been asked to talk about the philosophy behind the student movement. There can be no gain-saying of the fact that we confront a crisis in race relations in the United States. This crisis has been

Reprinted with permission from The Rhetoric of Racial Revolt, Roy L. Hill, ed. (Denver: Golden Bell Press, 1964).

precipitated on the one hand by the determined resistance of reactionary forces in the South to the Supreme Court's decision in 1954 outlawing segregation in the public schools. And we know that at times this resistance has risen to ominous proportions. At times we find the legislative halls of the South ringing loud with such words as interposition and nullification. And all of these forces have developed into massive resistance. But we must also say that the crisis has been precipitated on the other hand by the determination of hundreds and thousands and millions of Negro people to achieve freedom and human dignity. If the Negro stayed in his place and accepted discrimination and segregation, there would be no crisis. But the Negro has a new sense of dignity, a new self respect, and new determination. He has reevaluated his own intrinsic worth. Now this new sense of dignity on the part of the Negro grows out of the same longing for freedom and human dignity on the part of the oppressed people all over the world; for we see it in Africa, we see it in Asia, and we see it all over the world. Now we must say that this struggle for freedom will not come to an automatic halt, for history reveals to us that once oppressed people rise up against that oppression, there is no stopping point short of full freedom. On the other hand, history reveals to us that those who oppose the movement for freedom are those who are in privileged positions who very seldom give up their privileges without strong resistance. And they very seldom do it voluntarily. So the sense of struggle will continue. The question is how will the struggle be waged.

[3] Now there are three ways that oppressed people have generally dealt with their oppression. One way is the method of acquiescence, the method of surrender; that is, the individuals will somehow adjust themselves to oppression, they adjust themselves to discrimination or to segregation or colonialism or what have you. The other method that has been used in history is that of rising up against the oppressor with corroding hatred and physical violence. Now of course we know about this method in western civilization, because in a sense it has been the hallmark of its grandeur, and the inseparable twin of western materialism. But there is a weakness in this method because it ends up creating many more social problems than it solves. And I am convinced that if the Negro succumbs to the temptation of using violence in his struggle for freedom and justice, unborn generations will be the recipients of a long and desolate night of bitterness. And our chief legacy to the future will be an endless reign of meaningless chaos.

[4] But there is another way, namely the way of non-violent resistance. This method was popularized in our generation by a little man from India, whose name was Mohandas K. Gandhi. He used this method in a magnificent way to free his people from the economic exploitation and the political domination inflicted upon them by a foreign power.

[5] This has been the method used by the student movement in the South and all over the United States. And naturally whenever I talk about the student movement I cannot be totally objective. I have to be somewhat subjective because of my great admiration for what the students have done. For in a real sense they have taken our deep groans and passionate yearnings for freedom, and filtered them in their own tender souls, and fashioned them into a creative protest which is an epic known all over our nation. As a result of their disciplined, non-violent, yet courageous struggle, they have been able to do wonders in the South, and in our nation. But this movement does have an underlying philosophy, it has certain ideas that are attached to it, it has certain philosophical precepts. These are the things that I would like to discuss for the few moments left.

[6] I would say that the first point or the first principle in the movement is the idea that means must be as pure as the end. This movement is based on the philosophy that ends and means must cohere. Now this has been one of the long struggles in history, the whole idea of means and ends. Great philosophers have grappled with it, and sometimes they have emerged with the idea, from Machiavelli on down, that the end justifies the means. There is a great system of thought in our world today, known as Communism. And I think that with all of the weakness and tragedies of Communism, we find its greatest tragedy right here, that it goes under the philosophy that the end justifies the means that are used in the process. So we can read or we can hear the Lenins say that lying, deceit, or violence, that many of these things justify the ends of the classless society.

[7] This is where the student movement and the non-violent movement that is taking place in our nation would break with Communism and any other system that would argue that the end justifies the means. For in the long run, we must see that the end represents the means in process and the ideal in the making. In other words, we cannot believe, or we cannot go with the idea that the end justifies the means because the end is pre-existent in the means. So the idea of non-violent resistance, the philosophy of non-violent resistance, is the philosophy which says that the means must be as pure as the end, that in the long run of history, immoral destructive means cannot bring about moral and constructive ends.

[8] There is another thing about this philosophy, this method of non-violence which is followed by the student movement. It says that those who adhere to or follow this philosophy must follow a consistent principle of non-injury. They must consistently refuse to inflict injury upon another. Sometimes you will read the literature of the student movement and see that, as they are getting ready for the sit-in or stand-in, they will read something like this, "if you are hit do not hit back, if you are cursed do not curse back." This is the whole idea, that the individual who is engaged in a non-violent struggle must never inflict injury upon another. Now this has an external aspect and it has an internal one. From the external point of view it means that the individuals involved must avoid external physical violence. So they don't have guns, they don't retaliate with physical violence. If they are hit in the process, they avoid external physical violence at every point. But it also means that they avoid internal violence of spirit. This is why the love ethic stands so high in the student movement. We have a great deal of talk about love and non-violence in this whole thrust.

[9] Now when the students talk about love, certainly they are not talking about emotional bosh, they are not talking about merely a sentimental outpouring; they're talking something much deeper, and I always have to stop and try to define the meaning of love in this context. The Greek language comes to our aid in trying to deal with this. There are three words in the Greek language for love, one is the word Eros. This is a beautiful type of love, it is an aesthetic love. Plato talks about it a great deal in his *Dialogue*, the yearning of the soul for the realm of the divine. It has come to us to be a sort of romantic love, and so in a sense we have read about it and experienced it. We've read about it in all the beauties of literature. I guess in a sense Edgar Allan Poe was talking about Eros when he talked about his beautiful Annabelle Lee, with the love surrounded by the halo of eternity. In a sense Shakespeare was talking about Eros when he said "Love is not love which alters when it alteration finds, or bends with the remover to remove; O' no! it is an ever fixéd mark that looks on tempests and is never shaken, it is the star to every wandering bark." (You know I remember that because I used to quote it to this little lady when we were courting; that's Eros.) The Greek language talks about Philia which was another level of love. It is an intimate affection between personal friends, it is a reciprocal love. On this level you love because you are loved. It is friendship.

[10] Then the Greek language comes out with another word which is called the Agape. Agape is more than romantic love, agape is more than friendship. Agape is understanding, creative, redemptive, good will to all men. It is an overflowing love which seeks nothing in return. Theologians would say that it is the love of God operating in the human heart. So that when one rises to love on this level, he loves men not because he likes them, not because their ways appeal to him, but he loves every man because God loves him. And he rises to the point of loving the person who does an evil deed while hating the deed that the person does. I think this is what Jesus meant when he said "love your enemies." I'm very happy that he didn't say like your enemies, because it is pretty difficult to like some people. Like is sentimental, and it is pretty difficult to like someone bombing your home; it is pretty difficult to like somebody threatening your children; it is difficult to like congressmen who spend all of their time trying to defeat civil rights. But Jesus says love them, and love is greater

than like. Love is understanding, redemptive, creative, good will for all men. And it is this idea, it is this whole ethic of love which is the idea standing at the basis of the student movement.

[11] There is something else: that one seeks to defeat the unjust system, rather than individuals who are caught in that system. And that one goes on believing that somehow this is the important thing, to get rid of the evil system and not the individual who happens to be misguided, who happens to be misled, who was taught wrong. The thing to do is to get rid of the system and thereby create a moral balance within society.

[12] Another thing that stands at the center of this movement is another idea: that suffering can be a most creative and powerful social force. Suffering has certain moral attributes involved, but it can be a powerful and creative social force. Now, it is very interesting at this point to notice that both violence and nonviolence agree that suffering can be a very powerful social force. But there is this difference: violence says that suffering can be a powerful social force by inflicting the suffering on somebody else; so this is what we do in war, this is what we do in the whole violent thrust of the violent movement. It believes that you achieve some end by inflicting suffering on another. The non-violent say that suffering becomes a powerful social force when you willingly accept that violence on yourself, so that self-suffering stands at the center of the non-violent movement and the individuals involved are able to suffer in a creative manner, feeling that unearned suffering is redemptive, and that suffering may serve to transform the social situation.

[13] Another thing in this movement is the idea that there is within human nature an amazing potential for goodness. There is within human nature something that can respond to goodness. I know somebody's liable to say that this is an unrealistic movement if it goes on believing that all people are good. Well, I didn't say that. I think the students are realistic enough to believe that there is a strange dichotomy of disturbing dualism within human nature. Many of the great philosophers and thinkers through the ages have seen this. It caused Ovid the Latin poet to say, "I see and approve the better things of life, but the evil things I do." It caused even St. Augustine to say, "Lord, make me pure, but not yet." So that that is in human nature. Plato, centuries ago said that the human personality is like a charioteer with two headstrong horses, each wanting to go in different directions, so that within our own individual lives we see this conflict and certainly when we come to the collective life of man, we see a strange badness. But in spite of this there is something in human nature that can respond to goodness. So that man is neither innately good nor is he innately bad; he has potentialities for both. So in this sense, Carlyle was right when he said that "there are depths in man which go down to the lowest hell, and heights which reach the highest heaven, for are not both heaven and

hell made out of him, ever-lasting miracle and mystery that he is?" Man has the capacity to be good, man has the capacity to be evil.

[14] And so the non-violent resister never lets this idea go, that there is something within human nature that can respond to goodness. So that a Jesus of Nazareth or a Mohandas Gandhi, can appeal to human beings and appeal to that element of goodness within them, and a Hitler can appeal to the element of evil within them. But we must never forget that there is something within human nature that can respond to goodness, that man is not totally depraved, to put it in theological terms, the image of God is never totally gone. And so the individuals who believe in this movement and who believe in non-violence and our struggle in the South, somehow believe that even the worst segregationist can become an integrationist. Now sometimes it is hard to believe that this is what this movement says, and it believes it firmly, that there is something within human nature that can be changed, and this stands at the top of the whole philosophy of the student movement and the philosophy of non-violence.

[15] It says something else. It says that it is as much a moral obligation to refuse to cooperate with evil as it is to cooperate with good. Non-cooperation with evil is as much a moral obligation as the cooperation with good. So that the student movement is willing to stand up courageously on the idea of civil disobedience. Now I think this is the part of the student movement that is probably misunderstood more than anything else. And it is a difficult aspect, because on the one hand the students would say, and I would say, and all the people who believe in civil rights would say, obey the Supreme Court's decision of 1954 and at the same time, we would disobey certain laws that exist on the statutes of the South today.

[16] This brings in the whole question of how can you be logically consistent when you advocate obeying some laws and disobeying other laws. Well, I think one would have to see the whole meaning of this movement at this point by seeing that the students recognize that there are two types of laws. There are just laws and there are unjust laws. And they would be the first to say obey the just laws, they would be the first to say that men and women have a moral obligation to obey just and right laws. And they would go on to say that we must see that there are unjust laws. Now the question comes into being, what is the difference, and who determines the difference, what is the difference between a just and an unjust law?

[17] Well, a just law is a law that squares with a moral law. It is a law that squares with that which is right, so that any law that uplifts human personality is a just law. Whereas that law which is out of harmony with the moral is a law which does not square with the moral law of the universe. It does not square with the law of God, so for that reason it is unjust and any law that degrades the human personality is an unjust law.

[18] Well, somebody says that that does not mean anything to me; first, I don't believe in these abstract things called moral laws and I'm not too religious, so I don't believe in the law of God; you have to get a little more concrete, and more practical. What do you mean when you say that a law is unjust, and a law is just? Well, I would go on to say in more concrete terms that an unjust law is a code that the majority inflicts on the minority that is not binding on itself. So that this becomes difference made legal. Another thing that we can say is that an unjust law is a code which the majority inflicts upon the minority, which that minority had no part in enacting or creating, because that minority had no right to vote in many instances, so that the legislative bodies that made these laws were not democratically elected. Who could ever say that the legislative body of Mississippi was democratically elected, or the legislative body of Alabama was democratically elected, or the legislative body even of Georgia has been democratically elected, when there are people in Terrell County and in other counties because of the color of their skin who cannot vote? They confront reprisals and threats and all of that; so that an unjust law is a law that individuals did not have a part in creating or enacting because they were denied the right to vote.

[19] Now the same token of just law would be just the opposite. A just law becomes saneness made legal. It is a code that the majority, who happen to believe in that code, compel the minority, who don't believe in it, to follow, because they are willing to follow it themselves, so it is saneness made legal. Therefore the individuals who stand up on the basis of civil disobedience realize that they are following something that says that there are just laws and there are unjust laws. Now, they are not anarchists. They believe that there are laws which must be followed; they do not seek to defy the law, they do not seek to evade the law. For many individuals who would call themselves segregationists and who would hold on to segregation at any cost seek to defy the law, they seek to evade the law, and their process can lead on into anarchy. They seek in the final analysis to follow a way of uncivil disobedience, not civil disobedience. And I submit that the individual who disobeys the law, whose conscience tells him it is unjust and who is willing to accept the penalty by staying in jail until that law is altered, is expressing at the moment the very highest respect for law.

[20] This is what the students have followed in their movement. Of course there is nothing new about this, they feel that they are in good company and rightly so. We go back and read the *Apology* and the *Crito*, and you see Socrates practicing civil disobedience. And to a degree academic freedom is a reality today because Socrates practiced civil disobedience. The early Christians practiced civil disobedience in a superb manner, to a point where they were willing to be thrown to the lions. They were

willing to face all kinds of suffering in order to stand up for what they knew was right even though they knew it was against the laws of the Roman Empire.

[21] We could come up to our own day and we see it in many instances. We must never forget that everything that Hitler did in Germany was "legal." It was illegal to aid and comfort a Jew, in the days of Hitler's Germany. But I believe that if I had the same attitude then as I have now I would publicly aid and comfort my Jewish brothers in Germany if Hitler were alive today calling this an illegal process. If I lived in South Africa today in the midst of the white supremacy law in South Africa, I would join Chief Luthuli and others in saying break these unjust laws. And even let us come up to America. Our nation in a sense came into being through a massive act of civil disobedience, for the Boston Tea Party was nothing but a massive act of civil disobedience. Those who stood up against the slave laws, the abolitionists, by and large practiced civil disobedience. So I think these students are in good company, and they feel that by practicing civil disobedience they are in line with men and women through the ages who have stood up for something that is morally right.

[22] Now there are one or two other things that I want to say about this student movement, moving out of the philosophy of non-violence, something about what it is a revolt against. On the one hand it is a revolt against the negative peace that had encompassed the South for many years. I remember when I was in Montgomery, Ala., one of the white citizens came to me one day and said—and I think he was very sincere about this— that in Montgomery for all of these years we have been such a peaceful community, we have had so much harmony in race relations and then you people have started this movement and boycott, and it has done so much to disturb race relations, and we just don't love the Negro like we used to love them, because you have destroyed the harmony and the peace that we once had in race relations. And I said to him, in the best way I could say and I tried to say it in non-violent terms, we have never had peace in Montgomery, Ala., we have never had peace in the South. We have had a negative peace, which is merely the absence of tension; we've had a negative peace in which the Negro patiently accepted his situation and his plight, but we've never had true peace, we've never had positive peace, and what we're seeking now is to develop this positive peace. For we must come to see that peace is not merely the absence of some negative force, it is the presence of a positive force. True peace is not merely the absence of tension, but it is the presence of justice and brotherhood. I think this is what Jesus meant when he said, I come not to bring peace but a sword. Now Jesus didn't mean he came to start war, to bring a physical sword, and he didn't mean, I come not to bring positive peace. But I think what Jesus was saying in substance was this, that I come not to bring an old negative

peace, which makes for stagnant passivity and deadening complacency, I come to bring something different, and whenever I come, a conflict is precipitated, between the old and the new, whenever I come a struggle takes place between justice and injustice, between the forces of light and the forces of darkness. I come not to bring a negative peace, but a positive peace, which is brotherhood, which is justice, which is the Kingdom of God.

[23] And I think this is what we are seeking to do today, and this movement is a revolt against a negative peace and a struggle to bring into being a positive peace, which makes for true brotherhood, true integration, true person-to-person relationships. This movement is also revolt against what is often called tokenism. Here again many people do not understand this, they feel that in this struggle the Negro will be satisfied with tokens of integration, just a few students and a few schools here and there and a few doors open here and there. But this isn't the meaning of the movement and I think that honesty impels me to admit it everywhere I have an opportunity, that the Negro's aim is to bring about complete integration in American life. And he has come to see that token integration is little more than token democracy, which ends up with many new evasive schemes and it ends up with new discrimination, covered up with such niceties of complexity. It is very interesting to discover that the movement has thrived in many communities that had token integration. So this reveals that the movement is based on a principle that integration must become real and complete, not just token integration.

[24] It is also a revolt against what I often call the myth of time. We hear this quite often, that only time can solve this problem. That if we will only be patient, and only pray—which we must do, we must be patient and we must pray—but there are those who say just do these things and wait for time, and time will solve this problem. Well the people who argue this do not themselves realize that time is neutral, that it can be used constructively or destructively. At points the people of ill will, the segregationists, have used time much more effectively than the people of good will. So individuals in the struggle must come to realize that it is necessary to aid time, that without this kind of aid, time itself will become an ally of the insurgent and primitive forces of social stagnation. Therefore, this movement is a revolt against the myth of time.

[25] There is a final thing that I would like to say to you, this movement is a movement based on faith in the future. It is a movement based on a philosophy, the possibility of the future bringing into being something real and meaningful. It is a movement based on hope. I think this is very important. The students have developed a theme song for their movement, maybe you've heard it. It goes something like this "we shall overcome, deep in my heart, I do believe, we shall overcome," and then they go on to say another verse, "we are not afraid, we are not afraid today, deep in my heart

I do believe, we shall overcome." So it is out of this deep faith in the future that they are able to move out and adjourn the councils of despair, and to bring new light in the dark chambers of pessimism. I can remember the times that we've been together, I remember that night in Montgomery, Ala., when we had stayed up all night, discussing the Freedom Rides, and that morning came to see that it was necessary to go on with the Freedom Rides, that we would not in all good conscience call an end to the Freedom Rides at that point. And I remember the first group got ready to leave, to take a bus for Jackson, Miss., we all joined hands and started singing together. "We shall overcome, we shall overcome." And something within me said, now how is it that these students can sing this, they are going down to Mississippi, they are going to face hostile and jeering mobs, and yet they could sing, "We shall overcome." They may even face physical death, and yet they could sing, "We shall overcome." Most of them realized that they would be thrown into jail, and yet they could sing, "We shall overcome, we are not afraid." Then something caused me to see at that moment the real meaning of the movement. That students had faith in the future. That the movement was based on hope, that this movement had something within it that says somehow even though the arc of the moral universe is long, it bends toward justice. And I think this should be a challenge to all others who are struggling to transform the dangling discords of our Southland into a beautiful symphony of brotherhood. There is something in this student movement which says to us, that we shall overcome. Before the victory is won some may have to get scarred up, but we shall overcome. Before the victory of brotherhood is achieved, some will maybe face physical death, but we shall overcome. Before the victory is won, some will lose jobs, some will be called Communists, and reds, merely because they believe in brotherhood, some will be dismissed as dangerous rabble-rousers and agitators merely because they're standing up for what is right, but we shall overcome. That is the basis of this movement, and as I like to say, there is something in this universe that justifies Carlyle in saying no lie can live forever. We shall overcome because there is something in this universe which justifies William Cullen Bryant in saying truth crushed to earth shall rise again. We shall overcome because there is something in this universe that justifies James Russell Lowell in saying, truth forever on the scaffold, wrong forever on the throne. Yet that scaffold sways the future, and behind the dim unknown standeth God within the shadows, keeping watch above His own. With this faith in the future, with this determined struggle, we will be able to emerge from the bleak and desolate midnight of man's inhumanity to man, into the bright and glittering daybreak of freedom and justice. Thank you.

A Strategy for the Seventies:
Unity, Coalition, Negotiation

Whitney M. Young, Jr.

The late Whitney M. Young, Jr., for many years the executive direc-
tor of the National Urban League, delivered this speech on July 19,
1970, at the National Urban League Conference held in New York.
He reviewed the American scene, past and present; listed the achieve-
ments of the National Urban League; and discussed the strategies
used in the past and the strategy needed in the 1970's to gain the
dignity and rights withheld from minorities in America. His proposed
strategy is persuasive rather than coercive. Notice the language em-
ployed to "picture" the America of today and the need for a new
strategy.

[1] There comes a time in the life of every great nation when it finds
itself at the crossroads—on one side, the path of division, decline, and
oblivion; on the other, the path of progress, purpose, and decency. There is
every indication that this nation, almost two centuries after its birth by fire,
is at that crossroads.

[2] At every hand we see chaos instead of concern, drift instead of
decision, and hate instead of hope. It may well be that we are witnessing
the exhaustion of the American spirit; the full-scale retreat by a people nur-
turing false dreams of superiority; a retreat from the responsibilities and
decency that characterize true greatness.

[3] Six renowned historians recently probed the confused spirit of our
country in a national weekly. One called this "The Age of Rubbish." Another proclaimed "the end of the American era." Another said we are
experiencing "a massive breakdown." Yet another said we suffer from "a
case of hypochondria." All, Conservative and Marxist alike, agreed there is
a crisis of confidence. The overwhelming impression one gets from their
comments is doubt that the quality of national leadership today is adequate
to the magnitude of the challenges faced.

Reprinted with permission of the National Urban League.

[4] The signs, then, are unmistakable that this unhappy land, this bitterly polarized society, seems incapable of living up to the ideals and dreams that it purportedly held for so long.

[5] A hateful war that no one wants has spread to neighboring lands. A public inured to "body counts" and "enemy kills" has found that its own children—at Kent State and Jackson—form a new set of body count numbers.

[6] A country whose very survival depends upon the reconstruction of its young, its poor, and its neglected non-white minorities seems only capable of hate rather than love, isolation rather than reclamation, and killing rather than saving.

[7] Repression is rampant. Americans—for the first time in decades—now have their own "show" trials, political prisoners, and midnight police raids that kill people in their beds, people whose crime was dissent from a society that persecuted them.

[8] And fanning the flames of repression have been the mindless pseudo-revolutionists of the left whose idea of changing society is to plant bombs where they might kill the innocent—and the mindless pseudo-conservatives of the right whose idea of standing up for the democracy they are sworn to protect is to destroy it through division and hate. Those superpatriots who yell "America, love it or leave it" ought to recognize the words of the great French philosopher Albert Camus who said: "I would like to be able to love my country and justice at the same time."

[9] This is an America that generously supports a giant welfare subsidy program for the rich in the form of unbridled defense spending, space programs, and supersonic planes, while refusing funds to feed starving black kids in Mississippi or housing to shelter the poverty-stricken of the rural areas and cities.

[10] It is a nation whose answer to a disturbing inflation is to create an even more dangerous recession. It tinkers with the economic system to artificially induce unemployment, to bring housing construction to a virtual end, and to drive all hope from the hearts of the poor. And in so doing, it may yet create the Depression that will rob it of the wealth it tries so hard to protect.

[11] Beset by the twin evils of repression and recession, black people today are fearful that the limited gains of the sixties are in danger. We have seen that in spite of legal and legislative victories, racism is still alive in new and different forms.

[12] We know all too well that the cost of liberty is less than the price of repression, and that the cost of economic justice is but a fraction of the price of racial privilege and exploitation.

[13] It has become more clear than ever, that the black man's fight

for respect and for manhood is also a fight to right the wrongs of a bloated, sick society, and to bring it back to its senses.

[14] Our task at this Conference will be to devise the strategies that will ensure that the cause of equality, for which so much blood and tears have been shed, will triumph in this land. In our sessions and workshops we will question the prevailing myths that entangle current thinking on economic and political problems afflicting blacks and other minorities, and we will continue to move beyond the narrow limits of debate to get at the roots of the problem of bringing power to the powerless.

[15] I am hopeful that out of this Conference will come strategies for the seventies; the framework for organizing for results, results that will have an impact upon the millions of victims of racism and neglect, a neglect sometimes called "benign" but more accurately called "callous."

[16] The Urban League, at this stage of its history, has the responsibility to continue in its efforts to pull together America's minority communities in order to mobilize its enormous reservoir of talent and skills to win political, economic, and social victories.

[17] The Urban League is in position to assert such leadership not only because of its historic strengths, its dedicated staff of full-time experts and the devoted cooperation of its thousands of volunteers, but also because of its own experience with change; its own success in developing a new thrust into the ghettos of America.

[18] For, in this our sixtieth year, the Urban League has evolved far from the limited functions envisioned by its founders. The social services we once provided newcomers to the cities of the North have had to be supplemented and replaced by a much more comprehensive organization of the black community. Two years ago, we organized our New Thrust program to do just that. The Urban League moved into the ghetto—physically and spiritually—and is serving as an enabling vehicle for a black community determined to win unity, dignity, and power. We responded to that need. We responded with vigor, and with the realization that we exist to serve the community, to identify with it, and to provide the technical assistance and know-how to enable the community itself to organize for successful action.

[19] For we believe that "Power to the People" is but an empty phrase unless the people can be provided with the mechanism, technical assistance, and opportunities to make that power work for them in their own communities, on their own terms, under their own leadership. And a clenched fist is useless, if, when forced open, it is found to be empty of the resources of money, intellect, and the will to do the job.

[20] New Thrust has proved itself. In city after city, local affiliates have become more relevant to the needs of the ghetto. In city after city,

while continuing to keep vital channels of communication with the white community open, we have served as the catalyst that brought blacks together to win victories.

[21] The Urban League movement continues to be flexible, relevant, and vital. We have successfully shifted gears from treating the results of racism and poverty to mounting a full-scale attack on the causes of racism and poverty. The Urban League has taken on a commitment to change the institutions and the society that perpetuates injustice.

[22] And that is not a short-term commitment. The New Thrust activities that started as a laboratory for community change are now part and parcel of our movement. New Thrust is no longer a separate program; it is structurally a part of our ongoing operations, and its spirit and thinking permeate every facet of our movement.

[23] In order to insure our increased effectiveness, we have implemented structural changes within the National Office, beginning with the addition of a competent Deputy Director, that will increase our accountability and provide better planning and operating procedures. Our new Departments of Research, Personnel and Training, and our strengthened Washington Bureau—together with a redefining of our program planning and operating procedures—will make possible more effective services to our now-almost 100 affiliates.

[24] The past year also saw the Urban League initiate a broad coalition of groups to influence what we tried to make the first accurate Census count of non-white peoples in the history of the nation. The "Make Black Count" campaign was founded on the realization that by undercounting the actual numbers of blacks and browns in America, the government, in effect, was withholding from them the federal aid distributed on a per capita basis. Black communities across the land were not getting their fair share of hospital and school monies, or even proper representation in Congress and State Legislatures. The figures are not all in yet, but the "Make Black Count" staff will be "riding herd" on the Census Bureau to insure that blacks—blacks—for a welcome change—get a fair count.

[25] But equal to the importance of the count itself was the way the campaign was able to bring black people together, making it possible to deal with the Census Bureau from a position of strength.

[26] The "Make Black Count" campaign has been a unified effort of the black community. It has been a coalition of all representative groups —organized welfare mothers, street gangs, church members, sororities, civil rights organizations, and others. The Urban League was the catalyst, the enabler, the provider of resources and technical assistance. We were content to take a back seat in this. Our intent was not to hog headlines or be pictured on television. All literature, posters, publicity, etc., highlighted the coalition, not the Urban League. Our goal was to bring the community

together on a vital issue, and to set in motion the national and local coalitions that will become the basis for further cooperation and unity. Our experience in this campaign convinces me that our purpose has been successful, and we shall build upon it in the coming months.

[27] We joined, also, with others to mount campaigns to protest the willful murders of Black Panthers and black college students by our home-grown version of the SS, and to successfully protest the nomination of insensitive judges to the Supreme Court that protects our liberties from the very system of racism they represent.

[28] The Urban League is active on a broad series of fronts:

. . . At the request of key Congressional leaders we are submitting to the Congress a detailed agenda for an updated Domestic Marshall Plan which we first proposed in 1964 to do for the victims of American racism and the poor of all colors what America so willingly did for the European victims of World War II.

[29] . . . We have started the National Urban League Housing Foundation to expand the supply of low and moderate income housing and to give black people a share in the building and control of their own housing.

[30] . . . We took a giant step toward strengthening black colleges through the Black Executive Exchange Program that brings blacks who have made it in the competitive give-and-take of the professions and business to lecture and advise students and faculty at black institutions of higher education.

[31] . . . And we have served the needs of ghetto youth in a variety of ways, including consultation and assistance for Youth Organizations United, the national federation of over 200 city street gangs that is helping to channel the energies of these youngsters into constructive action on behalf of their communities.

[32] And, further serving youth, our summer student program brought 100 college student leaders again into the ghettos of America in a constructive program to help organize the black community, and to place the talent and spirits of campus youth at the service of their brothers and sisters.

[33] . . . We moved to fill the nationwide vacuum in child care through a Day Care Center Corporation that promises to fill a crying need for neighborhood day care centers operated and controlled by the community.

[34] . . . Our new Consumer Protection Program is designed at organizing the exploited minority community to a new awareness of making the most effective use of their scarce dollars and ending the callous preying upon the poor that typifies so much of the economic life of the ghetto.

[35] . . . The Urban League's pioneering Street Academies will come

to many more communities through the establishment of an Urban Education Institute that will provide the framework for planning and consulting with other institutions and the community in order to duplicate many times over our successes in helping deprived youngsters to recover from the failures of the heartless educational bureaucracies, and go on to higher educational goals.

[36] . . . Our Labor Education Advancement Program (LEAP) is responsible for the greatest breakthrough of black apprentices into the building trades in history, while at the same time creating and supporting black contractors.

[37] . . . Our On-the-Job Training programs are the most efficient in the country, with the highest retention rate at the lowest cost per trainee.

[38] Other Urban League programs are helping to develop black businessmen, bring new opportunities to returning veterans, and family planning and mental retardation services to the black community under its own control for the first time. And our various job placement and training programs pumped $400 million of cool, green cash into the black community in new and added wages and salaries.

[39] But we cannot be complacent about our successes, accomplished with limited resources. They represent a challenge for still greater efforts in the future; a base from which we must build the coalitions and unity without which racism will remain supreme, and poverty will possess the souls of the real forgotten Americans—the blacks, the browns, and the reds of the rural and urban ghettos.

[40] This new decade could bring promise of a new era in the relations between the races. Just as the nation as a whole is at a crossroads, so, too, black people face a new turning point, a decisive strategic moment that may put us on a new path to freedom. Just as there is some doubt whether the nation will choose the right path to greatness there must be doubts, especially in the light of the historic racism of America, that the seventies will bring true equality for black people. But while we may question the future, it becomes our duty to mobilize and steel ourselves for a new phase of struggle.

[41] Black Americans first pursued a *strategy of conciliation*. Fresh from the prison of slavery, the Freedmen and their sons tried to work with whites and convince them to act with decency. Whites remained in basic control of all matters affecting blacks, and the strategy of conciliation became, above all, a strategy of survival, a strategy to squeeze short-term gains under adversity.

[42] Then there came a *strategy of organization*. Blacks created the institutions without which there can be no community and no progress in a hostile society. These were the years that saw the birth of the NAACP, the Urban League, and educational, civil, religious and business associations.

The institutional structure of the black community took shape, and, abandoned by white society, blacks came together to build strength for the inevitable future confrontation with unbridled white power.

[43] The next phase was the *strategy of confrontation*, in which the institutions of the black community staged a frontal assault on the pillars of racism. This was the era of the boycott, the sit-in, ride-ins, wade-ins, lie-ins and all the other disruptive tactics that confronted Americans not with the pliant, silent oppressed blacks they wanted, but with the proud, determined black men and women who insisted on equality.

[44] We will be forever grateful for the dedicated, fearless warriors of CORE, SNCC, SCLC, the NAACP and the Urban League who fought the evils of racism on its home grounds—in the Southern Black Belt, and in the rigged courts and bigoted cities of the North.

[45] And, basically, this strategy worked. To it we owe the destruction of the formal, legal structure of racism in America. To it we owe the passage of laws and the legal decisions that provide a framework from which we can pursue the goals of complete equality. To it we owe the world-wide realization that America is plagued by racism, and our country has won not the respect, not even the envy, of the world's peoples, but their pity that so great a nation can be so incapable of morality and action to end poverty and bigotry.

[46] The suspicions harbored by black people of this Administration's intentions, suspicions that are supported by many of its actions, have led to intensified confrontations. Last year, at our annual Conference in Washington, I recited a long list of Administration actions and warned that black people would not stand for a reversion to official attitudes and actions directed against them. A few weeks ago Bishop Spottswood, chairman of the NAACP, reasserted the widespread black disillusionment with the Administration in a forceful indictment that accurately reflected much of the mood of black people today. This mood was further reflected in the Gallup Poll of last week which shows the overwhelming majority of black people dissatisfied with the current Administration.

[47] It is obvious that where blacks are concerned, the Administration faces a credibility gap of enormous proportions. But it persists in claiming that the record does not justify this suspicion; that progress is being made, and that it does not intend to abandon blacks to the evil expedient of a Southern strategy that tries to out-Wallace Wallace.

[48] The record is sometimes muddied. As critical as I have been of Administration actions, I do admit that there are some signs that elements of this Administration are moving forward to bring about change. In recent weeks there have been indications that tax-exemptions for the South's private "Hate Academies" will be cut off; that school desegregation might be implemented; that the government proposes to move more

strongly against job discrimination. And there are indications that agencies such as OEO and HEW will channel new funds and programs into black organizations that have the expertise and the community's respect to do the job that others failed to do.

[49] All these may be but straws in the wind, but it would be a mistake for us to fail to recognize that within every Administration there are contending forces. To cease to fight for our victories and to fail to negotiate with those in power is to leave the field to the political Neanderthals that so far seem to have dominated decision-making in the past few years.

[50] Early in his Administration, the President asked black Americans to judge him by his deeds and not his words. We have done that—and we have been greatly disappointed. Both words and deeds have left a bitterness that must now be transcended. Black people have—with justification—always judged white America with suspicion and disappointment. Promises have rarely led to performance, and words as well as well-meaning deeds have often been traps to further ensnare us.

[51] We have been forced by this Administration to react with defensive measures, if not actual confrontation, and perhaps now a new strategy would be more fitting. For these tactics were based on protest born of powerlessness. I believe that we have demonstrated that we do have some power now—power to make America sit and listen, and to negotiate with us as equal partners. America can no longer afford to ignore its awakened black masses. And no Administration—unless it is willing to preside over the destruction of American democracy, can afford to refuse the just demands of its neglected minorities.

[52] While we would hope that the nation's leadership would exercise the kind of determined, crusading sense of mission that is the hallmark of great leadership, it is a fact of life that there is developing a national stand-off between those of us who are fighting for justice and those who want to maintain the status quo.

[53] This is an impasse that leads nowhere, unless it be to further polarization, further division, further bitterness. White society has shown that it lacks the courage and the imagination to break this impasse by moving constructively. It is up to the black community to show the way.

[54] Our cause is just. But white America still possesses the power. We must forge the union of justice with power. In the words of Pascal: "Justice and power must be brought together, so that whatever is just may be powerful, and whatever is powerful may be just."

[55] I propose that the just and the powerful deal with each other as equals in a *strategy of negotiation*.

[56] White society has the trappings of power—its police, its army, its law. But blacks have demonstrated effectively that unless our just demands are dealt with, these trappings of power only make a society muscle-bound;

only drive it into displays of raw, naked power, displays that solve nothing and tear apart everything.

[57] The two Americas—black and white—need each other. Let us break the rigid confines of charges and countercharges, protest and neglect. Let us negotiate our way out of the impasse that threatens to split the country apart.

[58] By all means, we must continue to confront injustice. A strategy of negotiation does not imply weakness; on the contrary, it implies strength —the strength a unified black community can demonstrate. In the words of John F. Kennedy: "Let us never negotiate out of fear; but let us never fear to negotiate." Such a strategy demands from white America that it face up to the realities of a situation in which black young men are sent thousands of miles from home to fight and die for a cause labeled democracy, while democracy is denied them in the swollen ghettos of New York and in the sullen farmlands of Mississippi.

[59] It demands from white America that it implement a massive Domestic Marshall Plan that will rescue all Americans from poverty and disease.

[60] And above all, it demands from white America that it demonstrate the will, the honesty, and the sincerity to face its black brothers on equal terms, as peers in a joint effort to rid the nation of the cancer of racism.

[61] A strategy of negotiation demands from black America the power to negotiate from a position of strength. I believe we have demonstrated that power. In one sense, we have amply demonstrated a power to disrupt. In another sense, we have demonstrated, through the election of black mayors and legislators, political strength, and through the relentless accomplishment of our people against great odds, a changing economic and educational strength. We have made the most of the limited opportunities available to the point where we have the pride, the strength, and the accomplishments which should compel white leadership to sit down with us as equals.

[62] A strategy of negotiation demands of black leadership a sense of unity and purpose, without which we will be subject to the old divide-and-conquer tactics oppressors have always used. It will demand of us a discipline and a willingness to rise above differences of doctrine and personality for the greater good of all black people. We must, more than ever, impose upon ourselves and our organizations a community of spirit and a fraternal bond that will enable us to better negotiate from a base of strength and unity.

[63] Because we believe so strongly in the need for a unified black community to negotiate from a position of strength, we here and now issue a Call to Black Leadership to meet and to discuss an agenda for change.

[64] We want to arrive at a broad consensus of positions that can be negotiated with White America.

[65] We call for a meeting of blacks that includes all points of view from all shades of the spectrum of opinion.

[66] We would like to cooperate with our brothers and sisters of all persuasions. We seek peaceful dialogue, not only with those whose opinions we share, but with all representative elements of the black community.

[67] In unity there is strength, and we seek to help to bring about a unified black position with which White Society can be confronted and with which it must negotiate.

[68] It will not be easy to achieve such unity, because there are those whose experiences have led them to despair of white America ever acting in a decent way. But I have confidence that black people will muster the courage and the strength to make one last effort, based on our common sufferings, to stand united against the system that oppresses us.

[69] And for America, this may be the last opportunity she has to deal with black Americans and to negotiate with leaders responsible to their people, before the terrifying prospect of internal strife, armed suppression and needless destruction descend fully upon us all.

[70] Black unity is essential for black progress. This is no time for divisions. This is no time for us to mimic the polarization of white society. Only by unified action can we break the bonds that chain us. Only by unified action can we force America to become moral. Only by unified action can we forge the alliances across racial lines that promise progress.

[71] And only through unity can we cut through the undergrowth of myth and misunderstanding and unite with other minorities to forge a new coalition for a better tomorrow.

[72] I know that blacks have often been suspicious of such alliances. We have become contemptuous of an America that has "discovered" its problems so recently, although we have struggled with them for so long. We sense that other causes have higher priority than our own—that the motives of others are not always the same as ours, and that our suffering is so much more intense, and has been so prolonged.

[73] But we must not let ourselves become imprisoned by concepts of race that ignore the other causes of our misery. As W. E. B. DuBois pointed out: "Back of the problem of race and color lies a greater problem which both obscures and implements it: and that is the fact that so many civilized persons are willing to live in comfort even if the price of this is poverty, ignorance, and disease of the majority of their fellow-men."

[74] The economic and power dimensions of the problems facing us can be met through alliances with others in this twisted society who are hurting, too.

[75] The problems of poverty are not black alone. There is hunger in the tenements and shacks of whites and browns and reds as well. There is misery in Appalachian ghost-towns, in the barrios of the West, in migrant labor camps, and in Indian reservations. And there is misery here in New York's Harlem, South Bronx, and Bedford Stuyvesant.

[76] America has grown fat and heavy with the sweat and labor of all minorities; now she must grow proud and strong through an alliance based on our realism and sense of purpose. There is at hand the raw material for building the strong alliance for social justice that is essential if America is to be saved—and we must save her if we are not *all* to go down the drain. While it is an historic fact that we came here on different ships, it is imperative that we realize that we're in the same boat now.

[77] Coalitions for action can be formed with those whose frustrations may be somewhat different from those of minorities and the poor. White workers are hurting economically—just as we are. The top five per cent of the population makes twenty per cent of the income; the bottom twenty per cent makes only five per cent of the income. And that hasn't changed despite the New Deal, the Fair Deal, and all the other efforts at reform in the past. The white working class must be helped to understand that they, too, are dying in Vietnam; they, too, are hurting from the recession; and that they, too, are plagued by many of the problems that plague black people.

[78] The white working class can also unite with us to combat crime. For all the talk of crime in the streets, it is the black community that suffers disproportionately from crime. If you are black, the chances that you will be robbed are triple those if you are white; the chances you'll know burglary and car theft are almost double. If you make less than $3,000 your chances of being robbed are five times higher than if your income is over $10,000; your chances of being raped are four times as high; and your chances of being burglarized, double. Blacks and whites can join together to combat the fear that grips both our communities.

[79] Moreover, the deep frustrations caused by the expanding war; the horror of the Jackson and Kent State killings; the growing unemployment and recession; the stock market's steep decline; and the dissatisfaction with the rampant materialism that poisons the environment have convinced millions of Americans that you cannot tolerate injustice to the few without encouraging the erosion of justice for the many. Affluent Americans are beginning to see these connections and they are beginning to listen to their children, who are not only concerned with the poverty of the ghetto, but also are angry at the poverty of the spirit that afflicts their elders.

[80] I believe that the time is now for broad coalitions.

[81] I believe that the many disparate and contending forces in our society today, the diverse people and groups trying to change some small

corner of American life, can be brought to see how racism and mindless materialism work hand-in-hand to turn the American dream into a nightmare.

[82] And I believe that—whether because they pursue their own self-interest or because they move their idealism to a higher, more realistic plane—a new coalition can be forged that will once more return America to a sense of purpose and a will to justice.

[83] I believe the time has come when black people must unite, must create coalitions in order to negotiate a peace that will settle the issues that divide the country and, by so doing, bring us together.

[84] The proud black spirit of today seeks justice and decency. It seeks to move beyond racism to a new era of progress and reconciliation. It seeks power not for its own sake, but in order to use it wisely and to prevent its misuse by racism. It seeks peace with honor, justice with respect. It seeks a newer world, and a better tomorrow.

> And for that tomorrow,
> God, give us men,
> Men who are proud of their Godliness,
> Yet humble in their humanity;
> Men who know themselves, but who in knowing themselves
> Do not ignore others;
> Men who are conscious of others, not only of what
> They can derive from them, but also give to them;
> God give us men,
> Men like Abraham Lincoln, Frederick Douglass,
> Franklin D. Roosevelt and John Brown
> Who would not stop at the cheap art of espousing causes,
> But who championed men among the anonymous mass of men;
> Men like these whose piety
> Lay not only in credal affirmation, but rather in the
> Confirmation of their deeds.
> To this end,
> We need Thy help,
> And with Thy help we may yet, all of us, become men;
> All of us brothers,
> All of us Thy children;
> All of us truly human.

Immorality, Racism, and Survival

Charles G. Hurst, Jr.

Charles G. Hurst, Jr., president of Malcolm X College, delivered this speech at the annual summer conference of the Speech Communication Association, July 11, 1970, in Chicago. The audience consisted primarily of white college professors, and Hurst spoke to them about racism, young people, and needed changes in college education. Can you discern the speaker's purpose and strategy? How well is this speech adapted to this audience? How does the speaker enhance his credibility with this audience?

[1] For a time I didn't know quite what to talk about to this illustrious group, although I thought a lot about potential topics. Then just a few days ago I learned that President Nixon had signed another treaty with the Indians. This caught my attention because in the past when treaties were signed with the Indians it cost them such assets as New York, Boston, Chicago, San Francisco, Denver, Texas, and a few other valuable pieces of real estate. This thought led me to reflect: "All those poor Indians have left are their reservations, could it be that this treaty will cause them to lose these, too"? A silly thought?

[2] I reflected then on some other recent newspaper articles. One in particular stated that five years ago the United States and Soviet Russia each had a nuclear arms stockpile sufficient to kill every man, woman, and child in the world twenty times over. Five years from now, the article continued, each power will have five times as many. I began to speculate on how interesting it might be to talk about what we're going to feel like when we've all been killed a hundred times.

[3] I recalled another article in which the Pope called on all to fight "racialism" as the most dangerous threat to world peace because it "disfigures man's image, twists consciences, violently separates men from each

Reprinted by permission of Charles G. Hurst, Jr.

other, and divides nations." I felt a certain comfort in learning that the Pope has become concerned enough to speak out unequivocally on this most important source of human conflict. Maybe an international conscience, I contemplated, can accomplish what has become an apparent impossibility for the national conscience of America.

[4] On a nearby page of the same newspaper I saw still another headline that appeared at first glance to be a cause for hope—"Minority Group Students Up 25%." Twenty-five per cent of anything ought to be quite a bit, I said to myself. But a closer look at the details revealed that the increase was only from 3.7% to 4.5%. Well, I mused with a sense of disappointment, things are getting better. I guess a little bit of freedom is better than none at all. Or is it?

[5] Then another headline caught my eye: "A Word or Two about Agnew." No one can ignore Vice President Agnew these days. He is a man whose vitriolic phrases, stilted though they may be, have reignited some old hatreds and recreated some antiquated racial myths. Reading about the vice president's excursions in semantics, hyperboles, and nonsequiturs left me a little cold and forced me to speculate anew about the seeming hopelessness of our present plight as a nation divided. It occurred to me that under the circumstances I could select no more appropriate topic than one related to the nature and causes of the strife that is hurtling this country toward extreme repression.

[6] I decided to begin by talking about the new attitudes of Black people, because everywhere I go people ask such questions as: "What do you think about Black separatism"? My response to this, of course, is that separatism is a long-standing reality forced upon the Black masses by a recalcitrant white majority. After long years of struggling, and even shedding blood, for the dream of full integration into the American mainstream, Black America has shifted gears and has decided that Black is beautiful, and that black communities *can become* beautiful communities by their own efforts—in the economic sense and in every other possible sense.

[7] Rather amazingly to me, when Black America announced the intention to struggle for selective integration and equal opportunity in certain economic, political, and educational areas, while striving for optimal self-sufficiency in their own community, the white community recoiled. Posturing as if the black community had demanded for itself all these years degrading slums, inferior schools, poor economic opportunity, and generally fourth-class citizenship, the white community with indignant piety spoke out against what they call "black separatism." Still refusing, we should note, to integrate the ghettos themselves or build housing projects in their own suburban retreats. Is it any wonder that the young people of this decade are condemning deceit?

[8] Thinking along these lines leads me to conclude that there is a host of problems threatening the integrity of education as a profession in this country; these issues of integrity, must also be viewed as the prime responsibilities of this Association, because they concern, at least in part, the relationship between our speciality, communication, and the moral values constituting the proper foundation of any nation worth saving. In consequence, if we are to hope for a future superior to the present and the past, professional Associations such as ours must lead the way in recognizing that the major crises in our country are based in a breakdown in human communication and moral values. This breakdown has occurred despite all of the attention that has been given by highly sophisticated professionals such as yourselves. Essentially, I think that the universities and colleges of our nation are going, first and foremost, through a crisis of moral values. And the breakdown of human relations and communications observable all around us constitute the major victims. Only a very heroic effort by the moral as well as the intellectual forces of our Association, indeed our entire nation, can create the new hope needed to avoid continued and even more bitter conflict than we have experienced during the past several years.

[9] Obviously the crisis of confidence and the total breakdown of intergroup communication grows out of a larger concern than that represented by the narrow specialty of a single profession. Involved is something that demands the attention of the entire area of higher education. Yet someone must lead the way.

[10] We must realize also in analyzing the existing state of affairs that the causes of the present crises are intertwined in a rather complex way with the revolutions of nations, nature, technology, and people that have created violent change in a time span of unprecedented brevity. The last two decades have seen change and a growth of knowledge which was not even imaginable in earlier periods. Centuries, as measured by past human achievement, have been compressed, as it were into the years of the recent decades. We now have a growth rate that finds knowledge doubling at least every eight years, or maybe less. An estimated 90% of all scientists the world has ever known are living today.

[11] In sharp contrast to these exciting phenomena of human achievement are the seriously depressed social, economic, and educational conditions existing for so many millions of people in all parts of the world. These conditions, that we seem to be able to do little or nothing about, are steeped in racism, widespread illiteracy, ignorance, disease, and malnutrition, and comprise in varying degrees a hopelessly subhuman type of existence for a majority of the people of the world. Surprisingly all of these conditions exist in varying degrees right here in the United States. Yet, too many of us are unconcerned, if not totally oblivious.

[12] I want to quote to you something about Albert Szent-Györgyi,

the Hungarian-born American biologist, and I think that this is very indicative of the kind of conditions prevailing today.

[13] "Man is a very strange animal; in much of the world half of the children go to bed hungry, and we spend a trillion on rubbish: steel, iron, tanks. We are all criminals. As stated in an old Hungarian poem, if you are among criminals and you are silent, then you are a criminal yourself."

[14] Györgyi goes on to point out that at present we are on the road to self-extermination. A great part of newspapers is taken up by war, murder, nuclear bombs, bacterial agents, nerve gases, napalm, defoliants, and so on. Seemingly, we have become de-humanized, or at least insensitive, to the meaning of all of this—the inevitable end toward which we are being led.

The conditions I cite must disturb all enlightened persons in this country, irrespective of race, color, or creed. Particularly in the area of education, for years the center of humanistic influences, should there be disturbed contemplation as to where we are heading.

[15] Even if we do not concur with theses concerning the inevitable self-destruction of mankind, should we not be grieved over conditions that we ought to be able to do something about? I think the only answer is a resounding yes. Moreover, a feeling that something may be done stirs, if only feebly, because of the inspirational vision provided by such people as the Hungarian-born biologist. Among the words that I treasure as a source of inspiration are the following. "You have only to wish it, and you can have a world without hunger, disease, cancer, and toil. Wish anything, and it can be done—or else we can exterminate ourselves." I believe this to be true. If we match determination with an indefatigable will a new hope for the future is bound to emerge.

[16] The only way in which we can survive, however, is to make some new beginnings. Making a new beginning difficult is the fact that the human brain tends to freeze up for new ideas at a certain age, around forty. Since the entire governing mechanism of our society is over this age, we cannot really expect a profusion of new ideas. The only people who can make the turn is youth, our present youth. Therefore, we must preserve and cherish them, despite any abrasiveness on their part or differences between us.

[17] If we live long enough, if our human kind is not exterminated, our youth will make the turn. And where would we expect that they begin this, except in the university? Yet, in the universities is just where activities are germinating that divide us even more from our youth.

If education cannot respond with humane wisdom to the present crises, what hope is there from any other source? Through the ages, men of wisdom and vision, and young people of compassion, have turned to education as the principal means of coping with the ills of mankind. And education has always responded—although sometimes lethargically.

[18] I think that today's confused responses by administrators of education reflect the effects of an absence in our colleges and universities of a clearly defined, explicit, and accepted social mission. Our young people realize this. I am suggesting that because the important social objectives of human efforts as taught in our schools, the hierarchy of human values, are ill-defined, or confused, or not well supported, the country and almost every campus in it are beset by irreconcilable conflicts. The failure to meet social responsibilities head-on also emphasizes why as a country we are in a state of debilitating moral crisis. The crisis is also based, of course, on the racism that has become an inherent part of our system.

[19] The failure by our schools to develop a contemporary ethic upon which an honest morality structure can be built to combat racism and other barriers to the elimination of injustice, has left this country and its leaders in a state that finds benign paternalism, materialism, and repression superseding all else, while concern is almost nonexistent for such values as human life, human dignity, and the unimpeded opportunity to pursue happiness. These conditions exist also for a variety of very explicit reasons, most of which cannot be detailed here because of space or time limitations.

[20] It may be important to interject at this point my firm recognition that one very important role of education is the training of people to fill the professional and technical manpower needs of our society. But as our young people are constantly pointing out to us today, this is not the most important role of education. It should be elementary that the educational process must, above all else if it intends to produce human beings, help provide answers to problems such as those of poverty, race relations, peace, and personal identification. This competence can only grow out of a willingness on the part of education as an institution to humanize itself, and to function as an agent of dynamic and radical social change.

[21] In the decade since Sputnik we've seen an unprecedented escalation of world-wide tension, uninhibited fratricide in Vietnam, Africa, the Middle East, and now Cambodia, a year of rebellion by the youth in the United States, flaming explosions of discontent in the streets of our major cities, and all of the ingredients for a final resolution of our problems through adopting police-state tactics. This is what we have become, and the frightening future that we face ought to be alarmingly clear unless we develop some new directions.

[22] The present situation, brought on, in part, because education was caught bringing up the rear on countless humanistic and educational issues, is an intolerable one. It must be accepted that if we are to aspire to any kind of real freedom in this country, the education enterprise as repre-

sented by you here today, must reassert its responsibilities for providing moral leadership in all human affairs, and reaffirm its accountability to people for the behavior of the institutions that play such an important role in shaping lives, attitudes, personal characteristics, and most importantly, the national perspective. But then again, in order for education to effect the kinds of critical reappraisal of current practices that are needed, I think that some new approaches to desired solutions are necessary. Again, educating for change must become a top-priority item—change that will improve life conditions for the unhappy millions of deprived people in our country as well as in the rest of the world. And education must demand that all concerned people set aside matters of self-interest and parochialism, and promote the causes of justice and humanity in every possible way. In short, the education enterprise must exist as a revolutionary force serving a counterrevolutionary function to immense efforts to enslave mentalities and corrupt irreparably the psychological will of the masses.

[23] In essence, education as it stands today is without doubt in a state of despairing disgrace. It is tragic, for example, that education did react with sharp indignation as it should have when college students were ruthlessly slaughtered during frantic expressions of their despair and discontent—or when the black citizens of Augusta, Georgia, were shot in the back—(we still don't hear much about that today). Similarly, the matters of poverty, discrimination, war, human exploitation, ecological corruption, and gross disparities and inequities among people of the world are valid arenas of concern and must be kept constantly visible by the present education enterprise, or else we must look elsewhere for the kind of institution that will support our hopes for the future.

[24] I think that probably the most shameful chapter of recent vintage has been the lethargic response to pleas by young people—black, white, yellow, red, for educational programs that are relevant; programs that speak directly to the kinds of concerns needed to fulfill all of us.

[25] Two common threads run through all of the questioning by students and minority spokesmen and their demands for relevant curricula. The first is a violent reaction to deception, and the second is the demand for a new form of humanism expressed through a desire to transform all existing institutions so that they really and directly serve to improve the quality of human life in all of its dimensions. Products of the resulting system would certainly reject racism and war as unworthy of man's potential. We are confronted today by a very different kind of student who will accept no less than this.

[26] I want to cover at this point just a few of the specific problems that I think many of you choose to ignore on a regular basis. I am talking about the general problem of Black America in a very specific way in order that some recommendations might emerge as to what people in an organiza-

tion such as this ought to be about. I'm talking about the fact that the situation of Black America is getting worse with every single passing day, rather than better.

[27] To their discredit, we have a President, we have a Congress, we have many in education and religion, who are debating and continuing to debate as to whether Black people shall be given justice and equal rights. The tale of oppression has been documented in many ways over the past months.

[28] I want to quote a great American, Buell Gallagher, former President of the City College of New York. In a recent address he warned of the nation's apparent inability to solve the critical problems of race, pollution, overpopulation, violence, war and drugs. Of racism and violence he noted that: "He would be a bold man indeed who tried to assert on the record that we have made more progress than we have lost ground in the months since the Kerner Report was issued. On balance, we are losing the struggle against racism and its attendant violence. Such progress as we can discern is like sunlight glinting on a sea of blood and tears. Higher education in the coming decade must place those larger social problems on its agenda. The time is now; its now or never."

[29] Certainly we can all agree that the hoary conditions of the past are not adequate to the needs of the hour. Institutional inertia must be swept aside. Colleges and universities can no longer wait on the glacial movement of the generations, retreat into the ivory towers, rely on repression and indirection to get them through times of trouble. Administrators and faculty members and students together will come up with the answers to these problems together, or they will go down together with the sinking ship.

[30] As further evidence of the deteriorating human and civil rights climate that we must be willing to do something very forcefully about is the recent decision by a federal judge upholding the army's right to infiltrate civilian groups and compile intelligence reports on individuals ranging from Vietnam War protestors to Civil Rights activists. The judge ruled that the army activity was legal because, he said "It was essentially no different from that of newspapers gathering information on people and storing it in their files." During the court hearing, a Justice Department attorney actually acknowledged that the army compiles intelligence reports on individuals aimed at helping to identify potential troublemakers in the event that the army may be called in to deal with civil disturbances. Two former army intelligence officers, whom the judge refused to hear as witnesses, said that they helped compile reports on such persons as the prince of peace, the late Martin Luther King; Georgia legislator Julian Bond; folk-singer Joan Baez; and Dr. Benjamin Spock. And then, also, upon several army generals who oppose involvement in Vietnam.

[31] About all of this, another very concerned American, Senator Charles H. Percy, has said the following: "A society capable of sustaining its basic principles and of renewing itself will find a means to provide for and profit from dissent, rather than ways to repress it." And he cited proposals that are currently being made in the Senate to chip away at basic freedoms. He cited measures that would authorize preventive detention, to extend prearrest evidence-taking procedures, and to increase scrutiny of the mails. He said such proposals raise fundamental questions of civil liberties, and require us to decide on a continuing basis just what kind of society we are, or wish to be.

[32] Although the Senator mentioned no names during his speech, the measures he cited have either been proposed or actively supported by the Nixon administration. One of the most troublesome was introduced by Senator James O. Eastland, the Mississippi Democrat. Mr. Percy conceded that the problem of how to deal with the dissident and disaffected elements of society becomes more difficult at a time like the present when dissent rises to politically volatile levels. He insisted, however, that we must realize that freedom itself could be irretrievably lost through repression. To assert that a government may ignore basic human rights to some degree and in some cases, so that it may most expeditiously deal with outrages and irresponsible elements is to show an underlying contempt for our democratic processes. He called for a rejection of the politics of fear, and its replacement with solutions based on greater responsiveness.

[33] You can discern from these citations, if not from my other remarks, what is going on in the United States today; not as stated by an alarmist Black Revolutionary, but as stated by concerned Americans of every echelon of life. These are the obvious reasons why I am irrevocably committed to efforts to revolutionize education, rehumanize our society, and eliminate racism as a factor in the institutions which shape and control the lives of our people.

[34] But aims such as mine can only be accomplished if the society as a whole becomes willing to incorporate at every level an intellectual honesty that recognizes fully the rights of all Americans—Black Americans, red Americans, yellow Americans—all Americans, to be free and equal participants in this country's affairs.

[35] The road to the needed insights certainly will not be easy because of the sad state of prevailing affairs. But it is we, ourselves, members —concerned members—of organizations such as ours, who can turn things around in this country. To achieve such a goal we must be more willing to pay the price in the future than we have been in the past. And there are certain essential understandings that must undergird whatever determinations we develop to do something about present conditions.

[36] Far too few people recognize, for example, that all of the

minority students in the country are being educated in an environment which is hostile to their development as members of their own community. Teachers, administrators, and others influencing important educational decisions do not realize that these young people are being trained to participate in a society to which they do not belong, and are being taught to become alienated from those to whom they owe primary allegiance. This is the kind of condition that we seek to eliminate as a direct outcome of the kinds of changes we are striving for in educational curricula.

[37] Further, educators specifically, but the white community generally must come to know a great deal more about what happened and the significance of what happened in the Black revolution of 1960's. There were tremendous and most profound implications in the protests of the 60's, for what our educational institutions ought to look like. There are some who would say that we had a mini-preview in the 1960's of what was going to happen on a massive scale in 1970, and I would agree. The Black revolutionary of the 1960's created an educational institution to fit his own needs and those of his people, a kind of university of the streets that make doing and thinking and learning inseparable. Formal education should learn from this experience. Educators must come to recognize that the education of people—Black people, white people, and all others—must go on inside and outside of the classroom. The educational experience must encourage all people to acquire the skills to humanize their own existence and protect their right to be whom they need to be. The requirements of the kind of education that I'm talking about must also include everything that is essential for human liberation. To fail to educate for humanity and liberation is merely to turn people against each other and gradualize their mutual destruction. Moreover, failure to provide a proper educational experience is to guarantee the gradual destruction of our total society.

[38] Specifically, the education of all people must free them from psychological dependence on all other people, and teach them to think and to act on their own. The ability I speak of does not reside only in intellectual talents, but also in all of the relevant nonintellectual factors that can help an individual rid himself of the need to be controlled by those who have power over him. Thus, the educational enterprise should provide students with an opportunity to select out, design, and articulate their own values, and to discern the impacts of these values on their behavior, their attitudes, and their relationships with others.

[39] It may be that much of what I've had to say may have upset many of you. Some might even be saying: "This man is a pessimist who has no hope for the future." On the contrary, I am very optimistic. Despite the Agnews and the Eastlands, and even the Nixons, I am highly optimistic. And my optimism is reaffirmed constantly and nourished deeply by such words as those uttered by the late Lillian Smith, author, who in speaking

of her own awakening to the idea of world-wide brotherhood said the following: "And it was there in China that I heard of Gandhi and Tagore, and suddenly, when in China I was also in India, in the minds of its two greatest leaders, and slowly and yet almost suddenly the whole earth opened to me, and I saw us as one people; as human beings all reaching toward the light of truth, all wanting to love and be loved."

[40] These are the beautiful words of inspiration that should give all of us the hope and determination needed to create the will that can bring about positive change in our society. But, again, we shall not have positive change and peace as long as we continue to tolerate narrow-minded bigotry and discrimination.

[41] I was asked earlier about the outcome of a particular address that I gave not too long ago at a high school commencement exercise. The audience was white, upper middle-class (not hard-hats), with an average income of $20,000 per year. I talked to this audience about love; I talked to them about brotherhood; and I talked to them about survival. Suddenly, out of the audience came a cry: "If you don't like this country, leave it!"

[42] I said to myself, "Oh, sweet charity. This is the kind of attitude that creates the potential for us to destroy ourselves." And I said in response to him as I say to you: a man does not leave his house to someone else simply because there are some serious defects in its structure. He tries to straighten out those defects, and fix the things that are wrong. He does not leave his house, and he does not burn it down because it offends him and shames him before other people. He does what we must do in America so that Black people and all other people will someday enjoy the full fruits of freedom. He tears out the rotten planks, he resets the faulty foundations, he cleanses the windows of despair, and he brightens the house with the shining light of truth.

[43] I think that there are no more capable people in the United States, and in fact, in the entire world, than those of our profession, for keeping in focus those elusive freedoms without which we cannot survive as a nation, and should not want to survive as a people. If only the right kind of leadership can emerge in our Association as a result of the summers of sacrifice that some of you have undergone, we should soon be able to see some new insights, some new understandings, and some new approaches—not just to the teaching of subject-matter in a classroom, but to the teaching of a new way of life. If the desired results do emerge, as I feel they will, a new kind of hope can spring up all over the country. The new hope I see is the kind that the children of tomorrow will have and appreciate if the people of today are willing to fulfill their responsibilities and their duties.

[44] If the people of today are willing to stand up and be counted, to protest in the most vigorous way, to demand of America the justice promised by the Constitution and guaranteed by the Bill of Rights, we can

look forward to a day when our children will know the sweet feeling of freedom and be able to hear the sweet song of liberty everywhere: in the ghettoes, on the reservations, in the barrios, and everywhere else in the United States where people reside. And when this time comes there will be no differentiating among people because of irrelevant considerations such as race, religion, creed, or any other irrelevant factors.

[45] The new humanity of which I speak will eventually derive because I truly believe that the people of America who are really concerned will demand it, and because they will thunder to the skies: we have the desire and we shall will that our country shall become a better place to live for everyone because racism shall no longer be permitted as part of our national life.

Index of Speech
Communication
Principles

This index notes the speech communication principles used in the selected messages found in Part Two of this book. The numbers specify paragraphs in the messages.

AMPLIFICATION AND CLARIFICATION

COMPARISON: Muskie 1, 4, 9; Rogers 21; Agnew 3, 6, 12, 25–27, 30–31, 45, 50; Stanton 8, 12, 14, 19, 26, 31; Bittner 3; Capp 3–4, 7, 11, 17–18, 25, 37; Zimbardo 28, 30; Dunbar 17–18, 26, 36, 52; King 10, 12.

DEFINITION: Stanton 12; Capp 12; King 9–10, 16–18, 22; Hurst 6.

QUOTATIONS: Campbell 4–6; Rogers 21; Agnew 12, 20, 29; Stanton 29; Dunbar 53; King 9–10, 13, 22, 25; Young 8, 54, 58, 73; Hurst 15, 39. (See *also* Supporting Materials)

REPETITION: Rogers 8; Stanton 1, 8, 30.

ATTENTION AND INTEREST FACTORS

CONTRAST-CONFLICT: Muskie 1; Agnew 8–9, 30–31, 40; Stanton 12, 14; Capp 42–44; King 12, 14, 16–19; Young 43, 81.

FAMILIARITY-PROXIMITY: Campbell 1, 4–7; Bittner 1.

HUMOR: Campbell 1, 5–6; Rogers 10; Capp 1–2, 9, 11, 16, 21, 25; Dunbar 12; Hurst 1–2, 5.

REPETITION: Muskie 2; Rogers 8; Stanton 1, 8, 30.

QUESTIONS

Bi-Polar: Zimbardo 1, 63; Dunbar 7, 15.

Closed: Zimbardo 65, 78, 82.

Leading: Zimbardo 7, 15–16, 18, 24, 44, 51, 53, 59; Dunbar 50, 65.

Loaded: Zimbardo 14, 20, 26, 31, 38, 41, 47, 63, 76, 81.

Mirror: Zimbardo 51; Dunbar 4, 28, 35, 44, 61.

Open-Ended: Zimbardo 12, 57, 70; Dunbar 1, 24, 46, 55, 63.

Probing: Zimbardo 3, 5, 11, 13, 22, 24, 34, 49, 53, 68, 73, 80, 84; Dunbar 20, 48, 59.

Rhetorical: Zimbardo 36, 40, 50, 55, 85; Dunbar 34. (*See also* Interest Factors)

SUPPORTING MATERIALS

Anology: Muskie 2, 4; Agnew 8–9, 30–31; Stanton 14, 26; Capp 19–22, 40–41; Dunbar 26, 36.

Authority: Campbell 9; Rogers 6; Agnew 19, 22–23, 29, 31, 33–35, 37; Stanton 10–12, 15, 17–18, 21, 24–25, 29, 32; Bittner 2, 12; Capp 32, 40; Young 3, 73; Hurst 3, 13, 28, 30–31. (*See also* Amplification and Clarification)

Factual Illustration: Muskie 5; Campbell 11; Rogers 1–6; Agnew 2–5, 34–36; Stanton 2–5; Bittner 3, 7; Capp 9–11, 15–21, 35–36; King 22; Hurst 30, 41–42.

Hypothetical Illustration: Rogers 16, 21; Bittner 8–10; King 19.

Specific Instance: Muskie 2; Campbell 4–7, 12; Agnew 16–17; Stanton 15, 21–25; Bittner 1, 4, 11; Dunbar 8, 10, 57; King 4, 6, 18, 20–21, 25; Young 28–38; Hurst 1–5.

Statistics: Campbell 6; Rogers 7–8; Agnew 2, 11, 13, 30; Stanton 3, 5, 12; Bittner 3–5; Zimbardo 23, 31; Dunbar 47; Young 77–78; Hurst 4, 10.

STYLE

IMAGERY: Muskie 7; Campbell 1, 3; Rogers 1–4, 21; Stanton 7.

INVECTIVE: Agnew 3, 7–8, 51; Capp 3, 5–6, 8, 21, 23–26, 28, 31, 38; Zimbardo 21, 27, 43, 72; Young 8, 13, 27, 35, 48–49.

LOADED WORDS: Muskie 1–5; Campbell 2, 9, 12; Rogers 12; Agnew 1, 3, 5, 7, 10, 20–21, 23–24, 32, 37, 41; Stanton 4, 8–10, 14–15, 17–19, 26–28, 30–32; Capp 3, 35, 40; Zimbardo 6, 27, 40, 54, 63; Dunbar 18, 27, 47, 51, 60, 64; King 3, 11, 23–24; Young 7, 12, 15; Hurst 5, 19, 22–23.

METAPHOR: Muskie 1, 8; Campbell 2–3, 7; Agnew 42, 48; Stanton 8, 17, 28, 31; Bittner 3, 6, 8–9; Capp 26, 34; Dunbar 39, 60, 64; King 25; Young 8, 13, 19, 44, 48–49, 56, 60; Hurst 6, 29.

SIMILE: Muskie 2; Agnew 6, 15; Stanton 20, 27; Capp 11, 18, 44; Dunbar 62; King 13, 25; Young 1; Hurst 42.

TYPES OF MESSAGES

PERSUASIVE SPEECHES: Campbell, Rogers, Agnew, Stanton, Capp, Young, Hurst, Muskie

INFORMATIVE SPEECHES: Bittner, King

PERSUASIVE INTERVIEWS: Zimbardo

INFORMATIVE INTERVIEWS: Dunbar